THE TOPOGRAPHY OF THEBES

THE TOPOGRAPHY OF

THEBES

FROM THE BRONZE AGE
TO MODERN TIMES

SARANTIS SYMEONOGLOU

PRINCETON UNIVERSITY PRESS
PRINCETON, NEW JERSEY

Copyright © 1985 by Princeton University Press
Published by Princeton University Press, 41 William Street
Princeton, New Jersey 08540
In the United Kingdom
Princeton University Press, Guildford, Surrey

All Rights Reserved
Library of Congress Cataloging in Publication Data will be
found on the last printed page of this book
ISBN 0-691-03576-8

This book has been composed in Linotron Sabon
with Linotron Gill Sans Light display

Clothbound editions of Princeton University Press books
are printed on acid-free paper, and binding materials are
chosen for strength and durability

Printed in the United States of America
by Princeton University Press
Princeton, New Jersey

TO THE MEMORY OF MY UNCLE

KONSTANTINOS SOUVATZOGLOU

WHO ENCOURAGED ME TO STUDY ARCHAEOLOGY

AND TO THE MEMORY OF

ANTONIOS KERAMOPOULLOS

CONTENTS

CONTENTS

3

THEBES IN THE IRON AGE,
ca. 1050 B.C. TO A.D. 300

4

THEBES IN THE CHRISTIAN ERA

CONTENTS

LIST OF TEXT FIGURES AND MAPS

CATALOGUE FIGURES

FOLD-OUT MAPS

LIST OF PLATES

LIST OF TABLES

LIST OF TABLES

CATALOGUE TABLES

PREFACE

This study was conceived in the period between 1964 and 1966 when I worked in Thebes as Epimelitis (Assistant Curator) of Antiquities of Boiotia. My original intention was to convince both the Thebans and the responsible officials in the Greek government of the importance of Thebes in the hope of saving some of the more important remains. The modernization of the city occurred much too rapidly, however: in the first fifteen years since modern construction methods were introduced (1960-1975), most of the ancient city had been dug clear to bedrock and then covered by cement. Consequently, my goal has been to study the city as completely as possible.

While working in Thebes, I was able to gather information on, or excavate approximately a hundred sites. Most of the excavations were salvage operations, performed under unfavorable circumstances, some of which will be clarified below. To the initial hundred sites, I have since added another 170. I have not included those sites that could not be accurately mapped, or about which the archaeological information was unreliable. Among the 270 sites, I have included all the churches of Thebes, because many of them have been built at or near ancient sites. Each site is described as concisely as possible in the Catalogue. I have discussed in considerable detail and at length only site 1, where Antonios Keramopoullos worked for twenty-seven years, although the results of his work were published only in preliminary reports; I consider this site the most important one excavated in Thebes.

The interpretive part of this book consists of three chapters: Thebes in the Bronze Age (ca. 2500-1050 B.C., chap. 2); Thebes in the Iron Age (ca. 1050 B.C.-A.D. 300, chap. 3); and Thebes in the Christian Era (A.D. 300 to the present, chap. 4). Within each chapter there is further division into periods, each accompanied by its own map. After I had catalogued the archaeological material according to site, I tabulated the data pertaining to each individual period before proceeding to write the text. The most meaningful and useful of the tables are published here. In interpreting the archaeological evidence, I made every effort to take into consideration relevant historical and mythohistorical information. I have tried to form and test my various hypotheses in accordance with what is known both about Boiotia, in particular, and about Greece, in general. Some of my arguments may nevertheless seem too speculative. I present them, however, because there is virtually no possibility that future archaeological work in Thebes will contribute to a more precise understanding: the city is almost completely covered by apartment buildings.

In using ancient sources, the work of Keramopoullos, especially his Θηβαϊκά *(Topography of Thebes, 1917)* was most helpful. He was a philologist by training and, despite his extensive excavating experience, maintained a philologist's viewpoint. He carefully analyzed the ancient texts and, on the basis of his excellent understanding of them, tried to interpret the archaeological remains. His few errors are partly the result of insufficient archaeological information, and partly the result of his too literal interpretation of the texts. For example, because Pausanias said (9.16.6) that the theater of Thebes was πρὸς δὲ ταῖς καλουμέναις πύλαις Προιτίσι (near the so-called Proitides gates), Keramopoullos looked for it in the immediate vicinity of the gates, even though there were neither visible remains of it, nor was the terrain suitable for constructing a theater. The only theater of Thebes was, in fact, 600 m north of the gates. Nevertheless, Keramopoullos made the first serious, and largely successful, attempt to bring order out of chaos; until his time, the topography of Thebes was usually regarded as a philological subject, and most studies concentrated on the locations of the famous seven gates. Having no archaeological evidence, all 19th-century scholars placed the seven gates along an imaginary wall. Keramopoullos was the first to place them on the Kadmeia (the akropolis of Thebes), and thus correctly interpret the topography recorded in the detailed description by Pausanias.

I do not repeat Keramopoullos' comprehensive analyses of ancient texts, but I do make frequent reference to his work on them, and discuss ancient sources whenever I wish to propose a new interpretation. Two ancient writers are of particular importance in connection with the topography of Thebes: Pindar and Pausanias. The writings of Pindar contain only a few indirect references to topographical features of Thebes, which, because he was a native, are very important to this study. I do consider Pindar primarily in the discussion of Classical Thebes (chap. 3). Pausanias, on the other hand, has written the most extensive description of Thebes, and his text preserves the most reliable record of what the Thebans knew about their own city in the second century A.D. The literary aspect of Pausanias' work is beyond the scope of this book and, in any case, has already been examined by Keramopoullos (in particular 1917) and in large measure by Frazer (1898), Gomme (1910), Philippart (1922) and Schober (1934). I do not know whether a fresh literary analysis of Pausanias would contribute anything new to their work. I am convinced, however, that the recent archaeological discoveries can give Pausanias' description of Thebes new validity. I found his text to be orderly and systematic. Although most of the monuments he saw are now gone, I can identify the approximate location of almost every one of them and thus bring up to date the earlier attempts to do so. With the help of the large amount of archaeological material presented here, it is possible to follow in Pausanias' footsteps. I have made many references to Pausanias in this study, and chapter 5 is devoted to an analysis of his description of Thebes.

During the initial stage of my research, I came upon a far greater number of bibliographical references to Thebes than I had ever anticipated. It soon became apparent, however, that many of the studies dealt solely with the literary aspects of Theban culture. It also became clear that if this study were to be cohesive, the research would have to be limited to archaeological concerns, and that questions of history, religion, and mythology could only be addressed if they helped clarify archaeological problems. This still left me with an enormous number of bibliographical references, and I decided, therefore, to follow the example of the scientists and document in parentheses. The advantages of this are that the flow of the text is not interrupted, and that references are made very selectively.

A word of explanation is in order regarding the maps. The fragmentary nature of the architectural remains made it impossible to produce topographical maps showing complete plans of buildings. I have therefore devised a system of symbols based on the Egyptian hieroglyph ⌐⌐ (*por* = house); each site is recorded on the maps by number, and the number is, in turn, enclosed in a symbol indicating the type of archaeological remains found at the site. I have given references to published plans and whenever possible have proposed reconstructions of plans. In this way, the extent and nature of the remains of each period, the location of identifiable public buildings, sanctuaries, houses, and cemeteries have been clearly indicated. There are two basic maps, which include all 270 sites and Theban toponyms: one of Greater Thebes (Map A) and one of the Kadmeia (Map B). These are the fold-outs near the end of the book. The period maps within the text show only those sites that have produced archaeological remains of the particular period under discussion. In connection with these, however, sites with remains of other periods are often discussed as well; these may be found on the fold-out maps once their locations, given in the Catalogue of sites, have been ascertained.

I have made use of the reports published in the *Deltion*; the last volume considered was 28 (1973), which reached me in 1979. This means that material published after the summer of 1980 could not be included for consideration. I seriously doubt, however, that the addition of a few more sites would significantly change the total picture shown by the 270 sites that I have included. I have personally marked all of the sites considered on an accurate map.

The archaeological dating of the remains is based primarily on pottery and architecture. I have avoided documenting dates by discussing or illustrating pottery as this would have made the book both difficult to produce and very cumbersome to use. The reader can, however, check the accuracy of my dating by consulting the many references to illustrated pottery.

In writing this book, I often wished that I could document the development of Thebes with more precise archaeological evidence. The paucity of data has been a constant frustration. Because the great majority of excavations were salvage operations, they had to be carried out in great haste. There were no laboratory facilities, nor was there even any possibility of collecting laboratory samples. Thebes was such an important agricultural center that it is particularly frustrating to have no data on local flora and fauna, on diet or skeletal remains, all of which would be expected from a modern excavation. For these reasons, I have tried to interpret the available evidence as conservatively as possible. In spite of the frustrations and shortcomings, it has indeed been inspiring to contemplate the changing fortunes of a city as celebrated as Thebes over a period of 4,500 years. I hope that something of what I have gained will be shared by the reader.

ACKNOWLEDGMENTS

Although writing a book involves many hours of working alone, an author cannot fail to remember and be grateful to the many who, in various ways, contributed to its completion. I thought about writing the *Topography* when I worked in Thebes from 1964 to 1966, but the research began in earnest when a grant from the American Philosophical Society (Grant #7362/75) enabled me to spend a summer there collecting data. On two subsequent occasions, Washington University provided me with travel funds. I deeply appreciate this assistance.

To Ioannis Gogos, a former official in the city government of Thebes, I am indebted for providing me with the aerial photographs published herein, and also to Konstantinos Kourkoutis, the current mayor, for providing the maps of Thebes, which I then used to prepare the illustrations. I owe many thanks to John Michael Palmer for his meticulous draughting, and to Konstantinos Konstantinopoulos for the photographs in plates 12, and 15 through 20.

The personnel of the Museum of Thebes have always been helpful to me, and I take this opportunity to thank them, in particular the chief guard, Ioannis Lambrou, for the many kindnesses extended to me. Kaiti Demakopoulou and Phanouria Dokoronia kept me informed of the results of their unpublished excavations in Thebes; their work is also acknowledged in the Catalogue of Sites.

I wish to thank John M. Fossey for reading the chapter on Pausanias, Homer Thompson for his valuable suggestions, especially those regarding the archaeological maps, and William Merritt Sale for his help in translating the passage of Herodotos 5.57-61.

In writing this book, I was indeed fortunate to have the collaboration of my wife, Rheba. While I struggled to make sense out of bits and pieces of archaeological, literary, and historical evidence, she spent countless hours, editorial pencil in hand, trying to produce a coherent text. If the reader finds the material easy to follow, it is because of my wife's work. Even when confronted with the necessity of rewriting or reorganizing entire chapters, she never lost heart. If there be fault to find with her effort, it is that having done her best to render the complexities of the subject as coherently and simply as possible, those who wish to disagree with me will see why they may do so all the more clearly.

Finally, I would like to thank R. Miriam Brokaw, Joanna Hitchcock, Robert E. Brown, and Elizabeth C. Powers of Princeton University Press for their interest and support.

SARANTIS SYMEONOGLOU
Washington University
November 1983

THE TOPOGRAPHY OF THEBES

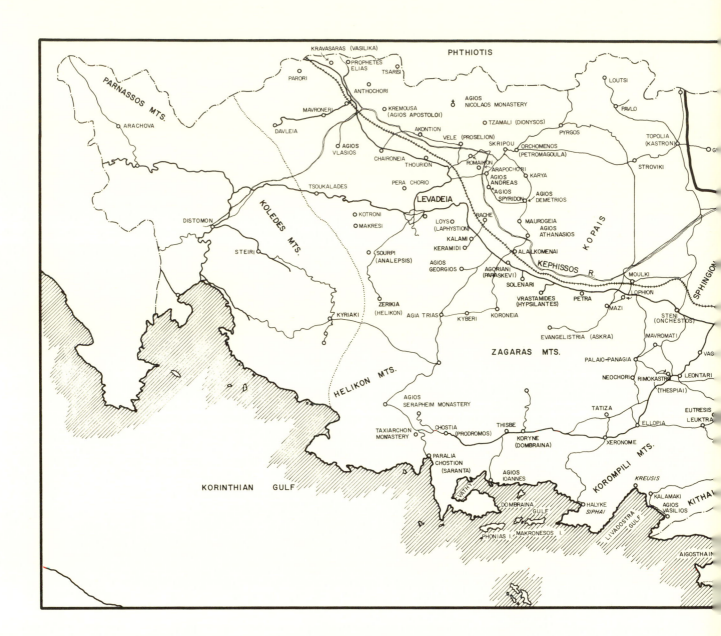

Fig. 1.1. Map of Boiotia

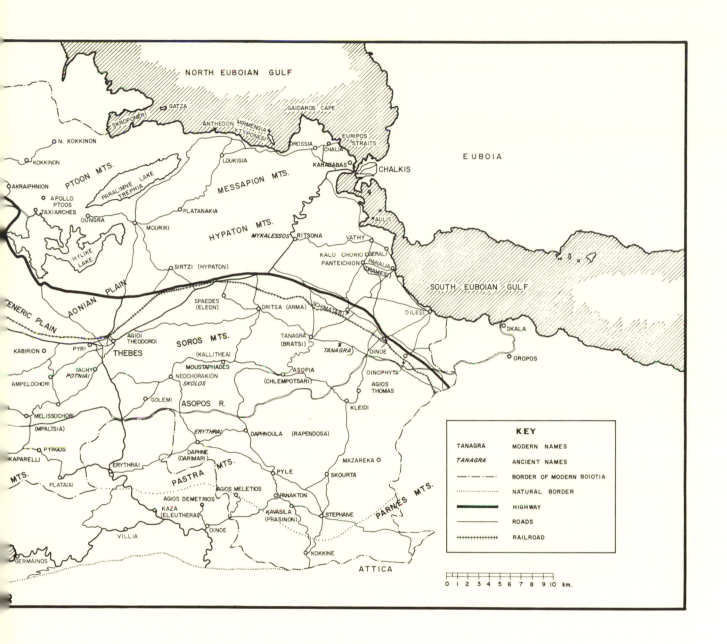

NORTH EUBOIAN GULF

GATZA

SKROPONÉRI

ANTHEDON MIRMENGIA
KTYPONESI

GAIDAROS CAPE

N. KOKKINON

DROSSIA

EURIPOS
STRAITS

CHALIA

EUBOIA

KOKKINON

LOUKISIA

KARABABAS

CHALKIS

AKRAIPHNION

PTOON MTS.

PARALIMNE LAKE
TREPHIA

MESSAPION MTS.

APOLLO
PTOOS
TAXIARCHES

OUNGRA

MOURIKI

PLATANAKIA

HYPATON MTS.

AULIS

HYLIKE
LAKE

MYKALESSOS RITSONA

VATHY

KALO CHORIO GERALI
PANTEICHION PARALIA
(DRAMESI)

AONIAN PLAIN

SIRTZI (HYPATON)

SOUTH EUBOIAN GULF

ENERIC PLAIN

SPAEDES
(ELEON)

DRITSA (ARMA)

SCHIMATARI

DILESI

KABIRION

PYRI

AGIOI
THEODOROI

SOROS MTS.

THEBES

(KALLITHEA)

TANAGRA
(BRATSI)

TANAGRA

OINOE

SKALA

OROPOS

TACHYO
POTNIAI

MOUSTAPHADES

NEOCHORAKION
SKOLOS

ASOPIA
(CHLEMPOTSARI)

OINOPHYTA

AMPELOCHORI

AGIOS
THOMAS

GOLEMI

ASOPOS R.

KLEIDI

MELISSOCHORI
(MPALTSIA)

ERYTHRAI

DAPHNOULA (RAPENDOSA)

PYRGOS

KAPARELLI

DAPHNE
(DARIMARI)

MAZAREKA

MTS.

ERYTHRAI

PASTRA MTS.

PYLE

SKOURTA

PARNES MTS.

PLATAIAI

AGIOS DEMETRIOS

AGIOS MELETIOS

KAZA
(ELEUTHERAI)

PANAKTON

KAVASILA
(PRASINON)

STEPHANE

VILLIA

OINOE

GERMAINOS

KOKKINE

ATTICA

KEY	
TANAGRA	MODERN NAMES
TANAGRA	ANCIENT NAMES
—·—·—	BORDER OF MODERN BOIOTIA
··········	NATURAL BORDER
▬▬▬	HIGHWAY
———	ROADS
+++++++++	RAILROAD

0 1 2 3 4 5 6 7 8 9 10 km.

1
GEOGRAPHY AND CLIMATE

The province that we refer to today as Boiotia is, for all intents and purposes, the same as the Boiotia of antiquity (fig. 1.1). The eastern border is marked partly by Mt. Parnes and partly by the Asopos River, which flows between the towns of Kleidi and Oinophyta all the way to the Gulf of Euboia; the mountain ranges of Helikon, Koledes, and Parnassos form a clear natural boundary to the west, although the modern administrative district extends far into Phokis; another range of mountains and the Gulf of Euboia marks the northern limit of Boiotia, and the southern boundary is formed by the Gulf of Korinth and the mountain ranges of Kithairon, Pastra, and Parnes.

Boiotia is thus encircled by the sea and large mountains situated in such a way as to leave several large plains in the center of the province. Only the Plain of Tanagra extends all the way to the sea. The plains are fertile and have abundant water, making them ideal for agriculture, in contrast to the coastal areas, which are generally rocky.

Not surprisingly, all the major Boiotian settlements have developed in the central plains, and these settlements have had to share the rich alluvial deposits there. Some of the best land has been submerged beneath lakes that are formed by the water that flows from the mountains directly into the plains where it collects, there being no channel to the sea. Today, there are only two large lakes, Hylike (or Likeri) and Paralimne. A third, the huge Lake Kopais, was drained in the late nineteenth century; it now seems likely that it was at least partially drained by the Mycenaeans in the late fourteenth or thirteenth century B.C. (Wallace 1969, 1973; Fossey 1974). For the greater part of history, however, the Kopaic plain was submerged under the Kopaic lake, and only the small plains of Orchomenos, Chaironeia, Levadeia, Koroneia, and Haliartos were viable for agriculture.

Western Boiotia, an area of 1,320 square kilometers (Kayser and Thompson 1964), the capital of which is Levadeia, is dominated by the Kopaic basin, which, so long as it is drained, is one of the richest districts of Greece. The Sphingion and Ptoon mountains act as a barrier to the waters that collect in the basin, and separate western Boiotia from eastern Boiotia. Eastern Boiotia, an area of 1,854 square kilometers, the capital of which is Thebes, has three series of plains situated parallel to one another in an east-west orientation. The largest is the northern series, bordered on the north by the Sphingion,

Ptoon, Messapion, and Hypaton mountains, and on the south by a chain of hills that continue the Helikon and Zagoras mountain ranges. This northern series includes the Teneric plain, which extends from Onchestos (just east of the Kopaic plain) to Kabeirion, the Aonian plain (or Plain of Thebes), which extends from Kabeirion to Mesovouni mountain (fig. 1.2), and the Plain of Tanagra, which extends from Dritsa to Oinophyta. Small valleys opening onto these plains, and a few narrow coastal strips are also arable.

The second series, consisting of two plains, is located south of Thebes. One extends from Thisbe to Eutresis and is named for Thespiai, the most important city in this area. Just east of Eutresis, at Melissochori, the valley of the Asopos River begins, and extends for over 30 km until it joins the Plain of Tanagra. The Asopos valley is narrow, but together with the surrounding hills there is a lot of arable land. These plains are blocked off in the south by the Korompili, Kithairon, and Pastra mountains. Between the Korompili and Kithairon mountains is the small Plain of Plataiai where the famous battle of 479 B.C. took place. The plain extends west of the town of Plataiai and, through a small valley, reaches the Gulf of Livadostra where the ancient city of Kreusis once stood. The Plain of Plataiai is watered by the many springs and streams of Mt. Kithairon.

Thebes is centrally located in eastern Boiotia, controlling the large, fertile Aonian plain. Thebes is also very close to the Asopos valley. The Teneric plain is only 7 km away, and it was part of Theban territory for the better part of history, although Thebes often had to fight for control of it. The cities of western Boiotia, especially Orchomenos, were in need of arable land because most of their flat ground was sacrificed to Lake Kopais. The rivalry between Thebes and Orchomenos, documented in numerous Boiotian myths and in historical accounts as well, can, for the most part, be attributed to a struggle for control of the Teneric plain. At the foot of the Sphingion Mountains (modern Phagas), where the Teneric plain meets the Kopaic basin was the ancient city of Onchestos (modern Steni—the narrows); here, at the sanctuary of Poseidon, was the center of the first Boiotian confederacy, at the place laid claim to by both the eastern and western regions.

Like most major Boiotian cities, Thebes is so far inland that access to the sea is problematic: the nearest harbors, Kreusis on the Korinthian gulf and Anthedon in the north Euboian gulf, are each about 22 km away. The mountainous road to Kreusis was too arduous to allow for regular communication with the Korinthian gulf; instead, it was preferable to reach the harbors of the Vathy bay by the longer but smoother road via Thespiai/Thisbe (Heurtley 1923). Easiest to reach, however, was the port of Anthedon on the Euboian gulf, by way of a road that went through the valley of Thebes and along Paralimne Lake (ancient Trephia). Anthedon was in antiquity a harbor of major importance, not only to Thebes, but perhaps to other Boiotian cities as well; in addition, the probability that the ancient road to Chalkis passed Anthedon gave it importance as a link in the land route (Schläger, Blackman, and Schäfer 1968). It was through Anthedon that Thebes communicated with other civilizations in the Aegean and the Near East as early as prehistoric times.

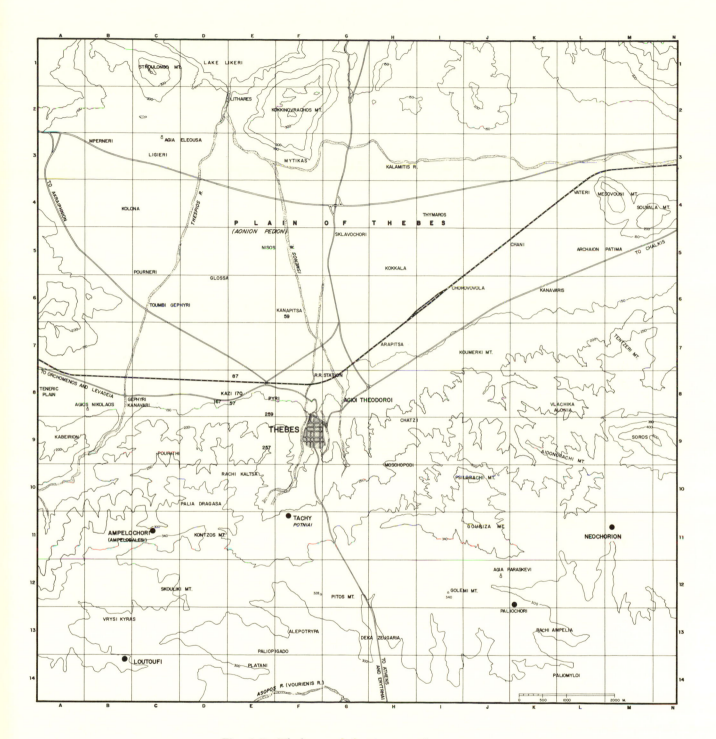

Fig. 1.2. Thebes and the Aonian plain

The climate of Thebes differs from the more typical Greek climate of Athens or the Peloponnese in that extremes of cold and heat are more pronounced. The mean annual temperature is 18° C (65° F); the coldest month is January with an average temperature of 10° C (50° F), while the hottest is July (27° C, 80° F). The annual rainfall ranges from 600 to 800 millimeters, or 24 to 32 inches (Kayser and Thompson 1964). Humidity levels are relatively high for Greece; in Thebes the mean is 67 percent.

Thebes stands on the north side of a chain of hills that begins at the Zagoras Mountains and ends at the Plain of Tanagra. In the area of Thebes, the hills are low and form a saddle, providing easy access to the Asopos valley in the north. The hills on which Thebes was built and the ones surrounding them are pleistocene formations of conglomerates, sandstones, sands, red loams, and similar deposits, while further east and south there are extensive formations of marls, clays, sandstones, and conglomerates (Tataris, Kounis, and Marangoudakis 1970; Philippson 1951:501). The Plain of Thebes is closed off in the west and north by much older geological formations of limestone, shale, chert, and dolomitic limestones; these formations provided Thebes with her most durable building materials, although transporting them must have been one of the thorniest problems facing the ancient engineers: the nearest source of limestone is Mt. Kotsika, 5.5. km west of Thebes (fig 1.2). As early as the prehistoric period stone was transported from here for use in the city's fortifications and also in domestic architecture.

As a major city, Thebes had an ongoing need to protect and defend itself. The location of the city made this difficult: not only was it necessary to transport stone for the fortifications from far away, but also the terrain on which one had to build the walls was soft, forcing the builders to dig all the way to bedrock for a solid surface. It was also irregular and low-lying, necessitating the creation of terraces and landfills and forcing the builders to give the walls extra height to provide any real protection. Yet, the difficulties of fortifying Thebes were not reason enough to move the settlement to a more easily defended location, even in later historical periods. In fact, no matter how often the city was destroyed, it was always rebuilt on the same site. Clearly, the overriding justification for this must have been very powerful, indeed, and we must give it due consideration.

A city like Thebes, which depended primarily on agriculture, had two essential requirements: arable land and a dependable supply of water (Bintliff 1977: chap. 5). The Aonian plain provided excellent farm land, and many settlements grew up around it, but only Thebes developed into a major city. I attribute this to an inexhaustible supply of water, which enabled the Thebans not merely to farm, but to practice agriculture on a large scale. This minimized the significance of other factors that usually contribute to the flourishing of a town, such as defensibility, climate, and a geographic location that favors trade and communication. Even when warfare made it imperative that very strong fortifications be erected, as it did in the Mycenaean period, the settlement was not moved.

The water, which was so highly valued, flowed from numerous natural springs in the vicinity and fed three rivers or streams; these flowed from the hills through the Aonian plain, into Lake Hylike (pls. 1-3, figs. 1.2, 3.6). The largest of the rivers was the Agianni (ancient Ismenos) in the east; second in size was the Plakiotissa (ancient Dirke) in the west, and the smallest was the Chrysorroas (ancient Strophia) which flowed between the other two. Almost the entire volume of the river water came from the springs; even during the rainy season there was little increase because the courses of the rivers were short. Today, the riverbeds are dry, as all the spring water is consumed within the town or in the factories that have sprung up in the plain. The riverbeds are quite deep, however, indicating that water flowed through them from the time the area was formed geologically, and throughout most of the city's history. The settlements and temporary military camps that were established outside the Kadmeia and eventually abandoned have been washed into these rivers; one can usually find ancient coins in the riverbeds after a heavy rain.

The Ismenos River was fed by the Oidipodia spring (pl. 39; Catalogue, site 244) located at Agioi Theodoroi, and by the Agianni spring (Catalogue, site 243), known in antiquity as the *Ismene spring*, or *Kadmos' foot*. We cannot precisely identify the location of the Agianni spring, because like all the springs of Thebes, it too has been capped in recent times at the spot marked on the map in figure 3.6. The flow of water, however, must begin further south; the remains of the aqueducts of Thebes (fig. 3.6) give evidence that the inhabitants of the Classical period were able to tap the spring south of its present location, where the ground is higher, and thereby divert some of the water towards the Kadmeia. Ever since the construction of the aqueduct, the Kadmeia has relied on this spring for its water supply.

The Strophia River never had more than a small amount of water, and was often completely dry; Ulrichs called it a "rainstream" (1863:5). This river, however, was fed by at least one spring near the southern part of the Kadmeia called *Pege*, which may be the one that in antiquity was called the *spring of Ares* (Catalogue, site 173). There may have been yet another spring further south feeding into the river: the sanctuary of Demeter Potnia was by the river, and the presence of a grove near it and statues on the river bank (Pausanias 9.8.1) give some indication that the stream was not dry. In connection with this sanctuary, Pausanias (9.8.2) discusses the *Well of the Mad Mares*, perhaps another source of water, so called because the horses that drank from it became hysterical.

The junction of the river with three roads may be identified as the crossroads where Oidipous killed his father (see also chap. 5, passages 1 and 18). The river flows west of the Kolonaki hill, curving in a wide arc around the Kadmeia where the riverbed still looks low in relation to the height of the Kadmeia itself (pls. 6-7). The river was probably called *Strophia* ("turn," or "twist"), and the road by the river was either *Schiste* ("divided") or *Koile* ("hollowed"). Each of these names reflects an aspect of the geographic environment. The name *Strophia* appears only once in Kallimachos (*Hymn Del.* 76) and for this reason there has been some reluctance to identify it with the river (Pagidas 1882:19-20). Keramopoullos (1917:366) did identify it as such because no alternatives exist. Although Kallimachos is our only source, he is not unreliable: in the same passage he also refers to Dirke, Strophia, and Ismenos, a clear reference to the three streams and perhaps their springs as well.

Until recently there were two springs west of Tachy, called *Kephalari* and *Pegadaki*, and another one to the north called the *Kati* spring (Ulrichs 1863:12-13). All three flowed into the third river, Dirke (pl. 2). Of these three, the Kati spring is the one closest to Thebes and perhaps the most important, because it was reputed to have had the best drinking water of all. Its ancient name is not known. Pliny (N.H. 4.12) mentions a Psamathe spring, the location of which is still undetermined, but there is no evidence to link it with the Kati spring. Pindar makes frequent reference not only to the river Dirke, but to a spring of the same name; his house was in the vicinity (modern Kalogeros, ancient Kynos Kephalai, Map A). The only spring in this area is the one called *Paraporti* (site 53), and its ancient name must have been *Dirke*, the most famous spring of Thebes after the *spring of Ares*. The Dirke spring is the source of water closest to the Kadmeia, and would have been the main source had not its position below the Kadmeia presented the difficulty of transporting the water up to the settlement. It was this difficulty that prompted the ancient Thebans to search for alternate sources. The spring was used, however, until recently, primarily because of its proximity to the city. Its present name (*Paraporti*, ''by the gate'') probably reflects its proximity to the medieval tower and gate of site 19.

There were four other springs in Thebes, but all have been recently capped. These were located northwest of the Kadmeia at Mpouka, Vranezi, Chlevino, and Pyri (the last in the public square just south of site 161). After having studied the remains of the Theban aqueducts, I began to doubt that these were natural springs; three of them are very close to line *A* of the aqueduct (fig. 3.6), while the fourth (Vranezi) is a little to the south and it too could have taken its water from a side conduit. There is no surviving reference in ancient literature to any spring in this area, and all of these may have been man-made fountains fed by the spring of Agianni.

Finally, one more natural spring exists, 1.5 km east of the Kadmeia, beyond the Ismenos River. The spring and its locality are called *Moschopodi*, and there used to be a small waterfall called *Kales Kyrades*. The water flows into a stream that runs parallel to the Ismenos River (fig. 1.2). Moschopodi is an attractive place, but because of its distance from the Kadmeia and its position in the infertile hills, it has not played any role in the history of Thebes.

The original settlers of Thebes, who confronted the difficulty of choosing terrain appropriate for construction, must not have had an easy time. Although there was probably considerable vegetation at the river banks, the land must have looked in antiquity very much as it does today in the unoccupied hills around Thebes (pl. 1): in a very irregular terrain we see few flat-top hills and many long, conical ridges with countless sloping depressions on either side. It is difficult to erect houses on such land, not to mention fortifications. Yet, the overriding benefit of the springs and the proximity to the rich Aonian plain were in some measure augmented by the protection afforded by the three rivers, and a settlement site within their bounds must have seemed the best compromise. Although the Ismenos River was the major source of water, the area between the Ismenos and Strophia rivers is only about 200 m wide. In contrast, the area between the Strophia and Dirke rivers is over 400 m wide, and the ground is higher, a strategic advantage. The drawback of being far from the waters of the Ismenos was offset by the proximity of two natural springs close to the southern part of the Kadmeia (Dirke and the *spring of Ares*). The numerous surviving myths attest to the importance of these two springs.

The pear-shaped area that we call the Kadmeia was not always occupied in its entirety. The archaeological evidence shows that settlement started in the southern part of the Kadmeia (fig. 2.1) where the highest point is currently marked by the church of Agios Andreas. This was probably the location of the sanctuary of Zeus Hypsistos ("highest"). From this hill, the Dirke spring is less than 300 m to the west, and the *spring of Ares* less than 500 m to the south. The area around this hill is relatively flat, but becomes steep towards the south and west, thereby offering the settlers the best possible option (in an area far from ideal) for constructing a settlement and fortifying it if necessary. The area deemed most suitable for this earliest settlement formed an oval, bound on the south by Drakos St., and on the north by Antigone St. In the west, the high ground ends at a steep incline that runs along a fairly straight line from site 199 to the Pouros hill (see Map B); in the east, the ground slopes gradually towards the Strophia River, becoming more precipitous at Pelopidas St. The earliest archaeological remains of Thebes have been found within this oval. The ground slopes gently towards the north. At Antigone St. there used to be a depression about 4 m deep, running east-west. This presented no serious obstacle, however, and the city quickly expanded northward beyond it.

From Antigone St. (present elevation 203 m) the ground continues to slope until the church of Agios Georgios (site 93, present elevation 190 m). Here there was a rather deep ravine along the line reconstructed in figure 2.5, which was enough of an obstacle to halt the northward expansion of the Kadmeia until the end of the Mycenaean period (see chap. 2). Keramopoullos had known of this ravine when he first worked in Thebes (1909A:107-108); he described the Kadmeia as a town built on four hills and, as did everyone after him, believed that the city of Thebes had always extended north to the Frankish tower (site 52), occupying the present pear-shaped area. The archaeological evidence presented here, however, shows that from the small community in the southern part of the Kadmeia, the city expanded gradually with the creation of landfills until the entire Kadmeia was occupied as seen today. Some low-lying areas, particularly in the western part of the Kadmeia, remained unoccupied for a very long time.

Although the Kadmeia is not a high, rocky outcrop but rather a flat akropolis, to this day it is possible to enter and leave it only through those places that have bridges or where landfills have been created. On the south side, where the ground slopes sharply, there is only one exit at the end of Epaminondas St., which leads by way of what appears to be an artificial landfill to the southern part of Thebes; the ancient name of this area was probably *Knopia* (Strabo 8.404; Keramopoullos 1917:266). From here one had access to the southern part of Boiotia. After passing the crossroads, one kilometer to the south, the road divides in two: the southeast fork leads to the towns in the Asopos valley, Plataiai and Athens, the southwest to Tachy and the towns around the Plain of Thespiai; this was also an alternate road to Delphi, according to Pindar who used it himself (see chap. 5, passage 18).

The east side of the Kadmeia is the least precipitous and allows for easy access to the eastern part of Thebes and to two major roads via three exits. At the southeast, one exits through the Elektrai gates (site 7); the road follows a gentle descent towards the Strophia River and leads by way of a bridge to the Ismenion hill and Moschopodi; after crossing the bridge one can also turn south and follow the Koile Hodos to the crossroads.

A second road from the east Kadmeia descends rather steeply along Oidipous St. and after crossing a bridge reaches the modern suburbs of Nea Sphageia (formerly Tekes, ancient Galaxion) and Astegoi; across the Ismenos River, this road leads to Myloi which, in antiquity, was protected by the Classical fortifications (cf. fig. 3.6); today there are only a few houses. Beyond Myloi is the modern suburb of Konakia. The third exit is located at the east end of Vourdoumpas (formerly Proitos) St.; the road crosses the Mouchlinas bridge (site 46, see Map B) and leads northeast towards the modern road to Chalkis. In antiquity the famous Proitides gates were in this vicinity (site 9); the ancient road lay between the Kastellia hills—Mikro Kastelli to the north, and Megalo Kastelli to the south. These were probably the hills referred to as *Dios Gonai* ("birth of Zeus") in antiquity (Keramopoullos 1917:397). East of the Kastellia hills are the locality called Graveza, the Oidipodia spring, and the suburb of Agioi Theodoroi. North of this exit are the suburbs of Synoikismos (Palaios and Neos), Polygyra, Gypsolakkos, and the railroad station. In antiquity there were important public structures here that one could reach from the Kadmeia only through the Proitides gates. This was also the main exit for reaching the Plain of Thebes, Anthedon, Chalkis, and the towns of northeastern Boiotia (Eleon, Tanagra, Aulis, etc.).

On the north side of the Kadmeia there is only one exit today; the road descends along Pindar St., zigzags around the Museum and the Amphion hill, and leads to the railroad station and the suburb of Pyri. The ground is steep here, and this exit was not used for most of the city's history.

Finally, there are two exits on the west side of the Kadmeia. One of them is at the western end of Vourdoumpas St., across from the Proitides gates. The road leads to Pyri, and on to Akraiphnion and Levadeia. In antiquity this exit was used heavily: from here one had access to the vast Northwest Cemetery, Kabeirion, the Teneric plain, and the Kopaic plain beyond it. The last exit is at the west end of Oidipous St. where the road descends steeply towards the Paraporti spring and the river Dirke. In antiquity, the area was sparsely populated, and the main function of this exit was to provide access to the spring.

Before proceeding to a discussion of the development of the city of Thebes, something must be said about the various names by which the city has been known. According to both Tzetzes and Stephanos Byzantios, a very early name was *Kalydna*, after Kalydnos, the first king of Thebes. Stephanos Byzantios also calls the city τεμμίχιον ἄστυ, city of the Temmikes, an ethnic name known from other sources as well (*FGrHist* 70 F119, 384 F1). The most widely used and most important name was *Kadmeia*, after Kadmos, the city's mythological founder, and it is this name that has been used to designate the core settlement throughout most of the city's history. As early as prehistoric times, the name Θήβη (*Thebes*) was introduced; its etymology is unclear (Schober 1934:1452). The name *Thebes* was used concurrently with *Kadmeia*. Although the reason for a double appellation is not entirely clear, there is a plausible explanation for it. According to ancient tradition, best summarized in the scholiast to Euripides' *Phoinissai* 114, Kadmos built the city and named it *Kadmeia*; Amphion and Zethos subsequently fortified it and named it after Thebe, the wife of Zethos. It is possible that this simple explanation is also the correct one.

In Classical times, the name *Kadmeia* (in the singular) was specifically used to designate the old city, whereas Θῆβαι/*Thebes* (in the plural) was used to designate the entire city, which by that time had expanded in several directions around the Kadmeia; Pausanias used the names in this way. But the name *Thebes* predominated in late antiquity and was the only one used in medieval times, when a Φ was sometimes substituted for the Θ (e.g., Leake 1835:221); in Turkish the town was called *Stifa*. The name *Kadmeia* has been forgotten by the modern inhabitants, in spite of the fact that the area their city occupied for most of the Middle Ages was that of the old city. In the pages that follow, I will use *Kadmeia* to refer to the old city even in medieval times, *Greater Thebes* to refer to the areas around the Kadmeia, and *Thebes* when referring to the entire city as a cultural unit. One must bear in mind that the Kadmeia was not merely the akropolis of Thebes, but the major area of habitation through most of the city's history.

2
THEBES IN THE PREHISTORIC PERIOD,
ca. 2500 TO 1050 B.C.

Ἀμφίονά τε Ζῆθόν τε,
οἵ πρῶτοι Θήβης ἕδος ἔκτισαν ἑπταπύλοιο,
πύργωσάν τ᾽, ἐπεὶ οὐ μέν ἀπύργωτόν γ᾽ ἐδύναντο
ναιέμεν εὐρύχορον Θήβην, κρατερώ περ ἐόντε.

ODYSSEY 11.262-265

Most of the prehistoric archaeological remains of Thebes date to the thousand years from the end of the Early Helladic II period (ca. 2100 B.C.) to the end of the Bronze Age (ca. 1200 B.C.). It was during this time that Thebes grew from a small community to one of the largest cities of Greece, famous for its extensive fortifications with seven gates. The prehistoric remains were relatively well preserved, not only because they were deeply buried, but also because their undressed masonry was not seen as worthy of recycling in later times. Both the remains themselves and the many surviving myths and legends attest to the great wealth of the city. They also make possible an attempt to answer the long-standing questions regarding the city's founding, as well as the extent of its fortifications and the number of its gates. Moreover, the legends pertaining to Thebes may be viewed in relation to the archaeological remains in order to reveal whatever actual history they may preserve.

NEOLITHIC

Unfortunately, the area around Thebes has never been surveyed, and this has left un-answered significant questions regarding her earliest history. At the northern end of the Kadmeia (site 52, Map B), a small quantity of pottery was unearthed and identified by Mylonas (1928:74-75) as Neolithic. There is no other evidence of a Neolithic presence on the Kadmeia itself. In the vicinity of the Archaic cemetery of Thebes (site 87, fig. 1.2), a Neolithic settlement was seen but not excavated. It is likely that there were several settlements scattered around the Aonian plain during the Neolithic period.

THEBES IN THE EARLY HELLADIC PERIOD,
ca. 2500 to 2000 b.c.

No remains dating to EH I or the beginning of EH II (periods corresponding to Eutresis levels III-VI; Caskey and Caskey 1960) have ever been found in Thebes. On the Amphion hill (site 121, Map A), Pharaklas found Early Helladic pottery, but the exact date is undetermined. It is conceivable that during the earlier half of the Early Helladic period, a small settlement existed on such a location as the Amphion hill. fig. 2.1

On the Kadmeia itself habitation began sometime in EH II on the south side. The earliest remains are of clay-lined pits, hearths, and postholes cut in the bedrock, signifying the use of a wattle-and-daub method of construction. In five sites (13, 112, 166, 184, 186) such remains are not associated with stone foundations, which do not make their appearance until the subsequent habitation phase. In two other sites (6, 12) the stratigraphic relationship between clay-lined pits and stone walls is not clear.

These humble and inauspicious remnants of the earliest habitation of the Kadmeia are clustered just north of its highest point, which is located at site 217 (Map B). They are contained in an area measuring approximately 120 m × 130 m, or 15,600 square meters (fig. 2.1). The small size of the settlement and the finds of food remains and of bone and stone tools attest to an economy based on subsistence farming. In fact, the relative poverty seen in this settlement may indicate that it was only an offshoot of a larger, more prosperous community nearby. It is possible that the early settlers moved to the Kadmeia from the lower territory of the plain; such small settlements, hamlets, or even single farmsteads scattered in the plains seem to be characteristic of EH II (Howell 1974:82).

We can next distinguish a phase in which houses were constructed on stone foundations and sometimes reached enormous dimensions. In three sites (3, 12, 101) the walls were thin and made with small stones, but in eight others (1, 2, 4, 6, 18, 166, 205, 245) large building stones and massive foundations were seen. The houses were provided with well-made floors of packed earth or tiles (sites 101, 245), benches, hearths, and columns (sites 2(?), 245). Those houses that were well preserved yielded rich quantities of pottery, some of it imported (sites 208, 245), and other finds attesting to wealth, such as the hoard of beautiful bronze tools found in site 2. Most surprising, however, is the development of an architecture in which stone is used as a building material, for there is no source of stone close to the Kadmeia, the nearest quarry being Mt. Kotsika, 5.5 km away (fig. 1.2).

The houses are seldom preserved intact, and it has rarely been possible to excavate the plan completely. In site 245, part of an apsidal house 5.50 m wide was uncovered; the pottery from its destruction level dates it to the end of EH II. A second apsidal house (site 2) was later (EH III) and bigger. Its main room was 7.5 m wide, one of the largest structures known in Early Helladic Greece. A fragmentary wall of yet another house ran parallel to it, was the same size, and was built of exactly the same stone. A doorway at

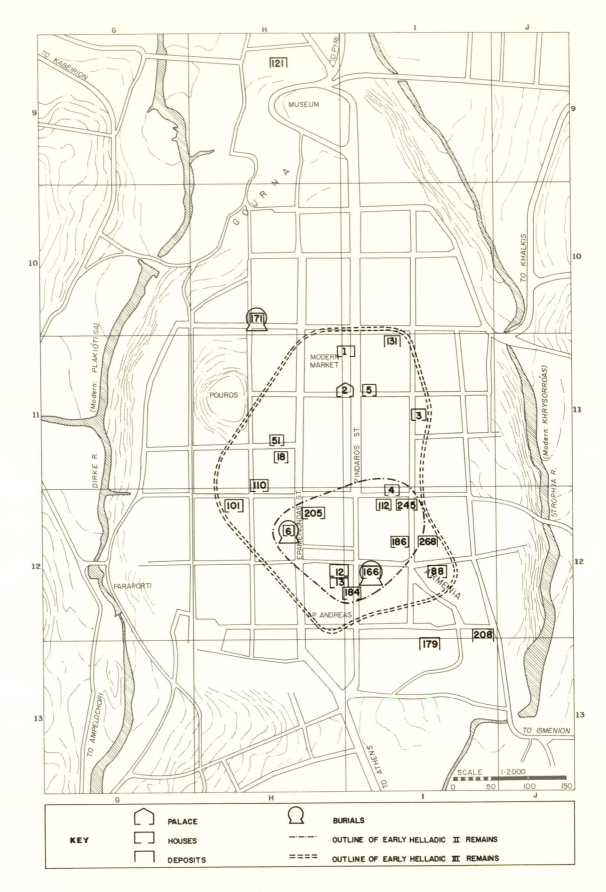

Fig. 2.1. Thebes in the Early Helladic period, ca. 2500-2000 B.C.

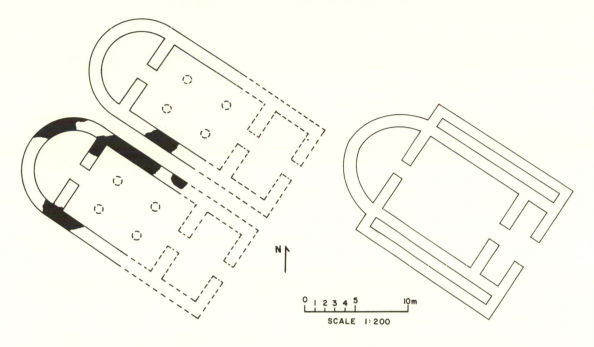

Fig. 2.2. Site 2, two suggested reconstructions of the Early Helladic apsidal house

the side of the first house faced the second and indicated communication between the two; it is likely that the fragmentary wall was part of yet another apsidal house.

Even in EH III, apsidal houses are rare. At Lerna, one was uncovered in the latest Early Helladic III occupation level (Caskey 1958:127, building *BC. 15*), and at Chasampali in Thessaly, two well-preserved houses were found (Theochari 1962; Sinos 1971:37, fig. 98). In the Middle Helladic period they are seen more frequently: at Eutresis there are the well-preserved houses C and X (Goldman 1931:35, figs. 37, 39). Of the several apsidal houses at Lerna, the most important is *98A* (Caskey 1957:149, fig. 4) the interior measurements of which are 3.25 m × 10 m. There is also one at Korakou (Blegen 1921:77, fig. 100), its main room measuring 3.80 m × 6.20 m. These houses are characterized by either a very long main room, or a main room and an anteroom. By comparison, if we reconstruct the plan of the Early Helladic III houses in site 2 of the Kadmeia according to the proportions of the remains, we see two buildings of monumental character, each achieving exterior measurements of 23 m × 10 m (fig. 2.2). The remarkably large dimensions of the main room (7.50 m wide and approximately 10 m long) could only have been achieved with the structural support of columns, possibly as many as four. There were columns even in the slightly earlier apsidal house of site 245.

Subsequent reoccupation of the area accounts for the poor state of preservation of the houses in site 2. Nevertheless, their sheer size, in addition to the isolated find of a hoard of bronze tools, marks them as structures fit for kings. As we shall see, the site at which they stood continued to be used for important buildings even to the Byzantine period.

Remains of other houses were too fragmentary to enable us to reconstruct their plans. However, they do reveal to what extent the settlement had grown. The Early Helladic remains occupy an oval, oriented southeast-northwest, that follows the natural shape of the land. The hill of Agios Andreas (site 217, see Map B), which is the highest point of the Kadmeia, marks the southeast point of the oval; the hill called Pouros tou Kavallari marks the northwest. The Early Helladic buildings follow the same orientation. By the end of EH III the area occupied by the settlement measured 200 m × 300 m, or 60,000 square meters, a fourfold expansion over the earlier settlement. This startling growth was accompanied by affluence, as seen in the monumental architecture and the related finds, and does not appear to have been a gradual development, but a sudden and surprising change. That the change must have occurred toward the end of EH II is supported by the pottery from site 245, where an apsidal house had been built and burned down by then.

There is no evidence that the Early Helladic settlement was fortified, although it is hard to imagine a large and rich town unprotected. If there were fortification walls during the Early Helladic period, then they must have encompassed the two hills of Agios Andreas and Pouros tou Kavallari. The walls could have offered no meaningful protection had the two high hills been left outside them in such close proximity.

Early Helladic Thebes has yielded relatively few movable finds in addition to pottery. There was a rather impressive array of sophisticated tools, including those from the hoard of bronze found in site 2; other tools have been found made of obsidian, flint, bone, copper, and stone (sites 6, 186, 245). A gold earring was found in site 186.

The Early Helladic pottery from site 166 has recently been studied (Demakopoulou and Konsola 1975). Both EH II and EH III were represented in the material. Most of the pottery was hand-made, but there were also a few wheel-made pots. The Early Helladic II pottery seems to date to the end of this period, and one observes a gradual transition to the Early Helladic III style. Demakopoulou and Konsola (1975:85-86) believe that the Early Helladic III style developed more slowly in Thebes than in neighboring Lefkandi in Euboia, or in the Cyclades; pottery from both of these areas was found to have been related to the pottery of Thebes.

Of the pottery types from this excavation, most common was the Slipped and Burnished ware (Caskey and Caskey 1960, groups VII and VIII) with red and black polish; the most frequently occurring shapes were small bowls with inverted rims, and large bowls with a T-rim, some with horizontal lug handles; there were also squat pyxides and other shapes. There were only a few sauceboats, and the quality of paint on them was not very good. A second type of pottery was the Glazed ware (*Urfirnis*) in shapes similar to the Slipped and Burnished pottery, and, in addition, a one-handled cup (*depas*), partly glazed jars with spreading necks, and cups with everted rims. A third type was the pottery with light-on-dark decoration (*Agia Marina ware*), which was quite common in Thebes and is associated with the Early Helladic phase. Finally, there was coarse ware in a variety of shapes, including large pithoi and amphoras, and small jars.

Cycladic imports have been found in Thebes (sites 208, 245), and there are relations between Theban and Cycladic pottery. The appearance of the potter's wheel may indicate the influence of the Lefkandi I culture (Howell 1974:85-86). Although the evidence is still insufficient to explain these connections, it is surprising that they are seen at all in Thebes, an inland Boiotian city; Boiotia is usually thought of as an isolated area (French 1972:43).

From the entire Early Helladic period, only five burials are known. Four of these were within the settlement (sites 6, 12, 166), and one may be called "extramural" (site 171) since it was located north of the inhabited area. Three were pit burials, and there was one cist tomb with two skeletons in it (site 166). The only offering was a cup for the deceased, at site 171. The empty pits excavated by Keramopoullos (1910B:250-252) west of the Kadmeia may belong to an Early Helladic cemetery. Empty pit graves with Early Helladic pottery within them were also found on the Amphion hill (site 121, see Map A).

THEBES IN THE MIDDLE HELLADIC PERIOD,
ca. 2000 TO 1600 B.C.

The more extensive preservation of Middle Helladic remains has enabled us to know more about this period than the previous one. In areas where later occupation has not disturbed them, the Middle Helladic deposits average 1.50 m in depth, an indication of a long and continuous period of occupation. At 18 sites, Middle Helladic architectural remains have been identified with certainty; 19 others yielded Middle Helladic deposits; there were Middle Helladic burials at 18 locations. The Middle Helladic architectural remains overlap with those of the Early Helladic town, but extend further to the north (sites 17, 171, 194) and south (site 179). It is clear that Thebes became larger, occupying an area of approximately 110,000 square meters. The density of habitation decreases as we move away from the center of the town.

fig.
2.3

A reconstruction of the basic size and plan of the Middle Helladic town depends in large measure on whether or not there were fortification walls. Many Middle Helladic sites are known to have been fortified (Scoufopoulos 1971:17-28); at Lerna, there are even fortifications that date to the early part of the Early Helladic period (Caskey 1958:132-136). Although no remains of fortifications have been found at Thebes dating to the Early Helladic or Middle Helladic periods, it is hard to imagine a city the size of Middle Helladic, or even Early Helladic Thebes in a vulnerable geographic location remaining long without walls. The fact that the town retained the same basic plan in both the Early and Middle Helladic periods (figs. 2.1, 2.3) could be interpreted as an indication that

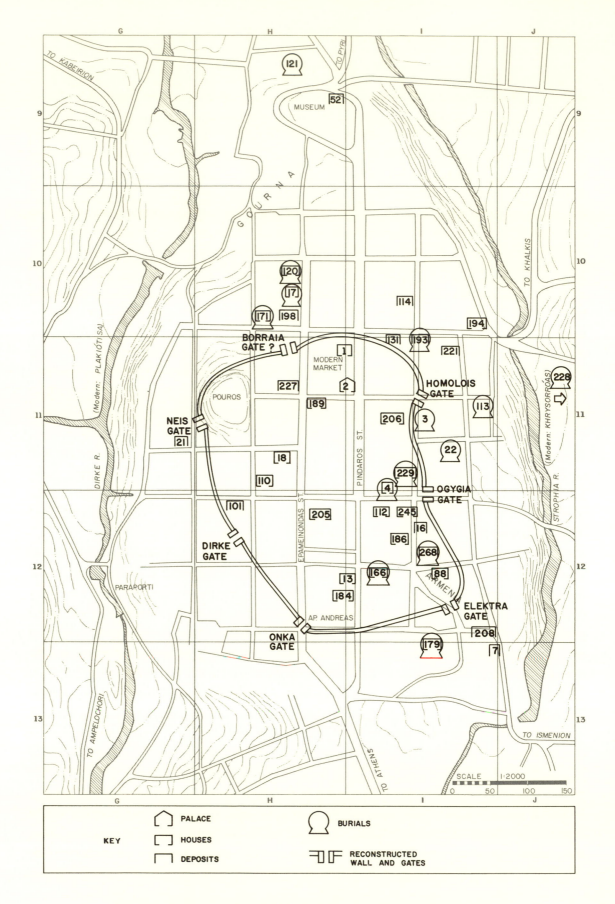

Fig. 2.3. Thebes in the Middle Helladic period, ca. 2000-1600 B.C.

expansion was limited by the presence of walls, and that the town might have been fortified as early as EH III. But a strong wall must have been built at least in the Middle Helladic period, when Boiotia (and other regions of Greece) felt the pressure of intensified warfare (Vermeule 1964:76-77; Howell 1974:75). We may conjecture that it was constructed of light materials, rubble and/or mud-brick, similar to those at Raphina and Askitario in Attica (Scoufopoulos 1971:19). Such materials are easily destroyed, if not by enemy invaders, then certainly by time. For this reason, in the Late Bronze Age different materials and construction methods were used to fortify major cities. Thebes, too, eventually built a huge Cyclopean wall. There is good reason to assume that any stone which remained from the earlier fortification walls was subsequently used in house construction. Stone is recycled everywhere, but in Thebes there is a more pressing need to do so, owing to the total lack of stone in the immediate vicinity. This may explain why so little has been found of the Theban fortifications from any period.

If we may assume that there was a wall around Middle Helladic or even Early Helladic III Thebes, we might attempt to reconstruct its outline. Although there are no remains of the actual wall, there is indirect evidence of its presence. For one thing, there is a close clustering of houses in the oval-shaped area described earlier; this shape was maintained over the entire period lasting about 500 years. It is bordered at the west by the two most prominent hills in this area: the hill of Agios Andreas (site 217, see Map B), and the hill of Pouros (fig. 2.3). Any wall protecting the town must, for defensive purposes, have encompassed these two hills. Moreover, the continuing proximity of the settlement to them may argue for the presence of a wall. The settlement might otherwise have expanded in another direction.

Another important consideration is the location of the graves. We observe that of the known burials, 70 percent have been found beyond the outline of the settlement; most of the remaining 30 percent were burials of infants within houses, a practice customary in the Middle Helladic period (Howell 1974:75-76). The extensive cemetery of site 3 (20 graves), together with other isolated graves in the vicinity (sites 22, 113, 193, fig. 2.3; and across the Strophia River, site 228, Map A), must have been outside the wall on the east site of the Kadmeia. To the north, there is another cluster of graves (sites 171, 17, 120, fig. 2.3; and further south, site 121, Map A), which must also have been outside the walls.

If the wall followed the general shape of the settlement, then it must have taken the line just west of the Pouros hill and, encircling site 101, turned southeast towards the hill of Agios Andreas. From here, again following the shape of the settlement, it would have turned east to enclose sites 184 and 88, and then north towards site 3. The Middle Helladic remains south and north of the proposed wall are scanty, and perhaps might best be considered extramural. Sites 7 and 208 to the south yielded only deposits; there were three burials at site 179 along with remains that might possibly be architectural.

North of the proposed wall there were scattered deposits, and remains of architecture in sites 17, 171, and 194 only.

The walled settlement thus outlined is about 80,000 square meters, a more conservative measurement than the total spread of the Middle Helladic archaeological remains (110,000 square meters). The wall could not have been much smaller than this because it must have enclosed the palatial structures of site 2 to the north, the dense clustering of houses to the south and east, and the two hills to the west.

The wall, as I have proposed its reconstruction, following the shape of the town (a shape maintained over hundreds of years), would have been approximately 1,150 m long. As such, its construction would have been an extraordinary undertaking for the period. The longest known fortifications are those of Malthi-Dorion in Messenia, which are 420 m long (Valmin 1938; Scoufopoulos 1971:20). Seen in this perspective, a Middle Helladic wall of the length I have proposed is an almost inconceivable achievement. We should, however, bear in mind that for the Thebans of the Middle Helladic period there was no realistic alternative to constructing such a wall. The Kadmeia was the only well-watered location in southern Boiotia, and if the Thebans wished to remain there and retain control of the Aonian plain, they had to fortify it. From a strategic point of view, the safest town plan is the one we describe, in that it puts the two highest hills to best advantage. The increase in population, estimated to have reached approximately 2,400 (table 2.6) in the Middle Helladic period, enabled the Thebans to undertake the fortification effort. They were compensated by the agricultural richness of the Aonian plain.

A wall encircling Middle Helladic Thebes must have had gates, although we have not enough evidence to suggest how many. What we can do, at least, is point out the natural exits from the town, which would have been likely locations for gates. At the southern end of Epaminondas St., adjacent to the hill of the church of Agios Andreas (site 217), remains of the Late Helladic period and a medieval tower were found (site 19, fig. 2.5), indicating continuous use of the area as an entrance into the Kadmeia from the south. In the western part of the Kadmeia, a probable location for a gate is near site 101, where the ground slopes gradually toward the Paraporti spring (by the gate), a major source of water. The name of the spring indicates that there was a gate here in the past, probably to give access to the spring itself. There may have been another gate near the Pouros hill, an easily defended location. There was a depression between the Pouros and the hill of the palaces (sites 1, 2). Another exit may have existed on the hill of the palaces, somewhere near the modern bus terminal (corner of Epaminondas and Vourdoumpas sts.). This would have been the most likely location of a northern gate, which would have given access to the plain of Thebes.

On the east side, there are two suitable places: the first is near the cemetery of site 3, the presence of which may indirectly indicate the position of the wall. Habitation remains have been found just east of here (site 206). A gate at this location would have given access both to the cemetery and to the road to Chalkis. The second probable location is in the vicinity of sites 4, 112, and 245, where there is still a road leading to the Strophia stream and to the hills east of the Kadmeia. Finally, a gate may have existed in the southeast corner of the settlement, near the later gates of site 7.

There may have been gates at all or some of these seven natural exits (fig. 2.3), although we ought not exclude the possibility that even more gates existed. If one were to judge by the six gates of Malthi-Dorion (Valmin 1938: plan 5), which is much smaller than Thebes, one might conclude that Middle Helladic civil engineers did not look upon the presence of numerous gates as a weakness to be avoided. It is, in fact, intriguing to associate the frequent ancient references to "seven-gated Thebes" with the town of the Middle Helladic period. Those ancient references are usually thought of in connection with Late Helladic Thebes, but in the Late Helladic period, the presence of so many gates would certainly have been considered a strategic weakness.

HOUSES

The Middle Helladic houses of Thebes were built on stone foundations that were usually adequate to support only a one-storey structure. The foundations rested on leveled ground, either the debris of earlier habitation, or bedrock. The floors were made of packed earth with one exception, where the floor was made of white plaster (site 166).

Eighteen of the 38 Middle Helladic sites yielded remains of houses, but unfortunately, no complete plans are preserved. Curved walls, which may have belonged to apsidal houses, were found in four sites: 17, 110, 112, and 166. The Middle Helladic structures were generally smaller and more modest than those of the previous period. In site 2, however, above the remains of the palatial Early Helladic buildings, the poorly pre-served remains of an important Middle Helladic building were found. It is possible to reconstruct the plan on the basis of the two large portions of the north wall, two small portions of the south wall, and two portions of a cross wall. This seems to be a house of the megaron type, 5.50 m wide, with a straight back wall. Similar structures, like house A of Eutresis (Goldman 1931, fig. 42), enable us to suggest a reconstruction of the plan to show a large room entered through an anteroom, probably without columns in front (fig. 2.4). The exterior measurements of the house were 7 m in width and approximately 16 m in length. Although it was not as large as the Early Helladic structures beneath it, it was, all the same, a very grand building for the Middle Helladic period of Thebes—not only because of its size, but also on account of its location directly above the Early Helladic "palace." It was destroyed by fire early in the Late Helladic period, and does not seem to have been built much before the end of the Middle Helladic period: in the south wall two construction phases are evident; the earlier is dated to the last

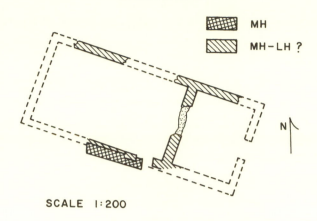

SCALE 1:200

Fig. 2.4. Site 2, suggested reconstruction
of plan of the Middle Helladic megaron

phase of the Middle Helladic period by the pottery associated with it; the use of regular masonry in this wall is probably another indication that it was built late in the Middle Helladic period.

BURIALS

The number of tombs found in Middle Helladic levels was far greater than that found in Early Helladic levels. Site 3, having the largest concentration of tombs, may be viewed as a true cemetery: 20 cist graves were clustered here, most of them with single adult skeletons in crouched position. One exception was tomb 1, a large grave holding several burials; another, tomb 13, held a man and woman in embrace; a third, tomb 15, held a mother and infant. The cemetery can be dated on the basis of tombs 6 and 18 (the latest stratigraphically), which contained Late Helladic I pottery, to the second half of the Middle Helladic period (see Catalogue, site 3). The examples of many other sites (Vermeule 1964:79-80; Howell 1974:75-76) show that true cemeteries like this one were located outside the settlements. The Middle Helladic cemetery of site 3 should also be considered extramural. A few additional isolated graves were found in the vicinity (fig. 2.3). North of the town, another cluster of graves was found, too few to constitute a cemetery.

Most of the cist tombs were provided with a pebble floor. Offerings to the dead seem to have become customary during the second half of the Middle Helladic period; by the end of the period, they were sometimes even quite luxurious. The offerings in the earliest Middle Helladic tombs were vases, or a nice potsherd; bronze jewelry was also quite common. The later tombs, however, contained objects made of glass paste, amethyst, carnelian, and even gold (site 3, tomb 3).

In common with many towns of the Middle Helladic period, there were also burials in the houses of Middle Helladic Thebes. Most of these were of infants, or of mother with child, and were found in floors, against walls, or inside stone benches. In addition, there were a few pithos burials: two at site 166, and one each at sites 193, 205, and 228.

On the Amphion hill, at site 121, was the most impressive tomb of all. It was a tumulus, the only one in Thebes. The large grave was lined with huge slabs of limestone and was covered by a huge slab of black limestone, which was not found in situ. It was surely intended for some member of the royal house of Thebes. Unfortunately, the published report of the tomb does not include a plan, or the size. The date of the tomb is also unclear: Spyropoulos, who excavated it, calls it Early Helladic, but the fact that it was a tumulus containing a cist burial, in addition to the style of the jewelry and pottery found within it, indicate a Middle Helladic date. Tumulus burials are known from many sites in Greece (Pelon 1976); according to Hammond (1973:24-25), they date to 1700-1300 B.C. One is tempted to identify this tomb, situated on the prominent Amphion hill and the only such monument in this area, as that described by Pausanias (9.17.4, 7) as the tomb shared by Amphion and Zethos, which was said to have been the most venerated tomb in Thebes (see chap. 5, passage 12). One may, of course, believe that this was the tomb Pausanias visited and still maintain one's skepticism regarding its original occupants.

It is difficult to tabulate the number of Middle Helladic tombs found in Thebes because so many of the published reports tell us nothing more precise than that "tombs were found." It is, however, possible to be sure of at least 49. If I have reconstructed the fortifications correctly, then 34 of these would have been extramural and 15 intramural, giving a ratio of 70 percent to 30 percent.

POTTERY

Rich deposits of Middle Helladic pottery were found, most notably at sites 2, 171, 179, 205, and 229. On the basis of the stratigraphy, it was possible to distinguish three phases at sites 2 and 18, and two phases at site 166. All typical Middle Helladic wares are represented in Thebes, though not all of the 20 classes listed by French (1972) have yet been identified. Gray Minyan ware is very common, and may be the most frequently occurring type (cf. Demakopoulou and Konsola 1975:66-70, pls. 31-32). There are a few examples of Black Burnished (or Black Minyan) and Yellow Minyan wares. The Red Slipped (or Red Minyan) ware is so well represented that Thebes may be looked upon as one of the centers of its manufacture.

Perhaps the second most common type of pottery is the Matte-painted ware, which includes several of the Polychrome categories (French 1972:33-36 lists six classes of this ware). The quality of the pottery is very high; most is wheel-made and the quantity of fine wares is sometimes surprising. In fact, on the basis of the pottery alone, one could conclude that by the Middle Helladic period, Thebes had developed into a prosperous and thriving town.

CHAPTER 2

THEBES IN THE LATE HELLADIC PERIOD,
ca. 1600 to 1250 b.c.

fig. 2.5 In comparison with remains of earlier periods, the Mycenaean remains were quite substantial. Mycenaean buildings were better preserved because stone was used not only for the foundations, but even for part of the upper structure. After Thebes was destroyed in the thirteenth century, most of the city remained abandoned for several centuries. When habitation resumed, regular masonry was apparently more desirable than the undressed stones of the Late Helladic buildings. Thus, Late Helladic buildings were not stripped of their stone in subsequent periods, as were Classical buildings.

Unfortunately, most of the Mycenaean Kadmeia has been completely built over, as a result of the construction boom that started in 1960. There is only one city block in the center of town, which has been left, in accordance with the recent town plan, as an "archaeological park." Under this block is part of the second Late Helladic palace, which may include a courtyard. Although this part of the palace may eventually come to light, it is doubtful that much more will be known about the Late Helladic town itself.

FORTIFICATIONS

Despite the fact that very little of the Late Helladic wall is visible today—nor was much more of it visible even in the nineteenth century—there is no real doubt that a Late Helladic wall did exist. Late Helladic towns were rarely unfortified, and Thebes, with its great wealth and vulnerable geographic position, could not have stood unprotected. If, as I have already argued, Thebes was fortified in the Middle Helladic period, the walls must have been reinforced in the Late Helladic period in response to increasing and widespread warfare. A unique underground aqueduct (discussed in greater detail below) was also incorporated into the fortifications. In addition, the increase in the population, which is attested in the archaeological remains, must have necessitated an enlargement of the perimeter of the wall.

Scholars of the nineteenth century attributed the celebrated seven gates to the much larger though short-lived fortifications of the Classical period (Forchhammer 1854; Brandis 1867; Pagidas 1882; Fabricius 1890; Soteriades 1900, 1914). Keramopoullos (1917) argued so persuasively, however, that the Late Helladic wall and its gates must have stood on the akropolis itself (i.e., the Kadmeia), that even the philologist Wilamowitz, who originally rejected the presence of the gates altogether (1891), was convinced that Keramopoullos was indeed correct (1922:23-31).

In discussing the problems relating to the walls and gates of Late Helladic Thebes, Keramopoullos (1917) had very little archaeological evidence to support his arguments. He relied heavily on the literary tradition, on the remains of monuments dating to subsequent periods, and on general topographical features. Of these last, he attached

26

considerable importance to "natural exits" from the Kadmeia, places that provided egress via a ridge, or a narrowing of rivers that could be easily bridged. Central to his argument was the evidence that many of the present-day roads leading out of Thebes followed the same path as the ancient ones. It was also his belief that remains of the Classical gates and medieval towers attested to a continuing tradition and preserved the locations of earlier fortifications, particularly when topographical features seemed to necessitate their presence. His attempts to excavate a portion of the Late Helladic wall, however, only once met with success (site 9). More recent work has brought to light additional evidence bearing on the location of the wall and gates, although we are still frustrated by our inability to uncover any segment of the Cyclopean wall in its entirety, anywhere.

In attempting to trace the line of the Late Helladic wall as it would have been shortly before Thebes was destroyed in the thirteenth century B.C., I have taken into account both recently discovered archaeological evidence and those elements and topographical features used by Keramopoullos that can still be considered valid. These items are listed below and will be described proceeding counterclockwise around the Kadmeia, beginning with the only visible remains of site 9 (see fig. 2.5):

W 1 (W = wall). In 1915, Keramopoullos excavated the remains of a wall at least 3.50 m thick, preserved to a length of 6.30 m (site 9). The individual, undressed stones were as long as one meter and were interlocked in the manner characteristic of Cyclopean masonry.

W 2. Just north of W 1, at site 194, a great heap of stones and Mycenaean pottery were found 5 m to 6 m below the surface.

W 3. Seven meters below the surface in site 23, a portion of the Mycenaean wall was discovered, only to be buried again, unfortunately, under a modern building. It was possible to see only the top of the wall, which was wider than the 3 square meters of the trench. The wall did not follow the northern line of the Kadmeia, but pointed west-northwest.

W 4. At site 47, architectural remains of undetermined character were unearthed; these may have been related to the fortifications.

W 5. At the northern end of the Kadmeia (site 52), Leake (1835:226) reported having seen substantial remains of the fortifications of Thebes, but Keramopoullos (1917:304) was skeptical of the fact that these remains were Mycenaean. By Keramopoullos' time, the wall was no longer visible, although he did see eight blocks that had apparently fallen from it. These he attributed to a polygonal wall of the sixth century B.C. (Keramopoullos 1907).

W 6. Nine boulders were found at site 188, possibly related to the remains of W 5.

W 7. Keramopoullos (1907) found a Classical wall here, similar to the Classical fortifications of Greater Thebes. The presence of a Frankish tower at this location may be seen in the context of continuous fortification of this area (cf. site 52).

W 8. Keramopoullos (1917:305) reported the presence of foundations for a city wall near Gourna made with medium-sized stones similar to those described by Leake (W 5). A lot of Mycenaean pottery was found in a nearby trench.

W 9. Keramopoullos (1917:305) excavated 100 m south of W 8 and reported finding the medieval wall built on isodomic foundations; inside it were undisturbed Mycenaean deposits and stone foundations of houses that he had hopes of excavating at some later date.

W 10. On the slope leading out of the Kadmeia, Cyclopean masonry and Mycenaean pottery were exposed by a bulldozer (site 104); this is probably very close to W 8 and W 9 described by Keramopoullos.

W 11. In the same general area are several thick deposits of the Mycenaean period, which may be interpreted as landfills. These were found in sites 45, 120, 17, 181, and 171, where bedrock lies 10 to 15 m below the modern surface. The landfills may indicate an intention to expand the city, and it is quite likely that a wall was erected beyond them. Isolated landfills were found in site 20 and perhaps site 110. Pappadakis (1919) reports finding another landfill somewhere in this vicinity.

W 12. At the southern end of Epaminondas St. was a Frankish tower, beneath which some Mycenaean pottery was found (site 19).

W 13. Frazer (1898:32) reported having seen a small portion of a wall, three feet high and six feet long, just east of W 12, that seemed to have been part of the fortifications.

W 14. This is the site of the Elektrai gates of the Classical period (site 7). The Late Helladic remains found at W 14 included part of a strong wall that Keramopoullos thought might have belonged to the Mycenaean fortifications (1917:27). The remains of Classical gates at site 7 strongly argue for the presence of fortifications in earlier periods.

W 15. Keramopoullos (1917:308) found another part of the Classical fortifications of the Kadmeia in the vicinity of the church of Agios Stephanos (site 219). The Mycenaean wall may have stood here, or a bit higher up the slope, closer to the landfills (W 16).

W 16. There is a series of landfills in the eastern part of the Kadmeia resembling those of the northwestern part (W 11). Sites 113 and 267 are in the center of the eastern part of the Kadmeia, while 194 is to the north, and 246 to the south. The Mycenaean wall should have stood just east of these landfills, the purpose of which was to terrace the irregular ground.

W 17. In this area, just east of W 1, a Frankish tower, a gate, and a bridge existed before 1904 (Keramopoullos 1917:361, 372). The location still retains the name of the old bridge of Mouchlinas (site 46, see Map A). The presence of these structures, and those of the Mycenaean wall at W 1 argue for the presence of fortifications and perhaps a gate at W 17. They also show that one area was used for the same purpose over a long period of time.

The features enumerated above take on greater significance when considered in conjunction with the remains of Mycenaean habitation. Architectural remains have been found at 32 sites, and deposits of Mycenaean finds have been uncovered at 30 additional sites (fig. 2.5). When compared with the town of the Middle Helladic period, Late Helladic Thebes shows clear expansion towards the north and east. There was a more modest expansion to the south, as seen in the substantial remains of sites 179 and 265. On the west side of the Kadmeia, only two deposits have been found (sites 20 and 21) beyond the line of the Middle Helladic town; remains of houses have been uncovered recently, but are still unpublished. At the northern tip of the Kadmeia (the area of the Archaeological Museum), no remains of habitation have been found except for those in sites 102 and 248, which are closer to the center of the town. Beyond the limits of the Kadmeia, only one house has been found (site 211) near the temple of Apollo Ismenios (fig. 2.12).

With all of this in mind (or, at least, in view, on the map of fig. 2.5), it is possible to trace the outline of the Late Helladic fortifications. As in the Middle Helladic period, the wall must have enclosed both the densest areas of habitation and those places that were strategically vulnerable. It is very likely that the difficulty of transporting stone must have played a significant role in determining the ultimate length of the wall. These difficulties and the expenses related to them must surely have dictated that thinly populated quarters and isolated houses be left unprotected. In trying to trace the wall, I propose to address questions regarding its position, proceeding systematically from the west side of the Kadmeia in a clockwise direction.

The 500-meter stretch between W 11 and W 12 on the west side of the Kadmeia gives no clue to where the Late Helladic wall stood. Keramopoullos proposed to place the wall at the edge of the present-day Kadmeia. While not impossible, this placement would have protected an area east of it that is 500 m long, and 100 m wide on the average, which has yielded very sparse Mycenaean remains. Had the wall indeed stood where Keramopoullos proposed, there should have been a denser concentration of houses, and with all the digging that has taken place in recent years, more would surely have come to light. My proposal would place the wall in essentially the same position as that of the Middle Helladic wall, holding a fairly straight line between W 11 and W 12. Although such a placement would significantly constrict the size of the Kadmeia, it would explain why no remains of habitation have been found west of this line. It would have been far

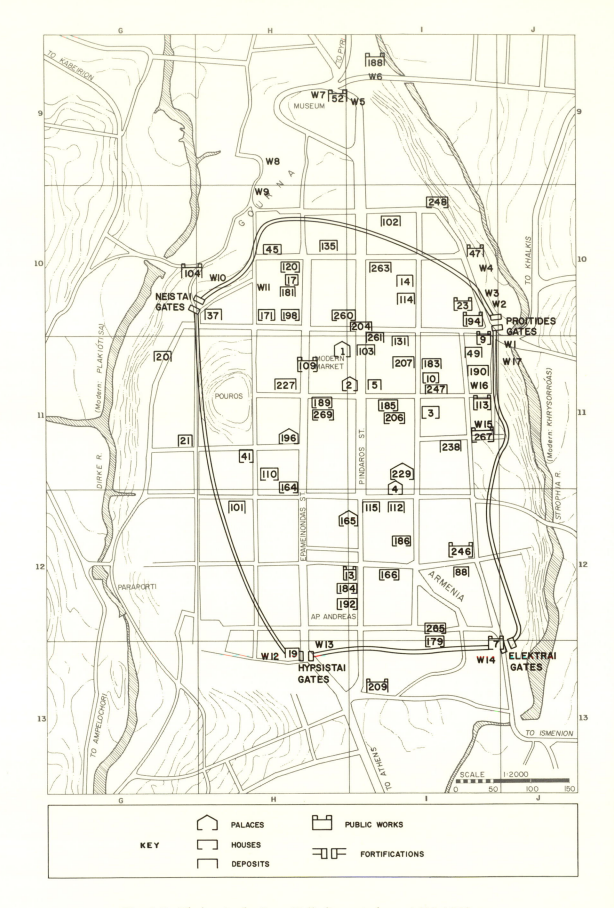

Fig. 2.5. Thebes in the Late Helladic period, ca. 1600-1250 B.C.

more economical to build the wall in this position, which also has the advantage of following an easily defensible high ridge connecting the hills of Agios Andreas (site 217, Map B) and Pouros.

North of the Pouros hill, it is again difficult to determine the position of the wall. A deep ravine running northwest-southeast between the Pouros and the high point marked by the church of Agios Georgios (site 93, Map B) makes construction especially problematic. The extensive landfills of the Mycenaeans (W 11) are evidence of their attempt to level the terrain. As they proceeded northward, they may well have repositioned the wall several times. By the end of the Mycenaean period, the wall probably passed just north of site 37, then curved toward site 45. Its direction after that, however, is something to ponder.

Keramopoullos again supposed that the wall must have stood at the limits of the modern-day Kadmeia, encircling the Archaeological Museum. Arguing against such a placement is the fact that the remains of the wall in the vicinity of W 5, W 6, W 7, and W 8 are *not* Mycenaean, as Keramopoullos conceded. In addition, Mycenaean remains are very sparse at the northern tip of the Kadmeia. There is only one house (site 248), a deposit at site 102, and the remains of houses excavated by Keramopoullos at an unspecified location (W 9). It is difficult to imagine the Mycenaeans erecting so long a stretch of wall to protect these isolated structures. They made no attempt to level the terrain north of site 45, although its current name *Gourna* ("trough") shows that it has always been a depression and remains so. These considerations, when viewed in conjunction with the westerly (rather than northerly) direction of the wall at W 3 (site 23) strongly suggest that after site 45, the Mycenaean wall turned sharply southeast, passed Agios Georgios (site 93), and continued towards W 3 (site 23). Although such a position would even further constrict the Kadmeia, it is supported by the evidence of dense occupation south of this line (i.e., inside the wall) and only sparse occupation north of it (outside the wall; see fig. 2.5).

On the east side, it is fairly certain that the wall held a north-south position, in a more or less straight line from W 1 (site 9), passing just outside of sites 113 and 246, and continuing in the direction of the gates at W 14 (site 7). The terrain is quite flat and chances are that the wall would have been higher, better built, and without gates or other openings. At site 7, the wall must have turned sharply west and followed a fairly straight line to site 19, as indicated by the features of W 12, W 13, and W 14.

The city enclosed by the wall as I have reconstructed it, though considerably smaller than that envisioned by Keramopoullos, is still extremely impressive in size, occupying an area of about 192,000 square meters, more than twice the size of the Middle Helladic town (ca. 80,000 square meters). Most of the Late Helladic expansion was to the north and east. Despite the great growth of the city, the total length of the wall (about 1,700 m) is only one half greater than that of the Middle Helladic period (1,150 m). This can be attributed not only to a phenomenon of geometry, but also to the fact that the wall was positioned along straight, rather than curving lines. In support of this reconstruction is the resulting orientation of the Mycenaean city, which retains essentially the same basic plan as the Middle Helladic town.

The only Mycenaean citadel larger than Thebes is the akropolis of Gla in the nearby Kopaic plain. Its wall of 2,500 to 2,600 m encloses an area of about 260,000 square meters. These measurements are derived from the very accurate maps published by Noack (1894, pl. 10) and Threpsiades (1958, fig. 2). They differ from the approximate measurements given by Ridder (1894:272, over 3,000 m and 200,000 square meters respectively), which have been repeated by others, including Threpsiades (1955:123). The town of Gla, built for military purposes, did not endure for very long; even its original name seems to have been forgotten. Although its walls represent a great engineering achievement, we should bear in mind that Gla sits on a rocky outcrop of the Kopaic basin, and stone was easily available. For our concerns, however, the importance of the walls of Gla is that they bear testimony to the presence of huge fortifications in Boiotia, which in turn attest to the presence of rich, highly organized cities. The celebrated walls of Thebes would not have been an isolated phenomenon, nor should they be viewed merely as a literary creation. In comparison with other Mycenaean fortifications, the walls of Gla are gigantic, and the walls of Thebes must have been no less so. The walls of Mycenae measure only 900 m, enclosing an area of 30,000 square meters; those of Tiryns and Athens are smaller still (Scoufopoulos 1971:82).

THE GATES OF THE KADMEIA

figs. 2.6 2.7 — Ancient writers made frequent allusion to "seven-gated" Thebes. Modern scholars, however, have called into question not only the location of the wall, but the actual number of gates. Although Keramopoullos convincingly showed that the gates were related to the akropolis of Thebes and not to the greater perimeter of Classical Thebes, his inability to find tangible remains of walls or gates left unanswered many doubts and questions about their location. His disposition of the gates, according to the seven traditional exits from the Kadmeia, is shown in figure 2.6. At each of the seven locations, archaeological remains of later periods were interpreted as evidence of earlier use of these areas for gates: there were Frankish towers at the locations of gates I and II; an old bridge at III; remains of Classical gates at IV; a Frankish tower at the end of Epaminondas St. (V, site 19), remains of which were found after Keramopoullos completed his scheme; and a spring at VI (*Krene* = "spring").

Keramopoullos was himself convinced that there were indeed seven gates during the Mycenaean period. Schober (1934:1429), however, objected that seven gates would have greatly weakened the fortifications. This is indeed a serious consideration: seven gates do seem too many for the Mycenaean period. Mycenae had only two, one of which was very small. Thebes, however, was so much larger a city that only two gates would not

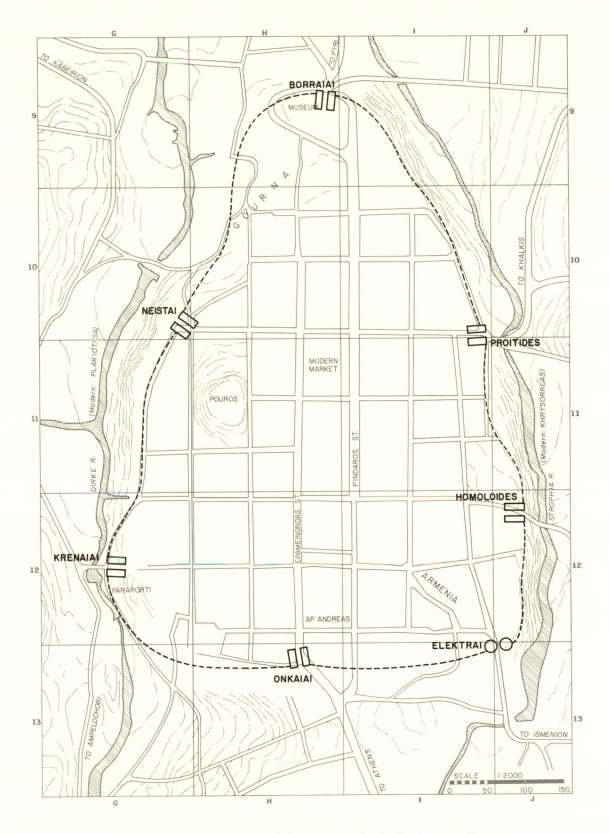

Fig. 2.6. The disposition of the gates on the Kadmeia according to
Keramopoullos (1917)

have accommodated comfortable ingress and egress of the population. The citadel of Gla, which was contemporary and of similar size, had four gates (one of which was double), spaced at regular intervals to allow for easy movement to and fro (Scoufopoulos 1971:124-126, plans 12-14).

The size of Mycenaean Thebes, determined by the position of the surrounding wall as I have reconstructed it, might well have called for no more than four gates. These might have been located more or less equidistantly at the four corners of a rectangle inscribed in the basic oval (sites 7, 9, 104, 19), all of which led to major roads. Medieval towers existed at sites 9 and 19, and there were remains of Classical gates and towers at site 7. Three of these locations (sites 7, 9, 104) can be shown to have had gates at the time of Pausanias. It is certainly possible that only three gates functioned during the Mycenaean period, but the parallel of Gla illustrates that four gates in a well-built and properly maintained fortification would not have resulted in diminished defense capability. More than four would be hard to justify. A gate in the low-lying north wall, in close proximity to the palace, would have constituted a great weakness. The short distances between gates known to have been located at the east and south sides (400 m and 300 m, respectively) would have made another gate unnecessary there. The long west wall may have had a gate to provide access to the spring of Paraporti (the Krenaiai gates are named with a spring in mind), but the Mycenaeans had constructed an aqueduct that brought water from the south into town, thereby diminishing the importance of this spring to the water supply of Thebes. It is therefore unlikely that a full-size gate existed here in the Mycenaean period, although it is possible that there was a smaller one, comparable to the Postern gate at Mycenae (Mylonas 1966:18). The Kadmeia, then, is rather more likely to have had three or four gates than seven during that period.

How, then, can we account for the traditional description of Thebes as seven-gated? Ancient authors not only allude to the number but also refer to each gate by name. As shown in table 2.1, ten of the gate names recur in ancient literature. Some of the names may have referred to the same gate. *Onkaiai* and *Hypsistai*, for example, must have been alternately used for the gate near both the sanctuary of Athena Onka and that of Zeus Hypsistos. The name honoring a spring, *Dircaea culmina* (no. 11), used by Statius is surely an alternate for *Krenaiai*. With the exception of Nonnus and Hyginus, each of whom offers an entirely different set of names, the ancient authors are in nearly complete accord, as shown in table 2.2. The names *Hebdomai* and *Borraiai*, which occur least frequently, may well have been alternate names for other gates. Keramopoullos' disposition of the names is seen in figure 2.6.

It is also possible, using the record left by Pausanias in combination with the archaeological and topographical evidence amassed by Keramopoullos, to assign many of the names to specific locations. Pausanias was quite orderly in referring first to the gates he actually used during his visit to Thebes: the Elektrai, the Proitides, and the Neistai (cf.

Table 2.1. The names for the seven gates of Thebes recorded in ancient literature

Names of Gates	Aischylos Seven	Euripides Phoin.	Pausanias 9.8	Pseudo-Apollodoros 3.68	Statius Thebais	Nonnus Dion.	Hyginus Fab. 69
1. Proitides	+	+	+	+	+		
2. Elektrai	+	+	+	+	+	+	
3. Neistai	+	+	+		+		
4. Homoloides	+	+	+	+	+		
5. Borraiai	+						
6. Hebdomai	+	+					
7. Onkaiai	+			+		+	
8. Ogygiai		+	+	+	+		+
9. Krenaiai		+	+	+			
10. Hypsistai			+	+	+		
11. Dircaea Culmina					+		
12. Hermaon						+	
13. Aphrodite						+	
14. Ares						+	
15. Zenos						+	
16. Kronou						+	
17. Astykratia							+
18. Cleodoxa							+
19. Astynome							+
20. Chias							+
21. Chloris							+
22. Thora							+

Note: Only the first ten names occur repeatedly.

Table 2.2. Frequency of occurrence of the gate names in the writings of the five ancient authorities who enumerate them (see table 2.1)

Gates	Authors in Agreement	Gates	Authors in Agreement
1. Elektrai	5	5. Ogygiai	4
2. Proitides	5	6. Krenaiai or Dirkaiai	4
3. Homoloides	5	7. Neistai	4
4. Onkaiai or Hypsistai	5	Hebdomai	2
		Borraiai	1

chap. 5). From the context of Pausanias' topographical associations, it is clear that the Elektrai were at site 7, the Proitides near site 9 (at the road to Chalkis), and the Neistai near site 104 (at the road to Kabeirion). The gates are mentioned in counterclockwise order. The locations of the remaining four gates, also mentioned in counterclockwise order, can be inferred: the Krenaiai should be situated near the spring of Paraporti (site 53, ancient Dirke), south of the Neistai gates. The Hypsistai must be at a high point near the southern tip of the Kadmeia, where there was a sanctuary of Zeus Hypsistos (Agios Andreas, site 217).

At this point Pausanias completes a full circle, having returned to the Elektrai gates once again. Although he does refer to the Ogygiai and Homoloides gates, their location is problematic. If they are placed in counterclockwise order, they fall between the Elektrai and Proitides gates. Keramopoullos (1917:472, 475) believed that only one gate could be accommodated there; he preferred to place the Homoloides in that location, owing to the documented existence of a cult of Zeus Homoloios (*IG* 7:2456). He assumed the Ogygiai gates were the same as the Borraiai, located at the northern tip of the Kadmeia. Thus, although he diverged from Pausanias in this regard, he did tally seven gates, in apparent accordance with tradition, if against strategic prudence for a Late Helladic fortification. However, there is another disposition that coordinates both tradition and a plausible fortification plan.

In discussing fortifications of the Middle Helladic period, we observed that having numerous gates did not seem to be viewed as undesirable, and that a city the size of Middle Helladic Thebes could well have had seven. I would suggest that some of the gate names we have been discussing originated with the gates not of the Late Helladic, but of the Middle Helladic fortifications. If the outline of the Middle Helladic town is superimposed on the outline of the Late Helladic town, the result is the configuration shown in figure 2.7. The names of the Middle Helladic gates are given in the singular in order to highlight their common peculiarity: all but the Borraia belonged to legendary Theban women, two of whom are associated with Kadmos, who founded Thebes, and four of whom are associated with Amphion and Zethos, who fortified it. Kadmos is said to have dedicated a sanctuary to Athena Onka in celebration of the founding of Thebes (Aischylos, *Hepta* 164; Pausanias 9.12.2). There are ancient references to Elektra as the mother of Harmonia, Kadmos' wife (Ephoros, *FGrHist* 70 F120). Of the four names related to Amphion and Zethos (who are said not only to have built the walls but also to have renamed the city in honor of Zethos' wife, Thebe), three are recorded as daughters: Neis (*FGrHist* 3 F125), Homolois (schol. Aischylos, *Hepta* 553; schol. Lykophron, *Alexandra* 520), and Ogygia (Hyginus, *Fabulae* 69). Dirke was the aunt of Antiope, who was the mother of Amphion and Zethos. We also observe in figure 2.7, that in startling accord with the account of Pausanias, the two Middle Helladic gates to which I have applied the names *Ogygiai* and *Homoloides* fall in counterclockwise order between the Late Helladic gates named *Elektrai* and *Proitides*.

36

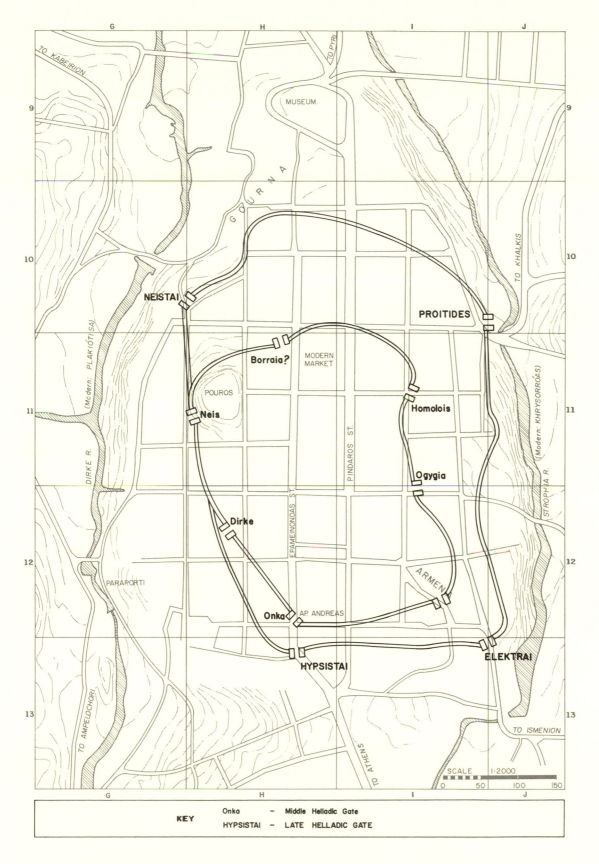

KEY   Onka   —   Middle Helladic Gate
HYPSISTAI — LATE HELLADIC GATE

Fig. 2.7. The disposition of the Middle Helladic and Late Helladic gates
on the Kadmeia

Not only would a seven-gated Middle Helladic fortification have been strategically acceptable, but as I will show below, the Middle Helladic wall probably had a very long life. I believe it most unlikely that in a culture relying significantly on oral memory, all the Middle Helladic gate names were dropped and forgotten when, in later times, the wall was renovated and repositioned. Some of the names must have been retained or used as alternates. Indeed, there is archaeological evidence to support continuing use of the name *Neistai*. The Neistai gates were in the northwest area of the Kadmeia, where massive landfills were needed in order to terrace a depression that was as deep as 15 m. Evidence of this activity is seen in the extremely deep deposits of sites 17, 120, 171, and 181 (fig. 2.5). The landfilling effort began in the Middle Helladic period; Middle Helladic deposits were very thick in sites 17, 120, and 171. The existence of Late Helladic terracing walls was confirmed in sites 17 and 45. It is likely, then, that as the landfilling was accomplished, the wall and the gates were gradually repositioned, and the gate name was retained. The name *Elektrai* may also have been retained with the gradual extension of the wall's perimeter. The two new gate names, *Hypsistai* and *Proitides*, honor male figures: Zeus Hypsistos and Proitos (Pausanias 9.8.4-5; cf. Schober 1934:1428-1434).

The completion of a Late Helladic wall with four rather than seven gates does not mean that the older gate names were discarded because the Middle Helladic gates were no longer in existence. The names may well have continued to be used to identify locations within the city, in much the same way that *Porta Maggiore* is used in present-day Rome, or *Porte Maillot* in Paris. The Onkaiai marked the location of the sanctuary of Athena Onka; the Homoloides, the sanctuary of Zeus Homoloios; the Dirkaiai, the spring Dirke.

I think it unlikely that there were two simultaneous rings of fortifications with gates placed one behind the other as in Tiryns and Athens. This notion was put forward by Robert (1909:173; 1915, vol. 1, 237) who rightly envisioned two rings to account for all the gate names. Had there been two simultaneous rings, however, some trace or indication, however slight, of the inner ring should have remained, whereas the purposeful dismantling of a Middle Helladic wall, which was being replaced, would account for its complete physical disappearance.

This complete disappearance must have occurred only after the wall had stood for a very long time. The evidence for dating the new Late Helladic wall is insufficient, amounting to only four sherds found in site 9 by Keramopoullos. It would, however, be safe to suggest that a Cyclopean wall 1,700 m long could only have been built when the technology to do so was available. Mylonas (1962A; 1966:25) has dated the earliest Cyclopean wall at Mycenae to the second half of LH III A:2. The Cyclopean wall of Thebes cannot have been built much earlier than this. As palatial Thebes was destroyed in LH III B:1, the Cyclopean wall could not have stood even as long as a hundred years. The earlier wall, however, built sometime in the Middle Helladic period, must have lasted through LH III A:2. Although the Cyclopean wall must have been an awesome spectacle, I think it more likely that the poetic references to a well-fortified, seven-gated Thebes recall the earlier fortifications that protected the city for so much longer a time.

Table 2.3. A summary of disposition and dates of houses and the two Mycenaean palaces

Sites of well-constructed houses	3, 13, 110, 166, 179, 184, 192, 198, 206, 265, 269
Sites where frescoes have been found	1, 2, 3, 13, 110, 179, 181, 184, 185, 192, 206, 265, 269
Sites of the first palace and related structures	1, 103, 204, 260, 261, 109
Sites of the second palace and related structures	2, 4, 165, 196, 229, 185(?)
Sites with evidence of destruction in LH III B:1 period	2, 3, 4, 165, 171, 229, 247
Sites with evidence of the LH III B:2 period	165, 185, 192
Houses with the same orientation as the second palace	171, 179(?), 229, 248

RESIDENTIAL ARCHITECTURE: HOUSES AND PALACES

The determination of the position of the Late Helladic wall just discussed is based on the density of the remains of habitation, which show considerable expansion of the city to the north and east, as well as a lesser expansion to the south, in relation to the Middle Helladic town. The area encompassed by the wall measures approximately 192,000 square meters and is, therefore, six and a half times larger than Mycenae and ten times larger than Tiryns. The reconstruction I have proposed indicates the existence of sparse extramural settlement, evidence of which is shown at the distant site 211 (fig. 2.12, J-12), perhaps at site 248 (fig. 2.5, I-10) and by the deposits at sites 20, 21 (fig. 2.5, G-11), and 102 (fig. 2.5, I-10). All other remains are intramural.

The depth of Late Helladic deposits varied from 0.40 m to over 2 m, depending on the location on the Kadmeia and degree of preservation. Those Mycenaean levels that were well preserved showed successive phases of occupation: as many as three phases in sites 4 and 110, and two phases in sites 3, 179, 185, and 206. The earlier Late Helladic houses were constructed much like those of the Middle Helladic period, on stone foundations set in shallow trenches that were usually dug in the debris of earlier periods. Toward the end of the Late Helladic period, larger stones were used, set in deeper foundation trenches, which sometimes went down to bedrock. The rough kind of limestone used was quarried at Mt. Kotsika, 5.5 km west of the Kadmeia (fig. 1.2). There is no closer source, and the quarrying and transporting of such stone in the huge quantities required, not only for the fortification but also for residential architecture, further attests to the tremendous economic prosperity and advanced social organization of Thebes during the Late Helladic period.

The upper structures were composed of mud-brick, sometimes reinforced with wood. Frescoes were found in many sites, another indication of widespread affluence (table 2.3).

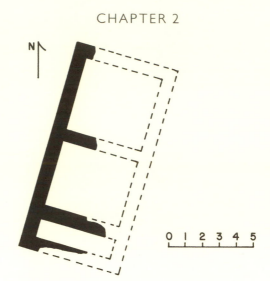

Fig. 2.8. Site 3, reconstructed plan of
Late Helladic megaron

Unfortunately, we are no more able to reconstruct the plans of Late Helladic houses than
those of earlier ones. The best-preserved house (site 3), built above a Middle Helladic
cemetery, was 12 m long and probably 6 m wide (fig. 2.8); a shallow porch provided
access to two consecutive square rooms and indicates a megaron design. The owner was
clearly someone of great wealth and power, able to afford not only decorative frescoes
and carved ivory furnishings, but also a collection of bronze weapons including a defensive
armor similar to that found at Dendra. As Chadwick has pointed out (1969:127), the
Linear B tablets found here constitute the local record keeping of a small storage building
and do not belong to the palace archives. This house, therefore, has no connection with
either of the palaces. It was destroyed along with palatial Thebes at the end of LH III
B:1 (see site 3 and table 2.3).

If the relatively well-preserved house of site 3 is a typical example of a wealthy family
residence in the densely populated Kadmeia, then the existence of other such houses at
numerous sites throughout the Kadmeia may well indicate the presence of a sizeable
upper class. Remains of well-built houses were found at ten sites in addition to site 3
and these do not include the sites related to the two palaces; nine of these sites produced
evidence of frescoes (table 2.3). Only two of these sites (185, 192) showed possible
evidence of reuse in LH III B:2 and this reinforces the idea that most of Thebes suffered
the destruction that marked the end of the palatial period.

THE PALACES OF THE KADMEIA

That there were two Mycenaean palaces on the Kadmeia is clearly shown by the differences in the way they were built, in their orientation, and, as I will show, by the separate

and distinct areas they occupy. It is not possible to provide a complete plan for either of these buildings. It was only in 1963 that the first part of the second palace was discovered (site 2), and only a few more portions have been found since (table 2.3).

Keramopoullos excavated as much as he could of the first palace (site 1). A re-analysis of his work (see Catalogue) has made possible a more complete reconstruction of that palace than he originally provided (cat. fig. 1). The excavated portion is clearly part of a larger building that may have extended to the east and north (see table 2.3 for possible sites associated with the first palace). The proximity to site 1 of sites 103 and 204 on Pindaros St., both of which yielded evidence of Mycenaean occupation, may allow us to consider them as belonging to the same building. Perhaps there is substance to the rumor that a part of this palace was found at site 261, because extensive storage facilities dating to the Mycenaean period were found in this area (site 260), very close to site 1. It is highly likely that all these sites belong to the same structure.

The portion of the first palace that Keramopoullos excavated is by far the best-preserved structure in Thebes of any period, having at least fifteen rooms on either side of a long, winding corridor. The orientation is south-southwest by north-northeast. The plan of the better-preserved western half is clear except for the northwest corner. The eastern half, much of which was destroyed, is problematic.

There seem to be two possible reconstructions: the first renders room *A* slightly greater in length than in width, in typical megaron style. The east facade would then be either straight with unusually elongated rooms, or indented, which I think more likely (fig. 2.9). The second possibility (fig. 2.10) shows a square room *A* and a straight east facade with rooms of balanced proportions. This is a symmetrical plan and the more persuasive reconstruction, not only because the wall on the west side is straight, but also because it calls to mind the palace of Gla, which has similarly straight or slightly indented walls (Threpsiades 1960:35, fig. 7).

The only certain entrance to the building is corridor *K*, which must have opened to the east facade; there is a similar corridor on the west facade (*Π*1). Both of these corridors lead to the long corridor that runs the length of the interior, curves around rooms *Θ* and *H*, and ends in room *B*. From room *B* one has access to the large square room *A*, and the narrow space *Γ*. Somewhere here there should be a main entrance to the complex. Keramopoullos (1921:23) suggests that room *A* belonged to a megaron, an interpretation that my reconstruction supports. This makes an entrance on the east side unlikely. The best possibility is in room *Γ*, where Keramopoullos initially expected to find a continuation of the long west wall. When he realized it was not there, he suggested that this area might be an entrance (1922:30). Curiously, he had found ten years earlier, in an undisturbed Mycenaean layer somewhere west of the building, an enormous stone slab of irregular shape, 2.10 m long and as thick as 0.75 m. On its flat side, an oval measuring 1.54 m × 1.36 m had been cut and raised by 0.105 m. Keramopoullos (1912:87, fig. 1) called it a keystone from a tholos tomb but Kavvadias (1912:76) recognized it as a

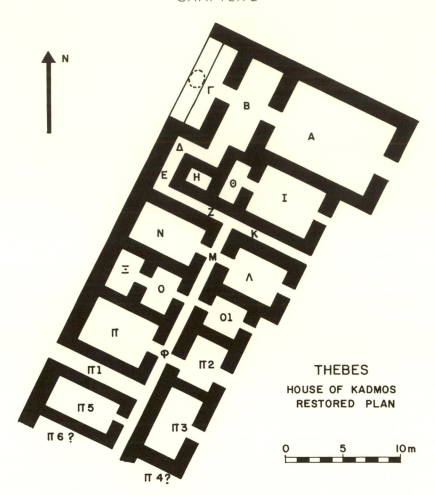

Fig. 2.9. Site 1, restored plan of the first Mycenaean palace
(first possibility)

column base that might have supported a double column. A similarly large base (diam. 1.42 m) was found at the propylon at Phaistos (Pernier and Banti 1951:320-321); this base is the largest known in Crete (Shaw 1973:119-121). Although the Theban column base was not found in situ, its orginal position may well have been room *Γ*. Room *Γ*, then, would have been the entrance to the complex, leading to the long corridor and the megaron-like room *A* with its anteroom *B*.

These last rooms were very poorly preserved and no finds are associated with them. Room *B* continues to the south with a 1.12 m wide corridor that contained a great many large stirrup-jars in its first two sections (*Δ* and *E*); overall, there were over 120 stirrup-jars found in the corridor, a third of which were inscribed with Linear B (Raison 1968:15).

From *Z*, the corridor continues in two directions: towards the east side through *K*, and towards the south through *Φ*. More pottery and frescoes were found here, but the most important find was a hoard of objects made of onyx in front of room *Π* (Kera-

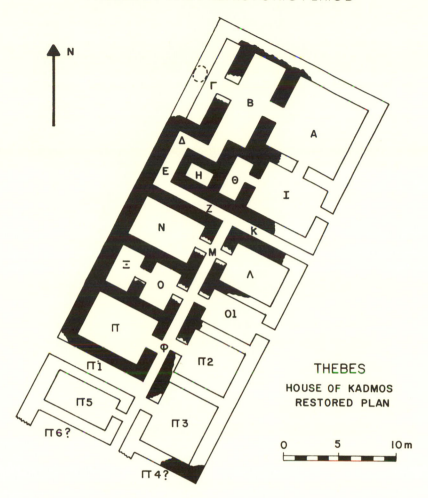

Fig. 2.10. Site 1, restored plan of the first Mycenaean palace (second possibility)

mopoullos 1930A). The corridor was found to continue for at least 6 m beyond the published plan, but it is only mentioned by Keramopoullos (1928:49-50). This allows for a reconstruction of the plan with additional rooms *Π1-Π6* (cf. fig. 2.10, cat. fig. 1).

Large quantities of pottery were found in rooms *Λ* and *Π*, and smaller amounts in practically every other room. Frescoes were found in rooms *Λ*, *Ξ*, and *Π*, the best-preserved in room *N*, showing a procession of women. Other finds included large numbers of glass-paste beads (rooms *N* and *Ξ*), gold jewelry and scraps of gold (rooms *N*, *Ξ*, and *Π*), bronze arrowheads and one spearhead (room *Ξ*), rock crystal (room *Ξ*), a stone carving and a stone vase (room *I*). Terracotta tiles were found in rooms *Λ*, *Ξ*, and especially *Π*. During a cleanup operation in 1965, we found by accident on the west wall of room *Π2*, 105 grams of gold wire that had originally been on a spool.

The building found by Keramopoullos was erected without proper foundations on leveled ground, in a manner reminiscent of Minoan buildings (Graham 1962:149). Protruding irregularities of the terrain were leveled off and cavities were filled with clay (Keramopoullos 1909A:86). The lower parts of the walls, which were of stone, were then built directly on the leveled surface. More clay may then have been added to further level the surface. Keramopoullos found a thick layer of clay in the low levels of the excavation, but was unable to locate doorways. This is probably because above the clay surface, there was a massive construction including floors, thresholds, and doorways, all made of wood, and held in position by the stone foundations. A large amount of wood was also used in the upper structure of the walls, together with small, irregular stones, and mud-bricks of assorted sizes. These diverse materials were bound together with clay mortar, and both transverse and horizontal wooden beams, a manner of construction known elsewhere in Greece (Mylonas 1966:48, fig. 11). The walls were then stuccoed and painted. Another characteristic of such construction is that the stone foundations are not bonded at the junctions, but simply lean against one another (Keramopoullos 1909A:84-85).

Although Keramopoullos originally conceived of the building as multistoried (1909A:89-90), he later proposed that it was single-storied (1927A:42). There are, however, several features that support his original conception, such as the clustering of small rooms at ground level, and the presence of thick walls that could well have supported a second storey (Graham 1962:114-117). Moreover, Keramopoullos did find two layers of burned debris (cat. table 1, nos. 2, 5), and two layers of plaster (cat. table 1, nos. 2, 4). In room *N*, which was the best preserved, jewelry and other small objects were found high above the floor, indicating that they had fallen from a second storey. Perhaps yet another indication of the existence of a second storey is the presence of a light-well (room *H*), next to which is room *Θ*, where there may have been a staircase to the second floor.

Terracotta tiles were found throughout the excavation (Keramopoullos mentions their presence in rooms *Λ*, *Ξ*, and *Π*), first referred to as "fired bricks" (1909A:70, 72). Two complete examples measured 0.32 m × 0.32 m and 0.03 to 0.05 m thick, and 0.27 m × 0.26 m and 0.02 m thick. The function of these tiles is unclear. In the context of the reconstructed stratigraphy (cat. table 1), they were found in the second layer from the top and the sixth layer, just above the floor. Although the sizes vary, Keramopoullos thought they might have been roof tiles, which would have meant that the building had had a sloping roof. This conception, though strongly supported by some in the past (Smith 1942; Dinsmoor 1942; 1950:7, n. 3), was so convincingly disputed by Blegen (1945) that today it is generally believed that flat and not sloping roofs were characteristic of Mycenaean architecture (McDonald 1967:373). No roof tiles have been found in Crete (Graham 1962:160), though square tiles were used in floors and as drain covers (Shaw 1973:204-205). Roof tiles of the Classical period were made large and heavy (Martin 1965:68-72) to minimize wind damage and reduce the need for frequent repair. The

Mycenaean tiles of Thebes are much smaller and thinner, and were probably used as Blegen suggested (1945:38-39), in floors or on drains, just as in Crete.

The excavated part of the first palace amounts to approximately 700 square meters. Although we cannot be sure of the plan of the entire building, those areas that may be associated with it occupy an additional 1,700 square meters, giving a minimum total of 2,400 square meters, not including whatever courtyards may have existed (fig. 2.11). The remains extend to the north and east in what appears to be an L-shaped plan, so that if there were a courtyard, it would have been west of the excavated portion. Such an arrangement is seen in the palace of Gla, which occupies 1,800 square meters. Keramopoullos did search in vain west of the palace for additional architectural remains.

The first palace of Thebes is thus much smaller than any of the Minoan palaces, occupying one sixth the area of the palace of Knossos, or a third of those at Mallia and Phaistos (Graham 1962:42). This is to be expected, however, if one bears in mind that unlike Minoan towns, the Kadmeia was fortified and space within the walls was limited. At Pylos, the main area of the palace of Nestor occupies 1,500 square meters, with the additional structures doubling the total space, making it comparable to the first palace of Kadmeia. The palace of Tiryns is also of comparable size if one includes the courtyard and all rooms north of the great Propylon. In this context, the palace of Thebes is certainly impressive.

THE FIRST PALACE IN ANCIENT TRADITION

Keramopoullos believed that the building he had unearthed was the famed house of Kadmos, and he published a lengthy explanation of the relationship between the excavated remains and the stories pertaining to Kadmos, Semele, and Dionysos (1909A:111-122). Best remembered are the myths that describe the destruction of the house of Kadmos and the ensuing birth of the god Dionysos. The most frequent account is that the house of Kadmos was destroyed when Zeus appeared to Semele in all the thunder and lightning of his true nature. Semele was herself consumed, but Dionysos, whom she was about to bear, was saved. This story was quite popular in antiquity, appearing in Hesiod (*Theogony* 940-942), and in Homer (*Iliad* 14.323-325); Aischylos based an entire play on it (Kirk 1970:2). In the *Bacchai* of Euripides (1-63), Dionysos relates that the site of the burned palace, called the tomb of Semele, continues to smolder from the fire of Zeus. Praising Kadmos for sanctifying the site, he claims that he himself covered it with vines, and also declares Thebes the first city in Greece to establish his cult.

The account of the birth of Dionysos is repeated several times in the *Bacchai*: by Pentheus (242-245), by Teiresias (274ff.), by Kadmos (330ff.) and by the chorus (522ff., 597f.). As if repetition of the telling were not enough, Euripides gives it even greater theatrical reality when he has Dionysos escape from the house of Pentheus, leaving it in

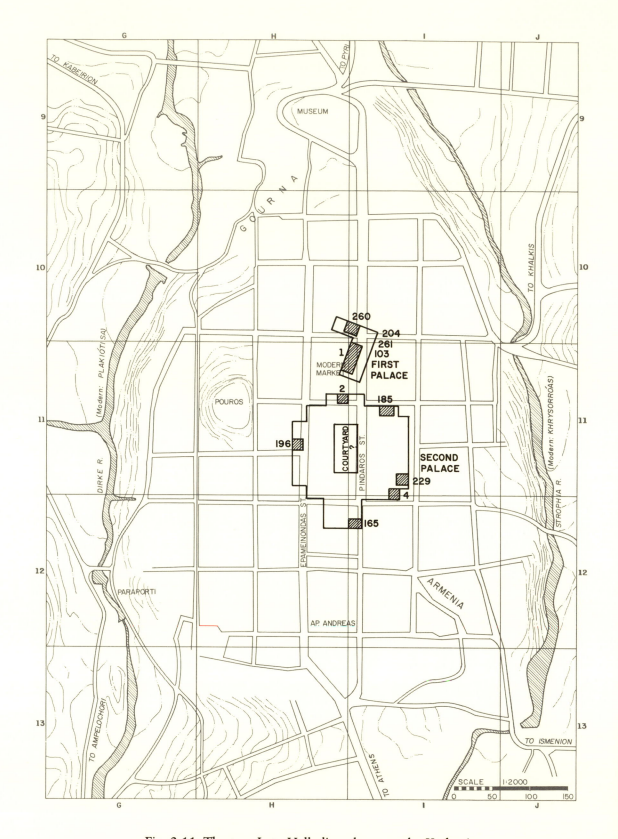

Fig. 2.11. The two Late Helladic palaces on the Kadmeia

ruins, and reactivate the fire on Semele's tomb, which is in full view on the stage (623-624). In a slightly different version presumably told by the Thebans (schol. Euripides, *Phoin.* 649), when the palace was destroyed by lightning, ivy suddenly grew up around the columns and also covered the infant Dionysos, protecting him from the fire. In this way Dionysos' epithet, περικιόνιος ("around the column"), is explained (indeed, there was a column fetish at the sanctuary of Dionysos Kadmeios during the Roman period: Pausanias 9.12.4). This version may also be seen to complement Dionysos' claim in the *Bacchai* to have covered his mother's "tomb" with vines (6-12). Lending credence to this story is the huge column base described above that may be linked to the column fetish seen by Pausanias.

Clearly, Greek literary tradition preserves the association of the destruction by lightning of the palace of Thebes with the birth of the god Dionysos, and with the subsequent maintenance of the site of the burned palace as an open-air sanctuary sacred to Dionysos. It is important to realize that the fire which destroyed the palace was an extraordinary one that affected later cult practices.

THE SECOND PALACE

When Pausanias visited Thebes in the second century A.D., he was shown palace ruins at an active sanctuary of Dionysos Kadmeios, and also, in close proximity, the ruins of another palace on which the sanctuary of Demeter Thesmophoros had been built. This second palace was discovered in 1963, only 30 m south of the first (cat. fig. 1). It was possible to excavate only a small part of it, but portions belonging to this building have been found in at least four, and possibly five, locations (table 2.3). The rich finds of site 2 made it clear that another palatial structure had been found: there was a large collection of lapis lazuli which included 36 Near Eastern cylinder seals, a large group of onyx jewelry, ivories, gold jewelry, and frescoes. Two storage rooms were found. Massive stone foundations reaching the bedrock and preserved to a height of over 2 m were associated with the finds.

At site 4, 150 m away (fig. 2.5), excavation uncovered a large collection of ivories, a workshop for gold and semiprecious stone jewelry, and a collection of well-made pottery. Here, there were remains of as many as three architectural phases in the Late Helladic period, the latest of which resembled the remains of site 2—massive foundations down to bedrock. There is clear evidence that the building was destroyed at the end of LH III B:1. The floor of the building had been renovated early in LH III B:1. This evidence and the possible association of a collection of ivories and pottery dating to LH III A:2 lead one to believe that the date of construction was sometime in LH III A:2. The monumental construction and the associated finds allow us to consider this structure a part of the second Late Helladic palace.

Related to site 4 are the finds of site 165: another workshop for fine jewelry was discovered here, and the finds included various tools, stone molds, rock-crystal beads, faience, onyx, and ivory. The pottery from the destruction level dated the building to the end of LH III B:1. The site is 170 m south of site 2; this must also be part of the second Late Helladic palace.

Two rooms from a structure similar to that found in site 4 were found in site 229, where the date of destruction was also LH III B:1. It is possible that the earlier remains of site 185 also belong to the second Late Helladic palace. Finally, in site 196, three rooms were found, one containing a bathtub, another 17 Linear B tablets; there were also frescoes, fine tools, figurines, and a large quantity of pottery. It is likely that these remains, located 90 m from site 2, belong to the same building. Although Spyropoulos (1970) (who identified the site as the palace archives) dated the destruction to LH III B:2, the published material from this site is consistently similar in style to that found in other parts of this building, and dates to LH III B:1 (see Catalogue, site 196).

The remains of the second palace, which we have been describing, occupy a large area in the central part of the Kadmeia; the longest north-south dimension is 170 m, and the longest east-west is 150 m (fig. 2.11). By comparison, the maximum dimensions of the palace at Knossos, which is the largest building known of prehistoric Greece, are 150 m x 140 m. At Knossos, the actual remains, including the central courtyard, occupy approximately 15,000 square meters, owing to the irregular outline of the building. The size of the second palace of Thebes could be as great as 21,000 square meters, assuming that the excavated portions do indeed belong to one building, as they seem to. A building so large is likely to have had one or more courtyards, as did the Minoan palaces; this design would make the second palace of Thebes a unique structure on the Greek mainland. The existence of the courtyards, however, must remain hypothetical until there is archaeological confirmation.

The architectural features of the second Late Helladic palace are remarkable for the time. The building rests on massive stone foundations, which, as we have already observed, required the transporting of heavy limestone blocks from Mt. Kotsika, 5.5 km away. In addition, the builders changed the orientation from the usual northeast-southwest to an exact north-south. For the first time in the history of the city, a building was oriented in a position drastically different from those surrounding it. Before the violent destruction of the city, there was time for a few more houses to be constructed in the new orientation (table 2.3). After the fall of the Late Helladic Kadmeia, however, all buildings were constructed in the new orientation and continued to be, right up to the present day. This can hardly be attributed to chance: it seems safe to assume that the ruins of the second Late Helladic palace were visible for a long time, providing a guide for the orientation of new buildings.

Keramopoullos (1929:61) suggested a date of LH II for the construction of the first palace on the basis of pottery found beneath a terracing wall in room *N*. He also distinguished a renovation phase late in LH II or early in LH III (Keramopoullos 1909A:105-

106; 1930A:33). On the basis of style, Reusch (1955) dated the frescoes from the palace to the early fifteenth century B.C. The method of construction also suggests a comparably early date. Evidence from the cemeteries confirms the fact that Thebes was prosperous in LH II, making the existence of a palace during that time very plausible.

Aspects of the chronological relationship between the two palaces are difficult to clarify. Platon and Touloupa (1964A:860) propose that there was a 30-year interval between the destruction of one and the destruction of the other, but that both were destroyed within LH III B. Spyropoulos (1970) asserts that there was only one palace and it was destroyed at the end of LH III B or the beginning of LH III C. Raison (1977) believes that both palaces shared a simultaneous destruction in LH III B:1.

In my earlier discussion of this subject (1973:73-76) I proposed that there were two palaces, which did not exist simultaneously; I dated the destruction of the second to the end of LH III B:1, a date now confirmed in three other parts of the palace (sites 2, 165, 229). I proposed that the first palace was destroyed early in LH III A:2, only slightly later than the date proposed by Keramopoullos (1909A:106) and Furumark (1941B:52), both of whom dated the destruction of the first palace to LH III A:1. Several considerations led me to conclude that the two palaces could not possibly have coexisted, and that the second palace was built at the beginning of LH III A:2, after the first palace had been destroyed. It is quite clear that the part of the second palace found in site 4 had already been built before the end of LH III A:2 (Symeonoglou 1973:17, 22, 62), and that part, which is 150 m away from the "Treasury Room" (site 2), may have been built somewhat later than the main part of the palace (i.e., site 2). Bearing in mind that Furumark assigned an early date to the pottery from the first palace, if we were to date the destruction of that palace to the end of LH III A:2 (the latest possible date), we would be implying that the second palace not only was built in its entirety, but also met its destruction, all within LH III B:1. Such a short life span seems to me unlikely.

Rutter (1974) and Snodgrass (1975) have reasonably objected that the evidence from site 4 is insufficient to date either the destruction of the first palace or the construction of the second palace to LH III A:2. I agree that dating the transition from one palace to the other must await clearer archaeological evidence. What does seem quite clear, however, is that the second palace was destroyed at the end of LH III B:1, and the part found at site 4 was in existence before the end of LH III A:2 (cf. Snodgrass 1975, Courtois 1976; Rutter 1974 does not accept the destruction date). It is also clear that the first palace was destroyed before the end of LH III A:2, meaning that its Linear B inscriptions are earlier than LH III B. Although Snodgrass (1975) does not find this surprising, Raison vehemently objects (1977) and adheres to the date of LH III B:1, which he earlier proposed (1968).

If Raison holds to this date, then he must also accept the overlapping existence of the two palaces and their simultaneous destruction in LH III B:1. In practical terms, this is not so far from Spyropoulos' view (1970) that there was only one palace. Yet, such a view rests on the assumption that the later structure is an extension of the earlier one. Many considerations argue against this: the part of the later structure that lies nearest the earlier one is 30 m south of it; the two buildings occupy altogether different areas (figs. 2.11, cat. fig. 1) and differ significantly both in orientation and in manner of construction. In addition, Theban tradition as recorded in Pausanias preserves the memory of two separate buildings (see chap. 5, passages 7 and 9). Finally, the coexistence of two palaces runs contrary to common sense and the constraints of practicality. Can one call to mind a single parallel in prehistoric Greece of a king who, in a crowded, walled city where space is at a premium, constructs a gigantic new palace while continuing to maintain the old one? Even Nero did not build his second palace until the first had burned down!

The Aqueduct

fig. 2.12

As there is no natural source of water on the Kadmeia, whatever was needed had to be brought into the city from the two nearest sources, the springs of Paraporti (site 53) and Pege (site 173, see Map A). But in the Mycenaean period water was needed inside the citadel in order to enable its inhabitants to withstand long periods of siege. We now have sufficient evidence to show that the Thebans constructed an underground conduit that brought water into the city from the higher ground south of the Kadmeia. Remains of it have been found in five sites (fig. 2.12). It is easy to distinguish it from the aqueduct of the Classical period because the Mycenaean is stone-lined and tapers upward.

A segment 12.50 m long was found in site 13. It had been stripped of most of its stones and was filled with debris that included a large quantity of Mycenaean pottery. The conduit had been cut in the rock 2 m deep and 1.30 m wide at the bottom. The segment in which the stone lining was preserved measured 1.10 m deep and 0.50 m wide at the bottom. The same kind of limestone was used in the aqueduct as in the foundations of houses; the stones were small in size with large slabs used as coverstones.

Other segments of this conduit were found in neighboring site 184 and in site 109. A portion of it was probably also found at the southern end of the Kadmeia (site 209) but the excavator found no evidence for its date and does not give the dimensions of the conduit. This site, however, together with the other three, forms a straight line that cuts diagonally across the Kadmeia in a southeast-northwest direction, which was the orientation of the city in the Bronze Age (figs. 2.1, 2.3, 2.5). In site 2, a small stone-lined duct oriented east-west was found, which brought water from the main aqueduct to the second Mycenaean palace.

Pappadakis (1911:141) excavated a portion of the Mycenaean aqueduct on the slopes of Kolonaki, west of the church of Agios Nikolaos (site 215, Map A). According to his description, the conduit was cut in the rock, approximately 2 m high and 1 m wide at the bottom, tapering toward the top. At the bottom of the conduit, he found a channel 0.32 m wide, lined with clay pipes that he described as being of "Roman date." These

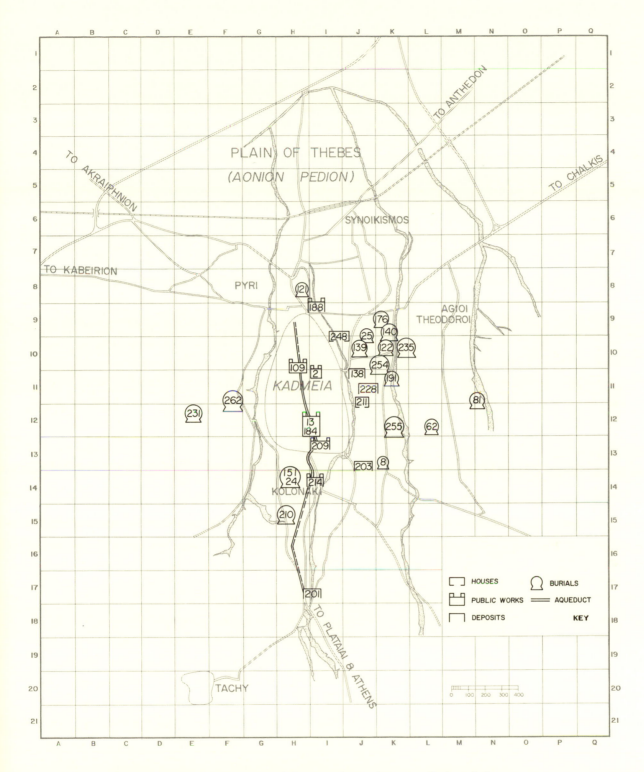

Fig. 2.12. The cemeteries and the aqueduct of Late Helladic Thebes

pipes show that at least a part of the Mycenaean conduit was rediscovered in later times and put into use. There was Mycenaean pottery in the conduit. Keramopoullos (1917:327-329) also reports finding another segment of this aqueduct farther south.

The Mycenaean aqueduct was at least 1 km long and brought an abundant and concealed supply of water to the city. The existing evidence does not allow us to confirm the date of its construction but it is possible that it was built at the same time as the extensive fortifications, the date of which I suggested was LH III A. It was, therefore, short-lived like the second palace of Thebes. The evidence from site 13 shows that the conduit on the Kadmeia was filled with debris shortly after the destruction of palatial Thebes. The conduit on Kolonaki, however, was reused in later times. Herakleides Kritikos (*FHG* 2.258 F12) refers to an aqueduct that was thought to be the work of Kadmos; perhaps he had in mind the Kolonaki segment of the Mycenaean aqueduct. The hill of Kolonaki has been used for aqueducts in many periods up to modern times. It is certainly possible that during construction of a later aqueduct (see chap. 3) the workers came upon a piece of the Late Helladic one and decided to reuse it. This may account for the presence of clay pipes of "Roman date," which Pappadakis saw; Keramopoullos (1917:327, fig. 192) mistakenly identified these as Mycenaean pipes.

The Cemeteries

fig. 2.12 The sandstone hills of Thebes are ideal for chamber tombs, and indeed, this is the only type one finds; no tholos or stone-lined tombs of any kind have been found dating to the Late Helladic period. Theban chamber tombs are similar to those found elsewhere in the Mycenaean world: there is an approach, or *dromos*, cut in the hill slope, and an entry blocked by stones; the chamber itself is usually round or of irregular shape, although a surprisingly large number are rectangular (Keramopoullos 1917: fig. 89; half the chambers shown are rectangular). Inside the chambers there are often pit graves; niches and benches are also cut from the living rock in the chamber walls.

There are, by my count, at least 79 separate tombs in the published record. An additional 160 are reported to have been robbed in the latter part of the nineteenth century (Philios 1897). No Theban tomb has ever been found intact; more often than not they are completely empty. Every tomb, however, originally contained large amounts of pottery. Offerings, when found, are typical of the Late Helladic period. Those from the cemetery at Kolonaki are on exhibit in the Museum of Thebes and are listed in the description of site 24 (see Catalogue). Among the more unusual finds from other locations are the frescoes from the tomb at site 254, numerous pieces from a helmet made of boar's tusk (site 25), and the terracotta sarcophagus and Canaanite jar from the well-preserved tomb at site 191. Pottery sherds dating to the Classical and even Christian periods have been found in many Late Helladic tombs, indicating reuse for some purpose, though not necessarily for burial.

Table 2.4. Periods of use of the cemeteries at Kolonaki and Ismenion hills

	A.ANNA 2	K4	K14	K26	K9	K15	K17	K21	K7	K1	K25	K10	K12	K16	I3	I4	I5	I6	I2
	19.0	34.5	16.1	15.4	21.6	21.6	8.1	14	4	5.2	19.9	3.2	4.4	6.2	12.4	5.3	12.2	16.2	6.7
LH I	│																		
II A	│	│	│	│															
B	│	│	│	│	│										│			│	│
III A1		│	│	│	│	│	│								│	│		│	│
A2		│	┊	│	│	┊	│	│	│						┊	│	│	│	│
B1	│	│	│	│		│		│	│	│	│								
B2	│	│								│	│								
C1		│										│	│	│					
C2																			

Note: The floor space of the burial chamber is indicated in square meters.

Only a few isolated Late Helladic burials have been found within the walls of the Kadmeia: two cist tombs (site 3) date to the transitional period from the Middle Helladic to the Late Helladic period. One burial of five infants was found in the Late Helladic level at site 17; there was a pit burial at site 112 and another at 120. All other Late Helladic tombs are found in the soft rock of the hills surrounding the Kadmeia. These tombs are concentrated in three cemeteries located outside the walls: the cemetery of Kolonaki to the south, the tombs to the southeast at the temple of Apollo Ismenios and the cemetery that extends east of it, and the cemetery of the Kastellia hills northeast of the Kadmeia.

The largest of these is the cemetery at Kolonaki (site 24), where Keramopoullos (1910B:210) saw 50 looted tombs, probably the same as those seen by Philios who had excavated three of them in an attempt to prevent further looting (1897). Keramopoullos excavated 30 of them, and these are the best published to date (1910A; 1910B; 1917:123-209). In 1966, three tombs were found at site 151, and one more at site 210.

Enough evidence was preserved in 14 of the 37 excavated tombs to allow us to draw some conclusions pertaining to their period of occupation (table 2.4). There is evidence of use from all periods with the exception of LH III C. Some of the tombs (4, 14, 26) show evidence of having been in continuous use, whereas in others (Agia Anna 2, Kolonaki 14, 15, 17) interruption of use is indicated by a hiatus in the pottery sequence. Many were clearly family tombs, comparable to those seen elsewhere in the Late Helladic period (Mylonas 1966:112-113).

The few finds, usually of pottery, do not enable us to infer very much about the original occupants of the Kolonaki tombs. The relative size of the tombs, however, when considered in conjunction with their date (table 2.4, cat. table 3) is somewhat illuminating.

The tombs that date to the first half of the period (LH I - LH III A:1) range in size from 8.1 to 34.5 square meters, and average 19.47 square meters. During the second half of the period (LH III A:2 - LH III C) the tombs range in size from 3.2 to 19.9 square meters and average 8.12 square meters. It is clear that the largest tombs are the earlier ones, and the largest of all, measuring 34.5 square meters, dates to LH II A. This is almost equal in size to the largest tomb found at Mycenae, which measures 6.50 m x 5.50 m, or 35.75 square meters (Mylonas 1966:112). In his discussion of the chamber tombs at Mycenae, Wace (1932:136) suggested that the size of a tomb depended on a family's wealth, size, social influence, and taste. It appears, then, that the largest and richest Theban families of the first half of the Mycenaean period buried their dead in the cemetery at Kolonaki. The tombs at the temple of Apollo Ismenios, ranging in date from LH II B to LH III A:2 and in size from 6.7 to 16.2 square meters (averaging 10.56 square meters), seem to be smaller than those of comparable date at the Kolonaki cemetery.

Regrettably, nothing is known about the cemetery at Myloi (site 62) which lies east of the temple of Apollo Ismenios. It was quite thoroughly looted; as many as 60 tombs were visible in the late nineteenth century (Philios 1897:95; Keramopoullos 1910B:210, 1917:100). Two empty chambers of unconfirmed date found at sites 81 and 255 may be related to this cemetery. The seven tombs at the temple of Apollo (site 8) were relatively well preserved, and it was possible to suggest dates for five of them (table 2.4).

In addition to a few doubtful chambers and a tomb excavated in the vicinity (see site 121), at least 31 tombs have been excavated at the cemetery of the Kastellia hills, most of them recently, and they are not yet published in detail (cat. table 4 provides a summary of the Kastellia tombs by site). Again, most of the tombs were empty. I know only the sizes of five and the dates of two of them: a small tomb was found in site 122 with a floor space measuring 4.8 square meters. It probably dates to LH III A:2. Keramopoullos excavated another small tomb (site 25) with a floor space of 9.6 square meters. The other three of known size are large: one excavated by Keramopoullos (1917:108-110, fig. 78; site 25) has a chamber measuring 6.12 m x 3.75 m (22.95 square meters); the chamber is rectangular and the tomb is well made, but the date is unknown. Another well-made, rectangular tomb was recently found at site 191 and was relatively well preserved; the dromos was 18 m long and 5.50 m wide, and the chamber 7.40 m x 5.40 m (39.96 square meters). It is larger than any of the tombs at Kolonaki and yielded finds of jewelry, pottery, and other objects. These have not been studied and the tomb is undated.

By far the most extraordinary tomb ever found in Thebes is that recently found at site 254. There are two dromoi, the larger of which is 25 m long and 4 m wide. The chamber is an enormous rectangle 11.50 m x 7 m (80.5 square meters), certainly the largest known chamber tomb in Greece. The two dromoi of differing length and the two different ceiling designs make it clear that half the tomb was a later addition. The unique fresco decoration shows floral and geometric motifs, a funerary procession, and a landscape. Spyropoulos, who excavated the tomb, dates it to LH III A:2 - LH III B:1.

In general, the tombs at Kastellia are larger and of later date than those of Kolonaki.

The evidence indicates that in the second half of the Late Helladic period, the Kastellia hill replaced Kolonaki as the main cemetery of Thebes. If there were other large tombs, they would surely have been found by this time with the amount of looting that took place in the nineteenth century and all the building activity that has taken place in recent years.

The areas north and west of the Kadmeia have very few tombs. There are some on the Amphion hill (site 121) but only a small one was excavated ; it was completely empty and had a floor space of 4.5 square meters. In the area west of Thebes (site 262) three empty tombs are known. I would also entertain the possibility that the chapel of Agios Minas (pl. 53), which is cut in the rock, could have been a chamber tomb; this little-known chapel is located 400 m west of the Kadmeia and has the appearance of a Mycenaean chamber tomb. The area in front of the chapel has been recently terraced, and there is no trace of a dromos; the chamber is roughly rectangular, with benches on three sides.

The Late Helladic cemeteries were located in close proximity to the inhabited area of the Kadmeia. On the Kolonaki hill, the tombs lie as close as 100 m and as far as 500 m to 600 m from the southern tip of the Kadmeia. The Kolonaki hill, with its soft yet sturdy bedrock, was ideal for the new type of chamber tomb, and it was easily accessible from the settlement. Other burial sites, too, were developed, especially to the east; the hill of the Ismenion, only 200 m from the Kadmeia, was one, and from here the cemetery extended to the north and east. It is not clear whether the cemetery of the Kastellia hills developed as an extension of the cemetery at the Ismenion, or whether it developed independently; its tombs are no further than 400 m from the settlement. The cemeteries east of the Kadmeia could only be reached by crossing the Strophia river, whereas the cemetery at Kolonaki could be reached more easily by crossing the small depression that was situated south of the Kadmeia.

Blegen (1937:228-229) observed that at Prosymna, the Late Helladic tombs were dispersed in four cemeteries, and offered two explanations: either the earliest tombs were those closest to the settlement, the later ones having to be dug further and further away, or each cemetery belonged to a different tribe. In Thebes, the areas nearest the settlement, perhaps nearest to the gates, seem to have been used first; the present evidence suggests that the Kolonaki hill, which is the most easily reached, became the first Late Helladic cemetery; the Hypsistai gates were here (fig. 2.7). The cemetery of the Ismenion hill, the next to be developed, was within easy reach of the Elektrai gates. Finally, the cemetery of the Kastellia hills was developed, very close to the Proitides gates. The few tombs on the Amphion hill and those west of Thebes could be reached from the Neistai gates.

A question must be raised concerning the burial places of the Theban royalty: were they buried in one of the main cemeteries, or in yet another, special cemetery? At Mycenae, there is a complete series of royal graves, the latest of which were monumental tholoi. Stone-lined tombs have been found throughout Greece (Vermeule 1964:120-126), including Boiotia; one of the largest, in fact, is located at Orchomenos, unquestionably a royal tomb. The largest of these tholoi were apparently visible for extended periods of time ever since they were built. If such tombs had been built in Thebes, they surely would not have escaped the attention of either the looters or the archaeologists. We must conclude, therefore, that there were none in Thebes, and that royalty and prominent families were buried in the same cemeteries as the rest of the population. It is likely that the largest of the excavated chamber tombs were those occupied by royalty. That the same cemeteries were shared by king and commoner alike may be explained by the fact that in Thebes, unlike most other Mycenaean cities, the entire population lived within the walls, sharing the limited habitation space. I would tentatively suggest that social stratification was not so clearly delineated at the extreme ends (king—slaves) as it was elsewhere in Late Helladic Greece.

CULT SITES

There are no Late Helladic Theban buildings to which we can ascribe a religious function. There can be no question, however, that the Thebans practiced a religion: ritual objects are commonly found in all Mycenaean cities; the names of gods have been identified in Linear B inscriptions (Vermeule 1964:291-297); and on Late Helladic works of art we can recognize religious scenes (Guthrie 1975). We also know that there were sanctuaries within the Late Helladic palaces, and even in private residences. Recently, religious sites or buildings have been identified at Mycenae (Taylour 1970), Tiryns (Kilian 1978, 1979), Phylakopi (Renfrew 1978), and Keos (Caskey 1971B:384-386; Caskey 1980). The building at Keos was used for religious practice as early as the Middle Bronze Age, and the god worshipped there, even at that early date, may have been Dionysos. The Middle Helladic Dionysos, in contrast to the god of the Classical period, was a god of fertility with a chthonic character (Caskey 1980). All of these shrines have been discovered recently through meticulous archaeological work. The shrines are small and might easily have been taken for houses had they not been so well preserved.

In Thebes, it has not been possible to identify such shrines, but it is probable that the sanctuary of Dionysos Kadmeios, which was well known in the Classical period, had been established long before then. The name, Dionysos, has been identified on Linear B tablets (Vermeule 1964:292). Hesiod (*Theogony* 940-942) considered the cult of Dionysos to be very old:

> Καδμείη δ' ἄρα οἱ Σεμέλη τέκε φαίδιμον υἱὸν
> μιχθεῖσ' ἐν φιλότητι Διώνυσον πολυγηθέα
> ἀθάνατον θνητή· νῦν δ'ἀμφότεροι θεοί εἰσιν.

> Semele, a Kadmeian, bore the god Dionysos, although
> she was herself a mortal; now both are gods.

In this passage, Hesiod shows that although Semele had been a mortal, by his lifetime she had become a goddess. The change in Semele's status could only have taken place over a very long time.

A cult site dedicated to the worship of Dionysos Kadmeios must have been established in Thebes soon after the destruction of the first Late Helladic palace, otherwise the identity of the site would have been forgotten. In the preceding discussion of the two Mycenaean palaces of Thebes, I proposed that the site of the first palace was left untouched after it had burned, and a second palace was built nearby. Here, I would like to emphasize that the fire which destroyed the first palace was extraordinary and may itself have provided the justification for establishing the sanctuary. This fire was so intense, and burned for such a long time, that it reduced the building materials to a density and hardness rarely, if ever, encountered in an archaeological excavation. Keramopoullos found the site covered by a cement-like crust one meter thick and almost impossible to penetrate. This was clearly produced by the large quantity of wood used in the two-storey structure burning and baking the equally large quantity of mud-brick. Although one reason for not re-building at the site was that the fire was seen as the work of a god, another practical consideration was that it was simply not feasible to clear the hard, massive heap of rubble after the fire died out. Yet another reason for not wishing to build on this site may have been that there was a need to establish religious sites within the city. The site of a destroyed palace was ideal for religious observance because it was already associated with religious rituals. In this instance, the story of Dionysos' birth may best be understood in relation to the establishment of a new cult site on the ruins of the very palace in which he had previously been worshipped. In Greece of the Classical period one can point to numerous ruined palaces that subsequently became temples. The consecration of the site of the first Late Helladic palace of Thebes may have renewed the vitality of an already existing cult. There is no reason (it is, in fact, counterproductive) to doubt the tradition that repeatedly claims that the sanctuary established on the ruins was dedicated to Dionysos. It was clearly an open-air sanctuary, and was known as such in the fifth century B.C. (as the *Bacchai* shows) and in the second century A.D., when Pausanias visited it. A third-century B.C. inscription from the Treasury of Thebes at Delphi (Bourguet 1929:195-201, no. 351) also identifies the sanctuary of Dionysos Kadmeios as an open-air sanctuary.

Although it is virtually impossible to provide archaeological proof of the great antiquty of an open-air sanctuary in this place, we should not disregard the presence of the huge column base that may have supported a column of the first palace, and then a fetish at the sanctuary that was preserved until the time of Pausanias (9.12:4). We must also not fail to remember that no structure was built at the site until the Byzantine period.

We know that during the Classical period there were many open-air sanctuaries in Thebes, and it is possible that some of them continued cult practices that started in the

Table 2.5. Sanctuaries of major deities of Thebes inside and outside the walls of the Kadmeia in the Classical period

Open-air Sanctuary on the Kadmeia	Sanctuary with Temple outside the Kadmeia
Apollo Spodios	Apollo Ismenios
Dionysos Kadmeios	Dionysos Lysios
	Dionysos Aigobolos
Demeter Thesmophoros (before Classical period)	Demeter and Kore Potniai
Birthplace of Herakles	Herakleion
Zeus Homoloios	Zeus Agoraios
Zeus Hypsistos	

prehistoric period, as did the sanctuary of Dionysos Kadmeios. The analysis of Pausanias' text shows a predominance of such open-air sanctuaries on the Kadmeia (table 5.1): there were seven inside and three outside the walls; by comparison, there were five sanctuaries with temples inside and eight outside the walls of the Kadmeia (table 3.1). The reason for this may be that the open-air sanctuaries were established earlier on the Kadmeia, before the city's expansion toward Greater Thebes in the eighth to sixth centuries B.C. Some of the sanctuaries may have been established on old ruins of great importance, such as those of the Mycenaean palaces. When it became customary to dedicate temples to the gods, the Thebans preferred to establish new sanctuaries in the more spacious areas outside the Kadmeia. The older, open-air sanctuaries in the city were not abandoned, however, and occasionally, if there was enough space, a temple was built on the Kadmeia, as at the sanctuary of Demeter Thesmophoros. The major deities of Thebes, whose cult sites are better known, had at least two sanctuaries—one, open-air, on the Kadmeia, and another with a temple outside the Kadmeia (table 2.5). Demeter probably shared the grove and temple with Dionysos at Potniai (see Catalogue, site 201) before a temple was constructed in her honor on the Kadmeia.

In most instances, there is evidence to show that the open-air sanctuaries were older than those with temples. The greater antiquity of the altar of Apollo Spodios, the sanctuary at the birthplace of Herakles, and the sanctuary of Zeus Hypsistos is indicated by the fact that all three cluster together with other religious sites in the southern part of the Kadmeia where the earliest habitation remains have been found and where one would therefore expect to find old relics warranting sanctification; this is indeed the case. In connection with the birthplace of Herakles, tradition has preserved specific associations with the house of Amphitryon, which may have been a Mycenaean ruin. Both the sanctuary of Dionysos Kadmeios and of Demeter Thesmophoros are firmly connected with the two Mycenaean palaces of Thebes.

While these associations with old ruins cannot prove that cults of each of the gods existed in prehistoric Thebes, they do allow for the possibility, and they strongly suggest continuity of worship. More importantly, these associations suggest the greater antiquity of the open-air sanctuaries than those with temples. Most of the temples outside the Kadmeia were built in the Archaic or Classical period at sites that had no previous religious associations (see chap. 3). The earliest known temple of Apollo Ismenios was constructed in the Geometric period at a site that had no obvious connection with a prehistoric site, but that was an idyllic location and was at the same time opposite the location I have suggested for the altar of Apollo Spodios (see chap. 5, passage 6).

The fact that the Kadmeia was continuously inhabited gives credence to the idea that cults continued to function for a long time. Keramopoullos (1917:341) suggested that had it not been for the almost complete break with tradition in Christian times, some of the religious monuments might have survived to the present day. Pharaklas actually discovered part of a Middle Helladic house that had been destroyed by fire. It was covered with a layer of earth in Mycenaean times, and a krepis was added in Classical times (see Catalogue, site 112). The poor state of preservation made it impossible to identify the site with any monument known through tradition, but it is likely that this ruin was only one of many on the Kadmeia that served as reminders of the past. Some of these may have been turned into sanctuaries either during the prehistoric period, or some time after the end of the Late Bronze Age. The House of Tiles at Lerna was destroyed by fire at the end of EH II, and a large, circular tumulus was made on top of its remains; the site was unused until new people arrived (Caskey 1956:165). This is one of the earliest and clearest examples of a practice that was common in ancient Greece. In Thebes, there may have been several sanctuaries that were established on important ruins. These will be more fully discussed in the following chapter. Here, however, I would like to call attention to the sanctuary of Demeter Potnia at site 201: Keramopoullos found three Mycenaean and two Geometric sherds there; recently, more Geometric pottery has been found there. The site, which is outside the Kadmeia, is far from any remains of habitation, so the pottery should not be viewed as intrusive. Instead, it is evidence of continuous cult activity. The name, *Potnia*, has occurred once on a tablet from Thebes (*Of* 36, Chadwick 1969), and it is almost certain that there was a Mycenaean cult of Demeter (Rocchi 1978).

Finally, we must consider the cult of the dead, the existence of which is generally assumed, although traces of its activities are not clearly identifiable in the archaeological record (Nelsson 1950:584-619). Keramopoullos considered niches and benches in chamber tombs (1917:109, 160), as well as the terracotta thrones (1917:190, fig. 135), indicative of the existence of the cult of the dead in Thebes. Now, however, they are recognized as elements of ordinary funerary practices, not practices of the cult of the dead (Mylonas 1966:176-186). In the local tradition recorded by Pausanias, many tombs were attributed to Theban legendary figures (table 5.1), but the extent to which these tombs were used as cult sites is hard to say. Keramopoullos (1917:77-79) suggested that the sanctuary of Apollo Ismenios was established where it was because of the existing ancestor cult at the chamber tombs. There is, however, no direct evidence of such a cult at the Ismenion, and according to Coldstream (1976), the earliest evidence of it in Greece first appears in the Late Geometric period.

THEBES FROM LATE HELLADIC III B TO THE SUBMYCENAEAN PERIOD, ca. 1250 TO 1050 B.C.

fig. 2.13 The period following the collapse of palatial Thebes is one of the most poorly documented in the city's history. Evidence from the tombs indicates that habitation continued, but the size of the city was drastically reduced. The name of the city was changed to *Hypothebai*, and as such Homer refers to it in the Great Catalogue (*Iliad* 2.505), giving it the epithet "well-built," which, under the circumstances, must be understood as a poetic description inspired by Mycenaean Thebes. The scholiast to Homer theorizes that the name *Hypothebai* may have reflected the city's reduced size after the war of the Epigonoi, or it may signify that Thebes itself was abandoned and the remaining population was absorbed by the village communities "below" Thebes. According to Strabo (9.2.32), Hypothebai was "below the Kadmeia in the flat plain."

In recent times, scholars have been puzzled by the name, and various explanations of it have been proposed. Wilamowitz (1891:237) believed that the name referred to the area of Greater Thebes below the Kadmeia; Fimmen (1912:541), the area outside the wall; Keramopoullos (1917:304) believed it was the name for the Homeric town that spread below the Kadmeia (also 1909A:110). The idea of a city below the Kadmeia is prevalent today as well (see, for example, Hope-Simpson and Lazenby 1970:30), but so far nobody has specified its location.

The archaeological evidence from this period is very scanty, but it can provide some information about the disposition of the city. Clearly, the thriving Mycenaean city of Thebes did not extend over the entire citadel as does modern Thebes, and the fortifications left unprotected its western and northern parts (fig. 2.5); occupation in these areas and beyond was extramural. There are indications that the fortified Mycenaean citadel continued to be occupied for a time during the Late Helladic III B:2 period. Large quantities of Late Helladic III B:2 pottery have been found at site 165, which was part of the second Late Helladic palace; this indicates that the area was used as a dump. Similar remains may have been found at sites 185 and 192 (cf. table 2.3). The continued or renewed active use of the Kolonaki cemetery indicates that the city had not been completely abandoned. There were at least eight tombs here (site 24), and one at the temple of Apollo Ismenios (site 8) that show occupation in Late Helladic III B:2 (cf. table 2.4).

Our main evidence of the Late Helladic III C period comes from a few burials at the Kolonaki cemetery, where pottery of Late Helladic III C style has been found in five tombs (table 2.4), one of which contained a cremation (T 16). On the Kadmeia itself,

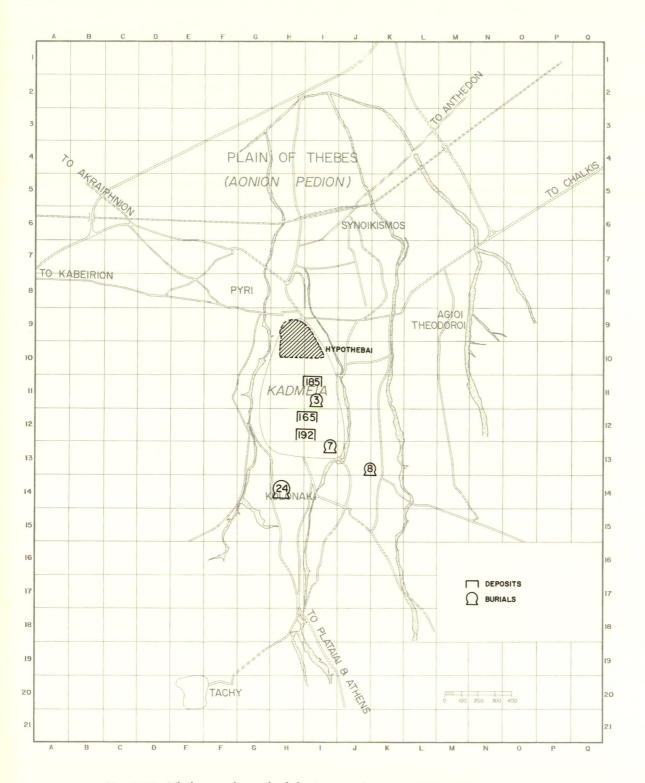

Fig. 2.13. Thebes at the end of the Bronze Age, ca. 1250-1050 B.C.

Late Helladic III C pottery has not been identified with certainty, despite claims to the contrary (Spyropoulos 1970).

Our knowledge of the Submycenaean period is also based solely on tombs; these, however, were found on the Kadmeia itself: a small cemetery consisting mainly of single cist burials was excavated by Keramopoullos at the Elektrai gates (site 7). The tombs range in date from the Submycenaean to the Protogeometric periods (Snodgrass 1971:134-135; Desborough 1972:69). Another Submycenaean cist burial was found recently, closer to the center of the Kadmeia (site 3). The center of the Kadmeia continued to be used for burial in the Protogeometric period as attested by the burial in site 10 (fig. 3.3). It is clear, therefore, that most, if not all, of the Kadmeia was uninhabited during the Submycenaean period, and, if the lack of Late Helladic III C remains is any indication, the Kadmeia may have been abandoned even earlier.

There are accounts of an exodus, most notably the one concerning the exile and return of most of the Kadmeians (Legras 1905:91-101; Buck 1979:46-49, 63). There is also the intriguing migration of Teiresias' daughter Manto, founder of Claros, and her son Mopsos, whose travels to Pamphylia and Cilicia have now been quite clearly confirmed by the bilingual inscription from Karatepe (Bossert 1948; Barnett 1975; Hammond 1975). Thebes must have been affected by the general decline and depopulation observed all over Greece (Snodgrass 1971:360-367). Very few settlements have been preserved because houses were poorly constructed, and, in addition, the same sites were reoccupied at a later date (Desborough 1972:261-265). The presence of tombs in Thebes ranging in date over the entire period indicates that there must have been a settlement there.

In my discussion of the Late Helladic wall of the Kadmeia, I included six elements that might have argued for its presence, but that proved to be unrelated (fig. 2.5, W 4-W 9). We don't know much about W 4, but since the wall W 3, just south of it, almost certainly turned west, W 4 must have been outside the Late Helladic wall. W 5 was the "Cyclopean" wall seen by Leake (1835:226), but Keramopoullos, who saw eight blocks that had fallen from it, thought it belonged to a polygonal wall of the fifth century B.C. (1907). The same is true of the nine loose boulders found at site 188. The segment at W 7 definitely dates to the Classical period, following the line of an earlier wall. At W 8, Keramopoullos (1917:305) found a wall, similar to W 5, associated with Mycenaean pottery. At W 9 (1917:305) he found only a medieval wall on isodomic foundation and remains of Mycenaean houses; unfortunately, this was never published because Keramopoullos thought he would return to excavate the area.

These scanty remains indicate that the northern tip of the Kadmeia was fortified sometime between the ends of the Mycenaean and the Archaic periods. The presence of Cyclopean stones, mistakenly identified by Leake as Mycenaean fortifications, strongly suggests that the wall was initially built of stones taken from the abandoned Late Helladic wall. I would suggest that this construction took place at the end of the Mycenaean period for two reasons: One is the presence of Mycenaean houses at W 9, although it is

Table 2.6 Population estimates for Bronze Age Thebes

Periods BC		150 per Hectare	300 per Hectare	400 per Hectare
EH II	2500	255	450	600
	2300			
EHIII	2100			
MH	1900	900	1800	2400
	1700			
LH		1200	2400	3200
	1500			
	1300	2880	5760	7680
	1100	630	1260	1680

Note: The lowest suggested density is 150 per hectare (McDonald and Rapp 1972); another study proposes 300 (Renfrew 1972), while 400 (Frankfort 1950) is possible in fortified cities.

not certain that they date to LH III C and it is possible that these were extramural houses of an earlier period. More importantly, however, the area between the Museum of Thebes and the church of Agios Georgios (site 93, Map B) is the only one where there is a bit of evidence that a settlement existed in the post-palatial period in Thebes. This area is low-lying by comparison with the Mycenaean citadel, and its western half is still called *Gourna* ("trough" or "depression"), a reasonable modern descriptive alternative for the name *Hypothebai*. This area was virtually uninhabited in the Mycenaean period and could therefore accept a new settlement. The settlers would not have had to confront the problem of cleaning up and terracing the debris that wars had left on the Kadmeia; at the same time, they would have had the advantage of taking easily accessible building materials, especially stone, to construct a protective wall. If we place Hypothebai at the northern tip of the Kadmeia, we may explain how this area came to be incorporated into the city of the Classical period. We also can see that it was from this nucleus that the Kadmeia was resettled during the Dark Ages. In addition, we can explain why there were gates named *Borraiai* ("northern"); these may have been the only gates of Hypothebai. Aischylos (*Hepta* 526-529) specifies that they were located near the tumulus of Amphion which, as I have suggested, was about 50 m from the northern end of the Kadmeia. Aischylos and his contemporaries may have thought that Hypothebai was part of the original (prehistoric) Kadmeia.

The Hypothebai settlement may have followed the outline of the hill, as does the modern one today, and may have overlapped at its southern limit with a portion of the Mycenaean wall that had survived or had been restored. The area thus outlined (fig. 2.13) covers about four hectares, dramatically smaller than the size of the Mycenaean settlement; the population of Hypothebai may have been about 1,200 (table 2.6), which in the Dark Ages was not unusually low. This Hypothebai continued to be the only Theban settlement for most of the Dark Ages (see chap. 3).

THE LEGENDS OF THEBES AND THE ARCHAEOLOGICAL REMAINS

There are a great many legends involving Theban personalities and Theban participation in events of the Bronze Age. Although a vast amount has been written on the philological aspects of the legends of Thebes, very little has been done with their historical qualities, so that in many ways they have remained an unexploited source of historical information. Notable exceptions are the work of Keramopoullos, and more recently Edwards (1979) and Buck (1979). These scholars, and a few others, maintain a general belief in the historicity of the Theban legends. The Greeks of the Bronze Age must have had a sense of history and a wish to preserve it, as did their Near Eastern neighbors with whom they were in contact. Whereas, however, writing had developed enough in the Near East to record literature, history, and poetry, the use of writing in Greece remained relatively undeveloped until the end of the Bronze Age. The oral tradition, on the other hand, developed in varied and sophisticated ways and became the predominent means for the dissemination of ideas. When the cultural record preserved by the oral tradition was finally written down, it formed some of the most wonderful literature of Greece, including the Homeric poems. Unfortunately, most of the oral tradition died with the collapse of the Mycenaean world and the Dark Age that followed. The remnants that have come down to us combine elements of history, religious ritual, social customs, and storytelling. During the Bronze Age, however, when the oral tradition was in full flower, there must have been diverse forms to preserve each of these aspects of the culture. Stubbings (1973:646) has proposed a differentiation in treatment between historic and religious subjects.

The importance of preserving the memory of historical events is clearest with regard to wars, which are remembered to the present day. Few would doubt that a conflict between Troy and Mycenae took place, remembered as the Trojan War; the palaces, royal burials, and fortifications of the two rival cities of Troy and Mycenae have been excavated. The oral tradition of Thebes preserves the memory of several wars: two of these occurred as certainly as did the Trojan War. The first, the War of the Seven against Thebes, was recorded in the epic *Thebais* (Bethe 1891; Legras 1905:1-21), now lost, and also inspired Aischylos' *Seven against Thebes* and Statius' *Thebaid*, which are extant. The War of the Seven was an unsuccessful expedition against Thebes by Argos and her allies who supported the exiled Theban king, Polyneikes. The second war, that of the Epigonoi, the sons of the Seven, resulted in the conquest of Thebes just before the expedition to Troy. This war may have been recorded in a separate epic (Legras 1905:21-23, 91-101).

Theban tradition has preserved the memory of several conflicts with Orchomenos, remembered in legends involving the Theban Herakles (Buck 1979:59-61). There was also the war over Oidipous' sheep (Hesiod, *Erga* 160-163). Yet another war, recorded by Pausanias (2.6.1-4), was between Thebes and Sikyon; because it involved altogether different personalities, it is not to be confused with any other. Scholars are not at all in agreement as to whether these wars were separate events, or whether the varying references are really to one and the same conflict. Schachter (1967A) combines all accounts to come up with one war that he places just before the Trojan War, whereas Vermeule (1964:190, 266, 269) sees them as separate events. Robert (1894:910) also believed they were separate, and that Thebes fought several wars against both Argos and Euboia.

Constant fighting during the Bronze Age, especially the Late Bronze period, is consonant with the archaeological evidence: cities were heavily fortified, weapons were commonly deposited in tombs, and warriors and chariots appear in numerous representations. If we consider how little is preserved of the oral tradition, we may well imagine that the wars in which Thebes is known to have been involved were but a small fraction of the city's military activities. Orchomenos alone would have kept Theban soldiers busy: there were constant border clashes for the possession of the Teneric plain (Buck 1979:61), and it is possible that when the Thebans finally won it, Orchomenos decided of necessity to drain Lake Kopais in order to increase the amount of arable land. The Thebans preserved the memory of these clashes in various ways: there is the myth of Herakles and Erginos; sanctuaries to Herakles Hippodetes and to Herakles Rhinokoloustes were dedicated to commemorate some battles; the tomb of the daughters of Antipoinos who sacrificed themselves to ensure a Theban victory was shown to Pausanias. The war over Oidipous' sheep was perhaps the final conflict between Thebes and Orchomenos (see below).

The reality of these wars attests the historical character of the legends, although we cannot use the legends for assigning dates or make clear associations with the archaeological record, as the legends preserve history in too fragmented a way. It does seem clear, however, that the War of the Seven and the War of the Epigonoi preceded the Trojan War because ancient tradition places them earlier by one generation (Schachter 1967A:1, n. 4, with many ancient sources).

Where Theban history is concerned, we can, by examining various traditions and by combining the legends to which they gave rise, put together a list of kings that may in turn be viewed in conjunction with the wars. Such a list may well prove more reliable than anything else available to us for classifying the historical elements in the legends and for dating events. However, because there are no reliable documents like those found in Egypt, such associations must be tentative. A major difficulty is the possible, even likely, repetition of the same name, both within a dynasty and outside a dynastic cycle. In the oral tradition, confusion may be introduced in distinguishing kings of the same name by epithets rather than by numbers, and by the alteration of some names through the ages. A further difficulty is the possibility that a historic event may be recorded in the style of an allegory; some have seen in the Labors of Herakles a record of military expeditions (Stubbings 1973:652). On the other hand, the Classical Greeks and Romans made the associations between kings and events with confidence; if there is general agreement among ancient sources, these associations must be considered seriously. Without ignoring the difficulties, I think it worthwhile to attempt an ordered list of Theban kings of the Bronze Age, starting with those of the latter part of the period.

The Last Two Dynasties of Late Helladic Thebes

Pausanias (9.5.13-16) tells us that there were eight kings after the War of the Seven, beginning with Laodamas, the son of Eteokles, who fought in that war. After him come Thersandros, son of Polyneikes, and Peneleos, both of whom died during the expedition against Troy; these are followed by Tisamenos, son of Thersandros; his son, Autesion; Damasichthon (grandson of Peneleos); his son, Ptolemaios; and finally Xanthos, son of Ptolemaios, after whose reign the monarchy was abolished in Thebes.

Although one may question the accuracy of the names, the order of succession, and lengths of reign, I believe Pausanias has correctly presented the eight kings who ruled Thebes after the War of the Seven. There is no reason to doubt that they ought to be associated with events such as the destruction of Thebes, the Trojan War, and the subsequent invasions that led to the total collapse of the Mycenaean world. This would mean that they must have lived during the period from LH III B:2 to LH III C. As an examination of the archaeological remains shows, the end of palatial Thebes can be dated to the end of LH III B:1, after which time the city, though not totally destroyed, was drastically reduced. It is during this period that we can place the founding of Hypothebai, perhaps by members of this dynasty.

At an even earlier period, beginning with the latest king, tradition refers to a certain Kreon, before whom were the twins, Eteokles and Polyneikes, their father, Oidipous, his father Laios, and perhaps Labdakos, whose name describes the entire dynasty (Statius, *Thebaid* 6.451); Several sources mention a certain Polydoros, son of Kadmos and father of Labdakos (Herodotos 5.59), who, according to Wilamowitz (1922:33), was an empty figure invented by the Labdakids in order to claim the throne. Pausanias (9.5.5-9), in an apparent attempt to create a single *stemma* or genealogy for all the Theban kings, places Amphion and Zethos between Laios and Oidipous, and Nykteus and Lykos between Labdakos and Laios. He is one of the few writers to include these characters in the Labdakid line. Yet, as I will show below, these four cannot possibly be included in the Labdakid dynasty, because they belong to a different dynasty all their own. Laios and Oidipous (and perhaps Labdakos before them) and the sons of Oidipous, Eteokles and Polyneikes, held power during the best remembered period of the Theban Bronze Age. Under these kings, the city achieved its greatest glory.

It is not the subject of this study to review the etymology of the names of these kings, or to explore their personalities, but I think their historical existence is as likely as that of the kings who were involved in the Trojan conflict. The historical details of their lives are distorted and remembered only vaguely not only because of the lack of written documents, but also because their civilization was destroyed. Perhaps another equally important reason for the distortion is the combination of a Bronze Age king's political function with his role as religious leader. He was not only the supreme ruler, but he and his palace were the main focus of religious activities (Nilsson 1950:483-487). Oidipous, for example, although tragically portrayed, may have been a relatively happy Mycenaean king, ruling one of the largest and richest cities of the time and controlling a fertile and relatively peaceful land. He had many children, and his religious duties may have included the fertility ritual of marriage to his "mother" (mother-goddess).

Whether or not the tragedy of Oidipous originated in a fertility rite, the archaeological record of Thebes clearly shows that some king, perhaps one named Oidipous, ruled Thebes during a period of great prosperity just before the city was destroyed in the War of the Epigonoi. In the earlier War of the Seven, Thebes had been victorious. An even earlier conflict, the War over Oidipous' Sheep, has been convincingly interpreted by Buck (1979:62) as one in the long series of confrontations between Thebes and Orchomenos. Conflicts between these two powers over the Teneric plain were renewed in the eighth century B.C. (Buck 1979:97-98), but these are poorly attested and should not be confused with those of the Bronze Age. If the war over Oidipous' sheep was the final conflict, as I believe it was, resulting in a much sought victory over Orchomenos, there should be some traditional reference to it. Perhaps the encounter between Oidipous and the Sphinx refers to it allegorically, in a way that the Labors of Herakles may refer to wars of the Argolid. The Sphinx was killed at Mt. Sphingion, which is near Onchestos, at the border between the territories of Orchomenos and Thebes. Just east of Onchestos (i.e., in the direction of Thebes) is the fertile Teneric plain, the cause of dispute between the rival cities.

The dynasty of the Labdakids, then, including Labdakos, Laios, Oidipous, Eteokles, Polyneikes, Kreon, and Laodamas (who is included here because he is of the generation of the Epigonoi who destroyed palatial Thebes), which ruled Thebes at the height of her power dominating most of Boiotia, may be associated with at least three costly wars. In terms of archaeological dates, these wars occurred in LH III A and LH III B:1, a period of tremendous affluence in Thebes, during which time the second Late Helladic palace was built and destroyed. Even the little we have uncovered of the second palace suffices to show that great wealth was required to produce it.

These last dynasties of Thebes are the best remembered mainly because they correspond with the end of the Bronze Age and the height of Mycenaean civilization. Yet, there are many other kings named in Theban legends, who must correspond to earlier periods. Tradition, though vague regarding the earlier dynasties, repeatedly and consistently refers to the founding of Thebes by Kadmos, and it is upon his date that the order of the remaining dynasties depends.

THE DATING OF KADMOS

The extensive controversy surrounding Kadmos is the subject of recent studies by Edwards (1979) and Billigmeier (1976), and will not be reviewed here. In the traditional story of Kadmos (as preserved, for example, in Ovid, *Metamorphoses* 3.1-137), Zeus abducts the daughter of Agenor, Europa, from Phoenicia and carries her to Crete. Her brother, Kadmos, is sent to search for her, but after a long journey (which also takes him to Crete), finally gives up and is advised by Apollo to establish a city at the site where a heifer sits down to rest. Kadmos obeys, eventually ending up in Boiotia, where he loses many of his companions to a serpent guarding the spring of Ares. He kills the serpent and, in obedience to instructions from Athena, sows its teeth in the earth. Armed men, the Spartoi, are born and fight each other until only five are left who help Kadmos build the new city.

Although the story certainly has elements of a fairy tale, one can, all the same, render a general historical interpretation: a foreigner arrives in Boiotia and, after subduing the local population, builds a new city. In support of such an interpretation is the persistence of names recalling Kadmos: there was a tribe of Kadmeiones, a province named Kadmeis, a sanctuary dedicated to Dionysos Kadmeios; the palace of Thebes was referred to as the "house of Kadmos," and the city itself as Kadmeia. All of these names were used until the end of antiquity, and one may say that in a general way, the story of Kadmos was believed. In modern times, however, serious doubts have been raised not only about the foreign origin of Kadmos, but also about his historical reality. Arguments have frequently been based on notions of racial purity: Kadmos the Phoenician, a Semite, establishing a Semitic colony and introducing a Semitic influence into Greek culture were unpalatable possibilities to a great number of scholars (for a full discussion of this, see Edwards 1979, and Billigmeier 1976).

It is certainly true that there is no evidence for foreign colonization of any type in Greece, in either the Mycenaean period, with which Kadmos is most often associated, or in the eighth century B.C., which has also been considered a possibility. Vermeule (1971) has argued eloquently against the historical reality of Kadmos, placing him entirely in the realm of fairy tale and adopting the position of Gomme (1913), that the story was a creation of poets of the seventh century B.C. These discussions, however, have ignored Kadmos' major achievement—the founding of Thebes. This is understandable: the archaeological evidence from the city itself has been too scanty and confusing to interpret. It is now possible, however, to discuss Kadmos and the founding of Thebes in a fresh and meaningful way.

Although there is much evidence of frequent commercial exchanges between Thebes and the Near East in the Late Helladic period, there is no evidence of a change in the character of Theban civilization that would indicate a foreign presence. In Thebes, as in the rest of the Mycenaean world, burial practices continued unchanged over the entire

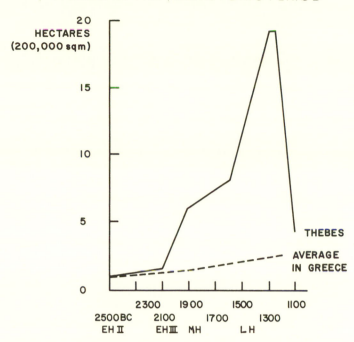

Fig. 2.14. Settlement growth in Thebes during the
Bronze Age (Estimates are based on the archaeological
remains within the walls.)

period; there was a clear preoccupation with warfare, as seen in the building of great fortifications and palaces. Art objects and pottery do not indicate a foreign presence. There are foreign objects that were imported, but these are found everywhere in the Mycenaean world. All of this should lead one to suspect that Kadmos and all that he represents were not related to the Mycenaean period as we know it. As to the placing of Kadmos in the eighth century B.C., this date was proposed only because Herodotus (5:59) mentions "Kadmeian letters," usually interpreted as a reference to the introduction of the Phoenician alphabet into Greece. The word "Kadmeian," however, can be shown to refer not to the person, Kadmos, but to the city named for him, Kadmeia (see below).

The founding of Thebes by outsiders clearly could not have taken place without some sign of change. The archaeological record shows no significant interruption of culture in either the Middle Helladic or the Late Helladic periods. There is, however, a striking development at the end of EH II, when a small community (the first settlement on the Kadmeia) is transformed into a large town (see fig. 2.1).

The estimated rate of the city's growth, based on the reconstructed size of the settlement during the Bronze Age, is shown on the graph in fig. 2.14. We see that the small settlement that was established in EH II gained sudden and dramatic momentum in EH III, setting the stage for the city's impressive development in the Middle and Late Helladic periods. The continuing, though slower, rate of growth in the Middle Helladic period brought the expansion of the walled city to an area of 80,000 square meters by ca. 1600 B.C. By

fig. 2.14

LH III B (ca. 1300), Thebes was at her zenith, and probably the largest walled city in Greece. The figures presented in figure 2.14 are based on conservative calculations of the extent of intramural remains. The dates are based on generally accepted correlations with Egyptian chronology (see, for example, Hood 1978:15).

Related to the size of the city are the population estimates for the different periods (table 2.6); three estimates are offered ranging from the lowest of 150 per hectare (McDonald and Rapp 1972), which has now been lowered even further (Carothers and McDonald 1979), to a high estimate of 400 (Frankfort 1950). For Thebes, we will consider the middle estimate of 300 as the minimum possible for two reasons: first, population density tends to be higher in settlements protected by fortifications and, second, no account is attempted of the extramural settlement that is known to have existed in certain periods.

Although changes in pottery style from EH II to EH III are as subtle in Thebes as in the rest of Greece (it took the careful and systematic work of Caskey at Lerna in the 50s to see them for the first time; see especially Caskey 1960), the Early Helladic III period in Thebes is distinguishably different from Early Helladic II in size of settlement and nature of artefacts. The archaeological evidence from Thebes supports the notion that EH III should be viewed as "Protominyan." Howell (1974:94) believes that the difference is sharp enough to suggest the arrival of new people and new traditions.

The changes in the pottery of Thebes from EH II to EH III are similar to the ones generally distinguished in southern Greece. Of interest is the presence of a couple of Cycladic imports and a hoard of beautifully made bronze tools (site 2, fig. 2.1; Branigan 1974), which, should they prove to be imports, would not suffice to prove foreign invasion. The sudden urbanization of the village community on the Kadmeia, however, coupled with a degree of affluence expressed in the construction of large, apsidal houses on solid stone, signals a development, the importance of which ought not to be minimized.

The Origin of Kadmos

Although foreign invasion seems a highly unlikely explanation for these developments, we should not rule out the possibility of an intrusion resulting from population movements within the Aegean, which are known to have occurred in Early Bronze II (Weinberg 1965:305; Caskey 1971B:787; Hood 1978:22). Such movements may have been in response to internal warfare (well documented for the period; Renfrew 1972:390-399) or overcrowding. It is certainly possible that the area around Thebes, situated inland and isolated, had not developed to its full agricultural potential and would have been attractive to a group with more highly developed agricultural skills. There is plenty of evidence of trade and communication within the Aegean during much of the Early Bronze II period (Renfrew 1972:449-455), making it easily conceivable that Boiotia was known to have been both underpopulated and underdeveloped. An Aegean group on the move from a

Table 2.7. The prehistory of Greece according to Thucydides

Period	Events
EBA	1. Pelasgians, first inhabitants of Greece.
	2. Migrations, expulsions; richest provinces undergo greatest changes: Thessaly, Boiotia, and the Peloponnese.
	3. Before Minos: settlements unprotected, entire Greece armed in response to piracy; the islanders (Karians and Phoenicians) were pirates.
MBA & Early LBA	4. Minos: establishes first sea power; eliminates piracy.
Late LBA	5. The Greeks unite. Expedition to Troy.
	6. Boiotians move to Kadmeis 60 years after Troy.
	7. Dorians move to the Peloponnese 80 years after Troy.

more advanced culture could account for the dramatic developments seen in Thebes in EH III.

The most likely place of origin of such a group is the Cyclades, or Crete. That Thebes enjoyed contact with the Cyclades is seen in the similarities of pottery styles and also in the fact that Cycladic pots were found in Thebes. The Karians and the Phoenicians, whose presence in the Cyclades is discussed by Thucydides (see table 2.7), also figure in Theban literary tradition (see table 2.12). On the Cycladic island of Keos there was a cult of Dionysos that may have been initiated as early as the beginning of the Middle Bronze Age (Caskey 1980).

The likelihood of Crete being the original homeland of migrants to Thebes is suggested for different and, I believe, more persuasive reasons. During the third millennium B.C., Crete had one of the densest populations in the Aegean (Renfrew 1972: table 14.x, figs. 14.11, 14.12) and was colonizing as early as EB II, as evidenced by the Minoan colony at Kythera (Coldstream and Huxley 1972). The large numbers of foreign objects found in Early Minoan Crete show that the island was even then quite cosmopolitan and conducted a vigorous trade with the Near East, perhaps the only Aegean culture to do so on a systematic basis (Renfrew 1972:444-449).

It is interesting to consider what is said about these connections by one of the most reliable historians of ancient Greece. In describing the early history of Greece, Thucydides (1.2-12) makes several distinct points that are germane to this discussion. His points are summarized in table 2.7: the last three (5-7) clearly refer to Mycenaean civilization at its height and to the events following its collapse, that is, from 1400 to 1100 B.C. Point 4 must surely refer to what we now conceive of as Minoan civilization during the period from 2000 to 1400 B.C. It seems very unlikely that these events can be dated to the Greek Dark Age as has been done in the past (Gomme 1945:100-108). There can be little doubt that the first three points refer to the Early Bronze Age or some part of it. The presence of the Pelasgians before the arrival of the Hellenes, and the turbulent migrations and expulsions, can be dated with some confidence to the end of EH II (Howell 1974). Also characteristic of that period are the absence of fortifications, and the frequent encounters with pirates. Thucydides accuses the islanders of piracy and specifically identifies them as Karians and Phoenicians, who inhabited the Cyclades. He also identifies the provinces that suffered most from attack, and among them is Boiotia.

When we consider the pains Thucydides took to be accurate, his identification of the Karians and Phoenicians gains in significance. It attests to the presence of "foreigners" in Early Bronze Age Greece. The presence of Karians, peoples from Asia Minor, should not be surprising: there is now archaeological evidence of frequent contact between Asia Minor and the Aegean throughout the Early Bronze Age (Renfrew 1972:449-453). As for the Phoenicians, this was the ethnic name used by Greeks of the Classical period for the inhabitants of coastal Syria and Lebanon. The Classical Greeks were unaware that those peoples were identified differently before 1200 B.C.; we now refer to them as Canaanites (Albright 1961:438). According to Thucydides, then, and almost every other ancient writer, Phoenicians/Canaanites were present in the Bronze Age. I propose that they were present in the Early Bronze Age, and that Kadmos is their representative in the literary tradition, according to which Kadmos stopped in Crete before giving up the search for his sister Europa. Kadmos led a group of Early Minoan Cretans, who were pressed either by internal constraints or simply by expansionism, into the relative vacuum of southern Boiotia. On the way, they may have stopped at the Cyclades and picked up additional migrants. They brought to Boiotia advanced agricultural skills along with the worship of Dionysos and Demeter.

CRETAN ORIGIN OF THE THEBAN DIONYSOS AND DEMETER

These two gods, who, in addition to Apollo, were the most important in Classical Thebes (Ziehen 1934:1509-1511), show most clearly the connections between Thebes and Crete in the Early Bronze Age. The Cretan origin of Demeter was generally accepted by the ancients, who also considered the mysteries honoring the goddess of the same origin. This is not disputed today (Guthrie 1975:885).

The worship of the Theban Dionysos bears striking resemblance to the worship of Cretan Zeus. The bull is symbolic of both (Nilsson 1950:573-574); the omophagia is characteristic of the worship of both; each was worshipped by orgiastic cults stimulated by wild music (Guthrie 1955:154-156). Further connecting Dionysos to Crete is the myth that records the god's marriage to Ariadne, the daughter of Minos, the marriage taking place, not insignificantly, in the Cyclades on the island of Naxos. Those elements of Greek tradition that point to the introduction of Dionysos into Thebes via Crete do not necessarily contradict the second tradition that suggests a Phrygian/Lydian origin for Dionysos (Nilsson 1950:565-577). The Theban tradition probably records an earlier arrival of the god by sea. The same god, or one like him, could also have come overland from Asia Minor and Thrace, descending into Greece and fusing with the earlier Dionysos. If we view the two traditions as complementing rather than contradicting one another, we may be better able to account for the different aspects of this complex god.

As early as the late third millennium, Dionysos was conceived of as a god of fertility, as the evidence from Keos shows (Caskey 1980). Although his character was more complex and even enigmatic in the Classical period, his continued importance in Theban fertility ritual is seen in the celebration of the triennial festival of Agrionia at the sanctuary of Dionysos Kadmeios (see chap. 3, p. 128). The close proximity on the Kadmeia of the sanctuaries of Dionysos and Demeter and the fact that they shared the sanctuary near Potniai show how closely linked was the worship of these two gods. In Thebes, both retained their predominantly agricultural character until late antiquity. Their prominence in Classical Thebes can be understood in relation to the frequent references to Boiotia as one of the richest and most systematically cultivated regions of Greece. I suggest that this was so even in the second millennium B.C., although the environmental studies that would provide the proof are lacking. Pausanias (9.25.1), however, does record the Theban boast that they were the very first to cultivate the grapevine and the pomegranate (symbols of Dionysos and Demeter, respectively). There is evidence that both of these plants were introduced into Greece in the third millennium, probably from the Near East (Renfrew 1973:125-131, the grapevine; 203, the pomegranate). It is likely that they found their way into Boiotia via Crete.

KADMOS IN ANCIENT LITERATURE

The association of Kadmos with the introduction of Dionysos and the sudden impetus seen in EH III is not only archaeologically sound, but also in agreement with the literary tradition. The ancients did not have names for the prehistoric periods, but they seem to have had a basic understanding of what was early and what was late. Kadmos was consistently thought of as early: he is the earliest figure in the Theban genealogy of Herodotos (5.59), and follows only Ogygos in the genealogies of Hekataios and Hellanikos (Buck 1979:51). Of even greater interest is his position in relation to other figures of Greek mythohistory, as seen, for example, in the arrangement of legends in Ovid's *Metamorphoses* (table 2.8). Ovid's attempt at chronological arrangement is evident: he begins with the creation of the world, and ends with the apotheosis of Caesar and a wish for his own immortality and that of his book. He undoubtedly arranged the myths in what he thought was a chronological order, although he had no intention of writing "history."

The first two books of the *Metamorphoses* include stories about the cosmogony, the flood, and the activities of several gods. Heading the stories about mythohistorical figures are those about Europa and Kadmos, and these are followed (Books 3 and 4) by stories

Table 2.8. The sequence of myths in Ovid's *Metamorphoses*

Book	Characters & Events	Date	Book	Characters & Events	Date
1	Creation			Baucis & Philemon	
	Four Ages			Erysichthon	
	Jupiter Intervenes		9	Achelous & Deianira	LH III
	Lykaon			Hercules, Nessus, &	
	The Flood			Deianira	
	Deucalion & Pyrrha			Hercules' birth	
	Apollo & Daphne			Dryope	
	Jupiter & Io			Caunus & Byblis	
2	Phaethon			Iphis & Ianthe	
	Jupiter in Arcadia		10	Orpheus & Euridice	
	The Raven			Cyparissus	
	Ocyrhoe			Ganymede	
	Mercury & Battus			Apollo & Hyacinthus	
	Mercury, Herse, & Aglauros			Pygmalion	
	The Goddess Envy			Cinyras & Myrrha	
	Europa			Adonis, Atalanta	
3	Cadmus	EH III	11	Death of Orpheus	ca. 1200 B.C.
	Actaeon			Midas	
	Semele			The Walls of Troy	
	Teiresias			Thetis, Daedalion, & Peleus	
	Echo & Narcissus			Ceyx, Aesacus, & Hesperia	
	Pentheus & Bacchus		12	Invasion of Troy	
4	Pyramus & Thisbe			Caeneus, Centaurs, & Nestor	
	Mars & Venus		13	Ajax, Ulysses & Troy	
	Helios & Leucothoe			after Fall	
	Salmacis			Polyxena	
	The Daughters of Minyas			Polydoros & Memnon	ca. 1100 B.C.
	Athamas & Ino			Aeneas, Anius' Daughters	
	The End of Cadmus	MH		Galatea, Polyphemus, & Acis	
	Perseus		14	Glaucus	
5	The Fighting of Perseus			Aeneas, Achaemenides	
	Minerva Visits the Muses			Picus, Diomedes, & Venulus	
6	Niobe			Apotheosis of Aeneas	
	Tereus, Procne, & Philomela			Rome	753 B.C.
7	Jason & Medea			Pomona & Vertumnus	
	War between Crete & Athens			Iphis & Anaxarete	
	Cephalus & Procris		15	Numa & Myrselus	
8	Nisus & Scylla	LH I-II (?)		Pythagoras	
	Daedalus & Icarus			Hippolytus	
	Calydonian Boar			Cipus	
	Meleager			Aesculapius	
	Return of Theseus; Achelous			Apotheosis of Caesar	44 B.C.

Note: The myths may be seen to correspond to historical periods.

Table 2.9. The women in *Odyssey* 11.234-310 and the order in which they approach Odysseus

Order	Woman	Father	Husband	Children
1	Tyro	Salmoneus	Kretheus	Pelias & Neleus
2	Antiope	Asopos	Zeus	Amphion & Zethos
3	Alkmene	——	Amphitryon	Herakles
4	Megara	Kreon	Herakles	Alkaids
5	Epikaste	——	Laios/Oidipous	Oidipodes
6	Chloris	Amphion	Neleus	Nestor
7	Leda	——	Tyndareos	Dioskouroi
8	Iphimedeia etc.	——	Aloeus/Poseidon	Otus & Ephialtes

Note: There are six more women mentioned in verses 311-332, but no genealogical details are given about them.

about related figures, mainly of Theban or Boiotian origin. This section concludes with "The End of Cadmus," inviting the inference that all the figures treated between the "End" and the opening story of Europa originated in Theban myth cycles. Following the "End of Cadmus" are various stories, some of which commemorate historical events, such as the war between Crete and Athens (Book 7), the Trojan War (Book 12), and the founding of Rome (Book 14). Archaeological periods or dates corresponding to these events are suggested in table 2.8 in order to show the historical validity of Ovid's arrangement.

Ovid was, of course, a poet, not a historian. I believe, however, that his arrangement of the *Metamorphoses* reflects a common ancient practice, and that mythological personalities were always thought of in some order. There are other genealogies relating in particular to Theban figures. In Book 11 of the *Odyssey*, Odysseus, after consulting with Teiresias, allows fifteen women to speak to him. The first is, as we may expect, his mother. The next eight women are presented in some detail (table 2.9), beginning with Tyro, grandmother of Achilles. The five who follow are Theban, the last of whom, Chloris, marries Neleus, the son of Tyro, thereby connecting her to Thebes as well. As did Ovid, Homer starts his list with the oldest legendary figures known to him, all women in this instance and all related to early Greek heroic figures (Stubbings 1973:646). It is probable that the five Theban women are themselves arranged in chronological order, as the discussion of the male figures associated with them will show. Of these, Amphion and Zethos are placed by Homer at the start of the list, followed by Amphitryon, Herakles, Laios, Oidipous, and his children.

In the passage of the *Iliad* (14.318-328) in which Zeus recounts his most important female conquests—also his earliest (Stubbings 1973:646)—Ixione, mother of Peirithous, and Danae, mother of Perseus, are followed by Europa, Semele, and Alkmene; the list

75

Table 2.10. Theban mythohistorical characters in Pindar.

Kadmos				
Semele	*Ol* 2			
Dionysos				
——				
Amphitryon			Iphikles	
Herakles			Teiresias	*Nem* 1
Teiresias	*Isth* 7			
Iolaos				
——			Laios	
——			Oidipous	*Ol* 2
Seven			Oidipodes	
Sons of Seven	*Pyth* 8		Thersandros	

ends with Leto. Again there is a sense of chronology in this list, and three of the six women play some role in Theban mythohistory, as did many of the women interviewed by Odysseus. One cannot fail to acknowledge the prominence of Theban legends in the ancient Greek conception of the prehistoric past. In the Great Catalogue of Book 2 of the *Iliad*, and the Little Catalogue of Book 13 (685-700), Boiotia is mentioned first not only because the expedition to Troy originated there, but also because the oldest memory of the Greek past was preserved in Boiotian legends. Ovid's *Metamorphoses* also seems to acknowledge this.

We might anticipate the most interesting testimony about the city's past from the celebrated Theban poet, Pindar. Unfortunately for our purposes, Pindar was too cosmopolitan a figure, and his references to Theban legends are few and random. Only four songs contain any genealogical information, but overlapping content enables us to make a chronological arrangement of the figures (table 2.10). These start with Kadmos and his descendants, continue with Herakles and his relatives, and end with the dynasty of the Labdakids. Although Amphion and Zethos are not mentioned directly, in fragment 64 Pindar tells us that the Lydian mode was created during Amphion's wedding, and in *Paian* 9.44 he refers to "the army of Kadmos and the city of Zethos." This may suggest that Pindar placed Kadmos earlier than the Dioskouroi.

In a recent study of early Boiotian legends, Buck (1979:45-72, esp. p. 51) distinguishes three traditions that, in his view, contradict one another. Actually, when elements of the three traditions are tabulated, they are found to be in general agreement (table 2.11). Hekataios and Hellanikos agree in every respect if we overlook the minor omission of Ogygos by Hekataios. The only major contradiction is seen in the tradition of Pherekydes, who places Kadmos after Amphion and Zethos. Pherekydes also errs in omitting the earliest tribes (Aones and Hyantes) and in interpolating the Phlegyans between Amphion/Zethos and Kadmos. Pherekydes' relative placement of Amphion/Zethos and the Phle-

Table 2.11. The early legends of Boiotia as preserved in the three major
historical traditions (cf. Buck 1979)

Hekataios, Ephoros	Hellanikos, Philochoros	Pherekydes, Homer
————	Ogygos & Ektenes (autochthonoi)	Ogygos
Aones, Hyantes, Temmikes, Leleges, Pelasgians	Aones, Hyantes	————
Kadmos Founds Kadmeia	Kadmos and Phoenicians Found Kadmeia	Amphion & Zethos Found Kadmeia
————	————	Phlegyans Destroy Thebes
Amphion & Zethos Found Eutresis	Amphion & Zethos, Kings of Thebes, Fortify Kadmeia	Kadmos Rebuilds Kadmeia
Polydoros, Labdakos, Laios, Oidipous	Laios, Oidipous	Polydoros, Labdakos, Laios, Oidipous
Seven against Thebes, Epigonoi	same	same

gyans is clearly anachronistic. In the other two traditions, the Phlegyans are placed after the Trojan War.

It is also interesting to note the position of Kadmos in the *Marmor Parium*, a document that records the Athenian view of history (*FGrHist* 239): Kekrops is mentioned first, after whom come figures and events related to the flood and Deukalion (nos. 2-6); Kadmos is next (no. 7), followed by Danaos, Erichthonios, Minos, Demeter's arrival in Athens under Erechtheus, and other Athenian kings. Here too, Kadmos is thought of as an early figure.

The Dynasties and Tribes of Thebes

In attempting to reconstruct Theban prehistory, it is also useful to take into account the names of the various tribes alluded to in Theban myths, particularly when they can be shown to have association with kings or historical events. Archaeological evidence does not help us clarify the relationship between these tribes and Thebes. It is known, however, that in other parts of Greece, Early Bronze Age tribes lived in small village communities that shared the wealth of fertile plains (Caskey 1971A:772). It is possible, therefore, that in Boiotia as well, tribes were dispersed around agricultural areas and that some of those tribes recorded in Theban tradition lived not only in the area of Thebes, but also in other parts of Boiotia. Archaeological evidence from Thebes clearly shows that the earliest remains of habitation are those of a small community of 450 people (table 2.6). It is

Table 2.12. The dynasties of Thebes with related figures, tribes, and major associated events.

Kings	Related Figures	Tribes & Clans	Events	Periods
——	——	Pelasgians, Leleges Karians, Temmikes	Establishment of Village Communities	EH I-II A
Kalydnos (?) Ogygos Kaanthos (?)	Ogygia (?) Melia (?) Elektra (?)	Ektenes Aones Hyantes	same	EH II B
Kadmos	Harmonia, Semele	Kadmeiones "Phoenicians" Spartoi	Founding of Kadmeia	EH III
Dionysos Athamas Echion Pentheus Aristaios Melampous(?)	Ino, Melikertes Agave Autonoe, Aktaion Other Spartoi			
Chthonios (?) Lykos Nykteus Epopeus Amphion Zethos Amyklas	Homole (?) Hyrieus (?) Dirke, Nykteis (?) Antiope Niobe Thebe, Neis Children of Niobe Chloris	Encheleans (?) Phlegyans (?) Niobids	Fortification of Kadmeia	MH
Amphitryon Herakles Iphikles Iolaos Proitos (?) Polydoros (?) Nykteis (?)	Alkmene Megara, Galinthias Children of Herakles Linos (?) Antipoinos Androkleia & Alkis	Herakleidai Alkaids	War against Sicyon (?) Wars against Orchomenos First LH Palace	LH I-III A:1
Labdakos Laios Oidipous Eteokles Polyneikes Kreon Laodamas	Teiresias Menoikeus(?) Iokaste Antigone, Ismene Melanippos & Asphodikos, Amphiaraos	Aiolians	LH Fortifications Second LH Palace War over Oidipous' Sheep Seven Against Thebes	LH III A-B:1
	Alkmaion, Manto (?)		War of the Epigonoi	
Thersandros Tisamenos Peneleos Autesion Damasichthon Ptolemaios Xanthos		Boiotians	Move to Hypothebai Trojan War	LH III B:2-C

interesting to note that Pausanias (9.5.2) reports that prior to the founding of the Kadmeia by Kadmos, the inhabitants did live in village communities.

The numerous tribes and clans that have been recorded in connection with Thebes are shown in table 2.12. Some can be traced to the time of their arrival in Boiotia (e.g., Kadmeiones, Boiotians). Depending on its size and the efficiency of its organization, a tribe or clan might survive a conquest and retain its identity even though another tribe might eventually dominate the region. The Kadmeiones of Kadmos, for example, not only gave their name to the citizenry of Thebes (*Iliad* 4.385, 391), but so dominated southern Boiotia that the region was referred to by their name for a long time (Hesiod, *Theogony* 162; Thucydides 1.12). A major upheaval occurred in the twelfth century B.C. when the Boiotoi conquered the region, giving their name to the land, and eventually to its inhabitants as well (Thucydides 1.12). The emergence of a new dominant tribe, however, did not necessarily cause the disappearance of the old tribes. After the conquest by the Boiotoi, the Kadmeiones were not forgotten, nor did they disappear, perhaps indicating that, for the most part, outbreaks of conflict were followed by periods of peaceful coexistence. It is not surprising, then, to find that a particular tribe is named in association with separate, chronologically distant events.

The names of exceptional kings also gained a more general circulation: the name of the founder of a dynasty, for example, might be given to descendants, or used as a dynastic title in much the same way as "Pharaoh" was used in Egypt. One may therefore infer that the palace referred to as "house of Kadmos" was not merely the palace of the original Kadmos, but the royal residence of succeeding rulers in his dynasty; this name seems actually to have become synonymous with royal residence in Thebes. Kings most likely to retain their historical identity long after they were gone were those who either established a dynasty or achieved something memorable.

In the context of the founding of the Kadmeia at the end of EH II and the early position of Kadmos in relation to other mythohistorical figures in Theban tradition, we can attempt to reconstruct the Theban dynasties by arranging all the legendary personalities who must come after Kadmos and before the Labdakids. Table 2.12 includes all known legendary kings and the figures related to them.

In many traditional accounts, Ogygos precedes Kadmos (see table 2.11). The two other figures listed with him in table 2.12 are more obscure: according to Tzetzes (*Ad Lyc.* 1209), Kalydnos preceded Ogygos as king of Thebes, and Kalydna is given as an alternate name for Thebes by Stephanos Byzantios (cf. Unger 1839:20). Kaanthos (son of Okeanos and brother of Melia) set fire to Apollo's temple and was killed by Apollo for doing so. His tomb near the spring of Ares was shown to Pausanias (9.10.5). He may have been a river god (Schober 1934:1450-1451; Wilamowitz 1922:45, n. 2) or a deified king. Ziehen (1934:1524) suggests that he may have been a pre-Greek deity superseded by Apollo and offers the intriguing possibility of a Karian origin for his name. The tribes of this period before Kadmos may have included the Aones, the Hyantes, and the Ektenes, who may have been preceded by such tribes as the Pelasgians.

The Dynasty of Kadmos

The great achievement for which Kadmos is remembered is the founding of the city that was named Kadmeia in his honor. His name also became the eponym of his tribe, the Kadmeiones. The numerous figures closely associated with him in Greek tradition may be viewed as his dynasty, although their significance is connected with religious ritual rather than historical development. The wedding of Kadmos and Harmonia, attended by all the gods and the nine Muses, was probably such a ritual, as was the union between his daughter, Semele, and Zeus, resulting in the birth of Dionysos, his divine grandson, and the subsequent death of Pentheus, his mortal grandson.

According to historical information suggested by the myths, there were other figures associated with Kadmos, and he and his descendants introduced new religious rituals into Thebes. These rituals had a lasting association with the city's history, most likely because they were an integral part of the new culture that also introduced the advanced methods of cultivation that spurred the agricultural economy of Boiotia. In Ovid's *Metamorphoses* (Book 4), Kadmos and Harmonia are in the end transformed into serpents. No existing literary document records a change of dynasty, and the two dynasties that follow Kadmos in table 2.12 have been reconstructed on admittedly little evidence.

The dynasty to supersede that of Kadmos was dominated by the Dioskouroi of Thebes, Amphion and Zethos, whose most memorable achievement was the construction of the first fortifications of the city. This must have occurred in the Middle Helladic period, by the end of which time the city had expanded to 80,000 square meters with a population of ca. 2,400 (fig. 2.14, table 2.6). Although not a single remnant of the actual wall has been found, it is doubtful that a city as large as Thebes would have remained unprotected; other fragmentary bits of evidence of a wall's existence have been discussed above. That the wall was astounding to behold and thought to have been beyond ordinary mortal capabilities to erect (it must have been 1,100 m long to encompass the whole city) is perhaps reflected in the myths of its construction: according to one account, Amphion's half of the wall was raised by the magic of his lyre (Pausanias 9.17.7). This may be a way of describing light construction, but it may just as well be an expression of amazement, bordering on disbelief, at the architectural achievement. Wilamowitz (1922:29) suggested that Amphion's lyre raised mud-brick rather than stone.

Zethos is also remembered for having renamed the city after his wife, Thebe. Other celebrated members of the family were Antiope, mother of the twins and the subject of a lost tragedy by Euripides, and Chloris, the daughter of Amphion, who married Neleus. All of these are mentioned by Homer (see table 2.9) who also tells of the construction of the wall (see quotation at beginning of this chapter). The tragic story of Amphion's wife, Niobe, and their children, the Niobids, is well known and frequently represented in art. The "earliest" recognizable characters of this small group are Lykos, Antiope's uncle, and Nykteus, her father. Pausanias (9.16.6-7) claims to have seen the "house of Lykos" in the area of the tomb of Amphion and Zethos and the tombs of the Niobids. However, he probably saw not the house (*oikia*) but the cemetery of the "dynasty (*oikos*) of Lykos" (see below, chap. 5, passage 10).

One further event that has been linked to this dynasty is a war with Sikyon. According to Pausanias (2.6.1-4), who provides the only extant record of that conflict, the beautiful Antiope was abducted by the king of Sikyon, thus precipitating a war which Thebes lost. We have no further information about the course of the war or its consequences, but its occurrence may explain the presence in Theban tradition of the figures of Amphitryon, Herakles, Iphikles, Proitos, and Linos. Not one of these seems to belong to the dynasties we have discussed; all are from the Peloponnese. Their presence could be more easily understood if Thebes had indeed been defeated by Sikyon, but the time of such a defeat is problematic. Could it have occurred at the beginning of the Mycenaean period? Stubbings (1975:166-168) suggests that the rivalry between the Argolid and Thebes might have started in the fifteenth century B.C. when Thebes was a major power and the Argolid was unified. The Boiotians and the Argives seem to have had many confrontations during the course of the Mycenaean period, and the War of the Seven may not have been a sudden and isolated burst of enmity, but the culmination of a long antagonism. Argive influence on the cults and myths of Boiotia (Buck 1979:61) may well have begun before the end of the Mycenaean period. The traditions surrounding the figure of Herakles may be a manifestation of this influence.

Herakles commands too prominent a role in Theban mythohistory to deny his Theban identity or to fail to distinguish a Theban Herakles from his Argive counterpart. The many cult sites and monuments associated with him (see table 5.1) show that whatever his ultimate origin, the Thebans viewed him as their own: he was worshipped in two separate sanctuaries, located in the Aonian and Teneric plains (Rhinokoloustes and Hippodetes); on the Kadmeia, the house of his parents, where he was born, was made a sanctuary; outside the Kadmeia, a temple was erected in his honor during the Classical period; the tomb of his children by Megara and the site where Hera nursed him were both civic landmarks. All of this leads one to consider a Theban Herakles separate from the Argive one. Ancient tradition did, in fact, distinguish between the two, portraying the Theban Herakles as a youth, the Argive as a mature man.

There are several reasons for placing the dynasty of Herakles at the beginning of the Mycenaean period. First, Herakles belongs to a group of heroes who have no connection with the dramatic developments that took place at the end of the period. Stubbings (1973:651-652) also dates Herakles to the early part of the Late Helladic period and connects him with the expansion of the Argolid, an early historical development that coordinates perfectly with events alluded to in Theban legends. In his view, the myths that declare Thebes the birthplace of Herakles reflect political tension between the two regions.

Archaeological evidence from Thebes can also be brought to bear on the issue of this dating: the tomb of Amphitryon and that of Iolaos, both referred to in Pindar (*Nem.* 4.20 and *Pyth.* 9.79-83, respectively) must have been located in the same cemetery as the tombs of the children of Herakles by Megara that Pausanias visited (9.11.1-9.12.2; see chap. 5, passage 6, for a full discussion of the topography). This must be the vast cemetery of Kolonaki (site 24) in which the largest tombs date from LH I to LH III A:1 (table 2.4). Keramopoullos (1917:324-327) reached the same conclusion and placed the tombs relating to Herakles there. Whereas the tombs of other legendary figures are associated with cemeteries east of Thebes, the Herakleidai are the only such figures associated with Kolonaki, thus reinforcing the view of Herakles as a hero of the first half of the Mycenaean period.

Herakles also figured prominently in the wars between Thebes and Orchomenos, the memory of which survived to the time of Pausanias, who saw the statue of a lion dedicated by Herakles after a Theban victory (9.17.1). We cannot be certain that the monument and that particular conflict were Mycenaean; clashes with Orchomenos continued into the Geometric period. In fact, the repeated involvement of Herakles in the Orchomenian conflicts suggests that his was a dynastic name that was passed on to his descendants. It seems certain, however, that there were several wars in the Late Helladic period alone between the two rival Boiotian cities, and they seem to have taken place in the earlier part of that period. They may have culminated in a major confrontation during the reign of Oidipous.

The kings of the Herakleidai dynasty probably built the first Late Helladic palace and may even have given it the traditional and prestigious name, "the house of Kadmos." That this dynasty was not more precisely remembered in Theban tradition may be attributed to the fact that the events at the end of the Mycenaean period were so striking that they overshadowed the memory of all that went before. Or perhaps there was a transfer of power from a "foreign" family to a "native" one, that is, one that claimed actual descent from Kadmos. The transitional figure may have been Labdakos. If the dynastic conflict were violent, perhaps it and not the traditional lightning caused the burning of the first Late Helladic palace.

Although there is no uncontestable evidence for the order of the dynasties given above, the general agreement between literary tradition and the fragmentary archaeological picture is of some significance, particularly in suggesting a coherent picture of Theban prehistory spanning a period of a thousand years. It is this *agreement* that is crucial when the physical remains are so poorly preserved and the literary evidence so often distorted and vague.

In the past, scholars suggested a late date for Kadmos because there was virtually no archaeological evidence to indicate otherwise. Myres (1930:fig. 13) dated him to 1400

B.C. on the basis of his study of the genealogies alone. More recently, Buck (1979:58, 68) dated Kadmos to LH III A:2 or early III B; these dates are even later than that of the *Marmor Parium*, which is 1518 B.C. (see Brillante 1980), and underestimate the validity of Theban tradition. In fact, what emerges from a study of the genealogies is the remarkable wealth of the Theban literary tradition. No other Greek city, with the possible exception of Argos, preserves such a long memory of events that go as far back as the third millennium B.C. A rich oral tradition undoubtedly helped maintain continuity, and Thebes may have been a great center for epic poetry in the second millennium B.C. (cf. Notopoulos 1960). The prominence of Thebes in the second millennium B.C. must have contributed to the flourishing of the oral tradition, which served to preserve the memory of a glorious past. Most of the monuments shown to Pausanias in the second century A.D. belonged to that great past, the longest and most consistent period of Theban prosperity. We can only regret that so much of the literary tradition was lost during Christian times and that so many of the monuments were destroyed in our own time. In spite of these irretrievable losses, this reconstruction of the dynasties may contribute to a better understanding of Theban prehistory.

3
THEBES IN THE IRON AGE,
ca. 1050 B.C. TO A.D. 300

The evolution of the city of Thebes from the time of the Protogeometric period (ca. 1050 B.C.) to the end of antiquity (ca. A.D. 300) may, in some ways, be viewed as a whole. The changes were, of course, gradual over the centuries, but the basic culture remained essentially unaltered in Thebes, as it did throughout Greece. From the Protogeometric period on, Thebes grew from a small village community to become the city that dominated Boiotia and, for a brief span in the fourth century B.C., the city that dominated all of Greece.

The archaeological remains of this period are even fewer and more poorly preserved than those of the Bronze Age for reasons that are easy to understand. Houses were generally built of mud-brick; whatever stone was used was invariably recycled in later construction. In common with people in other areas of Greece, the Thebans put their energy and resources into public buildings that were constructed with permanent materials, usually ashlar masonry. The stone from these buildings, however, was stripped for reuse during the Early Christian and medieval periods. Even in modern times, ancient stone has been much sought after for construction, and one can see numerous and varied ancient stones incorporated into modern churches. The deeply buried foundations of Classical buildings may survive, but in such a fragmentary state that one can but rarely determine the function of the structure.

Most regrettable is the almost complete destruction of Theban sanctuaries, which were undoubtedly of superior construction and potentially rich sources of information about the ancient city. Only one, the temple of Apollo Ismenios (site 8), has been identified with certainty, and it is very poorly preserved; even the foundations have been stripped, leaving only a few deeply buried blocks on the west side. Only traces remain of the other public buildings. The theater, which must have been quite large, has so completely disappeared that we can identify no more than its approximate location.

THE CEMETERIES OF THEBES

The cemeteries of Thebes are somewhat better preserved than the public and residential buildings and can contribute quite a lot of meaningful information about the city's

fig. 3.1

84

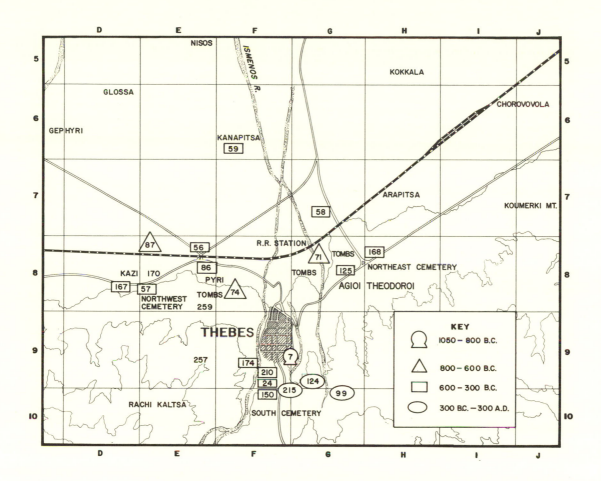

Fig. 3.1. The cemeteries of Thebes in the Iron Age

development. Some periods are, in fact, documented solely through finds from cemeteries: a few burials are known that date to the early part of the period, whereas no architectural remains of that time are preserved at all. Beginning with the Late Geometric period, however, although architectural remains of confirmed date continue to be rare, there is an increase in the number of excavated tombs. It is possible, therefore, to use the cemeteries as a source of information not only about Theban culture but also about the size and extent of the settlement during each historical phase. Present evidence suggests that in Thebes, as in all other Greek cities, intramural burials were the rare exception rather than the rule (Kurtz and Boardman 1971:188), and cemeteries were located outside the areas of habitation. Tombs of the Protogeometric period have been found in two locations on the Kadmeia. Of the eleven tombs in the cemetery at the Elektrai gates (site 7), two dated to the Protogeometric period; most of the others dated to the preceding Submycenaean period. One isolated burial was found in the east central part of the Kadmeia at site 10 (see Map B). In close proximity, at site 2, an isolated Protogeometric vase was found which could conceivably have belonged to yet another burial. Outside the Kadmeia in the Late Helladic cemetery at Kolonaki (site 24), a single Protogeometric skyphos was found in tomb 27. Although it was in no apparent association with a burial, the most plausible explanation of its presence is that Mycenaean tomb 27 was reused in the Protogeometric period.

The early part of the Geometric period is not represented, so far as I know, in the archaeological record. The only evidence from the Middle Geometric period is one published amphora (*Deltion* 1971, pl. 185:B) and a couple of sherds found at Kabeirion (Wolters and Bruns 1940:81, pl. 38:1-2); perhaps more will be known after the excavated material has been studied. Evidence of the eighth century B.C. is more plentiful: tombs of this period have been found in three locations, all north of the Kadmeia. Site 74, in the suburb of Pyri, contained a child burial and three Late Geometric vases, one of which was a beautiful large pithos. Although this is the only confirmed burial of the Geometric period in Pyri, it is likely that the tombs discovered in the late nineteenth century belonged to the cemetery in this area (Böhlau 1888; Wide 1899). At some point in the eighth century, another cemetery was established further west (site 87); most of the Geometric tombs here are at least three feet below the surface of the cultivated fields, and this has contributed to their preservation.

A third cemetery (site 71), just east of the modern railroad station, was cleared in Classical times for construction, but one tomb of the early seventh century was found intact. Keramopoullos (1917:297, n. 1) excavated a cremation burial with Geometric pottery near the theater, which is in the vicinity of site 71. This cemetery, then, was established in the eighth century and was also in use during the seventh. Our information about the seventh century B.C. comes primarily from the cemetery at site 87, which was in continuous use from the eighth until the beginning of the fifth century (cf. Keramopoullos 1917:297, n. 1). It is also likely that site 74, in the area of Pyri, continued to be used for burial during the seventh century.

During the Archaic period, three new areas were used for burial. One of them (site 57) lies south of site 87 and may be viewed as an expansion of the Geometric cemetery, which also continued to be used; the entire area became one huge cemetery that was used until the Hellenistic period. Another Archaic cemetery (sites 56, 86) was established between the huge one of sites 57 and 87 and the Geometric cemetery (site 74) of Pyri; here, many tombs have been uncovered. In the Classical period, this cemetery also extended to the south and continued to be used until the Hellenistic period. These two areas (sites 56, 86 and 57, 87) seem to have merged to form a vast burial ground, which I will refer to as the Northwest Cemetery. Keramopoullos (1917, map, and p. 297, n. 1) marks the presence of tombs even further to the south.

Just north of the seventh-century cemetery of site 71, a third Archaic cemetery was established (site 58): many tombs have been found there ranging in date from the sixth century B.C. to the third century A.D. This cemetery too seems to have extended southward in the Classical period: tombs dating to the Classical period were reported to have been found by the road to Chalkis, and numerous discarded tombstones have been found in the vicinity (sites 125, 168). This very large cemetery, which I will refer to as the Northeast Cemetery, lasted into Roman times: Keramopoullos (1910B:246-252; 1917:297, n. 1) found Roman tombs here, and Pappadakis excavated some Roman and Early Christian tombs north of here at the location called Chorovoivoda (the results were not published, but the excavation is mentioned by Keramopoullos 1917:297, n. 1).

During the Classical period, a new cemetery was established north of Thebes at the location called Kanapitsa (site 59). The tombs uncovered here range in date from the Classical to the Late Hellenistic period. Most of the tombs are deeply buried, however, and their discovery has been accidental. South of the Kadmeia, many tombs have been found dating to the Classical and Hellenistic periods. The Kolonaki hill, where there was an extensive Mycenaean cemetery, was reused: Keramopoullos (1917:210-252) excavated twenty tombs ranging in date from the fifth to the third centuries B.C. Eleven additional tombs of comparable date were found in the 1960s (site 24) and yet others have been discovered more recently still (sites 150, 174, 210).

Tombs of the Hellenistic period were found near the temple of Apollo Ismenios (sites 99, 124). Pappadakis (1911:140-141) excavated a few tombs in the vicinity of Agios Nikolaos (site 215). The main Hellenistic burial sites, however, are the Northwest and Northeast cemeteries. An empty Hellenistic tomb was found in Pyri (site 74).

Owing to the fact that burial practices of the Roman period resemble those of the Hellenistic period, tombs of the Roman period are not readily distinguishable; the tombs are sometimes tile-covered, and the offerings, if present at all, are poor. Keramopoullos (1910B:246-248) excavated three Roman tombs in the Northeast Cemetery; one of them was covered with tiles and drain pipes and the only offering was a plain vase. The other two were pit burials with offerings that included a lamp, a bronze coin, and four unguentaria. Funerary stelai of the Roman period have been found in Thebes, most often in the Northeast Cemetery.

Figure 3.2 lists the cemeteries of Thebes, arranged by location, and gives the approximate duration of their use. It is clear that certain areas ceased to be used for burial, while new cemeteries were established. Two developments are of particular importance in the evolution of Theban topography. The first is the moving of the cemetery from the Kadmeia to the area north of it (sites 71 and 74). The available evidence does not allow us to date this move precisely because there is a hiatus in the Early and Middle Geometric periods (ca. 875 to 740 B.C., according to Coldstream's chronology, 1968:330), but the cemetery was undoubtedly moved during this hiatus, perhaps ca. 800 B.C. This means that after 800 B.C. the Kadmeia was once more inhabited, perhaps in addition to Hypothebai which, as I have suggested, was the principal settlement during the Dark Ages. The moving of the cemetery to an area outside the Kadmeia may be viewed as an indication that the population of Hypothebai had grown sufficiently to warrant expansion of its living space. We must also observe that a Geometric cemetery was established at a considerable distance from the Kadmeia (site 87), perhaps for reasons related to the planned expansion of the settlement.

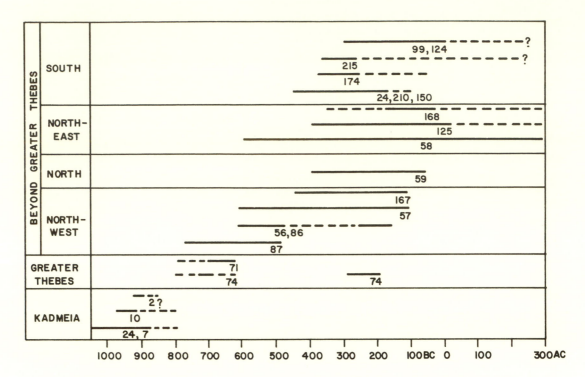

Fig. 3.2. The duration of the cemeteries of Thebes, arranged by location and period

The second important development occurred during the transition from the Orientalizing period to the Archaic, at which time the cemeteries in the areas of sites 71 and 74 ceased to be used. Burials took place at the Northwest and Northeast cemeteries, which are yet further away from the Kadmeia. In fact, there were no additional burials either on the Kadmeia or within the area of Greater Thebes until the end of antiquity. An occasional child burial or the empty tomb (a cenotaph?) of site 74 is the rare exception. No tombs have been found within the walls of Greater Thebes as Keramopoullos reconstructed them (1917, map); this is a good indication that his tracing of the wall is correct, although it is doubtful that this wall was constructed as early as 600 B.C. At that time, it is quite clear that there was a decision to move the cemeteries away from the immediate vicinity of the Kadmeia in order to allow the settlement to expand. It is possible that the initial need was for large spaces on which to erect public buildings; as we shall see, the largest public structures of Classical Thebes (the theater, new stadion and gymnasion, new agora, prison, and the hippodrome) are all to be found in the northern area of Greater Thebes, which continued to be occupied long after the great wall was destroyed in 335 B.C. Some public buildings were still in use in the time of Pausanias (second century A.D.), and there is evidence that there were houses in the area as well.

The evidence provided by the cemeteries suggests that the Theban settlement developed in a way that may be summarized as follows: During the Protogeometric period, the population was confined to the area of Hypothebai, protected by a wall that had been built during the Submycenaean period. In the Geometric period, the settlement grew and the Kadmeia was no longer used for burial; one may assume that sometime after this, perhaps between 800 and 700 B.C., a wall was built to protect the Kadmeia. At ca. 600 B.C., construction of large public buildings began in the area of Greater Thebes. By the beginning of the fourth century B.C., the city had reached its largest size. After the destruction of Thebes by Alexander the Great in 335 B.C., the population, though drastically reduced in number, continued to occupy the same area until the end of antiquity. The details of this evolution conform generally with the existing evidence from each successive period.

PROTOGEOMETRIC THEBES
ca. 1050 TO 875 B.C.

Of eleven tombs excavated by the east tower of the Elektrai gates (Keramopoullos 1917:25-32), two preserved no finds and seven were Submycenaean; the other two were Protogeometric. One (tomb 2) was a cist burial of an adult in which there were Mycenaean sherds, fragments of tiles, and a bronze ring; on the cover were two vases, a Protogeometric lekythos and an amphoriskos (Keramopoullos 1917, figs. 19, 20). Desborough (1952:196) thought the lekythos late Protogeometric and the amphoriskos Submycenaean. The other Protogeometric tomb (no. 9) was not intact, but it did contain a couple of bronze rings and a Protogeometric jug (Keramopoullos 1917, fig. 29). All the burials in this cemetery were inhumations with the skeletons in the extended position.

At site 10, a pit grave of unusual character was found: it contained an inhumation, the skeleton of an adult in the extended position, but between the legs was a Protogeometric amphora with the cremated remains of a second individual. The amphora (*Deltion* 1965B, pl. 283:a) was covered by two bowls. A Protogeometric skyphos discovered in a Mycenaean tomb (tomb 27) at the Kolonaki cemetery may have belonged to a Protogeometric burial (Keramopoullos 1917:203, fig. 148). This leaves us with a total of five burials dating to the Protogeometric period. We might also include in the body of evidence a trefoil jug of the late Protogeometric period from site 2; the close proximity of site 2 to site 10 may indicate that it, too, belonged to a burial.

This is certainly a small amount of material, but it provides at least some indication that Thebes existed as a community during the Protogeometric period. In common with neighboring Attica, inhumation and cremation were practiced, and individual burial was the rule. Desborough (1972:203) has observed evidence of connections with Euboia and Attica based on the pottery style; the lekythos from tomb 2 (site 7) may have been an Attic import (Snodgrass 1971:70). It is also possible that pottery continued to be made in the Mycenaean style into the Protogeometric period; Keramopoullos noted the presence

fig. 3.3

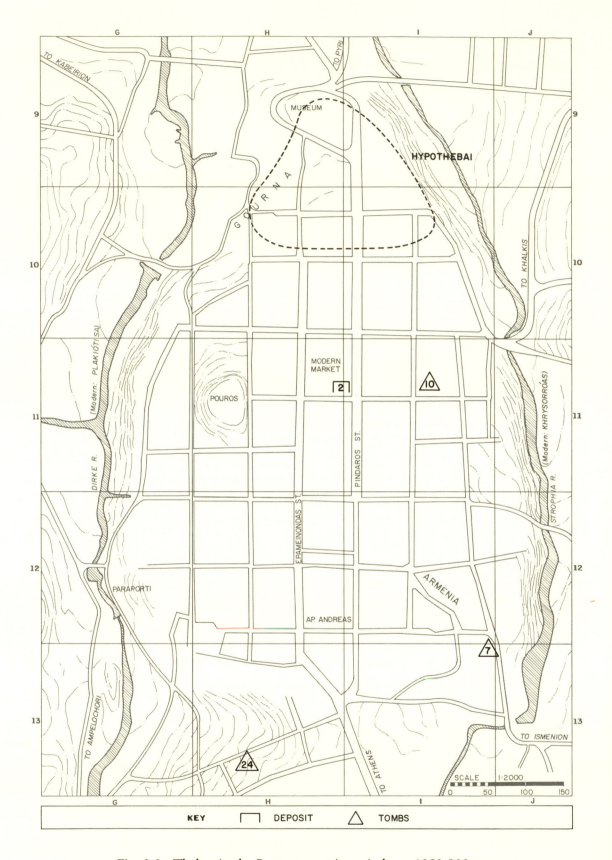

Fig. 3.3. Thebes in the Protogeometric period, ca. 1050-900 B.C.

of Mycenaean sherds in some of the other burials at site 7. In addition, there is the perplexing jug from tomb 3 (see Catalogue, site 7), which Snodgrass (1971:383) takes to be a cherished Mycenaean heirloom.

It is conceivable that in Thebes, the Submycenaean period lasted beyond ca. 1050, the date that marks the beginning of the Protogeometric period in Attica (Desborough 1972:133-158); if Protogeometric pottery was imported into Thebes, it is possible that both the Submycenaean and Protogeometric styles coexisted, as the material from tomb 2 (site 7) suggests. Had our evidence been more complete, we might well have been able to make meaningful comparisons with material from neighboring sites, in particular with Lefkandi (Popham and Sackett 1968; Popham 1980), which was occupied during the period from 1075 to 925 B.C. (Desborough 1972:188-199). Regarding the extent of the Theban settlement, the indirect evidence of the location of the cemeteries suggests that it was limited to a small section of the Kadmeia, possibly the northern tip, which I refer to as the Hypothebai of the Dark Ages. I believe that the Protogeometric settlement occupied the same area as that of the Submycenaean period, which was at the northern tip of the Kadmeia. It appears that the area occupied by the Mycenaean city was abandoned for a few centuries; isolated areas of it were used for burial. Those who survived the Late Bronze Age destruction continued to use old cult sites on the Kadmeia, or established new ones on the ruins of the more impressive buildings, such as the second Late Helladic palace. This would explain how so many sites associated with the Bronze Age continued to be remembered until late antiquity. It may also explain the preservation of so much of the Bronze Age oral tradition of Thebes. The few survivors inhabiting Hypothebai may be credited with preserving the memory of the glory of Thebes and contributing to its gradual revival.

THEBES IN THE GEOMETRIC AND ORIENTALIZING PERIODS, ca. 875 TO 600 B.C.

Again we are confronted with an almost total absence of architectural remains of the period. There is, however, abundant material from the cemeteries, and also objects that, although unearthed in illicit digging, can be traced to a Theban origin. There is also historical information about the city, but scholars do not agree on its interpretation. We do not have clear evidence pertaining to the Early and most of the Middle Geometric periods (ca. 875-740 B.C. according to Coldstream 1968:330), although there is stratified material that has not yet been studied (site 8; site 87, fig. 1.2), some of which may date to these periods. Three new burial sites were established north of the Kadmeia at some point in the eighth century B.C. (sites 71, 74, 87); as the Kadmeia itself was no longer used for burial, we may infer that it was inhabited once again, perhaps in addition to the area of Hypothebai as shown in fig. 3.4. The finds from site 187 at the southeast

fig. 3.4

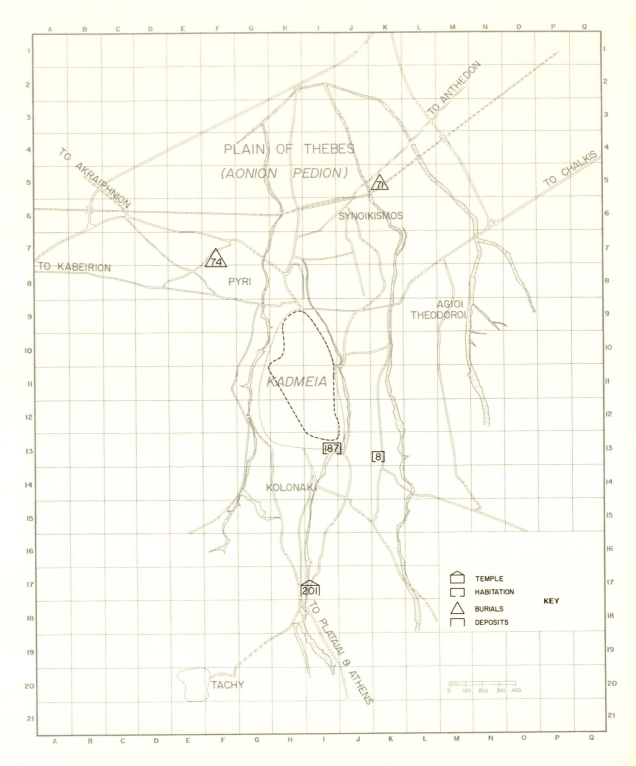

Fig. 3.4. Thebes in the Geometric and Orientalizing periods, ca. 900-600 B.C.

corner of the Kadmeia, which include a group of seventh-century Protocorinthian vases, and some tools and fragments of iron and bronze, were apparently in a context indicative of habitation. Unfortunately, the Kadmeia itself offers no further evidence pertaining to this period.

Aside from the material from the cemeteries, our best evidence comes from the sanctuary of Apollo Ismenios, a short distance southeast of the Kadmeia (see Catalogue, site 8, for detailed discussion). Keramopoullos' excavations of 1910 revealed that two temples were built consecutively during the Geometric period; a stratified excavation in 1966 (*Deltion* 1967:232, fig. 2) confirmed this. The first temple was erected on a terrace that contained Mycenaean and Geometric pottery; it was built of wood and mud-brick, possibly on foundations of poros stone. These materials were found in the destruction layer of the temple, in addition to large amounts of Late Geometric and Protocorinthian pottery, indicating that this temple was destroyed ca. 700 B.C. Hence, it must have been constructed in the eighth century B.C.

Keramopoullos (1917:73-75) believed that the second temple must have been built soon after 700 B.C. and was, in any case, in use by 600 B.C. It was built of poros stone with painted terracottas and was in the Doric style, but too little was preserved to allow for a reconstruction of its plan. It survived into the fourth century B.C., at which time it was replaced by a larger temple. Keramopoullos was able to distinguish the second temple from the later one on the basis of the different types of poros stone used in the construction of each. In addition to architectural fragments and roof tiles, he found part of a Doric column with 20 flutings, which had been stuccoed and painted red; this column was smaller than those of the later temple. The second temple, having been constructed in the seventh century, must have been the one that received the dedications recorded in ancient literature, as well as in the six fragmentary inscriptions known to us (see Catalogue, site 8); this was the temple that Herodotos visited, and the one known to Pindar and the fifth-century Greeks.

At yet another sanctuary (cf. site 201), Keramopoullos found two sherds of the Geometric period. Although evidence from this site dating to the Archaic and Classical periods is more substantial, it is possible that the sanctuary was established much earlier (cf. chap. 2). Keramopoullos (1910B:248-250) excavated a deposit of the Geometric and Orientalizing periods at Dragatsoula, about 1.5 km southwest of the Kadmeia; he thought that there might have been a sanctuary there. I do not know the exact location of this site or its relation to Thebes.

There is, relatively speaking, far more evidence dating to the Geometric and Orientalizing periods from tombs, many of which were discovered through clandestine digging. In the course of controlled excavations, however, a Geometric pithos burial of a child was found in the suburb of Pyri (site 74). Another pithos burial dating to the Orientalizing period was found in the suburb of Synoikismos (site 71). It is certain that these were not isolated burials and that there were cemeteries at both of these locations: damaged tombs were found near site 71, and many of the tombs discovered in the nineteenth century in Pyri were found in the vicinity of site 74 (cf. Böhlau 1888; Wide 1899).

At site 87 there is another, better-preserved Geometric cemetery, and important information will eventually emerge when the material excavated there has been studied. It seems that the tombs range in date from the eighth to the fifth centuries; they were rich in offerings, especially pottery. Of the 18 tombs excavated in 1966, eleven were pithos burials and seven pit burials, only one of which was a cremation. In the Geometric period, Thebans seemed to prefer to bury their dead in pithoi, a custom more closely related to burial practices of the Peloponnese than to those of Attica (Kurtz and Boardman 1971:180). One must not, however, generalize that inhumation was the funerary practice most common in Thebes throughout antiquity, because a large number of cremations dating to the Archaic period were discovered at another cemetery (site 56, fig. 3.5).

Because there are so few archaeological remains from the Geometric period, it is necessary to consider Boiotian objects in Greek and foreign museums, especially the material that is directly related to the evolution of Thebes as a city. Quite by accident, in 1878 a tomb was discovered intact in Pyri. Soon after the discovery, Furtwängler saw some of the finds from the tomb and we thus have reliable assurances that the tomb did, in fact, exist. The finds were later dispersed to various museums, quite a few ending up in Berlin; together with other Boiotian objects, they were published by Böhlau (1888). A few objects from Pyri housed in the Athens National Museum were published by Wolters (1892) and Wide (1899). These first publications of early Theban material spurred an interest in the more general subject of Boiotian pottery of the Geometric period, such as the work of Percy and Ann Ure (in particular, A. Ure 1932; P. Ure 1927A), Hampe (1936), and more recently Canciani (1965), Sparkes (1967), and Maffre (1975). Individual vases and small collections have been published in the *Corpus Vasorum Antiquorum*, most recently from the museums of Tübingen (Wellenstein 1973) and the Louvre (Waiblinger 1974), the latter with complete bibliography. Of the more interesting recent finds that have been published is the pithos with a representation of ritual dances (see Catalogue, site 74).

In one of the more complete studies of Boiotian pottery of the eighth and seventh centuries, Canciani (1965) examines 114 vases, only 33 of which are of known provenance; of these, 25 (i.e., 75 percent) are from Thebes. This is a very large proportion, which cannot be entirely coincidental. It suggests that in the Geometric period, Thebes had become a regional center, either importing ceramic wares in quantity, or, even more likely, manufacturing some and importing some.

Despite all these studies, not very much is known about Boiotian Geometric pottery because only a relatively small amount of material has been systematically excavated. Coldstream (1968:198-211), having studied the existing material, has proposed stylistic similarities with the pottery of Euboia and Thessaly in the Early Geometric period and influence from Attica beginning with EG II; the pottery of the Middle Geometric period is virtually unknown, and in the Late Geometric period, Boiotia produced very little pottery. Coldstream (1977:201-206) has recently reaffirmed his opinion that Boiotian Late Geometric pottery was slow to develop its own style because the local workshops remained under the influence of styles known to them through frequent imports. In his view, the Late Geometric style began ca. 740 B.C. with a Subgeometric phase lasting to ca. 670 B.C. In contrast, Boardman (1957) has proposed that Boiotia, Euboia, and the Cyclades shared a common style from the Geometric through the Archaic periods, whereas Courbin (1966:521-524) has seen stylistic similarities between the Geometric pottery of Boiotia and the Argolid.

Stylistic similarities seen in pottery are indicative of trade and cultural relations, but the evident disagreement among scholars of Boiotian pottery reveals the need for a more thorough study based on large quantities of systematically excavated material. Lacking this, it is difficult to envision Thebes during the Geometric period, because pottery is so basic a source of information. It has been possible, nevertheless, to identify pottery made in Thebes itself on the basis of what little we know: a group of oinochoai seems to have been made in a Theban workshop (Coldstream 1968:201, nos. 4-15). We may feel certain that far more pottery than this small sample was made in Thebes during the Geometric and Orientalizing periods.

Of a group of relief pithoi of the seventh century, four are known to have been found in Thebes (Hampe 1936:56-77, pls. 36-39). One of these, which is now in Athens (Nat. Mus. 5898), came from "the cemetery near Pyri" (Wolters 1892, pls. 8-9): it shows a *potnia theron* with two lions and two worshippers (also interpreted as Leto giving birth to Apollo and Artemis; Schefold 1966:32, pl. 12). Another pithos in Boston (Museum of Fine Arts 528; Fairbanks 1928) shows, according to Schefold (1966, pls. 25:b, 36:b), Achilles with the cattle of Aeneas on one side and the death of Aigisthos on the other. There are two in the Louvre (CA 795; CA 937, a fragment only), one of which shows a representation of the beheading of Medusa. Caskey (1976) proposes that these pithoi belong to a larger Tenian-Boiotian group and suggests that either they were all made in Tenos and exported from there, or they were made at their find spots by Tenian artisans.

In addition to vases, the Thebans were active in the production of terracotta figurines, many of which were discovered in Thebes in the past, and more recently at the cemetery of site 87. The well-known, bell-shaped idols were probably made here; two of them are known to have come from Thebes, one in Copenhagen dating to the early part of the eighth century (Higgins 1967:23, pl. 9:C-D), the other in the Louvre dating to the late eighth century (Mollard-Besques 1954:9, B 53, pl. VI).

Thebes is also known to have been active in the manufacture of a variety of bronze objects. Some bronze fibulae were found in Pyri (Böhlau 1888); others are simply said to have come from Thebes. The general subject of Greek fibulae was first explored systematically by Blinkenberg (1926); Boiotian fibulae in particular were the focus of a study by Hampe (1936), who found that as many as 57 of 159 Greek fibulae originated in Thebes. His view was that although the earliest fibulae may have been produced in Athens in the ninth century B.C., their manufacture from the middle of the eighth to the middle of the seventh century B.C. was dominated by the Boiotians. DeVries (1972), having studied the ten fibulae in Berlin, concluded that all ten may have come from Thebes, although he is not certain that all were made there; one of them may be dated as early as 800 B.C. (1972:114), while the remaining nine date to the liveliest period of Boiotian manufacture, ca. 730 to 675 B.C. DeVries (1974) identified one Theban workshop and also found that many fibulae of known provenance are from Thebes.

As for larger bronze objects, it is known that a few inscribed bronze cauldrons that were offered as prizes in funerary games have been found in Thebes (Jeffery 1961:94, nos. 2, 5). Cauldrons and tripods were offered as dedications to Apollo Ismenios during the festival of *Daphnephoria* (Ziehen 1934:1545-1549); such offerings were probably placed along the road leading from the sanctuary of Herakles to the temple of Apollo (Mommsen 1878:192). It is Guillon's belief that the Thebans introduced tripods as offerings at the sanctuary of Apollo Ptoios (1943:116-125). Cauldrons are, in fact, so typically a Theban offering that Jeffery (1976:79) believes the five fragmentary cauldrons found on the Akropolis of Athens were dedicated by Athenians who had won them as prizes in athletic competitions in Thebes.

By the Archaic period, Thebes had gained a reputation for the manufacture of chariots; as it is difficult to conceive of such a reputation materializing quickly, it is likely that chariots were being forged even earlier, yet another product of Theban bronze-working skill of the Geometric period.

One of the earliest objects known to have been dedicated to a god is the inscribed bronze statuette of a warrior that was dedicated to Apollo by Mantiklos (Boston, Museum of Fine Arts 03.997); it comes from Thebes and dates to ca. 700 B.C. (Richter 1960:41) or slightly later (Jeffery 1961:90-91, 94, n. 1, pl. 7). It was probably offered to Apollo Ismenios, as were the cauldrons and tripods; these are of particular significance because they too were accompanied by dedicatory inscriptions. In later periods, such inscriptions were common, but in the eighth and early seventh centuries they were rare. These objects, then, taken in conjunction with the few other inscribed dedications known (cf. site 8) and with the detailed account provided by Herodotos (5.58-61), who saw the old tripods when he visited the temple (see below, for a detailed discussion of Herodotos' visit), make it quite clear that the sanctuary of Apollo Ismenios was already of great importance by the eighth century B.C.

Wilamowitz (1922:44) believed that the oracle of Apollo Ismenios was established, or at least achieved prominence, earlier than the oracle at Delphi. It was primarily as a god of divination that Apollo was important in Boiotia, and many Boiotian sanctuaries were dedicated to him (Schachter 1967B). The practice of divination in Boiotia can be traced to the Mycenaean Age, when the preeminent seer was Teiresias, a Theban. That Thebes became an important center for divination and was so during the Dark Ages has been unappreciated for two reasons: first, the paucity of archaeological remains that could demonstrate the importance of the city, and second, the propaganda disseminated by Delphi that eventually succeeded in diminishing the importance of Apollo Ismenios. Defradas (1954:52-59) has already called attention to the fact that the *Pythian Hymn to Apollo* is an example of such propaganda, clearly intended to assert the antiquity of the Delphic Apollo: in its recounting of Boiotian cities visited by Apollo on his way to Delphi, Thebes is conspicuously excluded. Defradas believes that the poem was written at a time when Thebes as a political force had eclipsed all other Boiotian cities. Ducat (1973:63) has suggested that the First Sacred War (ca. 600-590 B.C.) may have broken out in response to Theban attempts to expand its influence beyond Boiotia, and the rivalry between the oracles of Thebes and Delphi may perhaps be viewed in this context. The outcome of the war was favorable to Delphi, which was able to expand its activities and establish the Pythian Games in 582 B.C.

Another poem, *Aspis* or *The Shield of Herakles*, is seen as an expression of the Theban point of view at about 600 B.C. In his monograph on the poem, Guillon (1963) suggests that the hero is the youthful Theban Herakles, who, until the time the poem was written, was distinguished from the adult Argive Herakles. During the period of Theban ascendancy (ca. 650-600 B.C.), the Theban Herakles became a Penhellenic hero and his identity was subsequently fused with that of his Argive counterpart. Guillon also believes that Herakles became the protector of the cult of Apollo in Boiotia (1963:81-83). Such a development would illuminate the old rivalry between the oracles of Thebes and Delphi; the frequently represented fight between Herakles and Apollo over the mantic tripod would take on new meaning as a political struggle between Thebes and Delphi for retaining the prestigious rights of divination (cf. Defradas 1954:134-136). The archaeologically documented dates of the two sanctuaries indicate that the temple of Apollo Ismenios was built earlier (i.e., eighth century B.C.) than the temple at Delphi, for which the earliest date is the seventh century (Defradas 1954:52). Divination was probably practiced earlier in each place but was only of local influence; the constuction of a temple would have increased the importance of the oracle, spurring competition or renewing rivalry. Such ongoing rivalry is probably revealed in Pindar's *Pythian* 11 written for a Theban victory in the Delphic games of 474 B.C. Pindar begins the ode by inviting legendary Thebans to a celebration at the temple of Apollo Ismenios, "the sanctuary of golden tripods, the treasury that Loxias honored most, and named Ismenion and made the true seat of diviners" (lines 3-6). Here Pindar clearly declares the preeminence of Apollo Ismenios over the Apollo of Delphi. The rivalry may have climaxed in the sixth century, but had already begun in the eighth.

The existing evidence suggests that in the eighth and seventh centuries B.C. Thebes was no isolated village community, but a rather lively city. While it is true that Thebes did not colonize, that does not mean she was without overseas contacts. Boardman (1957:9) suggests that Boiotia may have been involved in the founding of Metapontion (cf. Bérard 1941:345-348). Boiotians may also have been involved in the colonization of Sardinia (Bérard 1941:434-437), Kyme (Bérard 1960:72, 82), and Herakleia of Pontos (Burstein 1972). According to Pliny (*N.H.* 3.98) there was a Lukanian city called Thebes; this may have been a Boiotian colony. There is also reference of Pherekydes cited in Strabo (14.1. 3) indicating that Philotas of Thebes was the leader of the colony of Priene (cf. Bérard 1960:43, 142) and that Bias the Sage of Priene was supposed to be of Theban descent (Jeffery 1976:221). We must also remember the colonization of Cilicia by Mopsos, mentioned in the previous chapter.

According to Aristotle (*Pol.* 1265b, 1247a-b), Thebes of the eighth century B.C. is to be remembered for yet two other reasons: the Bacchiad Philolaos, exiled from Korinth, revised the laws of Thebes ca. 728 B.C. (Jeffery 1976:142) or slightly later (Buck 1979:95). At about that time, the old rivalry between Thebes and Orchomenos flared up once more; by the end of the eighth century B.C., Thebes was probably once again the victor (Buck 1979:96-98).

Within the region of Boiotia where poetry flourished (DeVries 1974), Thebes was a cultural center, preserving the memory of her glorious past throughout the Dark Ages in the form of oral poetry. Notopoulos (1960) has observed that there was a large body of oral Achaean tradition, some of which recorded the exploits of heroes in epic poems, but some of which treated the practical arts, sailing, and agriculture. Hesiod is the best known exponent of the latter. Boiotia, participating in this rich tradition, displays an enthusiasm for catalogues, genealogies, and the daily realities of practical life. Not in the least isolated, the Boiotians might have loved sailing; they were fond of painting ships on Geometric vases (Williams 1958). Thebes—with her ancient and revered oracle, her diverse industries, her agricultural wealth, and her various connections abroad—as the major city of Boiotia, must have been the cultural leader.

Geometric Thebes and the Introduction of the Alphabet

When Herodotos visited Thebes in the fifth century B.C., he described what he saw at the temple of Apollo Ismenios in a frequently quoted passage (5.57-61), making reference to the Phoenicians, Kadmos, and the introduction of the alphabet into Greece. I do not intend to address the large issue of the introduction of the alphabet into Greece, but Herodotos' observations have a bearing on the early history of Thebes, and also on the far-reaching and lasting Theban influence on Greek culture that resulted from her unique response to the potential of writing. Here, then, is Herodotos' account (cf. his *Historiai* in Oxford's 3d edition, Book 5, 57-61):

(57) Οἱ δὲ Γεφυραῖοι, τῶν ἦσαν οἱ φο-
νέες οἱ Ἱππάρχου, ὡς μὲν αὐτοὶ λέγουσι, ἐγεγόνεσαν ἐξ Ἐρετρίης τὴν
ἀρχήν, ὡς δὲ ἐγὼ ἀναπυνθανόμενος
εὑρίσκω, ἦσαν Φοίνικες τῶν σὺν Κάδμῳ
ἀπικομένων Φοινίκων ἐς γῆν τὴν νῦν
Βοιωτίην καλεομένην, οἴκεον δὲ τῆς
χώρης ταύτης ἀπολαχόντες τὴν Ταν-
αγρικὴν μοῖραν. ἐνθεῦτεν δὲ Καδμείων
πρότερον ἐξαναστάντων ὑπ᾽ Ἀργείων
οἱ Γεφυραῖοι οὗτοι δεύτερα ὑπὸ
Βοιωτῶν ἐξαναστάντες ἐτράποντο ἐπ᾽
Ἀθηνέων. Ἀθηναῖοι δέ σφεας ἐπὶ
ῥητοῖσι ἐδέξαντο σφέων αὐτῶν εἶναι
πολιήτας, (οὐ) πολλῶν τεων καὶ οὐκ
ἀξιαπηγήτων ἐπιτάξαντες ἔργεσθαι.

(58) οἱ δὲ Φοίνικες οὗτοι οἱ σὺν Κάδμῳ
ἀπικόμενοι, τῶν ἦσαν οἱ Γεφυραῖοι,
ἄλλα τε πολλὰ οἰκήσαντες ταύτην τὴν
χώρην ἐσήγαγον διδασκάλια ἐς τοὺς
Ἕλληνας καὶ δὴ καὶ γράμματα, οὐκ
ἐόντα πρὶν Ἕλλησι ὡς ἐμοὶ δοκέειν,
πρῶτα μὲν τοῖσι καὶ ἅπαντες χρέωνται
Φοίνικες· μετὰ δὲ χρόνου προβαίνον-
τος ἅμα τῇ φωνῇ μετέβαλον καὶ τὸν ῥυθ-
μὸν τῶν γραμμάτων. περιοίκεον δέ
σφεας τὰ πολλὰ τῶν χώρων τοῦτον τὸν
χρόνον Ἑλλήνων Ἴωνες· οἳ παραλα-
βόντες διδαχῇ παρὰ τῶν Φοινίκων τὰ
γράμματα, μεταρρυθμίσαντές σφεων
ὀλίγα ἐχρέωντο, χρεώμενοι δὲ ἐφά-
τισαν, ὥσπερ καὶ τὸ δίκαιον ἔφερε ἐσ-
αγαγόντων Φοινίκων ἐς τὴν Ἑλλάδα,
Φοινικήια κεκλῆσθαι. καὶ τὰς βύβλους
διφθέρας καλέουσι ἀπὸ τοῦ παλαιοῦ οἱ
Ἴωνες, ὅτι κοτὲ ἐν σπάνι βύβλων ἐχρέωντο διφθέρῃσι αἰγέῃσί τε καὶ οἰέῃσι· ἔτι
δὲ καὶ τὸ κατ᾽ ἐμὲ πολλοὶ τῶν βαρβά-
ρων ἐς τοιαύτας διφθέρας γράφουσι.

(57) The Gephyraioi, to whom the mur-
derers of Hipparchos belonged, came originally from Eretria, according to their own
account. I find upon inquiring, however,
that they are descendants of those Phoenicians who came with Kadmos to the land
now called Boiotia; they settled in part of
this region, after the territory of Tanagra
was apportioned to them. After the Kadmeians were expelled from here by the Argives, the Gephyraioi themselves were
expelled by the Boiotians and sought refuge in Athens. The Athenians accepted them
as citizens under certain conditions, that
placed but few restrictions on them, not
worth mentioning here.

(58) The Phoenicians who came with Kadmos, to whom the Gephyraioi belonged,
introduced to the Greeks a great many arts
after they settled in this region; most important was the alphabet which the Greeks
did not have, I believe, before that time.
At first, they introduced the characters
which all Phoenicians use as well; as time
went by, they changed both the pronunciation and the form of the letters. In most
of the areas at this time, the Greeks who
dwelt about them were Ionians; they
adopted the characters that were taught
by the Phoenicians, and used them after
making a few changes; they continued to
refer to these letters as "the Phoenician
letters," which is only appropriate since
they were introduced to Greece by the
Phoenicians. The Ionians still call the paper
rolls "parchments" because in the old days
paper was scarce and people used to write
on skins of goats and sheep; many foreigners write on skin even to this day.

(59) εἶδον δὲ καὶ αὐτὸς Καδμήια γράμματα ἐν τῷ ἱρῷ τοῦ Ἀπόλλωνος τοῦ Ἰσμηνίου ἐν Θήβῃσι τῇσι Βοιωτῶν ἐπὶ τρίποσι τρισὶ ἐγκεκολαμμένα, τὰ πολλὰ ὅμοια ἐόντα τοῖσι Ἰωνικοῖσι. ὁ μὲν δὴ εἷς τῶν τριπόδων ἐπίγραμμα ἔχει·

Ἀμφιτρύων μ' ἀνέθηκεν ἐὼν ἀπὸ Τηλεβοάων.

ταῦτα ἡλικίην εἴη ἂν κατὰ Λάιον τὸν Λαβδάκου τοῦ Πολυδώρου τοῦ Κάδμου. (60) ἕτερος δὲ τρίπους ἐν ἑξαμέτρῳ τόνῳ λέγει·

Σκαῖος πυγμαχέων με ἐκηβόλῳ Ἀπόλλωνι
νικήσας ἀνέθηκε τεῖν περικαλλὲς ἄγαλμα.

Σκαῖος δ' ἂν εἴη ὁ Ἱπποκόωντος, εἰ δὴ οὗτός γε ἐστὶ ὁ ἀναθεὶς καὶ μὴ ἄλλος τώυτὸ οὔνομα ἔχων τῷ Ἱπποκόωντος, ἡλικίην κατὰ Οἰδίπουν τὸν Λαΐου. (61) τρίτος δὲ τρίπους λέγει καὶ οὗτος ἐν ἑξαμέτρῳ·

Λαοδάμας τρίποδ' αὐτὸς ἐϋσκόπῳ Ἀπόλλωνι
μουναρχέων ἀνέθηκε τεῖν περικαλλὲς ἄγαλμα.

ἐπὶ τούτου δὴ τοῦ Λαοδάμαντος τοῦ Ἐτεοκλέος μουναρχέοντος ἐξανιστέαται Καδμεῖοι ὑπ' Ἀργείων καὶ τρέπονται ἐς τοὺς Ἐγχελέας, οἱ δὲ Γεφυραῖοι ὑπολειφθέντες ὕστερον ὑπὸ Βοιωτῶν ἀναχωρέουσι ἐς Ἀθήνας· . . .

(59) I myself saw Kadmeian letters at the sanctuary of Apollo Ismenios in Boiotian Thebes incised on three tripods and shaped very much like the Ionian. One of the tripods had this inscription:

'Amphitryon dedicated me, from the spoils of the Teleboans';

these letters would date to the time of Laios, the son of Labdakos, the son of Polydoros, the son of Kadmos.

(60) Another tripod says in the hexameter mode:

'Skaios, after winning at boxing, dedicated me to you, archer Apollo, a beautiful offering';

This might be Skaios the son of Hippokoon, unless it is someone else by the same name; this would be about the time of Oidipous, son of Laios.

(61) The third tripod says, also in hexameters:

'Laodamas, while king, dedicated this tripod to you, good archer Apollo, a beautiful offering'.

It was during the reign of Laodamas, the son of Eteokles, that the Kadmeians were expelled by the Argives and took refuge with the Encheleans. The Gephyraioi were expelled. . . .

In this long passage, Herodotos preserved some very important information about the introduction of writing; the events surrounding this development had already been obscured by Herodotos' time, and his inability to provide the reader with an accurate time frame led to a great deal of subsequent confusion. Even in later antiquity he was misinterpreted by Tacitus (*Annals* 11.14) who wrote that Kadmos and his Phoenicians sailed to Greece and taught the art of writing to the illiterate Greeks. Herodotos, however, does not associate Kadmos himself with the introduction of writing: it was the descendants of those who came with Kadmos that introduced the alphabet. Herodotos makes this clear by saying that it occurred "after they settled in Boiotia." He may confuse the reader by calling the letters "Kadmeian," but in context it is clear that 'Kadmeian' refers to the Kadmeia (the old city), and not to Kadmos. He saw the inscriptions at the sanctuary of Apollo in Thebes, the akropolis of which was called Kadmeia (cf. Wilamowitz 1922:24), and it was the akropolis that was inhabited at the time writing was introduced. Herodotos could have written Κάδμου γράμματα "the letters of Kadmos" if he had intended to attribute the introduction of writing to a person rather than to the city. Moreover, Herodotos does not say that he himself read the inscriptions, which allows us to wonder exactly what kind of writing he saw. Forsdyke (1957:40-41) argues that if it was Mycenaean script, the translation provided by the priests must have been a sham, since no one could read Linear B in the fifth century B.C., the reputation of the priests of Thebes for being excellent epigraphists notwithstanding. There is the possibility that the cauldrons were Mycenaean but the inscriptions were added to them in the Archaic period. Biesantz (1958) raises the possibility that the use of Linear B may have survived and may indeed be what Herodotos saw.

Most scholars believe, however, that there is something dubious about those inscriptions (to say nothing of Herodotos' account of them) and regard them as fakes (Guarducci 1967:489). We cannot, however, ignore the fact that seven centuries after Herodotos, Pausanias (9.10.4) saw among the tripods of the same sanctuary, one that was dedicated by Amphitryon, this one in honor of Herakles for having as a boy officiated at the festival of *Daphnephoria*. Each of these ancient eyewitnesses clearly thought that the objects were extraordinary. Herodotos went so far as to believe that they dated to some very remote era. Were the priests of Apollo actively deceiving their visitors, or did they too take the objects to be ancient? Herodotos' ability to compare the Kadmeian to the Ionian letters shows that they looked familiar to him, although he may not have been able to read them and thus had to rely on the priests for a translation of the inscriptions. Had the inscriptions been in Linear B, he could not possibly have found them similar to Ionian writing. This tells us that the writing was antiquated but not ancient at the time of Herodotos' visit. Even as literate a man as Herodotos could be expected to have difficulty reading a three-century-old inscription, made during the years when Greek writing was still a primitive skill, and written in a local dialect. Under the circumstances, Herodotos would be showing very good sense in relying on the translation of priests, who were, after all, expected to be knowledgeable about whatever concerned their own temple.

Forsdyke's suggestion that the tripods predate the inscriptions may raise more problems than it solves. If we entertain the possibility that the tripods were made early in the Geometric period, or even in the Mycenaean period, and that the inscriptions were added sometime after writing had been introduced, we are confronted with the question of how such bronzes managed to be preserved, especially if they were made in Mycenaean times, and whether, after so many centuries, they could have been in good enough condition to be dedicated at the sanctuary. On the other hand, we do know that cauldrons were commonly dedicated to this sanctuary during the Geometric and Orientalizing periods when Thebes was relatively affluent. It seems, therefore, more likely that the cauldrons were made at that time. If the inscripions were added later, it cannot have been very much later because Herodotos could easily have read a sixth-century inscription by himself. His need to rely on the priests indicates that the inscriptions were very early, perhaps eighth-century. It seems, therefore, most reasonable that both cauldrons and inscriptions must have been of eighth-century date. The only thing that ties them to a more remote era (i.e., Mycenaean) is the content of the inscriptions.

As to their authenticity, the inscriptions recorded by Herodotos are no less genuine than any other text of the historic era that transmitted to posterity those events of the Mycenaean period that the oral tradition had preserved through the Dark Ages. We don't look upon the Homeric poems as fake, nor do we regard the Archaic statues of Kleobis and Biton, characters of a past age (cf. Herodotos 1.31), to be false dedications to the temple in Delphi. There are countless such examples, which represent a genuine desire on the part of the Greeks to preserve in writing the precious little that was remembered of the glorious Mycenaean period. Some of these attempts may be clumsy, but they must be viewed with an appreciation of the excitement created by the discovery of writing. The Thebans of the Geometric period were able to draw upon a rich collection of myths about the Theban past. Among these were the myths alluded to in the inscriptions seen by Herodotos. The idea of preserving them by inscribing cauldrons may seem peculiar to us, but not if we remember that the cauldron was the typical offering in the Geometric period to the sanctuary of Apollo; the Thebans of that time would have understood that the dedications were made to commemorate some past event. If we were to add the words *in memory of* before the first word of each inscription, it would be clear that those who made the dedications did not intend to defraud. It is also easy to understand why these dedications were read in a different way, and perhaps exploited, centuries later: the priests of Apollo Ismenios must have been hard-pressed to establish the antiquity of their sanctuary, especially after it had lost much of its prestige to Delphi. By the time of Herodotos' visit, about three centuries had passed since the dedications were made, and those texts must have looked like ancient relics. Nevertheless, it is possible that even in Herodotos' time it was commonly understood that the cauldrons were commemorative. It seems clear that the reason Herodotos mentions the inscriptions is not to prove that they were Mycenaean/heroic antiques, but to show that Thebes was the place where writing was introduced into Greece. Such an assertion has, in modern times, called forth an almost mocking disbelief, and both Herodotos and ancient tradition have been viewed as essentially misleading.

Most recently, Jeffery (1976:26; 1961:5-10; Jeffery and Morpurgo-Davies 1970) has suggested that Crete was the place where writing was first introduced (for objections, see Edwards and Edwards 1974; Beattie 1975). Opinions vary regarding the date: some accept a dating from the eleventh to the tenth century B.C. (Naveh 1973; McCarter 1975) or late ninth (Guarducci 1967:73; Gelb 1963:180-181), but most accept an early eighth-century date (Jeffery 1961:12-21; Einarson 1967; Coldstream 1968:358). Perhaps the most convincing argument in support of an early eighth-century date was given by Young (1969), who believed that both the Greeks and the Phrygians adopted the alphabet in a West Semitic area and that this could not have occurred after 738 B.C. when the Assyrian King Tiglath-Pileser III caused interruption of trade in the area; a date before 800 B.C. would not agree with the evidence from Phrygia. Young pointed out that it was the Greeks in Western Asia who devised the alphabet. His view allows for the possibility of the simultaneous arrival of the alphabet in many Greek cities once it had been formulated in Western Asia.

In all of this controversy, it is important to make a clear distinction between the introduction of the letters into Greece, which could indeed have occurred suddenly and simultaneously in many areas as Young suggested, and the development of writing, which required the formulation of a system compatible with spoken Greek and perhaps the establishment of the first grammatical and syntactical rules. We should not assume that the introduction of the alphabet brought the immediate development of writing. Herodotos does, in fact, hint at a lag, in saying that at first the characters were used the way the Phoenicians used them and that later both their pronunciation and their form were changed. I take this to mean that at some time after the alphabet was introduced, those important modifications were made, some of which we recognize today, such as the addition or omission of certain letters and the introduction of vowels, which brought to writing a tremendous flexibility and greater representational precision. These developments—rather than the mechanical introduction of letters, which could have occurred anywhere—are the ones that gave the alphabet its broader significance.

The province of Boiotia in general, and Thebes as its major city in particular, must have contributed in a major way to the development of Greek literacy: Thebes was the mainland center for poetry during the period from 800 to 500 B.C. (DeVries 1974) and had perhaps the richest tradition in epic poetry (Notopoulos 1960; Huxley 1969). The enthusiasm for preserving the immense oral tradition in writing may be seen in that the largest number of early inscriptions are Boiotian, which, as Jeffery herself admits (1961:90), is startling. As she also observes, the scripts of Boiotian cities do not differ, and this homogeneity may be attributed to the early development of writing, the close contact between Boiotian communities, and the dominating influence of Thebes, Boiotia's most powerful city. Huxley (1969:189-190) notes that epic poetry may have been written down from 725 B.C. onward, and that other poetry and prose passages may have been incorporated in one and the same work, a rather sophisticated application of the skill of writing.

Thebes' role in acquiring the alphabet may be more clearly seen in the context of her activities during the Geometric period: in the eighth century, the city flourished as an agricultural center, as an important seat of divination, and as the most powerful Boiotian town. Renewed contacts between Greece and the Near East made it possible for the Theban descendants of the Phoenicians/Canaanites who came with Kadmos many centuries earlier to take advantage of the newly developed alphabet of their Phoenician contemporaries and adapt it to suit the Greek language. Implicit in Herodotos' text is an appreciation of the importance of the transition from a totally oral culture to one that could use writing. The change did not occur overnight; Herodotos calls attention to its beginning, which enabled him and other Greeks to use the alphabet not only for recording business transactions, but for recording poetry and prose as well. Thebes can lay strong claim to having been the place where Classical Greek literature began. No less a poet than Aischylos acknowledges this when he describes the city as Ἑλλάδος φθόγγον χέουσαν (*Hepta* 72-73), literally "the city that pours forth the speech of Greece." The passage is usually translated as the city that "speaks the language of Greece" but, if this were correct, it would be an odd thing for Aischylos to say about Thebes in 467 B.C. (the date of *Hepta*) when Pindar already had achieved recognition as a major poet of the Greek world. Dawson (1970:16) has acknowledged the awkwardness of this translation and has suggested that Aischylos may have had in mind the Persian wars during which Thebes was subjugated by a foreign power, yet still spoke Greek; he translates the line, "a Greek city with its established homes." The meaning of χέω, however, when used metaphorically to describe sound or utterance, is "to pour forth" or "to spread," as seen even in Homer (*Odyssey* 19.521, for the song of the nightingale). Weil (1903) correctly translated the line as "the city that pours forth the mother tongue of Greece." By Aischylos' time, the use of writing was barely three centuries old, and his audience would surely have recognized this line as a tribute to an old and important city where poetry flourished and where writing was first used to record it.

THEBES IN THE ARCHAIC PERIOD,
ca. 600 to 500 B.C.

fig.
3.5

After the First Sacred War (ca. 600-590 B.C.), several Boiotian cities formed an organization in connection with a religious festival celebrated at Onchestos in honor of Poseidon. Although we do not know exactly how it functioned (cf. Schober 1934:1457-1459; Cloché 1952:18-47), we do know that by the middle of the sixth century, at least part of Boiotia was unified; this is evidenced by the coinage, which shows that the emblem of the "Boiotian" shield was common to at least seven cities, Thebes among them (Head 1881:195). The coinage has been viewed as an indication that the Boiotian League, an early attempt at federalization, must have been formed in the first part of the sixth century B.C. The activities of the League toward the end of the sixth century are better known: when the Thessalians invaded Boiotia (probably ca. 520 B.C.; Buck 1979:107), the League successfully repelled them in the battle at Keressos. Because the League was capable of coordinating its military forces so successfully by the time of this battle, some feel that it must have been organized ca. 525 B.C. at the latest (Ducat 1973:71). By the end of the sixth century, Thebes had become its most prominent member.

Most of our information comes from accounts of the war over Plataiai, the southern Boiotian city that was unwilling to join the League and allied itself with Athens instead. This precipitated a confrontation between Thebes and Athens, and in the war that ensued, Thebes was defeated (506 B.C., Amit 1970; Adcock and Mosley 1974; Buck 1979:107-117). We may trace to this war the bitter rivalry between Thebes and Athens, which continued for the next hundred years until the conclusion of the Peloponnesian War in 403 B.C.; that war, too, started at Plataiai.

Some scholars now believe that the political thought of Greece in the Archaic period was considerably influenced by developments in Boiotia involving the League (Larsen 1955; Ducat 1973). The extent and value of the influence have been obscured as a result of the rivalry with Athens and the defaming of Thebes during the Persian wars. The archaeological evidence, though scanty, nevertheless suffices to document the power and diversity of Thebes during the Archaic period.

Most of the archaeological evidence pertaining to the Archaic period was found in the cemeteries. On the Kadmeia itself, only a fragment of an inscription was found (site 7), although there can be little doubt that the entire akropolis was inhabited. In Greater Thebes, the sanctuary of Apollo Ismenios provides the most meaningful information: the second temple, which had been constructed during the Orientalizing period, continued to be used and may have been renovated; the presence of roof tiles dating to the early sixth century is mentioned by Keramopoullos (1917:60); a terracotta anthemion that he had dated to the end of the sixth century B.C. (1917:52-53, fig. 51), Payne dated to the second quarter of the fifth century (1931:262). Three inscriptions on objects dedicated to the sanctuary have been dated to the sixth century (see Catalogue, site 8, nos. 1-3), while two others could date to the late sixth to mid-fifth century B.C. (nos. 4-5). Two of these objects are Doric votive columns, comparable to those found at Ptoon, which probably supported bronze tripods (Guillon 1943, pl. 4). A bronze phiale bears a dedication to Athena Pronaia, who, according to Pausanias (9.10.2) shared the sanctuary with Apollo. These few fragmented objects are a far cry from the multitude of offerings that have been described by reliable ancient writers.

The sanctuary of Demeter and Dionysos, located south of the Kadmeia, was also functioning during the Archaic period (site 201). A small area of it excavated by Keramopoullos yielded a large amount of pottery (1917:263, fig. 180), a bronze phiale (ibid., fig. 179), and terracotta figurines: a seated female figure (ibid., fig. 183: 4), two standing youths (ibid., fig. 183: 1, 3), and two protomes of bearded figures (ibid., fig. 182: 3, 6). Most of these seem to date to the late sixth century B.C. (see Catalogue, site 201, and also below, *Thebes in the Classical Period,* for more information on this sanctuary).

The finds at site 158 (fig. 3.6) in northern Pyri suggest that there was habitation outside

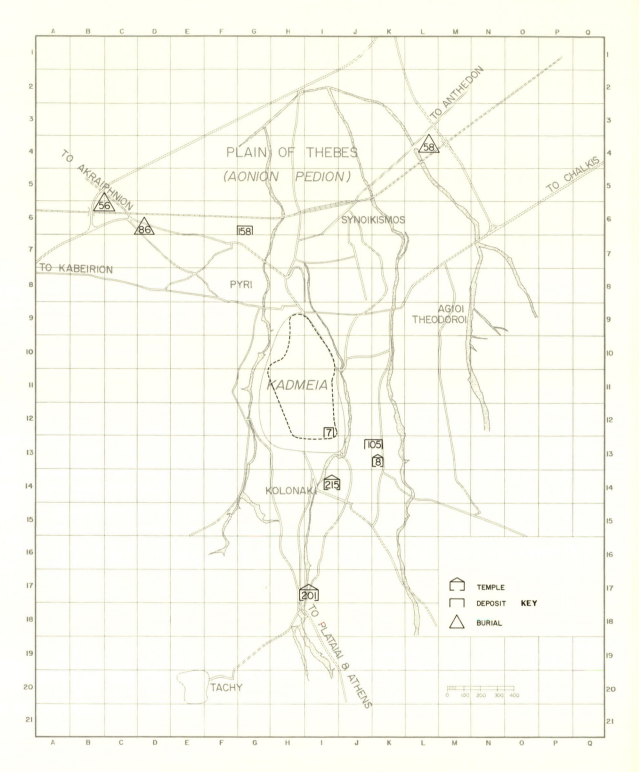

Fig. 3.5. Thebes in the Archaic period, ca. 600-500 B.C.

the Kadmeia: the remains of a house were discovered here, and although its main time of occupation was the Classical period, there was also a deposit of Archaic pottery. The disposition of the cemeteries also allows us to infer that the city extended beyond the Kadmeia. In addition, we know that Pindar (who was born in 518 B.C.) lived west of the Kadmeia. The fact that habitation remains are so meager suggests that the houses of these early periods were made entirely of mud-brick.

As I have shown earlier, the main burial sites of the Archaic period were the Northwest and Northeast cemeteries. An isolated child burial was found in Agioi Theodoroi (*Deltion* 1965:244). Despite the fact that the main cemeteries were located outside Greater Thebes, there is no evidence to support Keramopoullos' suggestion (1917:297) that a wall was constructed to protect the houses outside the Kadmeia. Those who lived in Greater Thebes during the Archaic period must have taken refuge on the Kadmeia in time of war.

The burial practices of the Archaic period vary somewhat from one cemetery to another. The few Archaic burials in the Northeast Cemetery (site 58) include inhumations (most of them in pithoi) and cremations. The offerings consist mainly of Boiotian and Korinthian pottery, and terracotta figurines. One funerary stele is known to have come from this cemetery (*Deltion* 1964:202, Mus. no. 13). At sites 87 and 57 of the Northwest Cemetery (fig. 1.2), there was a preference for pithos burials provided with great quantities of local and Korinthian pottery, and terracotta figurines. There were also pit burials with similar offerings. Only rarely have cremations been found. We observe different practices at the two sites that lie closer to Greater Thebes. There were mostly cremations found at site 56, with few pithos burials. Here too, there were great quantities of Boiotian and Korinthian pottery, but few figurines. The pottery found with the cremations was invariably broken, in contrast to the vases found intact with the inhumation burials. There were also some rich offerings of jewelry and bronzes, mainly daggers. At site 86, only inhumations have been found thus far, in pits, cists, and tile-covered graves. To judge by the offerings, these seem to have been the richest tombs of Archaic Thebes: the quality of Boiotian and Korinthian pottery was very fine, and there were many figurines and some imports, such as a Siana cup and a glass vase.

The burial practices of Archaic Thebes closely resemble those of Rhitsona (Burrows and Ure 1908, 1909; Ure 1910), except that deep shaft graves dating to the Archaic period have not yet been found in Thebes. The greater number of inhumations, if not coincidental, may indicate a Theban preference; in Athens, cremations were more prevalent in the Archaic period (Kurtz and Boardman 1971:71).

ANCIENT DOCUMENTS ABOUT THEBES
IN THE ARCHAIC PERIOD

The archaeological evidence of the Archaic period is clearly inadequate to document the life of a city that was as rich and powerful as Thebes was. That there were more than the two sanctuaries shown in the archaeological record of the Archaic period, and many other public buildings as well, is attested to by ancient texts.

According to Herodotos (8.134), there was in Thebes an oracle of Amphiaraos; those who wished to consult it spent a night sleeping at the sanctuary. Herodotos does not describe in detail the actual consultation, but *oneiromancy* (divination based on dreams) seems to have been practiced there. He includes this oracle among those consulted by Kroisos and tells us that the Thebans themselves were not allowed to consult the oracle: having been given the choice of having Amphiaraos either as an ally in war or as a diviner, the Thebans opted for the former. Herodotos also tells us (1.46, 49, 52) that Kroisos, satisfied with the response of the oracle, sent gifts of a shield and a spear of solid gold to the sanctuary. These, however, were stored at the sanctuary of Apollo Ismenios.

Some scholars have felt that in reporting that Kroisos' offerings were kept at the Ismenion, Herodotos reveals the unreliability of his information. Moreover, it seems to them unlikely that the Thebans could not consult their own oracle (for a discussion, see Ziehen 1934:1496-1497, who argues against the existence of a cult of Amphiaraos altogether). The oracle of Amphiaraos was in the open air, however (Pausanias 9.8.3), and consequently, no valuable offerings could be kept there; the temple of Apollo Ismenios was a short distance away from the probable location of this oracle, and it is plausible that the rich offerings of Kroisos were kept there. Attesting to the cult's existence are clear references to it by Pindar; in *Nemean* 10.9 he attributes to Amphiaraos the same two functions as Herodotos does, calling him "a prophet and a cloud of war"; in *Pythian* 8.38-60, he refers to a prophecy of Amphiaraos during the War of the Seven against Thebes and introduces Alkmaion (Alkman, in Pindar), the son of Amphiaraos, who shared his father's sanctuary. Alkmaion was also revered as a prophet in Thebes, and it was he whom Pindar consulted before going to Delphi (participating in divination through sleep, according to schol. *Pyth*. 8.55). Pindar even gives the relative location of the sanctuary by referring to Alkmaion as "my neighbor and protector of my wealth." Keramopoullos (1917:418-420) has explained that Pindar's house and property must have been in the vicinity of the sanctuary shared by Amphiaraos and Alkmaion. As I will show, the oracle was south of the Kadmeia, at or near the church of Agios Nikolaos (site 215).

Yet another sanctuary, dedicated to Herakles, must have existed in the sixth century; a stadion and a gymnasion were associated with it, forming a complex called the *Herakleion*. Many sources relate that a festival in honor of Herakles (the *Herakleia*) was held annually; Pindar confirms it: in *Nemean* 4 (composed ca. 473 B.C.), the Herakleion is described as being "near the tomb of Amphitryon," which must have been in the cemetery at the Kolonaki hill (site 24, fig. 3.6); in *Isthmian* 4 (composed ca. 474 B.C.), the *Herakleion* is described as being outside the Elektrai gates (i.e., southeast of the Kadmeia). The Herakleion must date at least to the sixth century B.C., since Pindar wrote about it in the early fifth century. It was probably in the open area between the sanctuary of Apollo Ismenios and that of Amphiaraos. This area is relatively small and, as I will show below, new athletic facilities were established in the valley north of the Kadmeia; these were to be named in honor of Iolaos, the nephew and companion of Herakles, and there was to be a festival named for him, the *Iolaeia*. There is some confusion in ancient sources (Ziehen 1934:1523) about the two festivals. It seems, however, that only the facilities were separate and that one festival was referred to by these two different names (Keramopoullos 1917:330). It is also likely that Iolaos was honored with Herakles during the festival/games at the old facility in the southern part of Thebes. According to Pindar (*Pyth.* 9.76-83), the tomb of Iolaos was also in the southern part of Thebes.

The presence of these public buildings demonstrates that the area south of the Kadmeia was quite actively used in the Archaic period: there were four sanctuaries, if we include the one dedicated to Apollo Ismenios and that of Demeter/Dionysos near Potniai; there was also a stadion and a gymnasion. This area, called *Knopia* in antiquity (Keramopoullos 1917:266), may also have been used for habitation, although remains of houses have not been identified. The Kolonaki hill, dotted with Mycenaean tombs, does not seem to have been used for burial by the Thebans in the Archaic period.

There were undoubtedly several sanctuaries on the Kadmeia during the Archaic period. Evidence of their existence can be found in Pausanias and other authors who refer to old cult images and statues of gods. Such statues, usually made of wood, were carved and dedicated to Greek sanctuaries in the seventh and sixth centuries B.C. At the sanctuary of Dionysos Kadmeios, there was a wooden image (*xoanon*) that was said to have fallen from the sky (Pausanias 9.12.4). There are also reported to have been three very old statues of Aphrodite (Pausanias 9.16.3) made of wood, which may have been Archaic, although the existence of a sanctuary dedicated to the goddess is not documented until later. The two stone statues of Athena Zosteria that Pausanias (9.17.3) saw in Greater Thebes and called "dedications of Amphitryon" were likewise probably very old. Keramopoullos (1917:375) suggested that they might have looked like a double Archaic Herm. An open-air sanctuary of Demeter Thesmophoros may have been on the ruins of the second Late Helladic palace; a temple was to be built later, but the existence of Demeter's cult is known from Pindar (*Isth.* 7.3) and must certainly predate him.

An agora probably existed on the Kadmeia during the Archaic period, perhaps near the sanctuary of Dionysos Kadmeios where Pausanias saw it (9.12.3). A second one was to be built in Greater Thebes in the fifth century.

Greater Thebes was probably sparsely inhabited, but there is no indication that public buildings existed there before the Classical period. Perhaps there were a few houses and some outdoor shrines. In addition to the statues of Athena Zosteria mentioned above, which may have been associated with a small shrine, there was perhaps a sanctuary of Themis in the vicinity of the Neistai gates (Pausanias 9.25.4); Pausanias mentions the sanctuaries of the Moirai and Zeus as though they were nearby. Pindar (frag. 30) also mentions these three deities together in an invocation. It is possible that cult sites in honor of Themis and perhaps the Moirai and Zeus were established in Greater Thebes during the Archaic period.

Another public structure that may have existed in Greater Thebes is the hippodrome. Knowing the importance of horses in Boiotia, it is likely that the hippodrome was established early, perhaps even before the Archaic period. Pausanias (9.23.2) saw it north of the Kadmeia and relates that Pindar was buried there. There are numerous references to horses in Pindar's poems: Thebes is called "mother of horses" (*Ol.* 6.85), or "chariot-loving city" (*Isth.* 8.20), Iolaos is called "master of horses" (*Isth.* 5.31), to give but a few examples. A hippodrome requires a lot of space, and this was available in the area north of the Kadmeia, perhaps east of site 158 (cf. chap. 5, passage 15).

Art and Sculpture

Numerous works of art and many artefacts were produced in Thebes in the Archaic period; unfortunately, not many have been found in controlled excavations. The general view of Archaic Boiotian sculpture is that it is provincial and not representative of a sophisticated artistic school (see Grace 1939:4-6 for a discussion of the problem). Karouzos (1934:7) has tried to balance this view, observing that in illuminating the dissimilarity between Boiotian work and that of other regions (Attica in particular), the negative and provincial aspects of Boiotian work have been overemphasized. This is not the place to reevaluate Boiotian art, but the activities of Thebes can be seen in a more reasonable perspective.

To the best of my knowledge, only two sculptural fragments dating to the Archaic period have been found in Thebes. There is the lower part of a female statue found near the church of Agios Georgios (site 93, fig. 3.7) now in the Thebes Museum (Museum no. 9; Körte 1878:308-309, no. 3; Karouzos 1934:14; *BCH* 1907:205, figs. 14-16), and the leg of a kouros found recently at Tachy (*Deltion* 1964:201, pl. 240:B). However, the sanctuary of Apollo Ptoios, which was under Theban control either from its inception (Pausanias 9.23.5; Guillon 1963:117-125) or for part of the sixth century (Ducat 1971:449-450), yielded an extraordinary number of kouroi; these have recently been the subject of an extensive study (Ducat 1971). Although many of the kouroi were fragmentary, approximately 120 individual works have been counted, compared to the 30 known kouroi from Attica (cf. Ridgway 1977:48). If sheer number is at all significant, it would seem that Boiotia specialized in this sort of sculpture.

Because they are so numerous, the kouroi of Ptoon raise some intriguing questions pertaining to Thebes in the Archaic period. Who commissioned the statues, and where were they carved? Why were so many of the dedications kouroi, rather than some other dedicatory object? Finally, in what way might Theban patronage of the sanctuary have influenced the type of dedication offered there? Before addressing these questions, I must point out that in spite of the fact that Langlotz, in his influential classification of early Greek sculpture (1927), did *not* distinguish a Boiotian workshop, Deonna (1909) had long since recognized one and had devoted a whole chapter of his book to it. More recently, Ducat (1971:209-210) has proposed that there was indeed a local school, though under continuous foreign influence.

Among the inscriptions at Ptoon are some that record the names of Theban artists, such as the sculptor Onasimos (Athens Nat. Mus. no. 11391; Ducat 1971:201-203, pl. 61), and Theban dedicators, such as Epichares (Ducat 1971:379-383, no. 232). A sculptor, Thebades, possibly a Theban, is known from an inscription on the Athenian Akropolis (Raubitschek 1949, no. 290). A Theban sculptor, Askaros, who may have worked at the end of the sixth and early fifth century, is credited by Pausanias (5.24.1) with having made a bronze statue of Zeus in Olympia (Overbeck 1868, no. 477; Grace 1939:6). Moreover, some of the earliest known inscriptions that record the names of sculptors have been found at Ptoon (Ducat 1971:379-385, nos. 232-235); the earliest of these dates to ca. 640-620 B.C. We cannot be sure that these were the names of local artists, but it is quite significant that they were working at Ptoon in the very period that saw the birth of monumental sculpture in Greece. This same period was the one in which the cult of Apollo was introduced at Ptoon, according to Ducat (1971:439-442).

The evidence suggests that kouroi were typical offerings to the sanctuary of Apollo Ptoos, and that at least some of them were made by Boiotian sculptors for Boiotian patrons. The various styles that characterize the kouroi of Ptoon indicate that sculptors from other parts of Greece worked here as well, perhaps for foreign patrons. The sculptors of Archaic Greece were probably itinerant, carrying their tools with them and applying the techniques of carving with which they were familiar. Ancient texts also characterize them thus; Pausanias (9.40.3) reports that Daidalos of Crete carved two statues in Boiotia, a Herakles in Thebes and the Apollo Trophonios in Levadeia. At Ptoon, the great number of statues of differing styles may be taken as an indication of foreign influence, but this view is countered by the evidence that there were indeed Boiotian sculptors, and that, in any case, sculptors were people who traveled and worked all over Greece. A more plausible view would be that Ptoon drew worshippers from many parts of the Greek world who brought dedications, or even their own artists, with them. In any place where large numbers of statues were dedicated, we should expect to see a variety of styles. What seems to be important is not that the styles varied, but that the dedication preferred at Ptoon was the kouros. This, I would suggest, was the typically Boiotian offering there. Furthermore, it is possible that the meaning attached to the kouros there may have differed from the meaning it carried in other parts of Greece. At Ptoon, the association of the kouros with the oracular god Apollo may have been particularly strong, at least when these statues were first introduced. Deonna (1909) may well have been right in suggesting that the kouroi were looked upon as statues of Apollo; this seems to be particularly meaningful in the context of Ptoon. The existing evidence suggests that the cult of Apollo was introduced there in the late seventh century B.C. (Ducat 1971:439-442), a time that coincides with the carving of the first kouroi.

According to Pausanias (9.23.5), Ptoon and its patron city, Akraiphnion, were "originally part of the territory of Thebes." Guillon (1943:117-125) believes that Thebes organized the cult of Apollo Ptoos and modeled the sanctuary on its own oracle of Apollo Ismenios. We cannot be certain that Thebes had complete control over Ptoon from the start; Ducat does not believe this could have happened until after 540 B.C. (1971:450). The relationship of Thebes to Ptoon, however, was but one aspect of a broad cultural bond that unified Boiotia during the seventh and sixth centuries B.C. Thebes, as the most influential of Boiotian cities, could be expected to play a very active role in the development of the new sanctuary of Apollo. In this context, we may explain the absence of kouroi in Thebes and their abundance at Ptoon: the older sanctuary of Apollo Ismenios continued to receive the traditional dedicatory tripods, while the new sanctuary of Apollo Ptoos became the primary recipient of the kouroi. Because Ptoon was part of a unified culture, there did not seem a need to initiate the new type of dedication in Thebes itself.

We also observe a scarcity of statues and reliefs among the funerary monuments of Thebes. Of the numerous stelai in the Museum, most are plain, bearing only the name of the deceased. A few are carved, however, such as the stele of a warrior from Pyri (Mus. no. 13; Heimberg 1973, pl. 2:A) and the two stelai now in Boston, one of a rider and one of a youth (Comstock and Vermeule 1976, nos. 16, 18; Schild-Xenidou 1972, nos. 2, 5, 8).

The head and wing of a terracotta sphinx, supposed to have come from a cemetery in Thebes, were purchased by the Louvre in 1895 (Mus. no. CA 637); they are now thought to have been architectural pieces from the temple of Apollo Ismenios (Mollard-Besques 1954:22, no. B 131, pl. 17), and they date to shortly after the middle of the sixth century B.C. The carving is very beautiful, and Payne evaluated this sphinx as the most important Korinthian work of the sixth century (1931:238-240, 260-261, pl. 49:3-4). Payne thought it had been imported because of its pale yellow clay, and because the refinement of style indicated that it had been made in a major artistic center that specialized in producing such objects. Van Buren (1926:63, 173, pl. 33), however, considered it a Theban work, and suggested that Thebes may even have been the artistic center for the production of such ornamental figures. The sphinx has recently been restudied and fully published by Billot (1977) who succeeded in joining the wing to the shoulder. Billot dates it ca. 530 to 520 B.C. and considers it an import, inspired by Athenian sculpture.

In questioning the origin of this sphinx, we must bear in mind that large terracotta objects are not easily transported; if one suspects an outside influence, one should consider the importing of the artist rather than the object. As sculptors did travel around Greece to work wherever they were commissioned to do so, it is entirely possible that a Korinthian or even an Athenian artist came to Thebes to make the sphinx and perhaps other terracottas as well. At the same time, we must acknowledge that inviting a sculptor of clay would have been far more unusual than inviting a sculptor of stone: every region of Greece had its own potters and terracotta experts, and Boiotia was, in fact, a province in which terracotta figurines were very popular in the Archaic period, as they continued to be later on. Boiotia is also known to have had several workshops for the manufacture of tiles (Felsch 1979). A great wealth of figurines has been found in the cemeteries of Thebes, and in Rhitsona (Ure 1934). Many different types have been found in Boiotia, and Thebes and Tanagra were the two most likely places for their manufacture. Many of the terracottas in the Louvre have reportedly come from Thebes, including an interesting collection of genre pieces and the familiar figurines with molded heads called *pappades* (Mollard-Besques 1954:11-23, pls. 8-17). To invite a foreign terracotta specialist to Thebes would seem altogether unnecessary. Moreover, the Theban sphinx is not unique: a large group of very similar sphinxes were found at nearby Halai (Goldman 1940:443-448, figs. 106-128), and there is no reason to believe that they were imported. Unless there is definite proof to the contrary, the Theban sphinx, like other terracottas, should be attributed to its place of origin. This does not exclude the possibility that the artist who made it may have been inspired by the art of another region.

POTTERY

There are large quantities of Theban pottery, both in the Museum and in other collections, much of it either decorated or modeled in unusual shapes. The Archaic pottery has not been analyzed, however, except in general studies of Boiotian pottery such as those of Ann and Percy Ure. Five Boiotian potters were identified by Hoppin (1924:17-24). In recent years, some special studies have been devoted to Boiotian pottery, the most extensive of which are by Sparkes (1967), Kilinski (1974, 1977, 1978A, 1978B), and Maffre (1975). One hopes the pottery that has been found in Thebes will also be studied before long.

BRONZES AND COINS

In the Archaic period, the Thebans must have been quite proficient in bronze casting. We learn from the elegy of Kritias (*Fragmente der Vorsokratiker* 88 F2), which mentions the sources of Athens' main imports, that in the fifth century B.C., Athens purchased war chariots from Thebes. By that time, Thebes had obviously acquired a reputation for the manufacture of such chariots. Because of the traditional Theban preoccupation with horses and chariots, it is certainly possible that this manufacture began as early as the sixth or even the seventh century B.C. Like most Greek cities, Thebes produced a variety of other bronze objects, such as the ones dedicated to the temple of Apollo Ismenios and the bronze periknemis dedicated in Olympia by the Thebans after their victory over the Hyettians (*Olympia Bericht* 1967:98-100, pl. 47).

There were four types of Boiotian coinage in the Archaic period, all of which bore the shield on one side (Ducat 1973:61). It has been suggested that the image of the shield originated in Thebes with the cult of Herakles (Head 1881:187). More recently, however, LaCroix (1958) has convincingly proposed that the shield was a more general symbol of Boiotia that evoked the grandeur of the great Mycenaean heroes and resulted from the continued manufacture of fine leather shields during the Dark Ages; he also proposed that the related etymology of Boiotia and *Bous* ("cattle"), from which the hide for the shields came, must have contributed to the adoption of the shield as a symbol. Even if the image of the shield did not originate in Thebes, the large quantities of coins found there indicate that the city was one of the principal members of the Boiotian League (Head 1881:193).

If we appraise the history of Thebes in the period before 500 B.C., we may say that the city, inspired by its glorious past and supported by its profitable agriculture emerged from the Dark Ages with enough vitality to assume a prominent position in Boiotia, and reached the height of its power with the formation of the Boiotian League. At the same time, it reached the limit of that power because its economy, so largely based on agriculture, allowed little possibility for further growth. Its rival, Athens, was in the meantime gaining strength by expanding its maritime trade and naval capability, which eventually led to the Athenian achievements of the fifth century and a dramatic change in the course of Greek history.

THEBES IN THE CLASSICAL PERIOD, ca. 500 to 335 B.C.

figs. 3.6, 3.7

In the sixty years following the Athenian victory over the Boiotian League in the war over Plataiai (506 B.C.), Thebes went through one of the worst periods of her history (Demand 1979). During this time, the rivalry and hatred between Thebes and Athens grew deeper, creating an almost permanent rupture in cooperative relations between them. During the Persian wars, Thebes, finding herself isolated, was forced to side with the Persians against the other Greek city-states. The unexpected victories of the Athenians over the Persians at Salamis (480 B.C.) and of the combined Greek forces at Plataiai (479 B.C.) brought Thebes the deepest humiliation. Only twenty years later, hostilities among the Greek city-states were renewed, and the Athenians again defeated Thebans and Boiotians in the battle of Tanagra (457 B.C.), after which the entire region remained under Athenian domination until 446 B.C. At that time, Athens suffered a defeat at Koroneia; the Boiotian Confederacy was then established, and Theban power and influence began to rise once again.

The prolonged Peloponnesian war (431-404 B.C.), in which Sparta and Thebes defeated

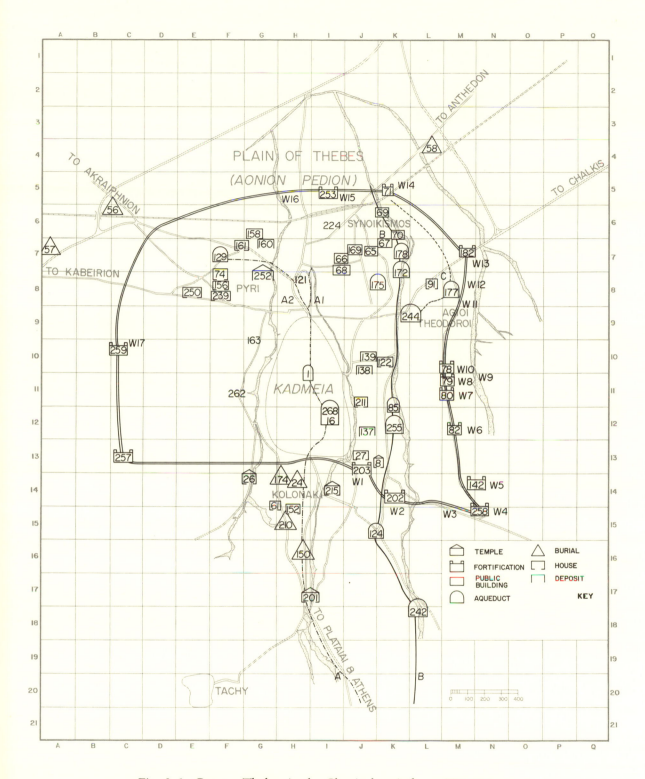

Fig. 3.6. Greater Thebes in the Classical period, ca. 500-335 B.C.

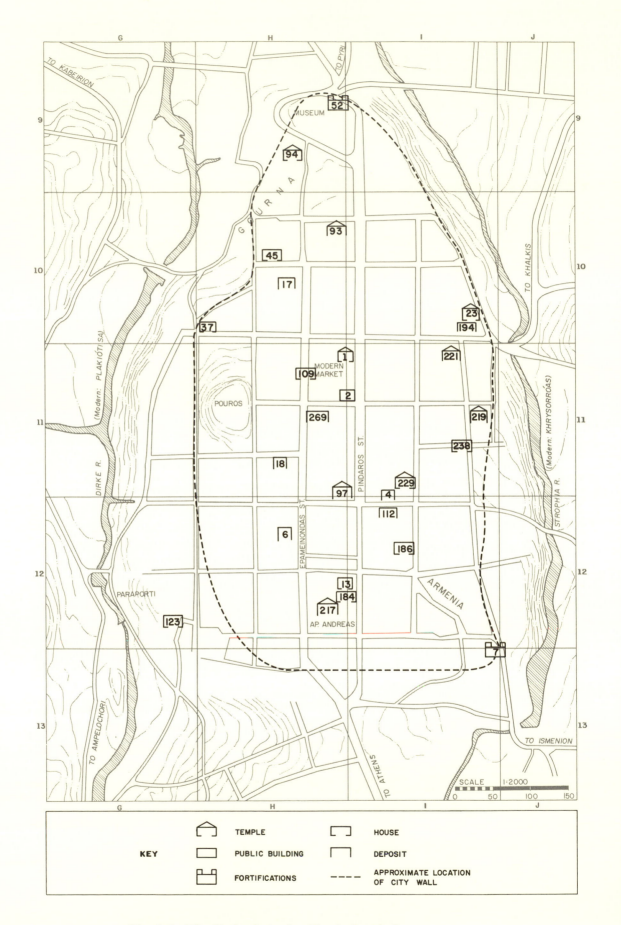

Fig. 3.7. The Kadmeia in the Classical period

the Athenians, did not spare Thebes its damaging effects. Nevertheless, the city was able to regain enough of her vitality to become a major power, and for a brief period to achieve the unification of the city-states of the Greek mainland in what is known as the Theban hegemony. Thebes consolidated her power between 386 and 371 B.C. (Hack 1976, 1978) and maintained the hegemony from 371 to 362 B.C. (Buckler 1980). The city continued to dominate Greek affairs until the battle of Chaironeia (338 B.C.), soon after which Thebes was destroyed by Alexander the Great (335 B.C).

The archaeological evidence of the Classical period in Thebes is adequate to document the city's activities. There are, however, no Classical buildings still standing, nor remains sufficient to show complete plans. In the late Roman and Early Christian periods, Classical buildings were being stripped of their well-made isodomic masonry, and this activity continued in later times as well. Only the deepest foundations remain, and even these are not well enough preserved to enable us to reconstruct a plan or to recognize the function of the buildings. Enough is preserved, however, to show that Thebes enjoyed a long period of prosperity; an unprecedented number of public buildings was erected within a short time.

I will attempt to identify or at least to suggest the locations of the buildings whose existence is known from literary sources. Pausanias' account of his visit to Thebes in the second century A.D. is of primary importance, and I will make repeated reference to my own detailed analysis of his text (chap. 5).

FORTIFICATIONS

Classical Thebes was protected by two rings of fortifications: the first, inner ring protected the old city, the Kadmeia, while the second encircled the area of Greater Thebes. The two rings were convincingly differentiated by Keramopoullos (1917:253-257, 266-298) on the basis of ancient references in conjunction with archaeological remains. Our clearest literary source is Arrian (*Anabasis* 1.7.4-1.10.2), who describes the siege and destruction of the city by Alexander. Alexander initially encamped north of the temenos of Iolaos outside the wall of Greater Thebes, while the Macedonian guard was trapped on the Kadmeia by the Thebans who occupied Greater Thebes. Alexander realized that the weakest point in the fortifications was on the south side where the two rings either merged or lay very close to each other; to compensate for this weakness, the Thebans had dug two deep trenches parallel to the wall. The Theban soldiers positioned themselves behind the exterior trench and were able to force the attackers, led by Perdikkas, to retreat. But the Macedonians, led by Alexander, returned once more and managed to push the The-bans behind the gates—in other words, behind the gates of Greater Thebes, since the Macedonian guard was behind the gates of the Kadmeia. The Thebans were forced to retreat towards the Amphion hill (site 121, see Map A) where they fought once more, surrounded by the enemy. The crucial battle, then, took place between the Elektrai gates (on the Kadmeia) and the unnamed gates of Greater Thebes.

Xenophon (*Hell.* 5.2.25-29) provides us with yet another description of the two rings of fortifications when he describes the capture of Thebes by the Spartans in 382 B.C. (Keramopoullos 1917:285-287; Bury 1951:559). The second wall, therefore, had been built by 382 B.C., but the date of its construction is not clear.

THE WALL OF THE KADMEIA

The Classical wall of the Kadmeia followed basically the same line as the Late Helladic fortifications, except that it encompassed Hypothebai, in addition. Hypothebai, as I have proposed above, probably became part of the city when the Kadmeia was resettled during the Geometric period. Some of the remains indicative of the presence of a wall, which were the basis for my reconstruction of the Late Helladic Cyclopean wall as well as the wall of Hypothebai, actually date to the Classical period (fig. 2.5, W 4 - W 9, W 14, W 15). The wall protecting the Kadmeia must have been rebuilt and repaired several times from the Geometric period on, and was substantially changed by Kassandros in 316 B.C. Some of it (like the portion seen by Leake) may well have been the original Late Helladic Cyclopean construction, or the Cyclopean wall of Hypothebai; parts of it were polygonal (W 5, W 8?), and other parts isodomic (W 7, W 9, W 14, W 15).

This wall enclosed an area of approximately 25 hectares, enough to accommodate a population of about 7,500 to 10,000 (see table 2.6). By the Archaic period, more space was needed and the city began to expand around the Kadmeia. No tombs later than 600 B.C. are found here, and a decision must have been made to establish cemeteries beyond the area of Greater Thebes. There is, however, no evidence for the construction of a protective wall, and the Kadmeia remained the only fortified area. Everyone must have sought protection there in times of trouble. By ancient standards this was not a small city; there are very few Archaic Greek cities with a population of ca. 10,000 that were protected by a wall. In Athens, for comparison, the residential area (excluding the rocky outcrops and the agorai) is estimated at about 20 hectares (Travlos 1960:41).

THE WALL OF GREATER THEBES

With the continued growth of the city, the need developed for a second ring of fortifications. This must have been considered a tremendous undertaking not only because of the lack of stone, but because of the difficult terrain: the area around the Kadmeia is either too flat and therefore vulnerable to attack, or too irregular and therefore problematic for building. When the wall was finally completed it proved to be a veritable wonder: the area protected was twelve times the size of the Kadmeia. The wall was 7,000 m long, encompassing an area of 328 hectares, enough to accommodate 100,000 people.

One wonders what the original expectations of the builders were, because it is doubtful that the population of Thebes ever reached more than a quarter of this number.

Evidence of the existence of this wall (most of it not visible today) can be summarized with reference to the following eighteen sites, beginning near the Elektrai gates and moving counterclockwise (fig. 3.6):

w 1. a tower or gate partially excavated by Keramopoullos (Catalogue, site 203)

w 2. a portion of the wall found by Keramopoullos (Catalogue, site 202)

w 3. two parts of the wall excavated by Kalopais (1892:42; Keramopoullos 1917, map)

w 4. the southeast corner of the wall of Greater Thebes (Catalogue, site 258) with gates, towers, and other military installations (Kalopais 1892:42, 44; 1893:19-21)

w 5. a portion of the wall still visible today (Catalogue, site 142)

w 6. perhaps a semicircular tower, still visible (Catalogue, site 82)

w 7 - w 10. remains of the wall (Catalogue, sites 77-80; site 77, Map A)

w 11 - w 12. parts of the wall mapped by Keramopoullos (1917)

w 13. a part of the wall (Catalogue, site 182)

w 14. a tower/cistern and portion of the wall (Catalogue, site 71)

w 15. a 15-meter stretch of the wall, no longer visible (Catalogue, site 253)

w 16. a small portion of the wall mentioned by Kalopais (1893:19)

w 17. a part found by Kalopais (Catalogue, site 259)

w 18. the southwest corner of the wall of Greater Thebes, found by Kalopais (Catalogue, site 257)

Although long stretches of the wall are gone, these remains suffice to trace its outline: near the Elektrai gates, the wall went southeast to enclose the temple of Apollo Ismenios; I disagree here with Keramopoullos who believed that the wall he discovered south of the Ismenion (site 202) was a later addition. I believe that the wall was purposely made to encircle a large area in order to encompass the sanctuary of Apollo, which must have been surrounded with many valuable offerings as well as auxiliary buildings. I would place the wall about 50 m south of the road that today leads to the Ismenion: it crossed the river at site 99 (Map A) and continued on top of a low ridge; at site 258 it turned sharply and continued north in a fairly straight line to the suburb of Agioi Theodoroi; from here it turned west in a wide semicircle, and then south and followed the high ridges west of the Kadmeia; at w 17 it turned sharply east towards the Kadmeia, perhaps passing close to the older wall but not necessarily touching it, as there was a separate gate in at least one spot, as the text of Arrian clearly indicates. It may seem surprising that the area south of the Kadmeia, where during the Archaic period there were many sanctuaries and public buildings, was not encircled by the fortifications. As the city developed, however, the northern area became more important than the southern because many houses had been built there; many public buildings and sanctuaries were also interspersed throughout. The city expanded toward the valley where there was plenty of space to erect large structures, and where the flat terrain facilitated construction.

The lower part of the wall was constructed of isodomic masonry, and the upper part, of mud-brick. There were tiles covering the top to protect the mud-brick. The isodomic masonry was made of local stone, either a soft poros or a conglomerate, which is brittle and tends to disintegrate when weathered; the portions excavated by Kalopais (1892, 1893) have collapsed into shapeless heaps by now. The wall was 2.50 to 3.20 m thick and of unknown height. The lower part consisted of two parallel rows of isodomic masonry filled in with stone debris.

The date of construction is not clear; Keramopoullos (1917:296-298) suggested that it had been built by 506 B.C. during the war with Athens. Soteriades (1914:19, 29) thought that the wall west of the river Dirke was built in 458/457, while Keramopoullos believed that only an extension was built at that time (cf. Catalogue, site 202). The archaeological evidence for dating is confined to the method of construction, which is characterized by regularity (in the size of the stone blocks) and precision of execution, indicative of Classical rather than Archaic work. Also, a project of such magnitude would not have been possible in the sixth century B.C. In the second half of the fifth century B.C., however, Thebes experienced remarkable growth. An important document offers some information about whether the construction of the wall was in some way related to that growth.

In discussing the federal constitution of Boiotia, the *Hellenika Oxyrhynchia* makes reference to circumstances that caused the redistribution of representation to the federal council (for a most up-to-date edition, see Bartoletti 1959). In 11.3, we read that Boiotia was divided into eleven districts, each contributing one representative: "Θηβαῖοι μὲν τέτταρας συνεβάλλοντο, δύο μὲν ὑπὲρ τῆς πόλεως, δύο δὲ ὑπὲρ Πλαταιέων καὶ Σκώλου καὶ Ἐρυθρῶν καὶ Σκαφῶν καὶ τῶν ἄλλων χωρίων τῶν πρότερον ἐκείνοις συμπολιτευομένων, τότε δὲ συντελούντων εἰς τὰς Θήβας." ("The Thebans contributed four, two for their own city and two for Plataiai, Skolos, Erythrai, Skaphai and other communities which had previously been allied with Thebes but were her subjects at that time.") The reasons for these circumstances are explained in 12.3: "When Athens began to fight Boiotia, the inhabitants of Erythrai, Skaphe, Skolos, Aulis, Schoinos, Potniai, and many other such communities moved to Thebes (συνῳκίσθησαν) because their towns did not have fortifications; this caused the size of Thebes to double."

The first editors of the text (Grenfell and Hunt 1908:226) believed that the two passages referred to circumstances related to the start of the Peloponnesian War (431 B.C.). Bruce (1967:106, 114) agrees that the migration into Thebes occurred at the beginning of this war, but prefers a date after 427 B.C., when Plataiai became subject to Thebes. It is possible that the movement of people from unfortified towns into Thebes recorded in the second passage (12.3) did occur at some point during the Peloponnesian War. The small communities listed in the first passage (11.3), however, are said to have been subject to Thebes at the time of the war between Boiotia and Phokis (396 B.C., the outbreak of the Korinthian war), although at some previous time (πρότερον) they had simply been allied with Thebes.

Grenfell and Hunt (1908:226) and Bruce (1967:106, 114) interpreted the passage to mean that the small communities were subject to Plataiai before 431 and to Thebes by 396 B.C., because they took the word ἐκείνοις to refer to Plataiai. Wickersham and Verbrugghe (1973:11) take the same word to refer to Thebes, and this seems far more reasonable in view of the fact that the three towns specified in this passage are closer to Thebes than to Plataiai. In addition, it is doubtful that they would have formed ties with Plataiai rather than Thebes at a time when Theban power was growing. Skolos and Skaphe (or Eteonos) were just north of the Asopos River on the Theban side, while Erythrai (modern Daphne or Darimari) was south of the river but still closer to Thebes than to Plataiai (Pritchett 1965:107-109; Buck 1979:15-18). The *Hellenika Oxyrhynchia* clearly refers to ties between Thebes and its immediate neighbors, the most prominent six of which are named. The inclusion of Aulis (about 24 km from Thebes) and Schoinos (perhaps modern Mouriki, 12 km from Thebes) shows that the influence of the city extended to considerable distances in the late fifth century. Erythrai is 12 km away also, while Skolos and Skaphe/Eteonos are about 6 km and 8 km respectively. Many other communities around the Aonian plain were forced to join Thebes in the creation of a large *polis* because of external threat (Fimmen 1912:541). The inclusion of Plataiai in this group in 427 B.C. may have caused the increase in the number of Boiotarchs but the bond between Thebes and the other small communities must have existed before that date.

The reason for this bond was the presence of fortifications in Greater Thebes, of which the author of the *Hellenika Oxyrhynchia* shows he was clearly aware by relating that the smaller places were not fortified, implying that Thebes had already built its large wall. The question that remains is when and under what circumstances was it built? *Hellenika Oxyrhynchia* provides a clue in pointing to the time when Athens *began* to fight Boiotia. It is unlikely that it was built at the time of the Peloponnesian War not only because the human and financial resources could not have been allocated for it at such a time, but also because had it been built then, Thucydides would surely have mentioned it. He does not. The author of *Hellenika Oxyrhynchia* clearly had in mind the hostilities of 458-446 B.C. In 458/457, the Boiotians were defeated at Tanagra, and their land remained under Athenian domination for the next ten years. This was plainly the most serious threat to Boiotia. Ephoros (by Diodoros 11.81) dates the construction of the wall to the time of the battle of Tanagra, and although this is not impossible (Wilamowitz 1922:36), it is difficult to imagine the Athenians allowing Thebes to grow and fortify while under their domination. It is much more likely that the wall was built after the victory of Thebes over Athens at Koroneia (446 B.C.), when Thebes emerged as the greatest power in Boiotia. It was then that the Confederacy was organized, and there is general agreement today that this occurred in 446 B.C. (cf. Buck 1979:154). The author of *Hellenika Oxyrhynchia* took for granted that the word πϱότεϱον would be understood as a clear reference to this time. In the hope of preventing future Athenian domination, the smaller towns near Thebes must have contributed manpower and funds for the construction of the Great Wall of Thebes with the understanding that it would be used to protect all of them if the need arose, as it must have in 431 B.C.

The protection afforded by the wall must have attracted inhabitants from all the small towns, causing the population of Thebes to double; there is no reason to doubt this (Bruce 1967:114) because the wall was specifically designed to accommodate 100,000 people. Thebes (cf. fig. 3.10) had a population of 7,500 to 10,000 before 446 B.C., and it may easily have doubled over the next twenty years.

It is clear that the wall of the Kadmeia was large enough to protect the population of Thebes at this time. The city had no need to construct another wall seven kilometers long, nor did it have the means to do so. Such a wall could only have been built with the cooperation of the neighboring towns. This partnership was not forced on the smaller towns by Thebes; it was rather the result of a need for protection and a need to consolidate efforts. Another manifestation of these needs was the federal organization of Boiotia, whereby the villages formed a city-state with the larger town or city in their area, at the same time keeping their individual rights, as Bruce observes (1967:166). In Attica, too, the small communities were unprotected, and a great fortification system was erected in Athens. Athens was completing a long wall of its own, which must have been a persuasive factor in the Theban decision to build one.

The text of *Hellenika Oxyrhynchia* provides us with the reasons for the city's sudden growth after 446 B.C. Although it does not directly discuss the wall, the reader cannot help but infer that it existed. The effect of the wall on the fortunes of Thebes cannot be overstated: without it the city could not possibly have expanded so dramatically, and Theban influence would not have extended over Boiotia and Greece to the degree that it did. It is no exaggeration to say that the wall provided the initial impetus that brought the city to its zenith from 371 to 362 B.C. when Thebes ruled the fortunes of the Greek mainland. This unique period in Greek history, which "marks the last significant effort of a Classical Greek state to win ascendancy in Greece" (Buckler 1980:1), can be seen to have started with the construction of the wall in 446 B.C or shortly after. The life of the wall was as short as the ephemeral Theban hegemony: after its destruction in 335 B.C. it was never rebuilt; the city shrank to its former size and withdrew behind its traditional fortifications on the Kadmeia.

SANCTUARIES

Most of the sanctuaries described by Pausanias in the second century A.D. were in existence in the Classical period; there are only two that he does not mention, but which we know

Table 3.1. The sanctuaries of Classical Thebes

	Sanctuaries with Temples	*Open-air Sanctuaries*
Kadmeia	Demeter Thesmophoros	Poseidon (?)
	Zeus Hypsistos (?)	Dionysos Kadmeios
	Ammon-Zeus	Zeus Homoloios
	Tyche	Birth Place of Herakles
	Aphrodite	Apollo Spodios
		Athena Onka
		Oionoskopeion of Teiresias
Greater Thebes	Apollo Ismenios	Amphiaraos/Alkmaion
	Herakles	Iolaos
	Dionysos Aigobolos	Moirai
	Dindymene	
	Dionysos Lysios	
	Artemis Eukleia (?)	
	Zeus Agoraios	
	Themis	

Note: This table shows predominance of open-air sanctuaries on the Kadmeia and of sanctuaries with temples in Greater Thebes.

about from other sources (see table 5.1). Pausanias remains our best ancient source, and thanks to him, we can in many cases verify the initiation of a new cult or the construction of a new temple. Most of this activity took place in the Classical period. Keramopoullos (1917) has written about the sanctuaries, and there are excellent summaries about them by Schober (1934:1434-1452) and on the cults and festivals of Thebes by Ziehen (1934). We can be fairly certain that there were twenty-three sanctuaries in existence in Thebes in the Classical period; twelve of these were located on the Kadmeia, and eleven in Greater Thebes. I have attempted to draw a distinction between the open-air sanctuaries and those within which temples were built; the disposition of these is seen in table 3.1.

While there were a greater number of sanctuaries on the Kadmeia, those with temples were more numerous in Greater Thebes; conversely, there were more open-air sanctuaries on the Kadmeia than in Greater Thebes. As I have explained in chapter 2, most of the open-air sanctuaries were established on ruins or religious sites of the prehistoric period; for a variety of reasons, shortage of space above all, temples were never built at these sanctuaries; instead, a second sanctuary with a temple was established in the uncrowded areas of Greater Thebes (cf. table 2.5).

SANCTUARIES OF THE KADMEIA

Demeter Thesmophoros. Pausanias (9.16.5) tells of the existence of a temple in which there was an unusual cult statue of the goddess visible only down to the chest; the shields from the battle at Leuktra (371 B.C.) were kept here. The sanctuary was located at the site of "the house of Kadmos and his descendants" which, according to my interpretation, had been the site of the second Late Helladic palace. It must have been established on the ruins of this palace soon after it had been destroyed; this sanctification of the site would have contributed to the preservation of the memory of the palace. We learn from other sources that Persephone and Ge were also worshipped at the sanctuary (Pindar, frag. 37; Euripides, *Phoin.* 685; *IG* 7.2452). Demeter shared another sanctuary with Persephone and Dionysos south of the Kadmeia, near Potniai, and a sacred grove was dedicated to her near Kabeirion. Demeter's main sanctuary, however, must have been the one on the Kadmeia.

Pindar (*Isth.* 7.3-4) refers to Dionysos as a neighbor of Demeter (πάρεδρος), perhaps an indication both of the proximity of the two sanctuaries and the affinity of the two deities. In the same passage, Pindar also uses the epithet χαλκοκρότος ("clasher of bronzes"), denoting the warlike aspect of the goddess. We cannot tell whether Pindar had a temple in mind, or simply the sanctuary. There is not in Pindar, nor in any other source, an indication of when the temple was built. Two considerations lead me to suggest a date in the second half of the fifth century. Despite Demeter's great importance to the Thebans, there was little opportunity to construct a temple in the first half of the fifth century, but after 446 B.C., there was a great burst of building activity and a temple of Demeter should have been a likely priority. The second consideration is based on the rivalry between Thebes and Athens: the construction of the Parthenon must have generated in Thebes the desire to build a monument to their main goddess, whom Wilamowitz called the genuine "Lady" of the city (1891:216). It is still possible, however, that it was built at an earlier time. It is surprising that more detailed information has not survived regarding this very important temple. Pausanias does not describe sculptural decoration or dedications of any kind, although he is careful to mention them in his account of other sanctuaries.

It has not been possible to identify remains of the sanctuary itself. The Classical building of site 2 was probably not a temple (see Catalogue), but was more likely a portico: its foundations resemble in plan the porticos of the Athenian Agora (Thompson 1937, pls. 1 and 2, Stoa of Zeus; 1968, pl. 16, Middle Stoa and South Stoa II). The sanctuary was probably south of site 2, perhaps at or near the church of Agios Ioannis (site 97). Two considerations support this suggestion: first, Pausanias discusses the sanctuary after having visited the other sites, which seem to have been arranged in a circular pattern, starting from the sanctuary of Dionysos Kadmeios and ending at the sanctuary of Demeter (see chap. 5, passages 7-9, and fig. 5.2); secondly, the sanctuary had occupied a large area left by the destruction of the second Late Helladic palace (fig. 2.11) and there was sufficient space to construct a temple here in the Classical period. I suggest that the temple preceded the Byzantine Cathedral (fig. 4.1), which itself may have been built at this location because there was space enough to do so. The *Thesmophoria* festival was celebrated in Demeter's

124

honor from the temple each summer (Xenophon, *Hell.* 5.2.29; Plutarch, *Pelop.* 5; Keramopoullos 1917:353-356; Ziehen 1934:1506-1508).

Zeus Hypsistos ("highest"). The sanctuary must have been located at the southern end of the Kadmeia, as indicated by Pausanias (9.8.5) who refers to it in conjunction with the Hypsistai gates, and by Pindar (*Nem.* 1.60) who places it near the house of Amphitryon. Euripides mentions an altar of Zeus Soter (*Herakles* 520-522) near the house of Amphitryon, and it is possible that he is referring to this sanctuary. If he is, it is possible that an altar was the main focus of the cult here; none of the ancient sources mentions a temple, but the presence of a small structure cannot be excluded because of the importance of Zeus Hypsistos and the prominent position of the site. Its location in the heart of the Bronze Age town lends credence to the notion that this was the oldest sanctuary of Zeus in Thebes. It was probably situated at the highest point of the Kadmeia where the church of Agios Andreas now stands, possibly supplanting the pagan sanctuary (site 217).

Ammon. The god was worshipped in Thebes as Ammon or Zeus/Ammon and had his own sanctuary and temple on the Kadmeia. Pausanias (9.16.1) saw the temple immediately after his visit to the sanctuary of Dionysos Kadmeios; he reports having seen the cult statue, a work of Kalamis, dedicated by Pindar after his stay at Kyrene, which he visited after King Arkesilas' victory in the chariot race at Delphi in 462 B.C. In honor of that victory, Pindar composed an ode (*Pyth.* 4) that begins with an invocation of Apollo Pythios whose priestess, "seated by the gold eagles of Zeus," predicted the founding of Kyrene in Libya by the men of Thera, who, upon their arrival there, were received at the temple of Zeus Ammon. The shift from Apollo of Delphi to Zeus and Zeus/Ammon is, I believe, purposeful: Pindar calls attention to the antiquity of the cult of Zeus/Ammon of Kyrene, which had already been established when the colonizers arrived; although he does not say so here, we may infer that Thebes had recently introduced the old cult of Zeus/Ammon from Kyrene. In honor of this Ammon, Pindar composed a cult song (frag. 17) which, according to Pausanias, he sent to Kyrene. The circumstances surrounding the initiation of the cult of Zeus/Ammon must have been known to Pindar's audience, perhaps even that the poet himself had dedicated a cult statue by a famous sculptor. The importance of all this is, I believe, quite plain: Thebes, having been overshadowed by Delphi as a center for divination in the sixth century B.C., was trying to regain some of her prestige by introducing an old and revered oracular cult. Pindar's ode is actually the earliest document recording the introducion of Ammon into Greece; the temple had already been built by the time Pindar dedicated the statue, and it continued to be important after the destruction of Thebes in 335 B.C. Ptolemy I dedicated an altar before it ca. 310 to 308 B.C. (Schober 1934:1485). In addition to the altar, Pausanias saw a triangular stele with Pindar's ode to Ammon inscribed on it. We do not know what Kalamis' statue looked like, but representations of the god on coins of Kyrene may give us some idea: the god had ram horns and a rather short beard (Franke and Hirmer 1964, fig. 383).

Regarding the location of the sanctuary, our only guide is the order in which Pausanias mentions the sanctuaries of the Kadmeia after visiting the sanctuary of Dionysos Kadmeios (see chap. 5, passage 8). If we are correct in placing the Oionoskopeion of Teiresias at site 23 (see below), I suspect that the sanctuary of Ammon was 120 m north of the sanctuary of Dionysos Kadmeios, at the site of the church of Agios Georgios (site 93). Ancient stones and remains of an old monastery have been found here.

Tyche. Pausanias (9.16.1-2) saw the sanctuary of Tyche and a cult statue that he described in detail: the goddess held the child Ploutos; the face and hands were made by Xenophon of Athens, the rest of the statue by Kallistonikos of Thebes. Pausanias does not tell us what the statue was made of, but he does compare it to the Eirene holding Ploutos by Kephisodotos, which may indicate that the Tyche was an early fourth-century work, although it may be earlier. This is probably the statue that was represented on Theban coins of the Roman period (Imhoof-Blumer and Gardner 1887:112). Keramopoullos (1917:349-350) suggested that this is the statue that Pindar refers to (*Isth.* 1.1; frag. 195) as Thebe. Wilamowitz (1922:306), however, doubted that a cult of Tyche could have existed as early as Pindar's time, and preferred a fourth-century date. Yet, the name *Tyche* could have been used alternatively for the name of a city in Pindar's time: the poet does use it once for the city of Himera (*Ol.* 12.2), and he wrote a hymn to Tyche (frags. 38-41) in which she is treated as a goddess. Although a fifth-century cult of Tyche cannot be ruled out, our knowledge that the sculptor Xenophon worked with Kephisodotos the Elder, who made the similar statue of Eirene holding Ploutos (Pausanias 8.30.10; Pollitt 1965:127-128), is an indication that the statue was probably made in the early fourth century. The presence of the statue leads us to infer that there was a structure to house it, a shrine or a temple. I suggest the vicinity of the church of Agios Stephanos as a likely location for the sanctuary (site 219; see chap. 5, passage 8).

Poseidon. Although Poseidon's cult is documented by Hesiod (*Aspis* 104-105), Aischylos (*Hepta* 130; cf. schol.), and *IG* 7.2465 (with the epithet *Empylaios*), Pausanias does not record a sanctuary. Perhaps there was one, but it may have been beyond Pausanias' route (see chap. 5, passage 8). Pindar (*Isth.* 1.52-54), in an interesting reference to Poseidon, calls him "a neighbor and benefactor," and uses the word *hippodromios*, which was, according to the scholiast, the god's epithet. Pindar's house was near both the hippodrome and the sanctuary of Poseidon (Keramopoullos 1917:357-358). The epithet *Empylaios* implies that the sanctuary was near a gate and I believe Keramopoullos was correct in placing it near the Borraiai gates (or a locality that retained the gate name; see chap. 2, p. 62, on Hypothebai), which overlook the hippodrome to the north and Pindar's house to the west.

These considerations notwithstanding, Poseidon, the protector of horses and the god of earthquakes (to which Thebes has always been vulnerable), must have had a cult in Thebes. That Pausanias does not mention his sanctuary may be explained by its isolated location, which I would place (with Keramopoullos) at the northern tip of the Kadmeia, in the vicinity of the church of Agia Eleousa (site 94). Perhaps it is not a coincidence that a mosaic showing the ocean with fish was seen in this vicinity (Keramopoullos 1917:120); we cannot take this as clear evidence that a temple was built at this sanctuary, but it is possible, because Poseidon was a god of great importance in Thebes.

Aphrodite. According to Plutarch (*Quaest. Rom.* 112), there was a sanctuary dedicated to Aphrodite in Thebes. Xenophon (*Hell.* 5.4.4-7) discusses in some detail the *Aphrodisia*, a festival honoring Aphrodite. We do know that in 304-302 B.C., the Thebans dedicated a temple to Aphrodite Lamia, in honor of the harlot-mistress of Demetrios Poliorketes, son of Antigonos (Athenaios, *Deipn.* 6.62. 253a-b). Pausanias (9.16.3-4) tells us that he saw three wooden statues of Aphrodite, each depicting a different aspect of the goddess (Ourania, Pandemos, and Apostrophia), that were said to have been carved from the prows of Kadmos' ships and dedicated by Harmonia. Pausanias does not describe a temple, but it is unlikely that the wooden statues were left outdoors unprotected. I believe that these statues were housed in the temple of Aphrodite; perhaps Pausanias says nothing about the temple because his ancient readers would have assumed that the statues of the goddess could only be within the temple dedicated to her. It is possible that Ares, who seems to have been closely associated with Aphrodite in Thebes (Hesiod, *Theogony* 933-937; Pausanias 9.5.2), shared the sanctuary. I believe that the large structure found in the east central part of Thebes (sites 229, 4) may very well have been the temple of Aphrodite.

Dionysos Kadmeios. Of all the open-air sanctuaries on the Kadmeia, the most important was the one dedicated to Dionysos Kadmeios. Pausanias' detailed description of it (9.12.3-6) may leave room for doubt about some of the particulars (the chambers of both Harmonia and Semele; the place where the Muses sang at the wedding of Kadmos and Harmonia), but it does record the presence of actual ritual objects: a log fetish decorated with bronze (the image of Dionysos Kadmeios), a bronze statue of Dionysos by Ona-simedes, and an altar made by the sons of Praxiteles. There were also statues of two famous Theban citizens: the flutist Pronomos, and the statesman Epaminondas. None of these objects has been preserved, but the image of Dionysos Kadmeios is represented on vases as a pillar with either a human mask (like a herm) or a double head of Dionysos on it (Frickenhaus 1912). The representations seen on vases show the image covered with ivy. The pillar-like appearance of the image and the depiction of two Dionysos heads, one on either side (cf. Keramopoullos 1917:342), seem to justify the god's epithet, *peri-kionios* ("around the column").

A third-century B.C. inscription from the Treasury of Thebes at Delphi provides our best information regarding the festival and games held in honor of Dionysos Kadmeios (Bourguet 1929:195-201, no. 351; for recent revisions, see Bousquet 1961, Gossage 1975, Robert 1977); a duplicate was supposed to have been in the chamber of Semele in Thebes. According to the inscription, the sanctuary of Dionysos Kadmeios was the center for artisans who worked at Isthmos and Nemea and who supervised the triennial festival and games honoring Dionysos in Thebes. The festival, one of the most important celebrated in Thebes, was called the *Agrionia* (Ziehen 1934:1543-1545); there were competitions in flute playing, dance, tragedy, and comedy.

In chapter 2, I presented sufficient evidence to show that the sanctuary of Dionysos Kadmeios was established on the ruins of the first Late Helladic palace (site 1). This location is confirmed by its position relative to the other sanctuaries described by Pausanias (chap. 5, passages 7-9, fig. 5.2), as well as by its proximity to the sanctuary of Demeter Thesmophoros.

Zeus Homoloios. The only sanctuary beside Poseidon's that Pausanias does not mention is the sanctuary of Zeus Homoloios. We have, however, a small column with a dedicatory inscription to this god (*IG* 7.2456), and the cult is also mentioned by the lexicographers. In Thebes, a month and a gate were named after the epithet *Homoloios,* and perhaps even a festival (Ziehen 1934:1550). An Athena Homolois is mentioned by the scholiast to Lykophron's *Alexandra* 520, and a Demeter Homoloia by Photios. It is highly likely that an open-air sanctuary dedicated to these three deities existed; Zeus would have been the main or the original god worshipped there (Ziehen 1934:1516). The sanctuary was probably located by the Homoloides gates (fig. 2.7), perhaps in the vicinity of the small chapel of Agios Georgios (site 221), which happens to be off the path of Pausanias as I have reconstructed it (fig. 5.2). Keramopoullos found Early Christian remains and a few Classical terracotta figurines here.

Birthplace of Herakles. Of all the marvelous events associated with the life of Herakles, it would probably be safe to say, on the basis of ancient literature, that the event of his birth was the most miraculous. For this reason, the various monuments that Pausanias visited inside the Elektrai gates (9.11.1-3), all of which are associated with Herakles' birth, ought to be regarded as a unit; these include the ruins of the house of Amphitryon with the chamber of Alkmene, the relief showing the Pharmakides (witches sent by Hera to prevent Alkmene from giving birth to Herakles), and the Sophronister (a stone thrown at Herakles by Athena to make him sleep and to keep him from killing his father).

According to Pausanias, the relief showing the Pharmakides had weathered by his time; perhaps it was a work of the Archaic or Early Classical period. In the chamber of Alkmene, Pausanias saw and recorded an inscription in hexameters that identified the architects of the house as Trophonios and Agamedes. These were the same architects who elsewhere are credited with the construction of the temple of Apollo at Delphi, destroyed by fire in 548 B.C. (Dinsmoor 1950:71-86). The inscription should be no more suspect than the ones seen by both Pausanias and Herodotos at the temple of Apollo Ismenios (see above, p. 101) and may be viewed as an attempt to affirm the great antiquity of the ruin.

Pindar frequently wrote of the marvels associated with the birth of Herakles: in *Nemean* 10.13-18, Zeus enters the αὐλάν ("courtyard") disguised as Amphitryon and bearing the seed of Herakles. Practically the entire *Nemean* 1 is devoted to the birth of Herakles and the miraculous strangling of the snakes; Amphitryon summons Teiresias who prophesies on the spot about Herakles' future. *Pythian* 9.83-88 tells of Amphitryon coming to dwell in Thebes, and Alkmene giving birth to her two sons who became worthy of praise and reverence. In *Isthmian* 4.104 Pindar places the house of Amphitryon "above the Elektrai gates," which means inside the Kadmeia. Although there is no direct reference to a sanctuary it would be surprising if none existed at the spot where Herakles was born, the snakes were strangled, and Teiresias prophesied. Wilamowitz (1895:52-54) would not accept the existence of a cult early in Theban history; he suggested that Herakles was a late-comer, and for this reason his sanctuary was established outside the Kadmeia. Keramopoullos (1917:324-327) also believed that there was only one sanctuary, and he too placed it outside the Kadmeia. Schachter (1973) agrees. Yet, it is difficult to imagine that for Alkmene the Thebans dedicated both a cult site (perhaps her "chamber") and a separate heroon (Ziehen 1934:1495), while no location was allocated for the worship of Herakles until a temple was built in the Classical period (probably the fifth century B.C.).

The ruins related to the birth of Herakles, that were shown to Pausanias inside the Elektrai gates must have constituted the main cult site before the construction of the temple outside the Kadmeia, near the stadion. The sanctuary on the Kadmeia would have been differentiated from the new sanctuary by virtue of its association with the Mycenaean past and the typically Theban focus of the Herakles cult, with its emphasis on the hero's early life. Substantial Mycenaean remains have been found here (cf. Catalogue, site 179; fig. 2.5). By the time of Pausanias' visit, its religious activities may have been transferred to the Classical temple, and it was no longer used as a cult site. It is clear, however, that its surviving components continued to be revered. When they were shown to Pausanias in the second century A.D., he thought them important enough to record.

Apollo Spodios. Our best source of information on the sanctuary of Apollo Spodios is Pausanias, who describes it in some detail (9.11.7-9.12.1): it was located near the Sophronister (i.e., the birth place of Herakles) and contained an altar made out of the ashes of the sacrificial victims; for this reason, Apollo was surnamed *Spodios* ("of the ashes"). Pausanias also tells us that at the site, clearly an open-air sanctuary, there was an oracle where divination based on voices and noises was practiced; he compares this oracle to a similar one at Smyrna. He also tells us that in antiquity (relative to his own time), the

Thebans sacrificed bulls to Apollo Spodios, whereas by the time of his visit they sacrificed working oxen. Holleaux (1898) did not believe that this sanctuary existed, and proposed that Pausanias had made a serious mistake in confounding two cult practices of Apollo Ismenios, for whom, and only for whom, a sanctuary was established in Thebes (see chap. 5, passage 6, for a discussion of the argument). I, however, cannot see how Pausanias could have confounded two sanctuaries in two different locations, both of which he describes in detail. I believe, in fact, that by recording a very old cult practice (the sacrifice of bulls), Pausanias was drawing a distinction between Apollo Spodios and Apollo Ismenios and informing us that the former had a more ancient cult. As I have explained above (p. 123), other major gods also had two sanctuaries (table 2.5), an older one on the Kadmeia and a later one in Greater Thebes (table 3.1). The open-air sanctuary of Apollo Spodios was probably the original oracle of the god and must predate the construction of the temple of Apollo Ismenios in the Geometric period. We do not know where on the Kadmeia the sanctuary of Apollo Spodios was located, except that it was near the sanctuary at the birthplace of Herakles, that is, near the Elektrai gates. If I am correct in suggesting that the earlier sanctuary of Herakles was west of the gates, directly opposite the later Herakleion (to the south), then the sanctuary of Apollo Spodios would have been north of the gates, opposite the sanctuary of Apollo Ismenios (to the southwest). A location in the vicinity of the church of Agios Vasileios (site 11, fig. 5.2) is likely.

Athena Onka. Sophokles (*Oid. Tyr.* 20) indicates that there were two temples of Athena in Thebes, and Euripides (*Phoin.* 1372) refers to "the house of Pallas." According to the scholiast to Euripides *Phoinissae* 1062, Kadmos himself established the sanctuary of Athena Onka because the goddess helped him overcome the Spartoi. Pausanias' text allows us to infer that it was established at the place where the cow Kadmos had been following collapsed, this being the signal that here he was to found a city. Pausanias (9.12.2) specifies that the sanctuary of Athena Onka was in the open air, and that there was an altar only; a statue of the goddess looked old enough to Pausanias to date to the time of Kadmos (Archaic?). It may be that a temple known to the dramatists had been made of mud-brick and wood, and had collapsed by the time of Pausanias' visit (Keramopoullos 1917:334-335).

Because the sanctuary was associated with the myth of the founding of Thebes, it may have been the one longest remembered there. That it was established very early is suggested by the presence of a gate named for it, which probably dated to the Middle Helladic period (chap. 2, p. 36). On the basis of the order in which Pausanias visited the various Theban monuments, we may infer that both the sanctuary of Athena Onka and the gate of the same name were located at the southern end of the Kadmeia, where the earliest remains of habitation have been found; the cult of Athena Onka may actually be as early as ca. 2100 B.C., the time when Thebes was established. A likely place for this sanctuary would be the vicinity of the church of Agia Aikaterini (site 218, fig. 5.2).

The Oionoskopeion of Teiresias. In ancient Greece, bird divination depended on the chance appearances of wild birds whose actions were then interpreted by professional augurs. The movement of birds being unrestricted, an omen might appear at any time and in any place (Pollard 1977:116-129). In the Roman period, there were several bird stations where augury could be practiced in a more systematic way (Bouché-Leclercq 1879:143). In the Classical period, however, there was only one such station, the bird observatory (oionoskopeion) of Teiresias in Thebes. The earliest and clearest reference to it is in *Antigone* (999-1005) when Teiresias says to Creon: "... for seated at my ancient observatory from which I survey every quarter of the sky I heard strange bird cries, as they screamed in dire rage and raised a barbarous din." It is clear to us that Sophokles imagined a Teiresias seated at a bird lookout with full view of the sky. He must have been assisted by someone who could see, while he himself paid particular attention to the cries of the birds.

Centuries after Sophokles, Pausanias (9.16.1) claims to have visited the bird observatory of Teiresias on the Kadmeia. Precisely where on the Kadmeia has been difficult to determine. Keramopoullos (1917:347-348) believed that the bird observatory was on the hill now called Pouros on the west side of the Kadmeia. From here, one certainly has a grand view towards western Thebes. But a grand view alone may be insufficient justification for locating a unique, permanent bird observatory on the Pouros. Other considerations speak against it. For one, we need not suppose that the lonely augur sat passively on the hilltop waiting for a bird to fly by. There are ways of attracting birds, thereby increasing the opportunities for prophecy. Birds of antiquity, like their modern counterparts, would be drawn to places where there was food, water, and protective vegetation. We know that there was systematic feeding at Roman stations, and a reference by Aischylos (*Hepta* 23) to Teiresias as "the feeder of birds" may justify an inference that feeding was practiced at the Theban observatory. Water might have been supplied by a nearby natural source, or a man-made installation. The Pouros hill not only lacks sufficient vegetative cover to be attractive to birds, but the nearest source of water is the river Dirke, which flows below the hill and is over 100 m away.

A more important drawback for divination on this hill is the fact that the Greeks characterized omens from the east, or right side, as bearing good fortune, and those from the west, or left side, as bringing bad luck. Of greatest importance archaeologically is that fact that although Pausanias describes several sanctuaries in topographical proximity to the observatory of Teiresias, to date no trace of a sanctuary has been found in the western part of the Kadmeia.

On the east side of the Kadmeia, however, archaeological remains not only attest to the presence of several sanctuaries, but reveal a cohesive topography when viewed in conjunction with Pausanias' descriptions (see chap. 5, passage 8). My analysis of his text leads me to believe that the northeast area of the Kadmeia was a likely location for the observatory of Teiresias. In 1964-1965, I excavated a site that seemed at the time to be an outdoor sanctuary (see Catalogue, site 23). There was evidence of continuous use of the site from the Classical to the end of the Roman period. The most striking feature at the site was an L-shaped wall, constructed at the beginning of the Hellenistic period. I originally thought that this was a sacred peribolos; while this is possible, a different interpretation may be suggested if the site was indeed a bird observatory: the long wall, which lies in an east-west orientation, may have marked the direction of the approaching birds. We may envision the augur seated at the west end of this wall, facing east. A bird approaching from the right side of the wall would be a good omen, from the left, a bad one.

The finds at the site, though few, attest to its importance (Catalogue, site 23). Its location is not only topographically related to the other sanctuaries cited by Pausanias, but is also most suitable for observing birds. Just below it flows the Strophia stream, which, though now almost dry, not only must have provided water for the birds to drink, but must also have sustained enough vegetation in antiquity to be attractive to them. Although my excavation did not investigate enough of the early levels thoroughly, it is certain that the bird observatory of Teiresias was not established in the Mycenaean period; in a small exploratory trench, the Mycenaean fortifications were found directly below the sanctuary. The observatory was probably established in the Archaic period. Sophokles' characterization of it as an "ancient observatory" is not entirely misleading, because it was indeed named for a legendary Mycenaean augur and because the old practice of prophesying from the cries of birds, in addition to the manner and direction of flight, was maintained.

THE SANCTUARIES OF GREATER THEBES

Apollo Ismenios. The second temple of Apollo Ismenios, which perhaps had been built ca. 700 B.C. (see above), was still in use in the fifth century B.C. Keramopoullos' excavations showed that a third temple was constructed in the fourth century B.C. to replace the second one (see Catalogue, site 8). The reasons for this were not clear, but the construction of a new and large structure may have reflected the city's prestige at the time of the Theban hegemony.

It was the second temple, however, that had received the wealth of offerings mentioned in ancient literary sources; Pindar (*Pyth.* 11.4) refers to it as "the treasury of golden tripods." The offerings were lined up along the road that led to the temple from the Elektrai gates. This was the same road taken by the procession of the *Daphnephoria* ("laurel bearing") festival, celebrated in honor of Apollo Ismenios every ninth year (Frazer 1898:41-43; Ziehen 1934:1545-1549). A boy whose parents were living was elected priest for the year of the festival, and he dedicated a tripod to Apollo at the end of his service. During the main procession, the closest relative of the boy-priest carried the κωπώ, an object similar to the Maypole of North European festivals. We know that Pindar held the pole for his son Daiphantos and composed a poem in honor of the occasion (frag. 104). We also know that a number of statues were dedicated to the sanctuary in the Classical period. Most important was the cult statue itself, made of cedar wood by Kanachos (Pausanias 9.10.2). Kanachos made an almost identical statue in bronze for the temple of Apollo at Didyma (Pollitt 1965:23-26); the god was shown nude with a bow in his left hand, and holding on to a stag with his right (Simon 1957; Bielefeld 1968). These statues were probably made in the early part of the fifth century B.C. Pausanias also tells us that near the entrance to the temple was a Hermes Pronaos by Pheidias, and an Athena Pronaos by Skopas; nothing more is known about these Classical works. There were also statues of Henioche and Pyrrha by unknown sculptors, and of unknown date.

Although the oracle lost much of its activity to Delphi, we know that it continued to function; Pindar (*Pyth.* 11.6) refers to it as the "true seat of divination." The sanctuary clearly retained its importance in Thebes and perhaps throughout Boiotia until late antiquity.

Herakleion. The Herakleion was located south of the Kadmeia. Pausanias refers to it together with many other monuments, most of which were on the Kadmeia, for reasons explained below (chap. 5, passage 6). This sanctuary, however, should be distinguished from the one that I have suggested was maintained at the birthplace of Herakles (see above). We know from Pindar (*Nem.* 4.19; *Isth.* 4.61) that a gymnasion, a stadion, and perhaps an altar, all named in honor of Herakles existed outside the Kadmeia. It was there that a temple dedicated to Herakles was built. We do not know its exact location, but it must have been near the sanctuary at the birthplace of Herakles because the gymnasion and the stadion of the Archaic period were known to have been south of the Kadmeia and not far from it (Keramopoullos 1917:329-330; Wilamowitz 1922:401, n. 1).

We cannot be certain when the temple was built, and Pindar does not refer directly to a temple. He does refer to Herakles' altars (*Isth.* 4.62), which indicates that there could at least have been an altar here in Pindar's time. In *Nemean* 4.24 he mentions "Herakles' court" by the tomb of Amphitryon (i.e., south of the Kadmeia). These are the two most explicit references to the Herakleion, written in 474 and 473(?) B.C. respectively, but they give no clue about the temple, which must have been completed by the end of the fifth century when a number of statues were dedicated. In 403 B.C., Thrasyboulos of Athens commissioned the sculptor Alkamenes to carve two colossal statues in Pentelic marble for the sanctuary: an Athena and a Herakles. Pausanias (9.11.6) reports that the pedimental sculptures of the temple showed the labors of Herakles; these were made by Praxiteles, perhaps the Elder, of the late fifth or early fourth century B.C. (Pollitt 1965:134). Eubios and Xenokritos, otherwise unknown Theban sculptors, carved a new cult statue of Herakles Promachos in marble. Most of this work seems to have been done in the second half of the fifth century B.C. when the political power of Thebes was growing, and it is possible that the temple itself was built after 446 B.C. Of all the known temples of Thebes, this one had the richest collection of sculpture, and its construction must have been an ambitious undertaking.

Dionysos Aigobolos, Demeter and Kore Potniai. The double sanctuary of Dionysos Aigobolos, and Demeter and Kore Potniai, located south of Thebes (site 201), which I described in the discussion of Archaic sanctuaries, was active for a very long time, and there are finds that prove it continued to be used in the Classical period (Keramopoullos 1917:261-266). The sanctuary was located at a crossroads, according to Keramopoullos (1917:419-420) the very crossroads at which Oidipous killed Laios (see chap. 5, passage 1). In the sanctuary's sacred grove, Pausanias (9.8.1-2) saw two statues dedicated to Demeter and Kore and a temple dedicated to Dionysos Aigobolos (the goat shooter). He relates that in a ritual honoring Demeter, young pigs were released, which were supposed to reappear in Dodona the following year (Ziehen 1934:1508). To honor Dionysos, goats were sacrificed in place of boys. Terracotta figurines of both pigs and boys were found at site 201. Two inscriptions referring to Dionysos were found in the southern area of Thebes: a fragmentary herm stele at the church of Agios Nikolaos (site 215), and an architectural fragment at the church of Agios Loukas (site 54, fig. 4.2). Both were found out of context, obviously in second use. Keramopoullos (1917:367-368; 1935:16, nos. 185, 189) attributed both references to Dionysos Lysios, for whom there was a sanctuary in the northern part of Greater Thebes, for reasons not clear to me. I believe that both originated at the nearby temple of Dionysos Aigobolos. The second inscription, in fact, is dedicated to]ροις καὶ Διονύσωι [καὶ τῆι] πόλει . . . Keramopoullos restored the first word to read Διοσκό?]ροις on the assumption that there was a cult of the Dioskouroi in Thebes; this is possible, but not clearly documented. I believe a more plausible restoration would be Θεσμοφό]ροις, which was the main epithet for Demeter and Kore in Thebes. It was used to designate their main sanctuary on the Kadmeia and the *Thesmophoria* festival, which was celebrated in their honor. It was also used, together with Potnia, in connection with this sanctuary (Pindar, frag. 37).

The temple dedicated to Dionysos was probably constructed during the period of Theban affluence, from 446 to 335 B.C. The sanctuary continued to function until the time of Pausanias.

Mother Dindymene. Pausanias (9.25.3) refers to a sanctuary west of the Kadmeia as sacred to Mother Dindymene. His reference to it immediately follows his mention of the house of Pindar, and this must indicate the proximity of the two. Pausanias also tells us that Pindar dedicated the cult image in which the goddess was depicted seated on the throne; it was made of Pentelic marble by Aristomedes and Sokrates of Thebes. Pausanias' report is confirmed by Pindar himself in *Pythian* 3.78-79, in which the goddess, whose sanctuary is near his house, is simply called "mother"; Pindar also names Pan and Korai (perhaps Charites) as companions of the goddess. Elsewhere (frag. 80), Pindar refers to "Kybele, mother of gods," perhaps the same goddess. Pindar does not give us any more information about this sanctuary, but a few scholars have suggested that he not only may have dedicated the statue, but may have actually started the cult (Ziehen 1934: 1532-1534). Wilamowitz (1922:270-272) believed that Pindar dedicated the statue upon his return to Thebes after the Persian wars. The most likely location for the sanctuary is the church of Agia Trias (site 26) where remains of an ancient structure, perhaps a temple, have been found (see chap. 5, passage 18).

Dionysos Lysios. North of the Kadmeia was the third sanctuary dedicated to Dionysos, this one to Dionysos Lysios. According to Pausanias (9.10.6) it was near the theater of Thebes and contained a temple within which Pausanias saw two statues. He skeptically reports that "the Thebans say that one of them is Semele." He says nothing about the other, presumably because it was of Dionysos. Because the temple in the southern part of Thebes was probably small, we may infer that the temple of Dionysos Lysios was the major temple dedicated to Dionysos in Thebes. Although we do know the general area of the theater, the temple has not been identified, and we have no clue regarding the date of its construction. Numerous Classical walls have been found in the area (cf. fig. 3.6, site 65), and the temple, too, may have been Classical. But Pausanias' lack of assurance in recognizing and naming the two statues may be an indication that they were Archaic (see chap. 5, passage 10, for a more complete discussion of the sanctuary). An inscription (*SEG* 15.328; Keramopoullos 1917:366) recorded the purchase of land for this temple by Eumenes II of Pergamon. The Lysian festival mentioned in Photius and Suidas may be related to the worship of Dionysos and to the activities of this temple (Ziehen 1934:1511).

Artemis Eukleia. Pausanias (9.17.1) saw the temple of Artemis Eukleia after having visited the temple of Dionysos and a cemetery that may have been on the Amphion hill (see Catalogue, site 121). He reported that the cult statue was by Skopas and that inside the cella was the tomb of Antipoinos' daughters, Androkleia and Alkis, who sacrificed their lives to ensure a Theban victory over the Orchomenians. In front of the temple, there was a stone lion said to have been dedicated by Herakles after his victory over King Erginos of Orchomenos.

From the presence of the tombs, we may infer that the Artemis worshiped here was probably a chthonic deity. The dedication of the lion would be appropriate to a *potnia theron,* an aspect of the goddess known from works of art found in Thebes, such as the relief pithoi (Hampe 1936; Schefold 1966) and vase paintings (Sparkes 1967). The cult of Artemis Eukleia is the only known cult of Artemis in Thebes, although the epithets *Hekate* and *Prostateria* ("protectress") do occur in ancient literature (Ziehen 1934:1503-1505). The temple has not been identified. Sophokles (*Oid. Tyr.* 160-161) seems to place the sanctuary near the agora of Greater Thebes; it ought to be in the vicinity of the Evangelistria chapel (site 252).

Zeus Agoraios. I have already discussed two sanctuaries of Zeus on the Kadmeia, but the one most likely to have contained a temple was that of Zeus Agoraios in Greater Thebes. Pausanias (9.25.4) mentions a statue made of stone, from which we may infer that there was a structure to house it. The epithet *Agoraios* indicates that the sanctuary was in or near the agora of Greater Thebes, where other monuments existed in the Classical period. By Pausanias' time, however, the use of the agora had already declined; perhaps it had even been abandoned except for this temple and a few isolated statues and ruins (see below). The most likely location of the temple and the agora would be the suburb of Pyri, perhaps the west side of it.

Themis. In referring to the sanctuary of Themis, Pausanias (9.25.4) also mentions the sanctuary of the Moirai and that of Zeus, leading one to infer that the three sanctuaries were in close proximity. Pindar (frag. 30) also mentions Themis, the Moirai, and Zeus in succession, which we may view as a verification of Pausanias' report. The presence of a statue at the sanctuary of Themis may indicate that there was a small temple or shrine. The sanctuary was probably located northwest of the Kadmeia or in the southern part of modern Pyri.

Amphiaraos. One of the three known open-air sanctuaries in Greater Thebes was dedicated to Amphiaraos. I have already included what is known about it in the discussion of Thebes in the Archaic period. The fact that Pausanias (9.8.3) describes it as a peribolos containing columns indicates that it continued to be used until his time. The sanctuary has not been found, but it was probably located in the southern part of Thebes, at or near the modern church of Agios Nikolaos (site 215).

Temenos of Iolaos. Pausanias (9.23.1) mentions a heroon dedicated to Iolaos, and nearby, a gymnasion and a stadion named in his honor; his text makes it clear that all of these were located north of the Kadmeia (see chap. 5, passage 14). Pindar (*Isth.* 5.32) confirms the existence of the cult and refers to Iolaos many times as Theban hero, athlete, and master of horses (see especially *Isth.* 1). According to Aristotle (frag. 97), lovers swore to be faithful at the heroon of Iolaos, and Aristophanes (*Acharnians* 867) tells us that Boiotians swore by Iolaos in general.

The *Iolaeia*, the festival and athletic games in his honor, is sometimes viewed as a celebration separate from the *Herakleia* (recently, Nisetich 1980:206, 219). Our best source of information about the *Iolaeia* is Pindar, who in three instances associates the celebration with a landmark (*Ol.* 9.98-99; *Pyth.* 9.79-83; and *Nem.* 4.20), the tomb of Iolaos and Amphitryon in the southern part of Thebes. This is where the stadion and gymnasion of Herakles were located, making it fairly clear that *Iolaeia* and *Herakleia* were alternate names for the same festival (Roesch [1975] reached the same conclusion). It is also safe to assume that until the temenos of Iolaos was established, both Iolaos and Herakles shared a common cult site in the southern part of Thebes. The separate temenos was probably established together with the new gymnasion and stadion after 446 B.C. Keramopoullos proposed to locate the heroon at the church of Agia Paraskevi (site 224, see fig. 5.1), in the area of which there are numerous foundations of Classical walls. The temenos itself, however, has not been identified.

Moirai. Pausanias (9.25.4) mentions the sanctuary of the Moirai between the sanctuaries of Themis and Zeus Agoraios, and specifies that it had no statues, which may be an indication that it was an open-air sanctuary. It was probably near the sanctuaries of Themis and Zeus Agoraios.

In addition to the numerous sanctuaries, there were other cult sites in Thebes, the documentation of which is much more difficult. Our best source for these is Pausanias, and a complete discussion of what he saw can be found in chapter 5. I have not discussed the sanctuaries of Demeter Kabeiria and of the Kabiroi because they do not relate directly to the topography of Thebes (see Wolters and Bruns 1940; Heyder and Mallwitz 1978; Schmaltz 1974; Haury 1908; Hemberg 1950).

PUBLIC BUILDINGS

The Old Agora. Pausanias (9.12.3) visited an agora in the general area of the "house of Kadmos" and the sanctuary of Dionysos Kadmeios. He gave no other information about it, unless in mentioning the statues of Pronomos and Epaminondas, he meant us to understand that they were in the agora, where one would expect them to be. This was the only agora functioning in Pausanias' time, whereas in the Classical period there was one other. Sophokles (*Oid. Tyr.* 19-20) alludes to two agoras, but gives no indication of their respective locations. Keramopoullos (1917:340, 371-379) believed that the one Pausanias saw was Roman because the five column bases he found west of site 1 (Keramopoullos 1912:86) dated to the Roman period. He consequently believed that Thebes had three agoras, because he considered the two mentioned by Sophokles to have been different from the Roman one. Although it is likely that the columns found by Keramopoullos belonged to the agora, they do not necessarily date the original building or the agora; they could very well have belonged to a Roman restoration or addition.

   The existing evidence makes it fairly certain that the main agora of Thebes was on the Kadmeia. It was probably established sometime during the Dark Ages and continued to function until Pausanias' time, having been refurbished several times over the course of its long existence. It should not come as a surprise that it was established in the vicinity of the house of Kadmos: the area of the two palaces remained unoccupied, except for the sanctuaries of Dionysos and Demeter, which were established on the ruins of those palaces. It is possible that the agora was established in the area west of the first Late Helladic palace (where Keramopoullos found the columns) and between the two palaces (fig. 2.11). The second agora known to Sophokles was in Greater Thebes and will be discussed below. There is no indication that a third agora existed.

The Federal Council. The *Hellenica Oxyrhynchia* (11.4) records that the federal council of Boiotia met on the Kadmeia. The council was composed of 660 members (Larsen 1968:35) and could therefore have been expected to meet in an enclosed structure or portico, perhaps in the agora. There was also a treasury (Bruce 1967:163), probably a separate building. It is conceivable that the poorly preserved foundations of the Classical building found in site 2 was part of the agora, or the seat of the federal council.

No other public buildings or public spaces on the Kadmeia are known to us from archaeological remains. Together with the sanctuaries, there is a total of fifteen places of public function, not a large number, especially if we consider that few of these occupied a large area. Keramopoullos (1917:269) believed that the Kadmeia was uninhabited in Classical times, but was covered with sanctuaries and public buildings. The opposite seems to have been true, however: the Kadmeia seems to have been so densely populated that there was little room for public buildings. For this reason, large public buildings and new temples were constructed in Greater Thebes.

The New Agora. The establishment of a new agora is documented in several literary sources: Arrian (*Anabasis* 1.8.6) indicates that the agora was beyond the Amphion hill as one approaches from the south. This is in accord with Pausanias who, though he does not make direct reference to the agora because it was not used in his time, does refer to Hermes Agoraios (9.17.2) and the sanctuary of Zeus Agoraios (9.25.4). One may assume that in each instance the epithet indicates that the temples were located in the agora.

Plutarch tells us (*De Gen. Sokr.* 33-34) that the agora had many porticos, one of which was constructed after the battle at Delion (424 B.C.); elsewhere (*Pelop.* 12) he tells us that near the agora were the shops of those who manufactured knives and spears. Xenophon (*Hell.* 5.2.29) says that on one occasion, the council of Thebes met at a stoa in the agora (of Greater Thebes) because the women were celebrating the *Thesmophoria* (at the temple of Demeter on the Kadmeia) on that day. He probably meant the portico built after 424 B.C., which was large and had many statues (Diodorus 12.70).

I believe that this agora was one of the projects initiated in the late sixth or early fifth century B.C. because Pindar dedicated there the statue of Hermes Agoraios. Several buildings and statues were added in the course of the Classical period—the temple of Zeus Agoraios, for example, and the statue of Apollo Boedromios, both mentioned by Pausanias. It is also possible that in or very near the agora were the two statues of Athena

Zosteria and the Pyre of the Seven, also mentioned by Pausanias. Keramopoullos (1917:372-373) placed the agora between the Kastellia hills and the Kadmeia, because he believed that the theater was also there. On the basis of Pausanias' account, I conclude that the agora was in the suburb of Pyri: the sanctuary of Zeus Agoraios was the penultimate monument Pausanias saw leaving the city on his way to Kabeirion. This is a likely place for Pindar to have dedicated a statue, because the agora was in his favorite neighborhood; his own house was just south of here. I believe that the most plausible location for the agora is the southern part of Pyri where some substantial archaeological remains have been found (sites 156, 239, 250). Unfortunately, very little of the agora survived; after the destruction of Thebes in 335 B.C., its buildings were probably among the first to be demolished so that the stones could be reused. Pausanias probably saw only the temple of Zeus and the few desolate statues that were left standing at the site.

A Prison. According to Plutarch, there was a prison near the new agora (*Pelop.* 12; *De Gen. Sokr.* 33); it had only one warden and may therefore have been a small structure.

The Theater. Keramopoullos believed that there were two theaters in Thebes, and that the main one was near the Proitides gates; he excavated in the area repeatedly in the hope of finding it, but without success (1917:362-364). He did consider the possibility that there may have been only one theater (1917:405-406), but the one theater known to him was not visible even though a large depression enabled him to identify its location. This, he supposed, was the Roman theater recorded by Plutarch (*Sulla* 19) who reports that Sulla, after his victory over Archelaos in 86 B.C., built a thymele ("stage") not far from the Oidipodeia spring. No trace of a second theater has been found to this date, and it seems that Sulla renovated the old theater and built a new stage there to celebrate his victory. This theater was located about 600 m north of the Proitides gates (cf. chap. 5, passage 11). All of its stone has been stripped, leaving us little hope for its recovery. A concentration of theater seats was found in site 66 and substantial foundations, which may be related to the theater, at site 68. Just south of these two sites there is still an open space that is shaped like the cavea of a Greek theater. Judging from the size of this space, the theater was quite large. Its construction must have been a major undertaking because there are neither high hills nor hard bedrock in this area. Between sites 66 and 68, there is an artificial hill, still preserved to a height of 10 to 12 m. This huge fill is probably part of the effort to construct the theater.

Regarding the date of the original construction, the literary record provides no clue. It is likely that it was built at the same time as the temple of Dionysos Lysios, that is, in the Classical period. I can only speculate that the construction of a very large theater with stone seating would not have been possible before 446 B.C., though this does not exclude the possibility that there was an earlier theater built of less permanent material.

Stadion and Gymnasion. North of the theater were a stadion and a gymnasion named in honor of Iolaos whose temenos was nearby (Pausanias 9.23.1). Foundations of Classical structures have been identified at many points in the area, but these do not present a coherent picture or a reconstructable plan. I suspect that sites 65 and 169 might be part of the gymnasion, and sites 67, 69, and 70, part of the stadion.

The construction date of both the stadion and gymnasion can be arrived at indirectly. Pindar knew only the stadion and gymnasion of Herakles in the southern part of Thebes; as he died after 438 B.C., it is very likely that the stadion and gymnasion of Iolaos were built after that date, perhaps after the completion of the great wall. It is understandable that these new facilities became the main site of the *Herakleia/Iolaeia* festival, since they were larger and were situated inside the new walls. Also, the southern area of Thebes seems to have declined in the Classical period; for the first time since the Late Helladic period, the hill of Kolonaki was again used for burials. The reason for the decline is related to the fact that the south area was not encompassed by the new fortifications. The stadion and gymnasion of Herakles were not forgotten, however; they were known to Pausanias, but it is hard to say how much they were used during and after the Classical period.

The Hippodrome. I have already discussed the hippodrome in connection with the sanctuary of Poseidon. In addition to the indirect references made to it by Pindar, we have the record of Pausanias (9.23.2), who located it "to the right" (i.e., west) of the stadion (see chap. 5, passage 15). He is the only one to tell us that Pindar's tomb was in the hippodrome; if this is so, its construction must predate Pindar's death, meaning that it was built in the early fifth or, more likely, in the sixth century B.C. From Pausanias we know that its approximate location was the northern part of Greater Thebes. It is possible that the 42-meter-long portion of an isodomic wall found by Kalopais near the railroad station was part of the hippodrome (see Catalogue, site 106).

The House of Pindar. Pindar's house was not exactly a public monument, but it was a famous landmark in ancient Thebes, and even Alexander spared it when he destroyed the rest of the city (Arrian, *Anabasis* 1.9.10). Pausanias (9.25.3) saw it in ruins outside the Neistai gates. Pindar was either born there (Philostratos, *Icones* 2.12), or, as is more likely, spent most of his life in this area called in antiquity *Kynos Kephalai* (Xenophon, *Hell.* 5.4.15). His house was built on a very large property that Pindar must have bought himself. The house was probably located between sites 163 and 262 (fig. 3.6). In his poems, the gods whose sanctuaries were near his property he calls his "neighbors": in *Pythian* 3.78 it is Mother Dindymene (perhaps site 26, approximately 500 m south of his house); in *Isthmian* 1.53 it is Poseidon (perhaps site 94, 400 m to the northeast, fig. 3.7); and in *Pythian* 8.56-58, it is Alkmaion (perhaps site 215, 800 m to the southeast).

The dates of these odes are 474(?), 458, and 446 B.C., respectively. In the last ode, Alkmaion is actually called "protector of my wealth."

Is it possible that Pindar gradually acquired property extending as far as the sanctuary of Amphiaraos/Alkmaion? One thing is clear: the poet felt a genuine devotion to the gods and heroes whose sanctuaries were in his neighborhood; he always addressed his poems to Dirke, the stream that flowed past his house, never to Ismenos (Wilamowitz 1922:36). Of the three statues that we know he dedicated, one was of Ammon (perhaps site 93, 400 m east of his house), another was Hermes Agoraios in the new agora (perhaps only 400 m north of his house), and the last one was Mother Dindymene, again in his neighborhood.

The ruins of the house of Pindar have not been identified. If they survived the Middle Ages, chances are they would not have survived the construction activity of modern times.

THE AQUEDUCT

In describing the geography of Thebes (chap. 1) I have already called attention to the fact that the higher ground to the south contains the sources of water that flow north in three streams. The citadel of the Kadmeia, built on higher ground, had no water of its own, but there was nothing to prevent its occupants from bringing water to it by means of a surface or underground conduit, which could easily be cut in the soft bedrock. An underground aqueduct was, of course, more desirable for strategic reasons: it would have been invisible to enemies and not vulnerable to attack. Such an aqueduct was actually built in the Mycenaean period (fig. 2.12); it is easy to identify not only because it was lined with undressed stones, but also because it had tapering walls. Another type of conduit, with barrel roof and straight walls, was also cut in the bedrock and has been found both on the Kadmeia and in many areas of Greater Thebes. The full extent of this system remains unclear, however, nor can we determine its date. In some places it is still visible and one can even walk inside it. I have traced on paper the parts of this system that are known to me, and the resulting network can be seen in fig. 3.6.

Although numerous recent archaeological reports make reference to conduits, I have included in my plan only those whose size I have been able to ascertain. Smaller conduits do exist, which distributed the water in an east-west direction, but there is not enough evidence to allow us to trace their path. The major conduits, however, present a clear picture: there are two long lines, one supplying the Kadmeia and western Thebes (line A), the other supplying eastern Thebes (line B); a third line (line C) may have gone a short distance.

Line A originated about 2 km south of the Kadmeia, on the east side of the road to Athens. The main water source of Thebes was in this area, and also the true ancient source of the Ismenos River. Line A was discovered in the 1920s by the locals, who cleaned a section one kilometer long for their own use. Karouzos (1926) observed the operation. The position of the conduit was not traced on a map; I have indicated its approximate course in fig. 3.6. The conduit was buried 18 m below the surface; about 50 m beyond the starting point, a second conduit was found running beneath the first at a depth of 25 m. At 110 m from the starting point, the upper conduit ended, while the lower continued northwest, crossing the main road to Athens. At about 370 m from the starting point, the conduit was fed by two side channels, the western one starting 42 m from the junction, the eastern one, only 10 m from it. The main conduit continues north, soon crossing the ravine (ancient Koile Hodos). For a short distance after crossing the ravine, the aqueduct once more has double conduits, then a single one, which soon branches off to the east; this eastern segment has not been followed. The western conduit was followed to a small rectangular room with a mosaic floor decorated with dolphins in black and red tesserae; the room is not visible today, but it is located at site 201. This conduit averages about 2 m in height and is from 0.40 to 0.60 m wide; it has a barrel-shaped roof, and there are small cavities for setting lamps at regular intervals in its upper part. Every 20 m there is a square shaft provided with footholes that were used for descending into the conduit for maintenance. These shafts or water mains are covered with stone slabs, some of which are funerary stelai; three stelai were transferred to the Museum. The western conduit was cleaned by the locals a few years after it was uncovered; we know that this occurred, but nobody actually observed the activity (Keramopoullos 1941).

It is clear that line *A* moved west from the sources of the Ismenos River in order to reach the Kolonaki hill, which is not cut by ravines and which is joined to the Kadmeia by a narrow ridge at the end of Epaminondas St. This is the only route by which water can be brought to the Kadmeia. The conduit had to be started at a great depth in order for it to run beneath the main obstacle in its course, the Koile Hodos. The presence of double conduits seems to indicate that after the enterprise had gotten started, there must have been a change of plan, because one of the two is abandoned. The side conduits were probably opened in order to provide access to additional sources of water.

There is no evidence to tell us what happened to the conduit after it reached the Kolonaki hill, but there are two possibilities. The first is that it continued on the ridge until it reached the Kadmeia; the second is that at some point it met the old Mycenaean conduit and was joined to it, thereby eliminating the necessity for digging a new one. This second possibility is highly likely, not only because there is a reference to such an occurrence (Herakleides Kritikos *FHG* 2.258 F12), but also because an excavated section of the Late Helladic conduit was found lined with carefully fitted terracotta pipes. Although Keramopoullos (1917:327-329, fig. 192, drawing of a pipe) believed that the pipes could have been Mycenaean, there are no such pipes lining the Late Helladic conduit inside the Kadmeia (site 13, 184, see fig. 2.12), whereas this does occur in remains of the Classical period (Wycherley 1969:210). All of this suggests that at least some part of the Mycenaean aqueduct was discovered and reused.

At the point at which the conduit enters the Kadmeia, there is a difficult transition to be made: the Mycenaean aqueduct had entered perhaps at site 209 (see fig. 2.12), but turned in a north-northwest direction. The Mycenaean conduit was found undisturbed and filled with Mycenaean debris at site 13. This means that the Classical Greeks either lost track of it, or for some reason decided to continue its course in a northeast direction. At sites 16 and 268, the conduit had been dug through the deep prehistoric levels, and an additional 4 m into the bedrock in an apparent attempt to channel through the hill of the southern part of the Kadmeia.

The only other site where line *A* has been found on the Kadmeia is site 1. Keramopoullos (1909A:71) reports that it was found during the construction of the Daoutis house (cat. fig. 2). From site 1, the conduit moved north. To the best of my knowledge, the next known part of the conduit was discovered at site 121, where a shaft as deep as 20 m was found leading to a square room from which two conduits branched out to either side of the Amphion hill. The excavator, Spyropoulos, considered the shaft and the room an Egyptian-style tomb, but there can be no doubt that it is really part of the aqueduct: Keramopoullos (1917:320, n. 2) was actually aware of two conduits emerging from the north side of the hill. The eastern branch (fig. 3.6: *A 1*) continued northwards in order to supply the northwest area of Greater Thebes with water. Two, or possibly three fountains, active until only recently, may attest to the course of line *A 2*: the "Mpouka spring" at the foot of the hill, the "Chlevino spring" north of the road to Pyri, and the fountain of Pyri, which lies beyond this line and could only be reached if the conduit had crossed the Dirke stream. A segment of the aqueduct found west of Dirke (site 129) may indicate that the conduit did cross the stream and continued southwest. I doubt that a separate line was established in western Thebes.

Line *B* may also have started in the vicinity of line *A*. One can only trace it today as far south as site 242; a little further south the locals have tapped the water for current use (site 243, see Map A). The conduit of line *B* was not cut as deeply below the surface as line *A*; it was cut into the west bank of the Ismenos River. In a few spots where the bank has eroded, the conduit is visible. At site 242, the conduit measured 1.55 m high and 0.55 m wide. It was found further north at site 124 and also on the property of A. Kavallas, the exact location of which I do not know, but it must be in the area. Potsherds of the Classical period, including some in the Red Figure style, were found in the conduit.

Next, the conduit was found west of the church of Agios Loukas (Keramopoullos 1917:321) and at sites 255 and 85 just north of the Ismenion hill. Its course can be confidently reconstructed along the left bank of the Ismenos River continuing along the chain of hills that begins at the Ismenion and ends at the church of Agia Paraskevi (site 224). The conduit was found in sites 172 and 178. At site 172 the conduit measured 1.00 m high and 0.5 m wide.

Line *B* supplied water to eastern Thebes, in particular to the new gymnasion and other important public buildings of the Classical period. The presence of a conduit west of line

B at site 175 may be viewed as a side branch bringing water to the area of the theater. The main conduit would have emptied into the Ismenos River.

Line *B* was clearly designed to move water to the newly developed area of Greater Thebes. The engineers opened the conduit very intelligently, probably after careful planning and ground surveying, in a most convenient line that poses few technical difficulties. When complete, line *B* would have been about 4 km long. It differs from line *A* in that it has many air holes, but not as many main-shafts. Air holes were found at sites 124 and 175, a shaft at site 178. The barrel-shaped roof and the lamp cavities are the same as those in line *A*.

It is also possible that there was a third conduit, line C. Keramopoullos (1917:398) reports that a tunnel was followed for 100 m south of the Oidipodia spring (site 244). Because the spring is east of the Ismenos River, there seems to be no connection between this conduit and line *B*. It is possible that line C was opened for a specific purpose and that it took its water from sources east of the Ismenos, or from the river itself. A conduit has been found northeast of here at site 177, and Keramopoullos (1917) marks the presence of other conduits west and north of site 177 on his map. It is possible that this line was meant to provide water for the inhabitants of the section of Greater Thebes that is furthest east. The Oidipodia may have existed as a natural spring before the opening of line C.

Keramopoullos (1917) maps a few other locations where a conduit existed, but I have not been able to verify any other aqueduct. The area west of the Kadmeia was sparsely populated in antiquity, except for the valley of the Dirke River; even today, there are only a few houses in this area.

Dating the aqueducts is a problem. Keramopoullos was undecided, but Karouzos (1926) proposed that line *A* dated to the time of Hadrian; Hadrian is known to have constructed an aqueduct in Athens (Travlos 1971:242). We know, however, that the area of Greater Thebes was only sparsely populated in the time of Hadrian and a construction project of such magnitude would seem unwarranted. There is no doubt that line *B* was an element in the planned expansion of Thebes in 446 B.C., and that it was meant to provide water for Greater Thebes. Line C may have been opened later, but still within the Classical period. Line *A*, which was meant to supply the Kadmeia primarily, may either predate line *B* or be part of the fortification effort under Kassandros in 316 B.C. The earlier date is more likely for two reasons: The fact that the conduit extends beyond the Kadmeia indicates that even western Thebes, which was abandoned after 335 B.C., was included in its original planning. The awkwardness of its construction indicates that it was built in the early days of such engineering efforts; the sixth century is more likely, and one immediately thinks of the aqueduct engineer, Eupalinos, from nearby Megara (Dinsmoor 1950:118). Could line *A* have been one of the achievements of his youth?

Table 3.2. A summary of houses in Classical Thebes with their characteristic
architectural features

	Site Numbers	
	Kadmeia	*Greater Thebes*
Houses	13,37,45,109,123,184,186,194,238	27,61,71,74,91,122,152,158,161,211
Deposits	4,6,17,18,193,269	129,137,138,139,160,170,210
Foundations of Ashlar Masonry	13,45,123,184,186	61,71,74,122,161
Pebble Floors	——	27,71,158
Cisterns	——	71,152
Drains	37,194	71
Stone Water Mains	18,23	71

RESIDENTIAL BUILDINGS

It is not easy to differentiate residential buildings from small public structures because they are similar in manner of construction and are, in any case, poorly preserved. Although some of the remains I am about to discuss could conceivably be those of small public buildings, it is certain that the large majority were residences. The two-step krepis found at site 112 was probably a small shrine built around an old ruin, but its poor state of preservation and the lack of a literary reference to it make it impossible to identify more precisely. The other remains under consideration, however, have yielded some indication of their residential character; these are described in the detailed discussion of individual sites in the Catalogue.

In order to avoid repetition, I have summarized the distribution of Theban houses in table 3.2 and pointed out a few outstanding characteristics. The 19 houses and 13 deposits constitute a small part of the total, and I believe demonstrate the poor state of preservation of Classical remains. Sometimes the remains are so fragmentary that the excavator does not even think it worthwhile to mention them.

Half of the houses tabulated were built on foundations of ashlar masonry. Although such masonry is usually associated with public buildings, its presence in areas where there were no public buildings and the discovery of objects of domestic character indicate that ashlar masonry was also used for residential foundations. This probably began after the fortifications of Greater Thebes had been erected, when huge quantities of such masonry were used. The presence of ashlar masonry does not necessarily indicate that the house belonged to a rich Theban: it is found side by side with other types of foundations at site 71. But it is also true that some of the better houses (sites 45, 122, 158, 161) were built on ashlar foundations.

Unfortunately, we do not have any complete plans for the houses of Classical Thebes. We may distinguish some features, however, like the ones shown in table 3.2. The houses were, generally speaking, of modest size and not luxurious: no marble columns, rich mosaics, or any such expensive decorations have been found. The houses were raised on stone foundations, probably with mud-brick and wood in the upper structure. This would account for their poor preservation. A few houses, especially those in Greater Thebes, had pebble floors, fine drains, and even their own cisterns. Some houses have been found with neatly plastered floors and walls (site 71); one house had two hearths (site 158). Roof tiles were found in large quantities at only one site (122), but the presence of roof tiles at many sites indicates that most houses had sloping roofs.

There were some large houses, perhaps villas, in Greater Thebes (sites 122, 158, 161). The perishable furnishings are missing from the archaeological record (there has been no opportunity to excavate in a way that might recover them), and we can only imagine the beauty of the gardens filled with flowers and fruit trees for which Thebes was famous in antiquity. According to Herakleides Kritikos (*FHG* 2.258 F12), who visited the city sometime between 260 and 230 B.C., Thebes had a greater number of gardens than any city in Greece. He comments on the large quantity of fruit and summer vegetables, on the underground channels for water, on the cool and pleasant summer weather, and the cold and muddy winter. He describes beautiful blonde women, whose eyes and feet alone were visible in public, and constantly quarreling men, who enjoyed 30-year law suits!

In spite of Alexander's destruction of the fortifications in 335 B.C., Greater Thebes continued to be inhabited. No doubt the greater space, which allowed for larger properties with gardens, remained an attraction. The Kadmeia, which was protected by its own fortifications in the Classical period, was densely populated, judging from the disposition of the remains. In fact, it is likely that the entire Kadmeia was occupied, an area of approximately 30 hectares, sufficient to accommodate 9,000 to 12,000 people. As I have already suggested, the installation of new fortifications after 446 B.C. would have allowed the population to double, but it is doubtful that it ever exceeded 24,000, a density that lasted for about 100 years.

The Cemeteries

figs. 3.1, 3.6 As I have shown at the beginning of this chapter, the cemeteries of Classical Thebes extended over a wide area around the northern perimeter of Greater Thebes, reaching as far north as Kanapitsa (site 59), 1.5 km beyond the wall. The old Mycenaean cemetery at Kolonaki was reopened, and this may indicate that Knopia (the suburb south of the Kadmeia) was not as important a site of habitation in the Classical period as it was in the Archaic period. The burial practices of the Classical period were similar to those of the Archaic. Cremations persisted, especially at the old cemetery of site 87; at the new cemetery of site 24, only five out of twenty burials were cremations, and it is possible that the popularity of the practice diminished in Thebes in the fourth century B.C., just as it did in Athens (Kurtz and Boardman 1971:96). Most of the burials at Kolonaki were pit graves and about 25 percent of them were tile-lined. Cist graves, lined with beautifully cut stone, existed elsewhere (site 58).

The offerings to the dead consisted mainly of pottery and terracotta figurines, but there were also bronzes and jewelry. The pottery was usually locally made, and there was a preference for black glazed vases, especially kantharoi. The funerary stelai were simple, showing the name of the deceased in the upper part and sometimes a painted representation below; the paint is usually not preserved, but in the later fifth century, the representation was sometimes delicately incised or punched, and this has preserved the image (Keramopoullos 1920; Karouzos 1934, figs. 24-26). Carved stelai did exist but were relatively rare (Karouzos 1934:25, no. 30, fig. 22; Schild-Xenidou 1972, nos. 10, 28, 30, 33, 40-42, 47, 53, 60, 67, 69, 77, 79; Heimberg 1973, no. 5, pl. 5:a), as were painted vases (cf. sites 59, 150). Towards the end of the period, a new type of stele was introduced, the architectural stele, which was to become very popular in the succeeding period. An inscribed lion of monumental size was installed over a grave; this may have been a public monument (site 59).

CULTURAL ACTIVITIES

The literary sources supplemented by the fragmentary archaeological evidence show that Theban economic activity increased in the Classical period. The city's prominence in the fourth century B.C. further enhanced her economic growth. Thebes enjoyed a rich cultural life, different in character from that of Athens. The city seems to have favored musicians and poets, the most celebrated of which was Pindar. Her great appreciation of music is evidenced in the dedication of a statue to Pronomos, the fifth-century B.C. flutist, which stood by the statue of the great statesman Epaminondas, a celebrated flutist himself (Cloché 1952:189). The names of many other Theban musicians are known; most famous among them was Antigenidas (Dinse 1856), considered the finest flutist of his time, that is, in the second quarter of the fourth century B.C. (Cloché 1952:189-190).

Although Thebes was not a major center for sculpture, the city nurtured a long list of native artists, some of whom have already been mentioned in the discussion of the sanctuaries. There is a fourth-century inscription (*IG* 1:1578), which is probably a catalogue of Theban sculptors (Overbeck 1868, no. 1568); the names of fifteen artists are preserved (cf. Decharme 1869). Among the Theban painters are two of the highest caliber, who lived in the fourth century B.C.: Nikomachos, a son of Aristeides the Elder (Pollitt 1965:172), and the great Aristeides the Younger (Pollitt 1976). Although a detailed study of the cultural contributions of Thebes in the Classical period is beyond the scope of this book, even a modest appraisal reveals that her cultural activity was impressive in view of the fact that the city continued to rely primarily on agriculture, in contrast to Athens, which accumulated great wealth through trading and commerce.

THEBES IN THE HELLENISTIC AND ROMAN PERIODS, 335 B.C. to ca. A.D. 300

figs. 3.8, 3.9

In 335 B.C., Thebes was thoroughly destroyed by Alexander the Great. Fortifications and residences were leveled to the ground, and those inhabitants who could not escape to neighboring towns were either sold into slavery or killed (Arrian, *Anabasis* 1.10.2; Diodoros 17.14). Only the sanctuaries and the house of Pindar were spared. Both Pausanias (9.7.4) and Diodoros (19.54) relate that Kassandros rebuilt the "ancient" wall twenty years later. There is no question that the wall to which they refer was that of the Kadmeia. Thebes is no longer described as a large city, and both Strabo (9.2.5) and Pausanias (9.7.6) say that the area of Greater Thebes was deserted. Keramopoullos (1917:267-276) also concluded that Kassandros rebuilt or restored the wall surrounding the Kadmeia, and doubted that it had been completely leveled by Alexander. It was possible to restore the houses with the help of contributions from many Greek cities, the names of which survive in a partially preserved inscription (*IG* 7.2419; Holleaux 1895, 1938). By the end of the fourth century, Thebes had become active in politics and warfare once again, though she never recovered the power she held in the Classical period.

It is impossible to identify the wall of Kassandros on the basis of the existing archaeological evidence. Only at the Elektrai gates (site 7) did Keramopoullos think he had found evidence of Kassandros' restoration (1917:23, 273). I would only suggest that the wall of the Kadmeia retained the same outline that it had in the Classical period. From Hellenistic times on, the wall of the Kadmeia has been the city's only protection, and settlement was basically confined within its perimeter. Only in periods of extended peace were houses built outside the wall of the Kadmeia.

The sanctuaries spared by Alexander continued to be used at least until the second century A.D., as Pausanias' account indicates. There are no noticeable changes in either the archaeological or the literary record that would indicate changes in the use or the appearance of these sanctuaries. It is possible that the temple of Aphrodite was renovated in 304-302 B.C. to honor the hetaira of Demetrios Poliorketes (*FHG* 3.120 F15); at that time, the goddess was given the epithet *Lamia*. It is also possible that the importance of particular sanctuaries diminished, and for this reason, Pausanias did not mention them (e.g., Zeus Homoloios, Poseidon). In any case, there is no clear indication that any new construction took place in the sanctuaries of Thebes, nor is there much evidence that new public buildings were erected; the unexcavated remains at site 55 and the fine structure at site 12 are likely possibilities, and the remains of hypocausta found at sites

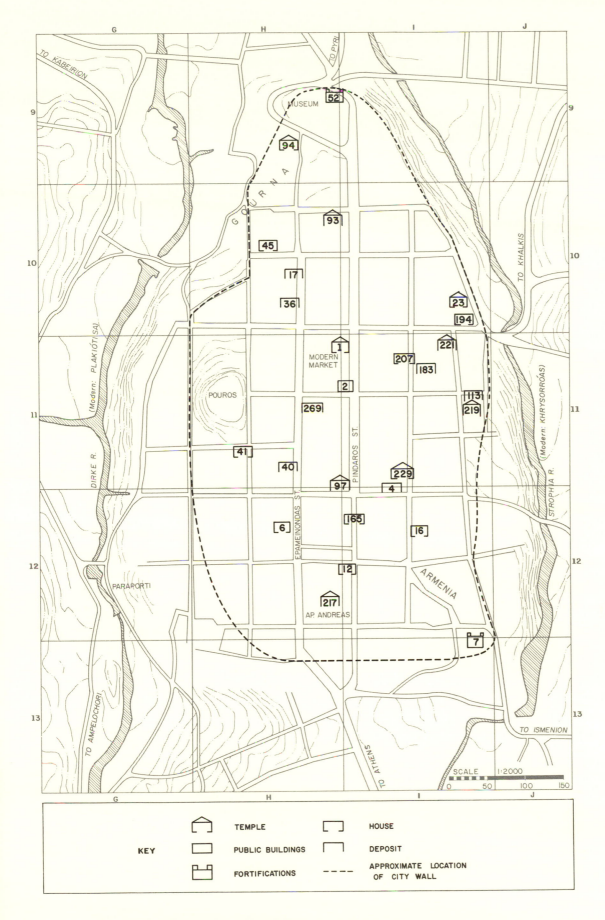

Fig. 3.8. The Kadmeia in the Hellenistic and Roman periods, ca. 335 B.C.
to ca. A.D. 300

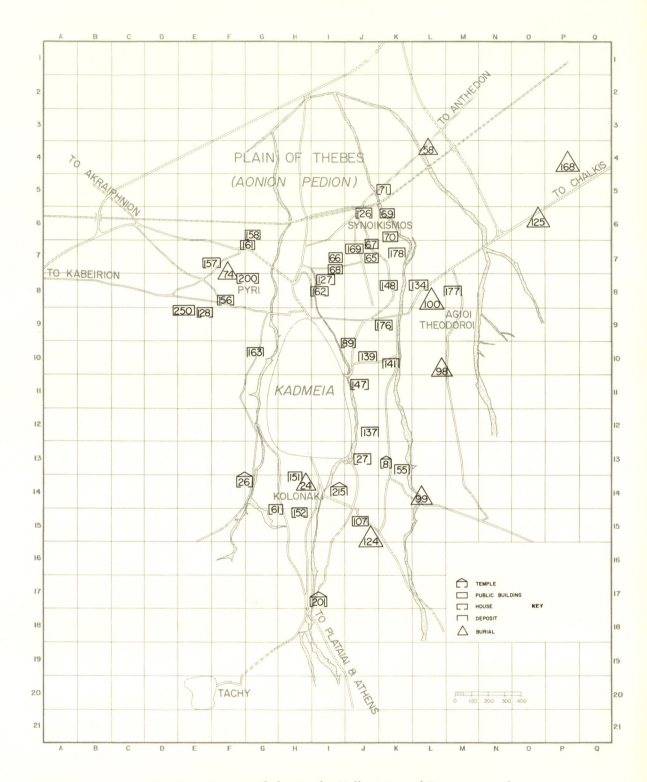

Fig. 3.9. Greater Thebes in the Hellenistic and Roman periods

Table 3.3. Houses of the Hellenistic and Roman periods

| | Site Numbers | |
	Kadmeia	Greater Thebes
Houses	6,12(?),16,17,41,45,112, 165,194,207(?)	27,61,71,89,126,128,134,147,148,152, 156(?),157,158,161,162,176,200
Deposits	36,40,113,183,269	55,137,139,141,151,163,177,178,250
Villas	——	127,134,161(?),200
Houses with Cisterns	——	134,148,152,176
Hellenistic and Roman	——	156,157,177(?),200(?)
Hellenistic	194,207	61(?),71,89(?),152,158,161,176
Roman	12,16,17,41,45	162,165

Note: Keramopoullos (1930C) excavated a Hellenistic/Roman house at the railroad station. As the exact location is not known, however, no site number was assigned.

2 and 107 may have belonged to public buildings. The consul Sulla built a stage for the theater of Thebes, as I have already indicated. The Emperor Hadrian came to Thebes in A.D. 125 and built a structure above the Oidipodia spring (Keramopoullos 1917:398).

Finds of pottery and coins allow us to identify many remains as those of houses (table 3.3). No house was sufficiently preserved, however, to enable us to reconstruct a complete plan. Most of the houses have been found in Greater Thebes, primarily because there was constant rebuilding on the Kadmeia, causing the obliteration of Hellenistic/Roman remains in subsequent periods. It has not been possible to accurately date the houses within this period, but it seems likely that most of the houses in Greater Thebes date to the Hellenistic period. The city is known to have suffered during the Roman conquest of 146 B.C. and again at the time of Sulla in 86 B.C. (Ziehen 1934:1489-1490; Cloché 1952:259-260). This is born out by the datable remains (table 3.3), which show that the number of houses outside the Kadmeia diminished dramatically in the Roman period. The population of the city must have stabilized in imperial times, but even then it was basically confined to the Kadmeia.

Thebes enjoyed a degree of affluence in the Hellenistic period and participated in international trade, as evidenced by the find of two hoards of coins (Hackens 1969). A series of inscriptions from Thebes honoring Roman emperors or members of their families indicates that the city continued to be important until the early fourth century A.D. (table 3.4). Its prominent position is also indicated by the fact that the Phokeans selected it as the place to honor the Emperor Hadrian in A.D. 125 (IG 7.2497).

The remains of the houses further suggest conditions of modest affluence. At four sites, there seem to have been large villas, all located in Greater Thebes. The one at site 127

Table 3.4. Inscriptions from Thebes with decrees honoring
Roman emperors and members of their families

Claudius	*IG* 7:	2493
Vespasian		2496
Titus		2494
Domitian		2495
Hadrian		2497
Caracalla		2500
Geta		2501
Claudius II		2502
Edict of Diocletian in A.D. 301		2417
Valeria, daughter of Diocletian		2503
Constantius Chlorus & Maximinianus		2451
Crispus, Constantinus, & Licinius		2451
Licinius		2504

was built on ashlar foundations, had floors of brick set in concrete and walls covered by red-painted plaster. The villas at each of the other three sites had similar features; one of them even had its own cistern (site 134). There were yet other houses with cisterns, a feature that may indicate the properties were country estates.

There were a few houses in Greater Thebes that continued to be occupied from Hellenistic to Roman times, but only two were found with Roman pottery alone; we may contrast this with the five houses of the Roman period found on the Kadmeia; the numbers, though small, may suggest the gradual abandonment of Greater Thebes after the Roman conquest. As we will later see, many sites in Greater Thebes that were inhabited in Greco-Roman times were used as cemeteries in the Early Christian period. It is interesting that most of the houses of Greater Thebes were built bordering the three lines of the aqueduct system, which was the most important attraction for settling outside the Kadmeia in post-Classical periods.

The cemeteries of the Classical period continued to be used and expanded in Hellenistic and Roman times. A new cemetery may have been established in the southeastern part of Thebes (sites 99, 124, and 215). The Hellenistic tomb at site 74 is an isolated example of a burial within the settlement. The funerary stelai found at sites 98 and 100 did not mark graves, but were reused for some other purpose; they were probably taken from the nearby Northeast Cemetery. We observe no major changes in the burial practices from those of the Classical period. There seem to have been fewer cremations, and offerings to the dead gradually diminished in quantity. One of the richest known tombs is of the "Macedonian" type (site 59, see fig. 1.2).

The funerary monuments of this period are characterized by their simplicity, even austerity. Most typical is the architectural stele, which was introduced in late Classical times and became the preferred monument throughout Boiotia. These monuments have been studied in detail by Fraser and Rönne (1957) who propose 300 to 100 B.C. as the main period of their use. There are many variations among the architectural stelai of Boiotia, but they all share simplicity of design and lack figured decoration with the exception of an occasional ornament. Characteristic of the Theban stelai is the use of the Doric frieze. Inscriptions are limited to the name of the deceased. Funerary stelai with figured decoration do exist, but are rarer and usually considered the work of non-Boiotian artists (Fraser and Rönne 1957:35). A group of twelve recently found stelai was published by Evi Touloupa (*Deltion* 1964:202-203). A large number of Hellenistic funerary stelai from Thebes were published in the 19th century by Körte (1878) in his catalogue of Boiotian sculptures, and a few were included in the catalog of Karouzos (1934). Others can be found incorporated in the construction of churches, most noticeably the church of Agios Demetrios (see Catalogue, site 212).

Theban pottery of the Hellenistic and Roman periods has not yet been studied, but a superficial overview reveals no differences from the pottery of other parts of Greece. Sizable amounts of Hellenistic pottery were found at sites 23, 161, and 163, and of Roman pottery at sites 2 and 23.

The names of only a few Theban artists who worked at this time have been recorded. Of the three known sculptors, only Myron is famous; he worked at Pergamos in the late third century B.C. (Six 1913). Theron and Timon (Overbeck 1868, nos. 1576 and 1577) are less well known. Xenophantos is the best-known musician: he accompanied the body of Demetrios Poliorketes to Korinth in 283 B.C. (Plutarch, *Dem.* 53.5) and played the flute in Delos the following year (*IG* 11, 2.106).

The history of Thebes in the Hellenistic and Roman periods is documented by literary and inscriptional evidence that has already been summarized (Schober 1934; Cloché 1952). Thebes did not have full control of the Boiotian Confederacy as she had in the Classical period (Roesch 1972:269). Her socio-political and military organization as a member of the Boiotian federation and as part of the Roman Empire was probably very much like that of Thespiai, which has already been studied (Roesch 1965A). Boiotian inscriptions of the Hellenistic period are numerous and have been the subject of several studies (Keramopoullos 1935, 1936; Feyel 1942A, 1942B; Roesch 1970; Salviat and Vatin 1971, to mention the most extensive ones). Unfortunately, there has been no comprehensive study of the inscriptions from Thebes.

The size of the population of Thebes in the Hellenistic period can be deduced indirectly. Most informative are the lists of army conscripts from Boiotia, which indicate that the average number of men between 20 and 50 years of age was about 15,000 (Feyel 1942A:209-218); this is well below the total of 23,000 men required by the federal constitution in the Classical period (Salmon 1953) though probably rarely reached (Larsen 1968:35, n. 1). If we assume that the average life span was about 60, the number of conscripts represents approximately one fourth of the total population of Boiotia, which can then be estimated at about 60,000; this should be considered a conservative estimate because it does not include slaves, or men unable to fight. Pappadakis (1923) proposed a population of 65,000 in the third century B.C., while Beloch (1886:162-172) proposed a range of 61,000 to 75,000 free individuals in the same period. Beloch believed, however, that a large number of slaves were kept in Boiotia, and he proposed a total population of 150,000 in the Classical period, but fewer than this in the Hellenistic. Boiotia, all the same, did not have nearly as many slaves as Athens did, primarily because as an agricultural state, it did not need as many as did an industrial state (Jardé 1925:108). Also, it is doubtful that the total ancient population was very different from that of today: the census of 1961 showed a total of 114,256 (a density of 36 inhabitants per square kilometer) in the province of Boiotia, which now encompasses a larger area than its ancient equivalent. It is far more likely that in the Hellenistic period, the total population was around 75,000. This number must be divided into eleven parts, corresponding to the ancient districts, which were more or less of equal population (Roesch 1965A:46-71). This gives us 6,800 inhabitants per district and indicates that the population of Thebes could not have exceeded this number in the Hellenistic period; more likely it was about 5,000. This fits well with our suppositions about the Classical period, when Thebes and its dependencies accounted for four of the eleven districts, and its population at some point soared as high as 24,000. This estimate would indicate that the Kadmeia was not as densely populated as it was in the Mycenaean period, when it was the main area of habitation. In the Hellenistic period, a significant part of the population seems to have resided in Greater Thebes, which, though unfortified, had ample space for more gracious living. These inhabitants would have moved inside the Kadmeia in times of war.

The pattern of fluctuation in Theban population from the Protogeometric to the Roman period is shown in the graph of figure 3.10. The modest number of about 1,200 inhabitants (see fig. 2.14, table 2.6) in the Protogeometric period gradually grew to between 8,000 and 10,000 by 446 B.C., a very large population for a Boiotian city. The extraordinary increase after 446 B.C. may be attributed to the construction of the great wall. Many have taken 24,000 to be the average size of the population of Thebes, but it was clearly temporary, maintained for only a century. The average population of Thebes over a period of fourteen centuries may be calculated (on the basis of the information summarized in fig. 3.10) at about 4,500. If we exclude the period between 446 and 335 B.C. because it is clearly atypical, the number would be about 3,500. This, in my view, is a reasonable norm for Thebes, allowing for upper and lower variations ranging from 1,200 to 8,500. The validity of the estimate is affirmed by comparisons with recent population data (table 4.1).

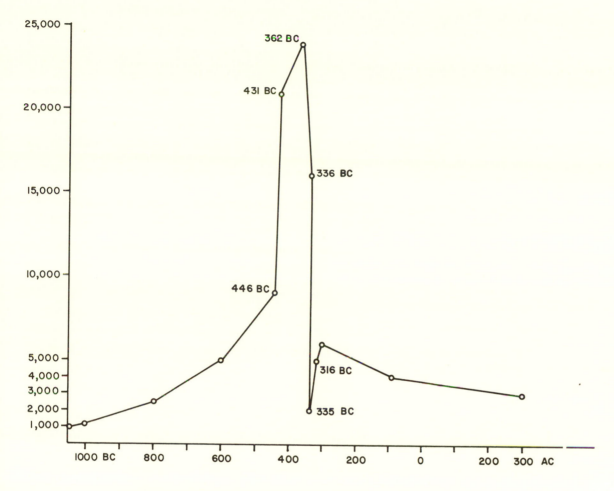

Fig. 3.10. Population estimates for Thebes in the Iron Age

4
THEBES IN THE CHRISTIAN ERA

The period from A.D. 300 to the modern age has left very thick deposits, especially on the Kadmeia, which was the primary site of habitation. It is very difficult to differentiate the individual periods of Christian Thebes because there are no detailed studies of the pottery; the tombs are normally without offerings, and the architecture does not show a distinctive development. It is also fair to say that most archaeologists have paid little heed to these remains, and the amount of collected material is miniscule in proportion to the thickness of the deposits. The reason for this neglect is not difficult to explain: the overwhelming majority of Christian remains consist of habitation debris and burials; with the exception of an occasional church, there are few public buildings, and of those, very little has survived of the original mosaic and fresco decoration. Some historical information about the city can be found in the work of Miller (1921), Schober (1934), and Delvenakiotis (1970), but there has never been a careful study of the history of Christian Thebes, despite the city's importance.

HISTORICAL SUMMARY

Thebes was one of the few cities to regain quickly its vitality in the fourth century. The bishop Julius represented Thebes in the synod of 343 in Sardika (Kominis 1968). A serious earthquake damaged the city in 375, but it was apparently in good enough condition to withstand the invasion of the Goths under Alarich in 395. It must have been relatively prosperous in the fifth century and may even have been a center for the manufacture of Early Christian mosaics (Sodini 1970). After the attack by the Huns and Slavs in 539, Justinian fortified Thebes once more, and introduced the silk industry (Miller 1921:33). The invasions of the late sixth and seventh centuries must have caused significant curtailment of the city's activities, but in 716 it was made the capital of the province (or thema) of Central Greece and Euboia. Its importance increased after the middle of the ninth century (Chatzidakis 1936). The church of Gregorios Theologos (site 11, see fig. 4.1) was built in 872-877.

The prosperity of Thebes continued to increase gradually, and by the eleventh century its silk industry had achieved international renown (Bréhier 1950). In 1081, the Venetians acquired the right to trade with a few Greek cities, and Thebes was one of them. In 1147 the Normans invaded Greece, conquered Thebes, and deported to Palermo the best of the silk workers and weavers, most of whom were Jews. Even after this setback, Thebes must have recovered quickly: the second half of the twelfth century was a period of great prosperity; Ioannis Kaloktenis, bishop of Thebes at this time, is the best-remembered figure of the city's more recent history (Delvenakiotis 1970; Schlumberger 1889:249). In 1160, the Jewish traveler, Benjamin of Tudela, found a population of 2,000 Jews in Thebes; among them were the most important manufacturers of silk and of purple cloth (purple dye was rare and precious), which were exported to places throughout the Mediterranean region. Among the Jews of Thebes were some highly esteemed Talmudic scholars, and also poets. There is still a neighborhood in Thebes (northwest of the Kadmeia) called *Hebraika* (Jewish neighborhood), and another (in the southeast part of the Kadmeia) called *Armenia* (Armenian neighborhood); both names may preserve the memory of ethnic neighborhoods of the Byzantine period. There is a location north of Thebes called *Morokampos* ("plain of the mulberry tree"); we know that the mulberry tree is basic to the needs of the silk industry. The modern village of Vagia, west of Thebes (fig. 1.1) used to be called *Morokampos*.

Genoese merchants were known in Thebes as early as 1169 (Gregorovius 1889). The wealth of Thebes attracted many foreigners. In fact, after the conquest of Greece in 1204, the city remained in the hands of western princes and adventurers until it was annexed to the Turkish empire in 1460. During the Frankish period, Thebes experienced many social and political changes. It continued to prosper under the Burgundian princes in the thirteenth century. Most prominent of these was Nicholas II de St. Omer, who came to Thebes in 1287, rebuilt its walls, and constructed a luxurious palace using the vast fortune of his wife, Princess Maria of Antioch. The only remaining monument of the period in Thebes today, the Frankish tower (site 52), is his work, and other archaeological remains attest to his reign.

The Catalans became masters of Boiotia after their victory in the battle of Kopais (1311). Thebes fell to them without a struggle. At about that time, the city was seriously damaged by an earthquake. The threat of Turkish aggression forced the Latins of Greece to call a meeting for unity in Thebes in 1373. In 1394, Thebes was one of a few cities to be controlled by the Florentine family of Acciajuoli, which remained there until the Turkish conquest. The most prominent member of the family was Antonio, who ruled Thebes from 1394 until 1435. This was the last period of prosperity; under the Turks (1456-1829), the importance of Thebes diminished: Chalkis became the capital of the province (the Negroponte sanjak), and Levadeia and Athens, as well as Thebes, were principal cities (Miller 1921:356). In Boiotia, Levadeia gradually superseded Thebes in importance.

Table 4.1. Census figures for Thebes

| Year | Population | |
	GSS*	Philippson (1951)
1889	—	5203
1897	3,496	—
1920	4,085	—
1928	7,113	10,862
1940	12,171	—
1951	12,582	—
1961	15,779	—

*Note: Greek Statistical Service.

A number of foreigners visited Thebes during the period of Turkish occupation: Spon (1678) and Wheler (1723) reported the presence of "ancient" fortifications; Giovanni Battista de Burgo described Thebes in 1687 as being "quite in ruins" (Paton 1951). He probably was witness to the damage caused by an extensive fire during the war between Venice and Turkey of 1684-1691.

In the War of Independence, Thebes revolted against the Turks and was liberated by Athanasios Diakos in 1821. In the following year, however, it was attacked and burned by the Turks. In 1826, the Turks made Thebes a military base, but the city was liberated in 1829, together with the other cities of central Greece.

During the modern era, Thebes has been the capital of eastern Boiotia, while Levadeia has been the capital of the entire province. The city has repeatedly suffered extensive damage from earthquakes; most serious were those of 1853, 1893, and 1914 (Skouphos 1894; Mitsopoulos 1894, Keramopoullos 1917:65; Philippson 1951:509). As far as I know, there is no structure in the city, except for the Frankish tower (site 52) that predates the year 1853. One church, Agia Anna (site 214), was probably destroyed in 1853; it was never rebuilt and is by now almost completely forgotten.

The population of Thebes has increased rather slowly over the last hundred years. According to figures provided by the Greek Statistical Service, the population rose from 3,496 in 1897 to 15,779 in 1961 (see table 4.1). The figures are lower than those provided by Philippson (1951), whose calculations are rather high because he added the population of the two suburbs, Pyri and Agioi Theodoroi, twice (Philippson 1951:510). The population of Thebes rose sharply after 1922 when great numbers of refugees from Asia Minor were settled in the Neos Synoikismos. In the nineteenth century, it was probably about 3,000; Leake (1835:222) estimated 700 families in 1805, 250 of which were Turkish. The city must have been depopulated during the War of Independence when it was used as a Turkish military garrison.

The census of 1961 showed that agriculture was of primary importance in the province of Thebes, 42.08 percent of which was cultivated. The relationship of the cultivated area to the size of the population was found to be the sixth highest of 146 provinces in Greece (Kayser and Thompson 1964). Emigration from Boiotia was only 1.98 percent in 1962, indicating strong ties to the land. The main products of the province of Thebes were wheat (32%), barley (6.97%), fodder crops (14.48%), cotton (10.90%), beans (4%), and wine grapes (4.86%). A count of livestock showed a predominance of sheep and goats, followed by hogs, beef, mules, and horses. The province ranked very high in the use of mechanized equipment, the use of irrigation, and consumption of fertilizer. Since the census of 1961, the economic conditions have changed dramatically: industrialization has arrived from Athens, via the new highway, into the plain of Thebes. Many of the former agricultural workers are now employed in factories, and the demand for workers has swelled the population of Thebes to over 20,000 for the first time since the Classical period.

THE ARCHAEOLOGICAL REMAINS OF CHRISTIAN THEBES

On the basis of the historical events I have just summarized, the period from A.D. 300 to the modern era may be divided as follows: Early Christian (300 to 800), Byzantine (800 to 1200), Frankish (1200 to 1456), Turkish (1456 to 1829), and Modern (1829 to the present). Beginning in Early Christian times, building materials from ancient structures have been reused, resulting in the almost complete destruction of ancient remains. In spite of this, evidence of new construction methods, which have been gradually introduced throughout the intervening period, can be used in conjunction with other finds for purposes of dating. During the Byzantine period, brick and stone set in mortar were quite common; during the Frankish period, foundations of lime and rubble concrete were most typical, while in the Turkish period and the nineteenth century, foundations, though made of stone, were usually shallow and flimsy.

Burial practices also changed during the period: At the beginning of the Early Christian period, catacombs were used together with pit graves, and bones from reused chamber tombs were gathered in ossuaria. Later in this period, tile-covered tombs were introduced and continued to be used for the poor into the Byzantine period. In the Byzantine period, there were, in addition to tile-covered graves, more pit graves, most of them covered with slabs, and we find burials in churchyards at least as early as the ninth century (Keramopoullos 1926:134-135). Most of the objects found in the tombs were of a personal character (fibulae, rings, earrings, etc.) and this type of object became more common in the Byzantine period. Pottery was also offered, especially in the Byzantine period—a nice jug or a lamp might be found inside a tomb, and a greater number of pots, usually coarse wares, outside it.

THEBES IN THE EARLY CHRISTIAN PERIOD
ca. A.D. 300 TO 800

figs.
4.1,
4.2
Remains of houses have been recognized at very few sites, most of them on the Kadmeia. A flimsy wall at site 4 may be dated on the basis of stratigraphy to the fourth to sixth centuries. At sites 17 and 22, there were walls made of reused ancient masonry. The remains found at site 109 could date to this period. The only certain trace of habitation outside the Kadmeia was found at site 143, where a mosaic floor was discovered at the lowest of four levels; the type of building to which it belonged was not clear.

Remains of churches and public buildings are also infrequent. Most important are the remains of a basilica found at sites 18 and 40 (see Catalogue); the mosaics found here date to the fifth century and are of such high quality that one surmises that Thebes may have been a center for mosaicists (Sodini 1970). Mosaics were also found at site 88 where a large structure may have stood. Early Christian churches may have existed at the chapel of Agia Aikaterini (site 218), and at the chapel of Agios Georgios (site 221), according to Keramopoullos (1917:207). It is also possible that there may have been a church underneath the Byzantine remains found in the adjoining site 270 and sites 32 and 266 (Map B); mosaics were reportedly found during construction of the modern city hall (site 270). There are no known remains of churches outside the Kadmeia, unless the mosaics of site 143 belonged to such a structure.

Tombs of the period have been found both inside and outside the Kadmeia. The large basilica of site 18 must have been destroyed at some time during this period, because directly above its remains was a cemetery. It is conceivable that the basilica was destroyed in the great earthquake of A.D. 551 (Keramopoullos 1917:309). A similar cemetery was found at site 4, above the remains of Early Christian houses and below those of the Byzantine period. The tombs at each cemetery were of the tile-covered type and devoid of offerings. Tombs are reported to have been found below churches (cf. sites 216, 218, 221, 270), and though their dates are not known, the Early Christian period is likely because in later times the Kadmeia was heavily populated and would not have been used as a burial ground.

Tombs outside the Kadmeia are numerous. At Kastellia (site 25), Keramopoullos excavated a large catacomb, at least part of which had been decorated with frescoes. The largest cemetery was established at the sanctuary of Apollo Ismenios, and many tombs were excavated there by Keramopoullos (1926). This cemetery provides our best evidence of burial practices in Christian Thebes (see also Catalogue, site 8). It has been in continuous use until the present and has been the main cemetery of Thebes for many centuries. It is enclosed by a wall and extends around the church of Agios Loukas (the Evangelist), who, according to local tradition, is buried in the church. There is no evidence to support this claim, but it serves to remind us of the antiquity and importance of the cemetery (see Catalogue, site 54). Isolated tombs have been found in the area between the Kastellia and Ismenion hills, most of them dating to the succeeding period, but one catacomb (see Catalogue, site 31) dates to the Early Christian period. Underground cuts in the bedrock on the hill of Kolonaki may have belonged to catacombs (see Catalogue, sites 60 and 136). There may have been yet another catacomb underneath the church of Agioi Theodoroi (site 220). Tombs have also been found at several other locations, but their date is uncertain and I will consider them below.

In the Museum of Thebes there are numerous Early Christian stone and marble carvings, most of them of unknown provenance. They originally belonged to interior architectural decorations of churches. Some of them were studied by Orlandos (1939A). Numerous coins of the period were found at site 22.

THEBES IN THE BYZANTINE AND FRANKISH PERIODS
ca. A.D. 800 to 1460

FORTIFICATIONS

We can be certain of the existence of three towers: one of them still stands (site 52), the only old structure that has survived; remains of a second tower were discovered at site 19, and a third is known to have existed until 1904 at site 46. The towers are at strategic locations: site 52 overlooks the plain of Thebes and corresponds to the proposed location of the Borraiai gates; site 19 controls the road to Athens, and site 46 the road to Chalkis; the last two sites correspond to the locations of the Hypsistai and Proitides gates (cf. fig. 2.7). Other remains of fortifications are not known, except for, perhaps, the wall at site 47 (see Catalogue). It is also possible that parts of walls, visible in the nineteenth century and thought to be Classical because of their isodomic construction, may have been Byzantine/Frankish built with classical masonry, as were the towers themselves. The fortifications probably followed the general shape of the present-day Kadmeia, except for the southwest area where no remains have been found of any period. The Kadmeia was densely populated, as shown in figure 4.1.

figs. 4.1, 4.2

THE PALACE OF THEBES

The most impressive structures in Thebes in the Christian era were undoubtedly churches. During the Frankish period, however, a palace was constructed by Nicholas II de St. Omer; it was supposed to have been very large, "the finest baronial mansion in all of the realm of Romania" (Miller 1921:76). The large structure discovered at sites 1 and 2 measures at least 29 m in length and continues further to the west, where it has not been excavated. It was demolished down to its deepest foundations, but what is left shows

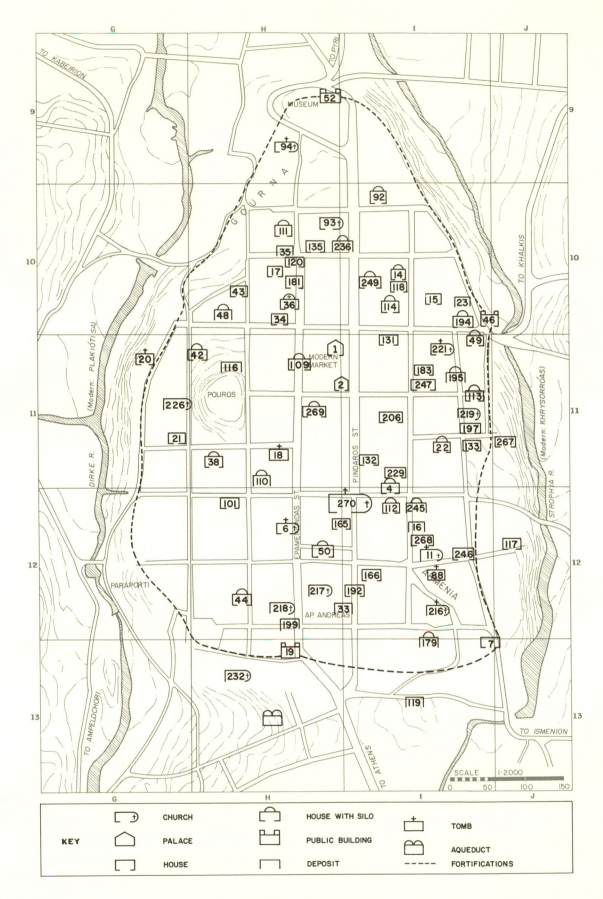

Fig. 4.1. The Kadmeia in the Byzantine and Frankish periods, ca. A.D. 800-1460

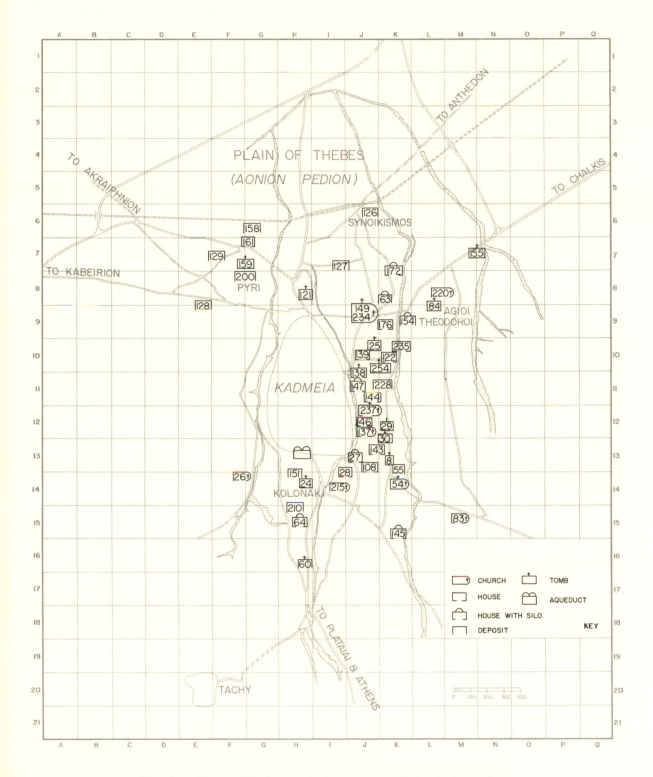

Fig. 4.2. Greater Thebes in the Byzantine and Frankish periods

massive construction of concrete, reaching the bedrock. These foundations are very thick and give little or no evidence of the plan of the building (cat. fig. 2.2), but I believe that these must be the foundations of St. Omer's palace (see Catalogue, site 2, for a full discussion).

The Churches of Thebes

It is surprising that none of the churches have survived to the present day, but remains of them have been excavated or found accidentally. Most modern churches have been built at the sites of older ones, sometimes even at the sites of ancient sanctuaries (see table 4.2). On the Kadmeia one can more easily see evidence of the continuous use of religious sites from antiquity to the present because there has been continuous habitation. This is not the case in Greater Thebes where habitation was interrupted in Early Christian times. Churches of the Early Christian period seem to have been continually rebuilt except for the basilica at sites 18/40 (see Catalogue). Of the 30 churches in modern Thebes, at least twelve and perhaps as many as sixteen can be shown to have been used continuously since the Byzantine period. Another four churches recently excavated seem not to have been superseded by modern ones: one was on the Kadmeia (site 6), and three were in Greater Thebes (sites 137, 75/237, and 234). These twenty churches are listed in table 4.2 together with their probably Byzantine names and the ancient sanctuaries that may have preceded them in the same location.

CHURCHES ON THE KADMEIA

Panagia Theotokos, or Katholikon. At the junction of Pindar and Oidipous streets, there is a cluster of sites containing well-built structures, some of which are of religious character; this strongly suggests that the celebrated cathedral, built in the twelfth century by the bishop Ioannis Kaloktenis stood here. A modern church at the northwest corner of the junction (site 97) has been named in honor of the bishop, while to the south, sites 32, 270, 115, 266, and 230, and perhaps even 165, seem to have been part of the cathedral and its administrative structures. (Of these sites, only 270 is shown on fig. 4.1; see also Map B.) The sanctuary of Demeter Thesmophoros probably occupied the area in antiquity, the sanctuary having been built on the ruins of the second Mycenaean palace of Thebes. The cathedral probably extended beyond the area outlined in figure 4.1, and it is very likely that the buildings and numerous silos found at sites 112, 245, and 4 once belonged to it (see individual site listings in the Catalogue for details, especially site 270).

Agios Gregorios (site 11, pl. 44). This single-nave basilica was built in 872 by Vasileios, the Byzantine emperor's local administrator. Soteriou (1924) excavated it. There are

Table 4.2. Sites where Byzantine churches are known or are likely to have existed.

Site	Modern Church	Byzantine Name	Ancient Name
KADMEIA			
232?	Soter	same?	——
218	Agia Aikaterini	?	Athena Onka
217	Apostolos Andreas	same?	Zeus Hypsistos
216	Panagia	same?	Birthplace of Herakles
6	——	?	——
11	Agios Vasileios	Agios Gregorios	Apollo Spodios
270 & 97	Agios Ioannis	Panagia	Demeter Thesmophoros
219	Agios Stephanos	same?	Tyche
226?	Agios Demetrios	?	——
221	Agios Georgios	same?	Zeus Homoloios
93	Agios Georgios	same?	Ammon Zeus
94	Agia Eleousa	?	Poseidon
GREATER THEBES			
215	Agios Nikolaos	same?	Amphiaraos
54	Agios Loukas	same?	Apollo Ismenios
83	Agia Photini	same?	——
137	——	?	——
75 & 237	——	?	——
234	——	?	——
220?	Agioi Theodoroi	same?	——
26?	Agia Trias	?	Mother Dindymene

Note: Many of the churches can be shown to have occupied the sites of ancient sanctuaries, although their original names are rarely documented.

burials associated with the church, one inside (Vasileios?) and at least five outside (priests of the church?). The burials found at site 88, to the south, may also be related. We know that the building was in continuous use because Turkish funerary stones were found during the excavations, and Soteriou (1924:9) has suggested that it may have been used as a mosque.

Agios Stephanos (site 219, pl. 7). The present-day chapel bears no sign that it supplanted an earlier structure, but substantial remains found to the north and south (sites 113, 197, 133, 267) may have been part of a Byzantine complex that included a church. Numerous silos have also been found in the vicinity (sites 113, 22, 195) and some of them may have been part of this complex.

Agios Georgios (site 221, pls. 7, 45). The previous existence of a Byzantine church has been documented by Keramopoullos' excavations in the courtyard of the present chapel.

The exact date of the remains is not certain, and the existence of Early Christian tombs may be taken as an indication that the church was even earlier.

Agios Georgios (site 93, pl. 5). The present church occupies a prominent location. Excavations at sites 135 and 236 to the south proved that at one time there were large Byzantine structures with kitchen and storage facilities, substantiating the local tradition that there was once a monastery here.

Agia Eleousa (site 94). Remains of a large structure with frescoes were found east of the present chapel (see Catalogue, site 130). Several Byzantine marble carvings were transferred to the Museum of Thebes from a wall just north of the chapel. These finds, and the presence of tombs and an ossuary strongly suggest that an earlier church occupied this site.

Agios Demetrios (site 226, pl. 46). The small chapel was preceded by another church as evidenced by the marble carvings inside and outside the chapel, and the old icons. There may have been a Byzantine church here (see Catalogue, site 226).

Anonymous Chapel (site 6). A nicely built chapel lasted from the tenth to the sixteenth centuries, judging from the excavated remains. There were numerous burials both inside and outside the chapel. No inscriptional evidence emerged to provide the name of the chapel.

Agia Aikaterini (site 218, pl. 34). The fact that this modern chapel is located near the tower of site 19 and near the highest point of the Kadmeia (site 217) almost invites us to infer that there must have been an earlier church here. No remains of such a church have survived, but cuts in the bedrock (catacombs?) have been noted.

Agios Andreas (site 217; pls. 8-10). The modern church is built at the highest point of the Kadmeia. There are a few ashlar blocks in the courtyard suggestive of the previous presence of a Byzantine church. Because of the prominent location, I have also suggested (chap. 3) that the sanctuary of Zeus Hypsistos was here in antiquity.

Metamorphosis Soteros (site 232, pl. 9). There may have been a Byzantine church at this site, or perhaps further north where there are two more modern churches (see Map B, sites 212, 213). Local tradition has it that a monastery once stood here that housed an icon made by the Evangelist Luke; that icon is now kept at the church of Agios Demetrios (site 212). It is covered with silver, leaving exposed only the faces of Mary and Christ (Vasileiou 1972, fig. on p. 9).

Panagia (site 216, pls. 7, 8, 10, 43). The present cathedral of Thebes is built above a cemetery that may be Early Christian (Keramopoullos 1917:64-65). This, along with other evidence (see Catalogue, site 216), leads one to suspect that there was an earlier church, possibly built in an open area just inside the Elektrai gates (site 7).

CHURCHES IN GREATER THEBES

In Greater Thebes, excavation has confirmed the presence of four churches; there is evidence allowing us confidently to infer the presence of four others.

Agia Photeini (site 83, pls. 49, 50). Orlandos (1939A, 1939B) excavated and restored a late tenth-century church. Architectural material may have been taken from the nearby southeast corner of the Classical fortifications (site 258, fig. 3.6). Water was also available here (site 153), perhaps carried by a secondary conduit of the Classical aqueduct.

Anonymous Chapel (site 137). The apsidal section of a small chapel was found here. It was probably associated with a cemetery (see Catalogue, sites 29, 30).

Anonymous Chapel (site 75/237). Another small chapel, just north of the one at site 137, it was also associated with a cemetery (site 237); a small duct or conduit found at site 76 (see Catalogue) may be related to it.

Anonymous Chapel (site 234). The remains of a well-built church were excavated just north of the Kastellia hills. Some frescoes were preserved, and there were numerous burials within. The burials found at neighboring site 149 may be related to it. The church dates between the twelfth and fifteenth centuries.

Agios Loukas (site 54). We can be fairly certain that there was an earlier church at this site, not only because of a few finds and references to it (see Catalogue, site 54), but also because this general area has been used for burial since Early Christian times (site 8).

Agios Nikolaos (site 215, pls. 8, 48). The present church occupies the site that I suspect to have been the oracle/sanctuary of Amphiaraos and Alkmaion (see chap. 3). There are Byzantine marble carvings inside the church, and architectural stones both inside and outside. A Byzantine church may well have preceded the current one.

Agioi Theodoroi (site 220, pls. 4, 51). It is possible that a Byzantine church was built over an Early Christian catacomb, the memory of which is preserved in local tradition (Vasileiou 1972:80).

Agia Trias (site 26). The "ancient foundations" on which the present church rests (Frazer 1898:48-49) lead us to suspect that there was once a Byzantine church here. This is the likely location of an ancient sanctuary (Mother Dindymene, see chap. 3).

PUBLIC WORKS

Few remains can be categorized as those of public works, as it is clear that most of the public finances were spent on fortifications and religious establishments. A stone-paved street was discovered at site 130, and it is possible that bridges such as those at sites 46, 240, 241, and 256, or fountains like that of site 53, which are of fairly recent construction, had Byzantine forerunners (see Catalogue). Well documented is the construction of an aqueduct by bishop Ioannis Kaloktenis: it consisted of twenty arches that linked the Kadmeia with the Kolonaki hills, whence the water came (Delvenakiotis 1970:73). This aqueduct was in use until the late nineteenth century and was seen by Frazer (1898:32); when an underground conduit was constructed, the arches were demolished to the dismay of the local antiquary, Epaminondas Papavasileiou (Keramopoullos 1917:123, n. 2). These arches entered the Kadmeia somewhere in the vicinity of the gate tower (site 19).

HOUSES

Remains of habitation dating to the Byzantine/Frankish period are very numerous on the Kadmeia (fig. 4.1). At sites where stratigraphy has not been disturbed by modern construction, Byzantine/Frankish deposits are two to three meters deep, and have usually penetrated into prehistoric levels. The deepest intrusions into earlier levels were made by the numerous silos, which can be as deep as five to seven meters. These are usually pear-shaped, with the narrow opening at the top; depending on the terrain, they can be partially cut in the rock, or dug in the earth and lined with stone or with plaster.

Most houses were of modest size, built on stone or concrete foundations, the upper structure having been mud-brick. Roof tiles did exist (cf. Catalogue, site 44). Some of the largest properties have been found near religious centers, such as the Cathedral, the church of Agios Georgios (site 93), and the church of Agios Stephanos. Other large properties did exist, however, in no apparent association with churches (table 4.3). Mosaic floors have appeared only in religious properties. Drains made of clay pipe were more common than indicated in table 4.3, but were not always acknowledged in excavation reports. Wells and cisterns were unusual because there was easy access to water in many parts of Thebes.

We know very little about interior furnishings, largely owing to the speed with which modern construction equipment has gone through the Byzantine levels. Pottery, glazed and household type, was very common and has been found in large quantity at several sites, most of which were not related to churches. Bronze objects have been commonly

Table 4.3. Important archaeological remains in Byzantine/Frankish Thebes

	Residential	*Religious*
Large properties	17,21,22,50,192,249 139	4,112,133,135,236,245,267
Multiple layers of occupation	34,92,111,131	
Mosaics		94,135,266,270
Drainage	116	112
Well	111 147	
Cistern		135
Rich pottery deposits	2,14,111,131,179,194 122,139,144	113,130
Coins	128 (Greater Thebes)	
Bronzes	21,111	

Note: The second line of site numbers in any group refers to Greater Thebes.

found, usually vessels, utensils, tools, and a few weapons. A large hoard of bronze objects was found inside a large pithos at site 21. Coins were also common; most interesting was the hoard of 620 coins from site 128 in Greater Thebes.

Habitation in Greater Thebes was limited largely to the area east of the Kadmeia, where a large number of houses were interspersed between burial sites. Most of these remains were found along the east side of the Kadmeia, between the Strophia and Ismenos rivers. It seems that with the exception of isolated remains to the north and south (farmsteads?) the medieval Thebans did not venture to build their homes far from the fortified Kadmeia, even at the height of Byzantine civilization. One of the finest and best-preserved houses was found on the Kastellia hills (site 139): there were at least ten rooms around a central courtyard; this was probably a one-storey house built on the ancient road to Chalkis, which was apparently still traveled. North of the Kadmeia, there were several deposits and one house (site 161), indicating minimal use of the area. To the south, there were a few deposits on the Kolonaki hill, and an isolated house south of the church of Agios Loukas (site 145).

CEMETERIES

Burials continued on the Kadmeia even after Early Christian times, though in all datable instances they were associated with a church. There were no cemeteries independent of a church on the Kadmeia during the Byzantine period. Many of the tombs were of the tile-covered type that was most common in Early Christian and early Byzantine times (fourth to tenth centuries; sites 18, 20, 36, 94), but there were also some more luxurious tombs that date to the Byzantine period (sites 6, 11). Two ossuaries have been found (see Catalogue, sites 36, 130), probably dating to the early Byzantine period.

The main cemeteries were located east of the Kadmeia. The Early Christian cemetery at the Kastellia hills ceased to be used some time during the early Byzantine period and became available for habitation; the fourteen pit graves found recently (site 25) probably date to the ninth to tenth centuries. The same is also true of the Early Christian cemetery in the suburb of Astegoi: remains of two chapels (site 75/237, 137) were surrounded by tombs, but the remains of Byzantine houses in this area indicate the end of its use as a cemetery. The Early Christian cemetery at sites 8 and 54 became the main burial site of Thebes and has continued as such to the present day.

There are other, smaller cemeteries in Greater Thebes: at Kolonaki some Mycenaean chamber tombs were reused (site 24), and there are other tombs perhaps as far south as site 60; to the north there are a few burials at site 121 (Amphion hill), at Pyri (site 159), a few isolated ones at the church of Agioi Theodoroi (sites 84 and 155), and at the newly excavated church (sites 234, 149). Some of these burials may be Early Christian.

THEBES IN THE TURKISH PERIOD

There has been minimal interest in the period of Turkish occupation; in any case, very little of it remains, owing to the poor quality of construction and the destruction caused by more recent building. Debris from this period is commonly found in excavations and is recognizable through the poor quality of its pottery, which rarely includes glazed examples, and through the numerous clay tobacco pipes. Habitation remains have been recognized at several sites, but excavators have mentioned only a few, such as sites 4, 7, 194, and 269, where, in addition to the architectural debris, objects have been found and saved. Some of the houses had silos at this time, but they are usually smaller than those of the previous period.

Many of the old churches continued to be used, such as the cathedral of Thebes, which was seen by foreign travelers (see Catalogue, site 270). Other churches were destroyed and never restored (sites 6, 234). We suspect that there were two mosques: the church of Agios Gregorios on the Kadmeia (site 11) may have been modified to serve as a small mosque, and in Greater Thebes there was a second mosque at the location called Tekes (site 255, Map A).

Some public monuments were probably constructed in this period: the fountain at the spring of Paraporti (site 53, Map B and pls. 9, 24-26) is quite charming, but no longer used. Near the spring of Agianni there are two arched footbridges (sites 240, 241, Map A and pls. 27-28). Agios Loukas (site 54) continued to be the main cemetery of Thebes, but it is possible that the cemetery of Agia Paraskevi (site 224, Map A), now abandoned, was established during the Turkish period. There are a few Turkish inscriptions in the Museum of Thebes, but these have not been studied.

MODERN THEBES

I do not intend to completely describe the modern city, but simply to summarize its development. The Kadmeia has continued to be the main habitation area, which completely occupies the land bordered by the Plakiotissa River (ancient Dirke) to the west, and the Chrysorroas (ancient Strophia) to the east. Smaller settlements were developed outside the Kadmeia in the nineteenth century, primarily at Pyri to the northwest, and Agioi Theodoroi to the northeast. The refugees from Asia Minor were settled between these two, in the suburbs now called Palaios Synoikismos and Neos Synoikismos. Settlements east and south of the Kadmeia are more recent; most of the houses have been built since World War II. West of the Kadmeia there are fewer houses; most of them were built as Pyri expanded southward toward the Kadmeia. I believe that the suburbs of Pyri and Agioi Theodoroi were settled because there was easy access to plentiful water. These suburbs lie directly on the line of the ancient aqueduct system (see fig. 3.6). With the exception of the Oidipodia spring (site 244), which may be natural, all other "springs" in the area take their water from the ancient aqueduct, which has provided Thebes with an unfailing supply of clean water since it was built.

Today, Thebes and the countryside around it appear rather barren, although trees have been planted in the last fifty years. In the nineteenth century the countryside was almost completely barren (Soteriades 1914, figs. 10-13). When Frazer (1898:32) refers to the city of Thebes as green, he clearly means not the suburbs, but only the Kadmeia, with the rich, verdant plain of Thebes in the background. In contrast to the verdure of Greater Thebes in antiquity, the modern landscape shows the effects of prolonged abuse of the land, partly the result of poor management, and partly the result of numerous wars.

Modern Thebes has thirty churches or chapels, two of which were built very recently, the chapel at the High School of Thebes (site 130) and the one at the new cemetery west of Pyri. Two others (sites 210 and 251) belong to the sect of the Old Calendrites. All those that may have had Byzantine or ancient predecessors I have already discussed (see table 4.2). Other churches that seem to have originated in the modern era and not to have superseded Byzantine churches are Agios Demetrios (site 212, pl. 42), Agioi Apostoli (site 222), Agios Athanasios in Pyri (site 96), and Agios Konstantinos in Palaios Synoikismos (site 223). There are also several chapels that have not yet been mentioned: Agios Charalambos (site 213, pl. 47), and Agios Nikolaos (site 225) on the Kadmeia; Evangelistria (site 253), Agia Paraskevi (site 224, pl. 52), and Agios Menas (site 231, pl. 53) in Greater Thebes.

Like many other Greek cities, Thebes has been modernized; apartment houses and factories are very much in evidence. Walking through the city, however, one can still see some of the ancient remains described in this volume, as well as buildings of the more recent past. There are still some nineteenth-century houses (pls. 29, 30, 35); one city block has remained as it was earlier in this century (pl. 29), and there are still some neoclassical two-storey houses, built in the 1920s and 1930s (pls. 33-34, 36-38).

Outside the Kadmeia one can find the Paraporti spring (pls. 24-26, site 53), the Oidipodia spring (site 244) with a water wheel in the background (pl. 39), and two old bridges by the Ismenos River (sites 240-241, pls. 27-28). On the first Monday of Lent, the city celebrates the Vlachikos Gamos ("wedding of the Vlachs," pl. 41), a festival that may well have pagan origins.

5
THE DESCRIPTION OF THEBES
BY PAUSANIAS

When Pausanias visited Thebes in the second century A.D., he was shown the most important religious, civic, and cultural monuments. What most interested him and his readers was not the precise topographical location of each monument, but its appearance, its history, and the mythology relating to it. Anyone who wished to see the monuments had only to visit Thebes and walk about. Pausanias had every expectation that these monuments would be preserved for all to see; in this, he was sadly mistaken. He acquired information about Thebes and her history from local guides and systematically described every section of the city. No major monument was omitted unless it was, by his time, no longer in use. In his work on the topography of Athens, Judeich (1931:13-15) also found that the description by Pausanias was orderly and that it could be divided into ten coherent sections, each dealing with a specific locality.

Pausanias' guidebook was the first of its kind and deserves our respect and admiration. The little archaeological evidence we have both confirms the accuracy of his description and attests to the remarkable continuity of tradition in Thebes. It is, therefore, well worth the effort to attempt to reconstruct the topography of Thebes on the basis of his account.

Because Pausanias' topographical indications are usually general and indirect, we must locate many of the sites he mentions by using his contextual clues and by noting the proximity of the sites to major monuments. In all, he identifies eighteen sanctuaries or cult places (if we include the sites associated with Amphiaraos, Aphrodite, and Herakles Rhinokoloustes, which he does not specify as sanctuaries); twenty mythohistorical sites, some of which may have been cult places without either temple or peribolos (the house of Amphitryon, or the Altar of Apollo Spodios, for example); fourteen tombs, some of which may have been cult sites (like the tomb of Zethos and Amphion, or the tomb of the children of Oidipous). If we count each of the gates as a separate entity, we find that Pausanias mentions only fifteen public structures. Finally, he mentions thirty-three statues (most of which are associated with temples), one monument in the form of a lion, and the pedimental sculptures of the temple of Herakles.

Of these 102 sites and monuments, we can today identify with certainty only the locations of three of the gates and the temple of Apollo Ismenios. A few other monuments can be associated with specific locations. We also know the locations of the spring of Dirke and the Classical wall of Greater Thebes, although Pausanias makes no mention of them. This is such a poor record of preservation that it may be hard to imagine that so many more sites were visible in Pausanias' time. If, however, in reading his text, we examine the order in which he has arranged his description of the monuments, we see that it is quite possible to map most of them on a plan of the modern town, and his text acquires considerable clarity. My analysis of the text divides the monuments into twenty groups, maintaining the exact order in which they appear in the text. Each group is preceded by a major topographical indication provided by Pausanias, and this is the clue from which we can make inferences about the location of each monument in the group. For example, when he moves from the south edge of the Kadmeia to "the site where the market is" we know he has reached the center of town. If, within a group, Pausanias gives additional topographical information, it too is quoted. Pausanias' walking tour can be followed on the general map of Thebes (fig. 5.1), and on the map of the Kadmeia (fig. 5.2). I have included the relevant passages in the original (Loeb edition); rather than translating the text literally, I have given in English a condensed version that enumerates the sites and monuments.

PASSAGE 1 (9.8.1-2)

Διαβεβηκότι δὲ ἤδη τὸν Ἀσωπὸν καὶ τῆς πόλεως δέκα μάλιστα ἀφεστηκότι στα-δίους Ποτνιῶν ἐστιν ἐρείπια καὶ ἐν αὐτοῖς ἄλσος Δήμητρος καὶ Κόρης. Τὰ δὲ ἀγάλματα ἐπὶ τῷ ποταμῷ τῷ παρὰ τὰς Ποτνιὰς . . .
Ἐνταῦθα καὶ Διονύσου ναός ἐστιν Αἰγοβόλου.

"After crossing [the river] Asopos and at a distance of ten stadia from the city [of Thebes]" the ruins of Potniai and "in these ruins" the grove of Demeter and Kore. The statues [stand] by the river which flows past Potniai . . . "Here [at the grove] is also" the temple of Dionysos Aigobolos.

Pausanias approached Thebes, crossing the Asopos River, 5 km south of the city. Although he mentions the ruins of Potniai, it is conceivable that he didn't actually go there but saw the town from a distance on his way to Thebes. Potniai is located, as he says, ten stadia (1.8 km) from Thebes and is today's Tachy (Keramopoullos 1917:260-261), a small suburb of Thebes (pl. 4). Recent finds such as the leg of an Archaic statue (*Deltion* 1964B:201, pl. 204:B) and tombs of the fourth century B.C. (*Deltion* 1971B:233) near the modern village attest to an ancient presence there. The grove of Demeter and Kore should be sought, as Pausanias says, by the river, probably in the area in which the river and the crossroads meet, northeast of Tachy (pl. 11). Four roads meet at this junction; the road Pausanias traveled is that which comes from Plataiai. An alternate and longer road from Plataiai to Potniai and Thebes goes through the modern villages of Pyrgos, Melissochori, and Loutouphi (fig. 1.1). It is clear that Pausanias did not take this one,

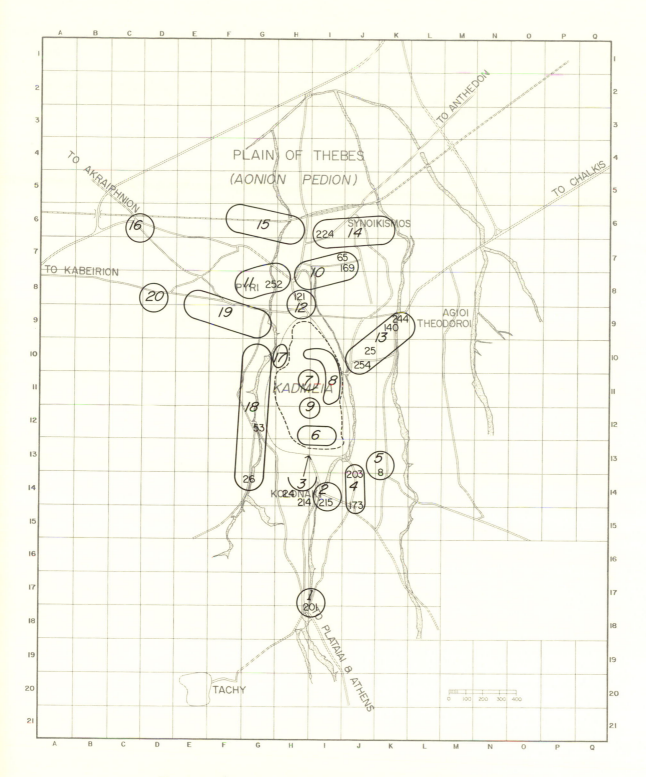

Fig. 5.1. The route of Pausanias in Greater Thebes

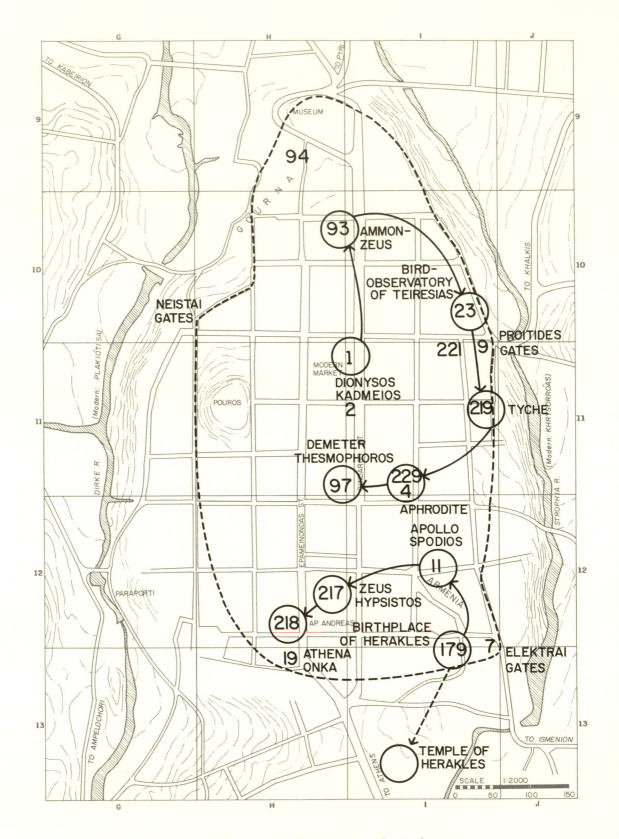

Fig. 5.2. The route of Pausanias on the Kadmeia

because he crossed the Asopos River 40 stadia (7.2 km) west of Skolos (probably modern Neochoraki; Pritchett 1965:107-109; Fossey 1971), which means he moved northeast rather than northwest from Plataiai. The other two roads that meet at the junction are the *Koile Hodos,* which runs through the Strophia valley to eastern Thebes (Keramopoullos 1917:261-262 calls it "road to Tachy B"), and the one that runs along the slopes of the Kolonaki hills to western Thebes ("road to Tachy A" in Keramopoullos).

This crossroads is significant in Theban mythohistory. According to Keramopoullos (1917:419-420), the crossroads where Oidipous killed his father, Laios, is this one. A passage attributed to Aischylos by the scholiast to Sophokles' *Oidipous Tyrannos* 733 refers to a road near Potniai named "Schiste" (a common name for roads in Greece). On Mt. Parnassos is another "Schiste," which goes to Delphi and which also leads to a crossroads; this has created confusion as to where the encounter between Laios and Oidipous took place. The importance of the crossroads near Potniai has been overshadowed, yet it seems that in antiquity, travelers frequently passed it on their way to Plataiai, Thespiai, Levadeia, and Delphi (see passage 18 below). Keramopoullos suspected that the sanctuary of Amphiaraos (one of the Seven against Thebes) was here, although his excavations in this area (fig. 5.1, site 201) were inconclusive. He himself admitted (1917:265) that the finds of terracotta pigs and seated female figurines (1917: figs. 182-183) rather indicated the worship of Demeter. Other finds of terracotta boys show that Demeter shared the site with Dionysos Aigobolos, to whom, according to Pausanias (9.8.2), the Thebans sacrificed a goat in substitution for a boy. Similar objects have recently been found on the property of S. Laliotis, which is in the vicinity (*Ephemeris* 1976, Parartema 12-17), giving support to the belief that both the sanctuary and the grove seen by Pausanias ought to be located near the crossroads.

From here, Pausanias moves south, probably taking what Keramopoullos calls the "road to Tachy A," which lies west of the modern road to Athens.

PASSAGE 2 (9.8.3)

Ἐκ δὲ τῶν Ποτνιῶν ἰοῦσιν ἐς Θήβας ἔστιν ἐν δεξιᾷ τῆς ὁδοῦ περίβολός τε οὐ μέγας καὶ κίονες ἐν αὐτῷ· διαστῆναι δὲ Ἀμφιαράῳ τὴν γῆν ταύτῃ νομίζουσιν . . .

"On the right side of the road from Potniai to Thebes" a not too big enclosure with columns in it; they believe the earth opened at this spot to receive Amphiaraos . . .

The ancient road passes the site of the church of Agia Anna of which no trace remains today (fig. 5.1, site 214). Directly east of Agia Anna, on the right side of the road, is a depression in which the church of Agios Nikolaos (site 215) now stands (pls. 8, 48). Keramopoullos (who has Pausanias moving on the "road to Tachy B") placed the sanc-

tuary of Herakles here (1917:267, 329-330), but I think it more likely that Pausanias'
Theban guides identified this depression as "the site where the earth opened" and Amphiaraos disappeared. It is "on the right side of the road" (to Tachy A), as he says. Had
Pausanias traveled south on the Koile Hodos as Keramopoullos believed, the depression
of Agios Nikolaos would have remained on his left, and the interpretation of the passage
would remain obscure. Pausanias does not describe anything else in this area at this time,
although, as we shall see, there were other monuments here that he prefers to discuss in
a different context (see passage 6). He pauses somewhere in the vicinity of Agios Nikolaos
(fig. 5.1, site 215) to admire the marvelous citadel of the Kadmeia with her celebrated
wall and seven gates.

PASSAGE 3 (9.8.4-7)

Θηβαίοις δὲ ἐν τῷ περιβόλῳ τοῦ ἀρ-
χαίου τείχους ἑπτὰ ἀριθμόν ἦσαν
πύλαι, μένουσι δὲ καὶ ἐς ἡμᾶς ἔτι.
Τεθῆναι δὲ τὰ ὀνόματα . . . ἀπό τε
Ἡλέκτρας ἀδελφῆς Κάδμου καὶ Προι-
τίσιν ἀπὸ ἀνδρὸς τῶν ἐπιχωρίων . . .
τὰς δὲ Νηίστας ὀνομασθῆναί φασιν ἐπὶ
τῷδε· ἐν ταῖς χορδαῖς νήτην καλοῦσιν
τὴν ἐσχάτην· ταύτην οὖν τὴν χορδὴν
Ἀμφίονα ἐπὶ ταῖς πύλαις ταύταις
ἀνευρεῖν. . . ἤκουσα καὶ ὡς Ζήθου . . .
τῷ παιδὶ ὄνομα Νῆις γένοιτο, ἀπὸ τούτου δὲ τοῦ Νήϊδος τὰς πύλας κληθῆναι
ταύτας. Πύλας δὲ Κρηναίας [. . .] πρὸς
δὲ ταῖς Ὑψίσταις Διὸς ἱερὸν ἐπίκλη-
σίν ἐστιν Ὑψίστου. Τὰς δὲ ἐπὶ ταύταις πύλας ὀνομάζουσιν Ὠγυγίας,
τελευταῖαι δέ εἰσιν Ὁμολωίδες· ἐ-
φαίνετο δὲ εἶναί μοι καὶ τὸ ὄνομα νεώ-
τατον ταῖς πύλαις ταύταις, αἱ δὲ
Ὠγύγιαι τὸ ἀρχαιότατον· τὰς δὲ Ὁμο-
λωίδας κληθῆναι . . . ἀπό Ὁμόλην,
ὀρῶν τῶν Θεσσαλικῶν . . .

"Along the perimeter of the ancient wall
of Thebes were seven gates which remain
to this day." The names of the gates
are: . . . *Elektrai*, named after Elektra, sister of Kadmos; *Proitides*, named after
Proitos, a native of Thebes; *Neistai*, named
after the harpstring called *nete* (Amphion
invented the string at this gate), or after
Neis, the son of Zethos; *Krenaiai* . . .
[Pausanias' explanation is missing from the
text, but the name referred to a spring];
Hypsistai, after the sanctuary of Zeus
Hypsistos which is nearby; *Ogygiai*, the
most ancient of the gate names [named for
Ogygos, the first mythological king of
Thebes]; *Homoloides*, the most recent gate
name . . . [Pausanias relates to it to Hom-
ole, a mountain in Thessaly where some
Thebans went after the war of the Epi-
gonoi.]

Rather than continue to describe sites and monuments outside the wall, Pausanias,
marveling at the citadel, chooses to discuss the walls and gates. In doing so from a vantage
point near the sanctuary of Amphiaraos, he created tremendous confusion for nineteenth-

century scholars, all of whom then placed the prehistoric walls and gates along a large perimeter around the Kadmeia (Leake 1835; Forchhammer 1854; Bursian 1862; Fabricius 1890; Frazer 1898). The Theban lawyer, Kalopais, tried in vain to convince the scholars that the wall of this large perimeter was Classical, as his own excavations proved (1892, 1893). But Soteriades (1914) continued to apply the names of the prehistoric gates to the Classical wall. Carl Robert was the only scholar who defended Pausanias' accuracy and placed the seven gates on the Kadmeia itself (1909:172-174). It was only when Keramopoullos published his extensive study on Thebes (1917) that the problem was solved. Even Wilamowitz, who had all along denied the actual existence of any of the gates (1891), was convinced by Keramopoullos' work and agreed with him about the presence of four gates on the Kadmeia (1922:24-31). Regardless of all this controversy, Pausanias' text itself is really not misleading: he specifies that the gates were on the *ancient* wall of Thebes (ancient, relative to his own time) and were seven in number. It is evident from the rest of his text that only three of the gates were actually used in his time; the others were either closed or only referred to as localities by the Thebans. He mentions the open gates in the order in which he used them: Elektrai, Proitides, and Neistai. There is little doubt about their location: Elektrai, opposite the Ismenion (fig. 5.2, site 7); Proitides by the road to Chalkis (fig. 5.2, site 9), and Neistai at the northwest side of the Kadmeia (fig. 5.2, site 104). These locations have been identified by Keramopoullos in an exhaustive discussion (1917:464-484). The problem of the remaining four gates has been discussed in connection with the archaeological evidence (see chap. 2).

Pausanias, not knowing he was to cause such a controversy (and outpouring of ink), now continues his walk in the direction of the Elektrai gates.

Passage 4 (9.10.1)

Πολυάνδριον δὲ οὐ μακρὰν ἀπὸ τῶν πυλῶν ἐστι· κεῖνται δὲ ὁπόσους κατέλαβεν ἀποθανεῖν Ἀλεξάνδρῳ καὶ Μακεδόσιν ἀντιτεταγμένους. Οὐ πόρρω δὲ ἀποφαίνουσι χωρίον ἔνθα Κάδμον λέγουσιν, . . . τοῦ δράκοντος, ὃν ἀπέκτεινε ἐπὶ τῇ κρήνῃ, τοὺς ὀδόντας σπείραντα . . .

"Not far from the [Elektrai] gates" the Polyandrion of the soldiers who fought against Alexander and the Macedonians. "Not far from it" the site where Kadmos . . . sowed the teeth of the dragon which he killed at the spring . . .

The Polyandrion was a memorial to the soldiers who died fighting Alexander the Great in 335 B.C. There is a detailed account of that battle by Arrian, who makes it plain that the fiercest fighting took place in the valley between the Herakleion and the Ismenion (*Anabasis* 1.8.1-5), south of the Kadmeia. In a very convincing analysis of Arrian's text,

Keramopoullos (1917:278-285) has shown that the Polyandrion must have been in the vicinity of the temple of Apollo (cf. fig. 5.1, and Catalogue, site 203). There is little doubt that Pausanias is now near the Kadmeia and southeast of it.

The place where Kadmos sowed the dragon's teeth from which sprang the Spartoi was not marked by a monument, at least, not in Pausanias' time, but it was probably a locality between the Polyandrion and the spring at which the dragon was slain. Pausanias does not name the spring here, but does discuss it in connection with his subsequent visit to the temple of Apollo. However, the famous spring has been identified as the spring of Ares by numerous other writers (Apollodoros 3.4.1-2: Apollonios Rhodios 3.1179-1180; Stephanos Byzantios; schol. *Iliad* 2.494; Pseudo-Plutarch, *De Fluviis* 1; Unger 1839: 103-120; Bursian 1862:226), and the location of that spring can be verified (see passage 5). Pausanias' text implies that the spring, the site of the Spartoi, and the Polyandrion were in close proximity to one another. It is plausible that he was shown the site associated with the Spartoi from the Polyandrion and then proceeded up the hill to the Ismenion.

PASSAGE 5 (9.10.2-3)

Ἔστι δὲ λόφος ἐν δεξιᾷ τῶν πυλῶν ἱερὸς Ἀπόλλωνος· καλεῖται δὲ ὅ τε λόφος καὶ ὁ θεὸς Ἰσμήνιος, παραρρέοντος τοῦ ποταμοῦ ταύτῃ τοῦ Ἰσμηνοῦ. Πρῶτα μὲν δὴ λίθου κατὰ τὴν ἔσοδόν ἔστιν Ἀθηνᾶ καὶ Ἑρμῆς, ὀνομαζόμενοι Πρόναοι· ποιῆσαι δὲ αὐτὸν Φειδίας, τὴν δὲ Ἀθηνᾶν λέγεται Σκόπας· μετὰ δὲ ὁ ναὸς ᾠκοδόμηται. Τὸ δὲ ἄγαλμα . . . Κανάχου ποίημα . . . Ἔστι δ' ἐνταῦθα λίθος ἐφ' ᾧ Μαντώ φασι τὴν Τειρεσίου καθέζεσθαι . . . Ἐν δεξιᾷ δὲ τοῦ ναοῦ λίθου πεποιημένας εἰκόνας Ἡνιόχης εἶναι, τὴν δὲ Πύρρας λέγουσι, . . . Τρίπους ἐστὶν Ἀμφιτρύωνος ἀνάθημα ἐπὶ Ἡρακλεῖ δαφνηφορήσαντι.
Ἀνωτέρω δὲ τοῦ Ἰσμηνίου τήν κρήνην ἴδοις ἄν, ἥντινα Ἄρεώς φασιν ἱερὰν εἶναι . . . Πρὸς ταύτῃ τῇ κρήνῃ τάφος ἐστὶ Καάνθου.

"To the right of the [Elektrai] gates is a hill sacred to Apollo Ismenios; the hill and the god are named after the river Ismenos that flows close by; at the entrance [to the sanctuary]" are the statues of Athena and Hermes both named Pronaoi; the statues were made by Skopas and Pheidias, respectively. "The temple is behind these statues" the [cult] statue . . . [of Apollo] is . . . by Kanachos; there is a stone called Manto's seat . . . and stone statues of Henioche and Pyrra; . . . a tripod dedicated by Amphitryon for Herakles. "Above the Ismenion" the spring of Ares . . . and the tomb of Kaanthos.

Inscriptional evidence has enabled us to identify the sanctuary of Apollo Ismenios with certainty. Keramopoullos excavated the remains of the temple of Apollo on the small hill 200 m southeast of the Elektrai gates (pls. 5, 18). The five statues seen and recorded by Pausanias indicate that the sanctuary was well preserved in his time, but the temple is in a poor state of preservation today (for details see Catalogue, site 8). The spring of Ares and the tomb of Kaanthos must have been in the same vicinity. Pausanias relates how Kaanthos was killed by Apollo when he tried to prevent the god from abducting Melia, his sister. He was buried by the spring of Ares which is, in Pausanias' account, clearly near the temple of Apollo (cf. Pindar, *Pyth.* 11.4-6). The story of Kaanthos and Melia was widely quoted in antiquity (Unger 1839:227-242). Keramopoullos (1917:320-321) suggested that the spring of Ares was also called the spring of Melia.

There is general confusion in ancient sources about the names and the locations of the springs of Thebes, and the spring of Ares in particular (for ancient references to the spring of Ares, see Unger 1839:103-120). That its location has remained uncertain is surprising because in the area of the temple of Apollo, there are only two springs to choose from. One is the source of the Ismenos River, the Agianni spring, which emerges about 1,200 m south of the temple. It is so far away that it could not possibly be the one in question (see the discussion of springs in chap. 1). The other is about 300 m southwest of the temple and is called *Pege* (which means "spring") to this day (Catalogue, site 173).

Keramopoullos discussed these two springs at length (1917:318-324), but decided not to attribute an ancient name to Pege, and suggested that Pausanias saw a third spring, east of the temple of Apollo, where there is running water by the mill of Koropoulis. There is no evidence, however, that a natural spring ever existed at this location, and the water we see comes from the aqueduct of the Classical period. Bursian marked Pege on his map (1862) and Pagidas was the only one to identify it as the spring of Ares (1882:13-17). Today, although this spring is almost forgotten, it is remarkable in that its waters emerge altogether unexpectedly in an area of bare bedrock; only an old tree grows near it. The first time I came upon it, I thought that a water main had broken and then realized that there was none in this area of Thebes. The water surfaces in a way that suggests the spring may have shifted from time to time. Somewhere in the vicinity, there may be an ancient structure associated with the water. Because of its proximity to the sanctuary of Apollo, and also because of the almost magical way in which the water appears, I believe that Pege was the spring Pausanias referred to in connection with Kadmos and the Spartoi (passage 4), and to which reference is made in this passage as the spring of Ares. Pausanias' clue that both references are to one and the same spring is the dragon: at 10.1, he told us that Kadmos killed it. Here, in 10.5, he tells us that Ares had posted it to guard the spring. The dragon Ares posted is the one Kadmos slew. Thebes had no other.

Having reported on what lies east of the Elektrai gates, Pausanias descends from the Ismenion towards the city (fig. 5.2).

Passage 6 (9.11.1-12.2)

Ἐν ἀριστερᾷ δέ τῶν πυλῶν ἃς ὀνομάζουσιν Ἠλέκτρας, οἰκίας ἐστὶν ἐρείπια ἔνθα οἰκῆσαί φασιν Ἀμφιτρύωνα
. . . καὶ τῆς Ἀλκμήνης . . . ὁ θάλαμος
ἐν τοῖς ἐρειπίοις δῆλος . . . Ἐπι-
δεικνύουσι δὲ Ἡρακλέους τῶν παίδων τῶν ἐκ Μεγάρας μνῆμα . . . Ἀθηνᾶν
δὲ εἶναι τὴν ἐπαφεῖσάν οἱ τὸν λίθον
τοῦτον ὄντινα Σωφρονιστῆρα ὀνομάζουσιν. Ἐνταῦθά εἰσιν ἐπὶ τύπου γυ-
ναικῶν εἰκόνες· . . . ταύτας καλοῦσιν
οἱ Θηβαῖοι Φαρμακίδας . . .

Ἐνταῦθα Ἡρακλεῖόν ἐστιν, ἄγαλμα
δὲ τὸ μὲν λίθου λευκοῦ Πρόμαχος καλούμενον, ἔργον δὲ Ξενοκρίτου καὶ
Εὐβίου Θηβαίων· τὸ δὲ ξόανον τὸ ἀρχαῖον Θηβαῖοί τε εἶναι Δαιδάλου νε-
νομίκασι . . . τὰ ἐν τοῖς ἀετοῖς Πρα-
ξιτέλης ἐποίησε τὰ πολλὰ τῶν δώδε-
κα καλουμένων ἄθλων· καὶ σφισι τὰ
ἐς τὰς ὄρνιθας ἐνδεῖ τὰς ἐπὶ Στυμ-
φάλῳ καὶ ὡς ἐκάθηρεν Ἡρακλῆς τὴν
Ἠλείαν χώραν, ἀντὶ τούτων δὲ ἡ πρὸς
Ἀνταῖον πάλη πεποίηται. Θρασύβου-
λος δὲ ὁ Λύκου καὶ Ἀθηναίων οἱ σὺν
αὐτῷ τυραννίδα τὴν τῶν τριάκοντα κα-
ταλύσαντες . . . Ἀθηνᾶν καὶ Ἡρακλέα
κολοσσοὺς ἐπὶ λίθου τύπου τοῦ Πεν-
τελῆσιν, ἔργα δὲ Ἀλκαμένους, ἀνέθηκαν
ἐς τὸ Ἡρακλεῖον.

Τοῦ δὲ Ἡρακλείου γυμνάσιον ἔχεται
καὶ στάδιον, ἀμφότερα ἐπώνυμα τοῦ
θεοῦ. Ὑπὲρ δέ τὸν Σωφρονιστῆρα λίθον
βωμός ἐστιν Ἀπόλλωνος ἐπίκλησιν Σπο-
δίου . . . Κάδμον . . . ἐνταῦθα οἰκῆσαι
. . . ἔνθα ἡ βοῦς ἔμελλε καμοῦσα ὀκλά-
ζειν· ἀποφαίνουσιν οὖν καὶ τοῦτο τὸ
χωρίον. Ἐνταῦθα ἔστι μὲν ἐν ὑπαίθρῳ
βωμὸς καὶ ἄγαλμα Ἀθηνᾶς· ἀναθεῖναι
δὲ αὐτὸ Κάδμον λέγουσι.

"To the left of the gates which they call Elektrai" the ruins of the house of Amphitryon . . . with the chamber of Alkmena; . . . the tomb of the children of Herakles and Megara; . . . the Sophronister, a stone which Athena threw at Herakles to stop him from killing his father; the relief of the Pharmakides . . .

"Here is" the sanctuary of Herakles with its marble cult statue made by Xenokritos and Eubios of Thebes, and the old wooden image by Daidalos; . . . the pedimental sculptures by Praxiteles show the twelve labors, but in place of the Stymphalian birds and the Augeian stables, Herakles is shown wrestling with Antaios. The statues of Athena and Herakles by Alkamenes were dedicated by Thrasyboulos of Athens . . . in Pentelic marble.

"Adjoining the Herakleion" the gymnasion and the stadion both named after the god. "Beyond the Sophronister" the altar of Apollo Spodios; the site where . . . the cow which Kadmos followed . . . sank down; the open-air sanctuary where the altar and statue of Athena Onka were dedicated by Kadmos.

Keramopoullos (1917:324-337) assumed that Pausanias, standing outside the Elektrai gates, faced them and described what he saw to his right and to his left. Although this was a perfectly reasonable assumption, it necessitates locating *all* of the monuments of the "left" group (which we are about to discuss) outside the Elektrai gates. Some of them, indeed, are beyond the gates, but as we shall see, most of these major monuments must have been *inside* the walls of the Kadmeia. This implies that when Pausanias points "to the right of the Elektrai," he must mean "east" or "outside" the Elektrai; when he points to the left, he must mean "west" or "inside" the gates. There are important reasons for which this must be so. For one thing, there is no trace of any major monument beyond the walls of the Kadmeia to the south. Within the walls, on the other hand, this area tells a different story: the archaeological remains can show that the original Early Helladic settlement of Thebes lay at the south side of the Kadmeia, just inside the Elektrai gates (fig. 2.1); Wilamowitz (1891:238-239) was able to infer its presence there through his study of philological material. Furthermore, had Pausanias been describing, at this point, monuments outside the gates, he could not have omitted mentioning the important tombs of Amphitryon and Iolaos, known from Pindar (*Nem.* 4.20, *Pyth.* 9.79-83) and probably associated with the large Mycenaean cemetery of Kolonaki.

Pausanias begins with a large group of monuments relating to Herakles, the first of which is the house of his birth. Pausanias probably was shown the ruins of a Mycenaean house; we are certain that there are no extensive traces of habitation during the Late Helladic period outside the walls of the Kadmeia. On the other hand, it is unlikely that the tomb of Herakles' children (all of whom he killed in his madness) was inside the walls. Herakles was a Mycenaean hero; there are no Mycenaean tombs within the Kadmeia. Pausanias may, of course, have been shown intramural burials of the Middle Helladic period, mistakenly identified as those of the children of Herakles; but it is more likely that the actual tomb was elsewhere (the Mycenaean cemetery of Kolonaki, or the Ismenion) and that a memorial was in the city.

After Herakles had killed his children, Athena threw a stone at him to prevent him from killing his father as well. The stone, called the *Sophronister,* was shown to Pausanias. His text implies that at the same place as the Sophronister, he was shown a relief representing the Pharmakides, witches sent by Hera to prevent Alkmene from giving birth to Herakles. The birth was eventually accomplished through the helpful intervention of Historis, the daughter of Teiresias, according to Pausanias. Other sources credit Galinthias, daughter of Proitos (*Anton. Lib.* 29). Either way, the birth of Herakles was believed to have been facilitated through the efforts of the daughter of a celebrated seer. It appears that the three monuments (the house of Amphitryon, the Sophronister, and the relief of the Pharmakides) were connected with one and the same site, which may have been a cult place, perhaps an open-air sanctuary, where Herakles was worshipped. His birth, his youth, and his madness may represent three aspects of his cult related to these monuments. This sanctuary was probably located inside the Elektrai gates.

The actual temple of Herakles must have been an impressive structure, and it is a great pity that not a trace of it has survived. Judging by the names of the sculptors whose works adorned it (Xenokritos and Eubios, Praxiteles, Alkamenes), it could have been built at the end of the fifth century B.C. Keramopoullos (1917:329) located the Herakleion in the valley south of the Kadmeia, which is the most likely location for it.

The length and detail of Pausanias' discussion of the monuments related to Herakles attest to his prominence in Theban religion and to the great antiquity of his cult. Holleaux (1898) pointed out the affinity between Herakles and Apollo, whose priest he once was. Altars made of the ashes of sacrificial animals were characteristic of the cult of Herakles elsewhere in Greece, but in Thebes, the one such altar is associated with Apollo. This is the one Pausanias describes as he walks "beyond the Sophronister." Although he has moved beyond the monuments of Herakles, he is still in the southern part of the Kadmeia and within the walls.

Pausanias tells us that the altar of Apollo Spodios was built from the ashes first of sacrificial bulls, and in later times of working oxen. Holleaux (1898) believed that the altar of Apollo Spodios should be located at the sanctuary of Apollo Ismenios, because no temple is mentioned in connection with the former, and no altar is mentioned in connection with the latter. He explains the different types of divination (*empyromancy,* divination from fire, at the Ismenion and *cledonomancy,* divination based on voices and noises, at the altar of Apollo Spodios) as the older and newer cult practices of one and the same god. Keramopoullos (1917:331, n. 1) disagreed, pointing out that the presence of an ash altar near the cult sites of Herakles strengthens the notion that we are dealing with the site of a cult distinct from that of Apollo Ismenios. He saw nothing unusual in the existence of two cult sites of Apollo. Wilamowitz (1922:45, n. 1) agreed with Holleaux, Schober (1934:1450) was undecided and Ziehen (1934:1501) sided with Keramopoullos.

The very first god to whom a temple was dedicated in the Geometric period was Apollo, and this is proof of how important he was to the Thebans. That his altar on the Kadmeia was still active in Pausanias' time (when the main temple was established elsewhere) indicates that the Thebans continued to maintain two cult sites in his honor, a common practice in Thebes for important gods (tables 2.5, 3.1). The order of Pausanias' walking tour suggests that the altar of Apollo Spodios should be located in the southern part of the Kadmeia rather than on the hill of Kolonaki (Keramopoullos 1917:330-333; Fabricius 1890:22). The vicinity of the church of Agios Vasileios (site 11) has already been suggested as a likely location for it (chap. 3, p. 130).

The next site indicated in Pausanias' journey is the spot where Kadmos, having been ordered to follow a cow until she sank from fatigue, founded the city of Thebes. If there was such a spot commemorating the cow's signal to Kadmos, it may well have been in this, the southern part of the Kadmeia, where the earliest remains of habitation have been found (fig. 2.1). The spring of Ares and the site associated with the Spartoi are not far, and a cohesive topographical picture emerges: all of the sites relating to the founding of the city can be located in the southern part of the Kadmeia, or just south of it. The very last site of this passage, the sanctuary of Athena Onka, is also related to the founding of Thebes. Pausanias tells us that Kadmos dedicated a statue of Athena at this sanctuary, indicating, perhaps, the initiation of her cult (see chap. 3, p. 130). The sanctuary may well have been at the same site as that of the exhausted cow, although Pausanias does not specify that this is so. The exact location of the sanctuary is unknown. The church of Agia Trias (fig. 5.1, site 26) has been proposed as a possibility (Fabricius 1890:28; Frazer 1898:48-49) but Keramopoullos (1917:333-336) preferred the area in the southwestern part of the Kadmeia where the Onkaiai gates must have been located and named after this sanctuary. He would place it with all the other monuments of this group, outside the walls; my interpretation of this passage as a whole leads to the same area, but inside the prehistoric wall, perhaps in the vicinity of the church of Agia Aikaterini (218).

There is reason to believe the sanctuary of Zeus Hypsistos, a major site that Pausanias does not discuss here in the context of the other monuments of this group, was also in this same general area (southern part of the Kadmeia). Pausanias did refer to it when he mentioned the gates of the same name (passage 3), and since topographical description was not his aim, having mentioned a site in one context, he may have seen no reason to bring it up again. Pindar (*Nem.* 1.60) places the sanctuary of Zeus Hypsistos near the house of Amphitryon, which we have located in the southwestern part of the Kadmeia. A short distance from the house of Amphitryon is the highest point of the Kadmeia, and it is possible that the sanctuary of Zeus Hypsistos ("the Highest") was established and named for it. The possible position of the Onkaiai gates (also called *Hypsistai*) is only 100 m from here (fig. 5.2, site 19).

Keramopoullos (1917:336-337) proposed that the gates in the southwest part of the Kadmeia were called alternatively *Onkaiai* and *Hypsistai*, after the sanctuaries in the vicinity. If my interpretation of this passage is correct, what Pausanias saw and described to the left of the Elektrai gates includes five major sanctuaries: the "old" open-air sanctuary of Herakles (including the house of Amphitryon, etc.), the "new" sanctuary of Herakles (with temple), the "old" cult site of Apollo (open-air altar of Apollo Spodios), the open-air sanctuary of Athena (associated with the founding of Thebes by Kadmos) and, finally, the sanctuary of Zeus Hypsistos. This is a fairly dense concentration of cult sites, corresponding to the equally high number of churches in the same area of modern Thebes (figs. 3.7, 4.1). If one compares this density with the heavy concentration of Early and Middle Helladic sites in this same area (fig. 2.1, 2.3), one must be hard put to call it coincidence or to insist that the sanctuaries Pausanias saw were not inside the walls of the Kadmeia.

Pausanias now abruptly leaves the southern part of the Kadmeia and goes directly to the heart of the town (fig. 5.2).

Passage 7 (9.12.3-6)

Φασὶ δὲ οἱ Θηβαῖοι, καθότι τῆς ἀκ-
ροπόλεως ἀγορὰ σφισιν ἐφ' ἡμῶν
πεποίηται, Κάδμου τὸ ἀρχαῖον οἰκίαν
εἶναι· θαλάμων δὲ ἀποφαίνουσι τοῦ μὲν
Ἁρμονίας ἐρείπια καὶ ὃν Σεμέλης
φασὶν εἶναι, τοῦτον δὲ καὶ ἐς ἡμᾶς
ἔτι ἄβατον φυλάσσουσιν ἀνθρώποις.
Ἑλλήνων δὲ τοῖς ἀποδεχομένοις ᾆσαι
Μούσας ἐς τὸν Ἁρμονίας γάμον τὸ
χωρίον ἐστὶν ἐπὶ τῆς ἀγορᾶς, ἔνθα δή
φασι τὰς θεὰς ᾆσαι. . . . Πολύδωρον δὲ
τὸ ξύλον τοῦτο χαλκῷ λέγουσιν ἐπι-
κοσμήσαντα Διόνυσον καλέσαι Κάδμον.
Πλησίον δὲ Διονύσου ἄγαλμα, καὶ
τοῦτο Ὀνασιμήδης ἐποίησε δι' ὅλου
πλῆρες ὑπὸ τοῦ χαλκοῦ· τὸν βωμὸν δὲ
οἱ παῖδες εἰργάσαντο οἱ Πραξιτέ-
λους. Ἀνδριάς τέ ἐστι Προνόμου . . .
καὶ Ἐπαμινώνδαν τὸν Πολύμνιδος
ἀνέθεσαν.

"The Thebans say that in the area of their akropolis where the market place stands today" the house of Kadmos stood in antiquity; preserved are the bridal chamber of Harmonia and Semele's chamber, which is maintained as a sacred place not to be entered; the site where the Muses sang is in the agora; . . . there is a log covered with bronze which is called Dionysos Kadmeios and nearby a bronze statue by Onasimedes, the altar [of Dionysos Kadmeios] made by the sons of Praxiteles, and statues of the flutist Pronomos . . . and of Epaminondas, son of Polymnis.

Pausanias asserts that he is within the citadel, and probably he is at the center of town because that is where a market usually is situated. Any attempt to locate it today depends on identifying and locating the house of Kadmos, which Pausanias describes in great detail. He makes it quite clear that near the market, in the center of town, was an open-air sanctuary dedicated to Dionysos Kadmeios. I have already explained the reasons that site 1, the first Mycenaean palace, ought to be identified with the house of Kadmos and the sanctuary of Dionysos Kadmeios (see chap. 2, fig. 2.11).

A careful reading of the passage reveals a distinction between the house of Kadmos itself, with both the bridal chamber of Harmonia and the chamber of Semele, and the apparently related area where the Muses sang, possibly a courtyard associated with the house of Kadmos. The statues of Pronomos and Epaminondas could have been in either place, or at yet a third site in the same general area. The bronze-covered log and the statue of Dionysos were apparently in Semele's chamber.

From the Mycenaean period, when the house of Kadmos was destroyed, until the Byzantine period, there is no evidence that the site was reused. During the Classical period, it was certainly considered important enough for the citizens to install there the statues of two famous Thebans: Pronomos, the flutist, and Epaminondas, the statesman. Even in Pausanias' time, the number of items shown him by his local guides indicates the continued importance of the site. The sanctuary of Dionysos Kadmeios was not merely the center of a cult long dead, but a place of lively activity: the center for the important festival of *Agrionia* and the base of a technicians' guild. The proximity of this site to the market made this area the commercial center of Thebes.

In continuing to describe the town, Pausanias gives no clue which direction he has taken.

PASSAGE 8 (9.16.1-4)

Οὐ πόρρω δέ ἐστι ναὸς Ἄμμωνος, καὶ τὸ ἄγαλμα ἀνέθηκεν μὲν ὁ Πίνδαρος, Καλάμιδος δέ ἐστιν ἔργον . . . μετὰ τοῦ Ἄμμωνος τὸ ἱερὸν οἰωνοσκοπεῖόν τε Τειρεσίου καλούμενον καὶ πλησίον Τύχης ἐστὶν ἱερόν· φέρει μὲν δὴ Πλοῦτον παῖδα· . . . χεῖρας μὲν τοῦ ἀγάλματος καὶ πρόσωπον Ξενοφῶν εἰργάσατο Ἀθηναῖος, Καλλιστόνικος δὲ τὰ λοιπὰ ἐπιχώριος.

. . . Ἀφροδίτης δὲ Θηβαίοις ξόανά ἐστιν οὕτω δὴ ἀρχαῖα ὥστε καὶ ἀναθήματα Ἁρμονίας εἶναί φασιν . . . καλοῦσι δὲ Οὐρανίαν, τὴν δὲ αὐτῶν Πάνδημον καὶ Ἀποστροφίαν τὴν τρίτην . . .

"Not far [from the group of monuments mentioned last] are" the temple of Ammon with the [cult] statue by Kalamis dedicated by Pindar; . . . the Bird Observatory of Teiresias; the sanctuary of Tyche, [the statue of Tyche] carrying Ploutos . . . made by Xenophon the Athenian (hands and face) and Kallistonikos of Thebes (the rest of the body).

"At Thebes" [connected with the previous monuments?] . . . three very ancient wooden images of Aphrodite offered by Harmonia; . . . the epithets of the goddess are Ourania, Pandemos, and Apostrophia . . .

Two of the four sanctuaries mentioned here may be identified with specific archaeological sites: the Oionospkopeion of Teiresias may well have been at site 23, and the sanctuary of Aphrodite with its three wooden statues may have been located at site 229 (see chap. 3). It seems likely, therefore, that Pausanias moved north from the sanctuary of Dionysos Kadmeios and visited these four sanctuaries in the east-central part of the Kadmeia, describing them in clockwise order. In this way, he reached the monuments that he describes in the subsequent passage.

The temple of Ammon (also referred to in Pindar, *Pyth.* 4.16) must have been located between the sanctuary of Dionysos Kadmeios and the Bird Observatory of Teiresias, perhaps at the church of Agios Georgios (site 93, pl. 5), 120 m north of the sanctuary of Dionysos Kadmeios. The Bird Observatory of Teiresias was presumably an open-air site. It is very likely that the remains of an open-air sanctuary found at the northeast edge of the Kadmeia (pl. 6) are those of this unique sanctuary (see chap. 3 and Catalogue, site 23). Close by was the sanctuary of Tyche, which had a temple and a statue of the goddess holding Ploutos. Considering the location of the following sanctuary, Pausanias must have moved south from the Bird Observatory of Teiresias along the east wall of the Kadmeia. The sanctuary of Tyche must have been between the Bird Observatory and the sanctuary of Aphrodite, perhaps in the vicinity of the church of Agios Stephanos (site 219). Pausanias tells us next about three wooden statues of Aphrodite, but says nothing about a sanctuary to house them. We know from other sources, however, that a sanctuary existed (see also chap. 3). It is very likely that the large structure found recently at sites 229 and 4 was the temple of Aphrodite; the remains were situated exactly on Pausanias' route.

In spite of the difficulty of clarifying the topography without more explicit help from Pausanias, our ability to place the Bird Observatory of Teiresias with some certainty begets a degree of confidence in assigning locations to all the sanctuaries referred to in passages 7 through 9 in relation to it. Pausanias has now reached the center of town once more.

PASSAGE 9 (9.16.5)

Τὸ δὲ τῆς Δήμητρος ἱερὸν τῆς Θεσμοφόρου Κάδμου καὶ τῶν ἀπογόνων οἰκίαν ποτὲ εἶναι λέγουσι· Δήμητρος δὲ ἄγαλμα ὅσον ἐς στέρνα ἐστὶν ἐν τῷ φανερῷ. Καὶ ἀσπίδες ἐνταῦθα ἀνάκεινται χαλκαῖ· Λακεδαιμονίων δὲ, ὁπόσοι τῶν ἐν τέλει περὶ Λεῦκτρα ἐτελεύτησαν, φασὶν εἶναι.

"At the site where once stood the house of Kadmos and his descendants" the sanctuary of Demeter Thesmophoros; a [cult] statue of the goddess visible down to the chest; Lakedaimonian shields from the battle at Leuktra.

Two important monuments are mentioned here, one serving as a topographical indication for the other. It would be easy to assume that Pausanias had returned to the same house of Kadmos he described earlier (see passage 7). This is, however, far from the case. For one thing, in the entire description of Thebes, Pausanias does not discuss the same monument in more than one passage. Secondly, he used a different name for each "house." This one, "Κάδμου καὶ τῶν ἀπογόνων οἰκίαν" is the house of Kadmos and his *descendants* (italics mine). The other, "οἰκίαν Κάδμου," was simply the house of Kadmos. Most important of all is his reporting that the site of the house of Kadmos was unused right up to his own time (ἐς ἡμᾶς ἔτι ἄβατον φυλάσσουσιν ἀνθρώποις) And the reason it remained unused, according to Pausanias, is that the thunderbolt of Zeus devastated it thoroughly. In contrast, the site of the house of Kadmos and his descendants was clearly occupied by the sanctuary of Demeter Thesmorphoros. This distinction was so plain to Keramopoullos that he not only believed in the existence of two Mycenaean palaces, but even predicted that the second would be found right next to the first (1917:355). A section of this second palace (fig. 5.2, site 2) was discovered in the winter of 1963-1964 only 20 m from Keramopoullos' excavations. I have already reviewed the question of the two palaces and have attempted to show that the archaeological evidence supports both Keramopoullos' prediction and Pausanias' description (1973:72-76; see also chap. 2 above). What is truly amazing is that the second Mycenaean palace, the house of Kadmos and his descendants—though we do not know how much was preserved in the time of

Pausanias—was nevertheless remembered by the Thebans 1,400 years after its destruction. Remains of this palace have now been discovered at several sites (fig. 2.11). The palace is so large that it would be difficult to determine where the sanctuary of Demeter might have been. Within the area it occupies, Classical foundations have been found at three sites: the structure found at site 2 was probably not a temple, and those at sites 4 and 229 belonged to one and the same building, possibly the temple of Aphrodite (see chap. 3). The most probable location of the sanctuary of Demeter is the vicinity of site 97, now occupied by the church of Agios Ioannis. The medieval cathedral of Thebes had stood here, and the site is centrally located on the Kadmeia (fig. 4.1). If this is correct, then the "walking tour" of passages 7 through 9 was very nicely planned: Pausanias started with one of the oldest and most venerated sites at the center of the Kadmeia. He then proceeded in a clockwise direction, describing as he went the monuments in the eastern part of the Kadmeia, and ended back at the center with another venerated site.

With the sanctuary of Demeter Thesmorphoros, Pausanias ends his description of monuments on the Kadmeia itself. There must have been others that he omitted, either because he didn't get to them or because he didn't think them worth describing. Both the lexicographers and a dedicatory inscription on a small column (*IG* 7.2456) attest to the existence of a cult of Zeus Homoloios (see chap. 3, p. 128). The most likely location of the sanctuary is the chapel of Agios Georgios (site 221), which is about 50 m west of the path Pausanias followed between the Bird Observatory of Teiresias and the sanctuary of Tyche. The cult of Zeus Homoloios may have died out by the time of his visit, or there may have been some other reason for this omission. A more perplexing omission is that of the sanctuary of Poseidon, known from several sources (see chap. 3). The sanctuary of Poseidon was in the vicinity of the church of Agia Eleousa (site 94) and was, therefore, outside Pausanias' route.

Leaving the Kadmeia, Pausanias visits the monuments in the vicinity of the Proitides gates.

Passage 10 (9.16.6-7)

Πρὸς δὲ ταῖς καλουμέναις πύλαις Προιτίσι θέατρον ᾠκοδόμηται, καὶ ἐγγυτάτω τοῦ θεάτρου Διονύσου ναός ἐστιν ἐπίκλησιν Λυσίου· . . . Ἐνταῦθα οἱ Θηβαῖοι τὸ ἕτερον τῶν ἀγαλμάτων φασὶν εἶναι Σεμέλης· . . . Καὶ οἰκίας τῆς Λύκου ἐρείπια καὶ Σεμέλης μνῆμά ἐστιν, Ἀλκμήνης δὲ οὐ μνῆμα· γενέσθαι δὲ αὐτὴν ὡς ἀπέθανε λίθον ... ... ἐνταῦθα καὶ τὰ μνήματα πεποίηται τῶν Ἀμφίονος παίδων...

"Near the Proitides gates" the theater; "very close to the theater" the temple of Dionysos Lysios ... with two statues: one of Semele [the other of Dionysos]; ... the house of Lykos; the tomb of Semele; ... stone [and heroon?] of Alkmena? ... the tombs of the children of Amphion.

The Proitides gates, though not preserved, can be located with certainty at the northeast exit of the Kadmeia, where the road to Chalkis begins (pl. 2; cf. Catalogue, site 9). The only theater ever found in Thebes is located 600 m north of these gates, a distance that by our standards cannot be described as "near." There have been attempts to locate a second theater, but these have come to nought. Pausanias refers to this one only, and we can be quite sure that in his day there was no other, or it would surely have been found by now. The reason he refers to it as "near" must be that, standing before the Proitides Gates, the theater was the largest, most important, and most easily visible monument in Greater Thebes and could therefore be used as a reference point for the other monuments in the vicinity.

The temple of Dionysos Lysios, located very close to the theater, has never been found, nor has anything resembling a temple been recognized in the vicinity of the theater, although there are Classical remains (see Catalogue, sites 65, 169). This, the only major temple of Dionysos, one of the most important gods of Thebes, may well have been a substantial structure.

The ruins of the house of Lykos, the tomb of Semele, the heroon of Alkmena, and, finally, the tombs of the Niobids were somewhere near the temple; no other topographical indication is given. The presence of a house among the tombs is puzzling, especially as no trace of prehistoric habitation has been found north of the Kadmeia. Lykos was the uncle of Antiope (mother of Zethos and Amphion, the Dioskouroi of Thebes) and grandfather of the Niobids. As we have seen, Zethos and Amphion were buried nearby in a common tomb that was much revered by the Thebans. Pausanias seems to have visited a small cemetery in which most of the tombs were those of the family headed by Lykos, its most ancient member and perhaps the founder of a dynasty. Is it possible that what was shown to Pausanias as the house of Lykos was in reality a group of tombs of the dynasty of Lykos? The word *oikia* can mean *dynasty* in Greek, just as *house* can mean *dynasty* in English. If this were indeed the case, we would have a homogeneous group of monuments consisting of tombs somewhere near the theater.

There was no tomb for Alkmene, only a stone marker. Pherekydes confirms this (*Anton. Lib.* 33) and tells us that there was also a heroon (Keramopoullos 1917:369). In this passage, Pausanias does no more than mention the tomb of the Niobids, but he is soon to relate it topographically to the site where he was told they were cremated: "the pyre of the children of Amphion is only half a stadion from their tombs" (9.17.2). This is most important because it means that all the sites in this group are near the theater. We know the location of the theater; therefore, it is rather simple to locate the cemetery: there is only one in the area and it is on the hill of Amphion, where several prehistoric tombs have indeed been found (cf. pl. 3, and site 121, fig. 5.1). The northern end of the hill is only 200 m from the theater.

PASSAGE 11 (9.17.1-3)

Πλησίον δὲ Ἀρτέμιδός ναός ἐστιν Εὐκλείας· Σκόπα δὲ τὸ ἄγαλμα ἔργον. ταφῆναι δὲ ἐντὸς τοῦ ἱεροῦ θυγατέρας Ἀντιποίνου λέγουσιν Ἀνδρόκλειάν τε καὶ Ἀλκίδα . . . Τοῦ ναοῦ δὲ . . . λέων ἐστὶν ἔμπροσθε λίθου πεποιημένος. Πλησίον δὲ Ἀπόλλων τέ ἐστιν ἐπίκλησιν βοηδρόμιος καὶ Ἀγοραῖος Ἑρμῆς καλούμενος, Πινδάρου καὶ τοῦτο ἀνάθημα. ἀπέχει δὲ ἡ πυρὰ Ἀμφίονος παίδων ἥμισυ σταδίου μάλιστα ἀπὸ τῶν τάφων· μένει δὲ ἡ τέφρα καὶ ἐς τόδε ἔτι ἀπὸ τῆς πυρᾶς. πλησίον δὲ Ἀμφιτρύωνος ἀνάθημα δύο ἀγάλματα λίθινα λέγουσιν Ἀθηνᾶς ἐπίκλησιν Ζωστηρίας.

"Near [the monuments discussed above] is" the temple of Artemis Eukleia, [cult] statue by Skopas; buried inside the cella are Androkleia and Alkis, the daughters of Antipoinos; . . . a lion of stone . . . is in front of the temple; "nearby" [the temple] the statue of Apollo Boedromios; the statue of Hermes Agoraios, another of the votive offerings of Pindar; the pyre of the children of Amphion "only half a stadion from the graves"; the ashes are still there. "Near this" [the pyre] two stone statues of Athena Zosteria, dedicated by Amphitryon.

Before turning back towards the Proitides gates, Pausanias describes the monuments that must have been located north and northwest of the Amphion hill. The temple of Artemis Eukleia with a cult statue by Skopas is the most important monument of this group. I suspect it was located at or near the site where the Evangelistria chapel stands today (fig. 5.1, site 252). The statues of Apollo, Hermes, and Athena, and the pyre of the Niobids, which Pausanias locates "nearby," are known from other sources to have been in or near the agora of Greater Thebes (Sophokles, *Oid. Tyr.* 161; Xenophon, *Hell.* 5.2.29). In Pausanias' time the agora was probably deserted. It is unlikely that the statues mentioned by Pausanias were associated with a sanctuary or cult site; rather, they were dedications within a public area.

Not everyone agrees that the pyre referred to here was indeed that of the Niobids, as Pausanias tells us. Pindar, in fact, speaks of seven pyres, thereby implying a connection with the War of the Seven against Thebes (*Ol.* 6:15-16; *Nem.* 9.24). Pindar lived nearby, and despite some confusion about the site (Keramopoullos discusses it in detail, 1917:374-376), there are several reasons to agree with him and not with Pausanias, here. Cremation was not the funerary custom in Mycenaean times. According to Mylonas (1962B:323-328), the Greeks became familiar with the practice of cremation during the Trojan War; Lorimer (1950:107) considered the practice "particularly suitable to the conditions of warfare on foreign soil." There are Mycenaean examples of cremation, but these occur toward the end of the period, and are limited to a few burial sites (e.g., at Perati, Iakovides 1969:32, 45-47, 87; 1970:15, 65, 78). In Thebes itself there is an isolated example of cremation, associated with a tomb of the Late Helladic III C period (Kolonaki tomb 16, Keramopoullos 1917:163-168; here, Catalogue, site 24). But the pyres of the Seven might well be explained through their association with a major war. After the defeat and flight of the attacking Seven, the Thebans must have been forced to collect and bury or burn the bodies on the field. Therefore, the pyres must have been those of the army of the attacking Seven (Schol. Pindar, *Ol.* 6:15-16), not merely the seven generals of the enemy. Keramopoullos (1917:379-381) placed the pyres (and the other monuments of this group) between the Kadmeia and the Kastellia hills because he believed that the theater was near the Proitides gates. But my location for the theater leads us northwest of the Amphion hill to the modern suburb of Pyri.

I have already suggested a strong relationship between the toponym Pyri and the pyres of the Seven (Symeonoglou 1973:79, n. 32). The cemetery of the Geometric period is in the same area, suggesting that cremation was practiced here over a long period. While it is possible that the discovery of such burials in recent times has given rise to the toponym, I rather doubt it, because Pindar refers to the site of the ἑπτὰ πυραὶ ("seven pyres"), and the name may easily have been used to designate the locality. Pausanias, seven centuries later, also associates the site with an important pyre, and even reports that the ashes were still visible. With the exception of *Thevai* (Thebes), the toponym *Pyri* may be the only one in the city that has survived in uninterrupted use since the Mycenaean period (toponyms such as *Ismenion* and *Amphion* are modern reinstatements of ancient ones). In addition to the pyres of the Seven, Pausanias, in a subsequent passage (see passage 17, 9.25.1-2), describes both the site where the sons of Oidipous dueled and the site of the Syrma of Antigone, each related to the War of the Seven and, as we shall see below, located in the vicinity of the pyres. Thus, the topography of the area coheres and even explains the power, significance, and permanence of its toponym.

Pausanias now returns to the Amphion hill and pauses to describe a single monument, the tomb of Zethos and Amphion.

PASSAGE 12 (9.17.4, 7)

Ζήθῳ δὲ μνῆμα καὶ Ἀμφίονι ἐν κοινῷ γῆς χῶμά ἐστιν οὐ μέγα . . . Τοὺς δὲ παρὰ τὸ Ἀμφίονος μνῆμα λίθους, οἳ κάτωθεν ὑποβέβληνται μηδὲ ἄλλως εἰργασμένοι πρὸς τὸ ἀκριβέστατον . . .	Zethos and Amphion are buried in a common grave marked by a small mound of earth . . . Roughly hewn stones are laid at the base of the tomb of Amphion [and Zethos] . . .

Pausanias gives a detailed account of the myths related to Zethos and Amphion, meaning to impress upon the reader the great importance of this site. It seems to have been the most venerated of all the tombs of Thebes. It is said that the Thebans kept vigil at the tomb so that the Tithoreans would not steal earth from it. If this was so, we have a rare glimpse of some form of funerary cult practice. The tomb was probably located on the most prominent part of the Amphion hill, close to the Kadmeia. I believe that the impressive tomb discovered recently at the highest point on the hill is the same as the one shown to Pausanias (site 121, fig. 5.1). The cemetery of passage 10 can be nowhere but on the same hill. Pausanias' tour, which started at the theater and made a circle, once again approaches the Proitides gates. From here, Pausanias moved east on the road to Chalkis.

PASSAGE 13 (9.18.1-6)

Ἐκ Θηβῶν δὲ ὁδὸς ἐς Χαλκίδα κατὰ πύλας ταύτας ἐστὶ τὰς Προιτίδας. Τάφος δὲ ἐπὶ τῇ λεωφόρῳ δείκνυται Με- λανίππου . . . τούτου δὲ ἐγγύτατα τρεῖς εἰσιν ἀργοὶ λίθοι . . . Τυδέα φασὶν εἶναι τὸν ἐνταῦθα κείμενον.

Ἑξῆς δέ ἐστι τῶν Οἰδίποδος παίδων μνήματα· . . . Θηβαῖοι δὲ καὶ Τειρε- σίου μνῆμα ἀποφαίνουσι, πέντε μά- λιστα καὶ δέκα ἀπωτέρω σταδίοις ἢ Οἰδίποδος τοῖς παισίν ἐστιν ὁ τάφος.

Ἔστι δὲ καὶ Ἕκτορος Θηβαίοις τάφος τοῦ Πριάμου πρὸς Οἰδιποδίᾳ καλουμένῃ κρήνῃ . . . Πρὸς δὲ τῇ πηγῇ τάφος ἐστὶν Ἀσφοδίκου.

"By the road from Thebes to Chalkis which starts at the Proitides gates" the tomb of Melanippos . . . and "close to it" three unhewn stones . . . which mark the tomb of Tydeus, according to the Thebans.

"Next" are the tombs of the children of Oidipous;—the cenotaph of Teiresias is fifteen stadia from these tombs;

the tomb of Hektor is "near the spring of Oidipous"; . . . by the fountain [of Oidipous] is the tomb of Asphodikos.

In antiquity, the road to Chalkis passed between the two Kastellia hills (Keramopoullos 1917:361). The tombs that Pausanias saw near this road fall easily into two groups: the first three are clustered in one area; the other two are by the spring of Oidipous. The two groups are related in that those buried here participated in the War of the Seven. In addition, Melanippos of the first group and Asphodikos (or Amphidikos in other sources) of the second were brothers (Apollod. 3.6.8). Included in each group is a tomb or cenotaph of the great opponents: in the first, three stones mark the tomb of Tydeus, the bravest of the Seven; in the second is the cenotaph of Hektor, greatest of the "Trojan" heroes. Pausanias seems to have arranged his description as though literary balance were his first concern. The description begins with the tomb of Melanippos and ends with that of his brother, Asphodikos. Second and penultimate are the memorials to Tydeus and Hektor, both foreigners. In the middle are the tombs of Teiresias and the children of Oidipous. Though the literary arrangement may appear artificial or contrived, the archaeological evidence and many other reliable literary sources attest to its integrity as a record of what Pausanias saw.

Homer mentions the tomb of Tydeus (*Iliad* 14.114). Robert (1915, 1:127) believed that Tydeus was an ancient god for whom Theban historians, in deference to Homer, established a tomb in Thebes. The three stones, in Robert's view, indicate an ancient fetish. Pausanias is careful to preserve a skeptical, or at least an objective stance in that he himself does not declare the site a tomb, but reports that "very near" the tomb of Melanippos he saw three stones "which, according to the Theban antiquarians, mark the tomb of Tydeus." He then explains the relationship between the two characters by relating that Tydeus was slain by Melanippos in the War of the Seven. It is interesting to remember that according to Herodotos (5.67), king Kleisthenes of Sicyon established a hero cult for Melanippos.

What seems to have been of far greater importance for the Thebans than the existence of the tomb of Tydeus, or the precise identification of any of the other tombs, was the memory of the war. Even the existence of a hero cult appears less important than that. If the Thebans pointed out the tomb of Tydeus to visitors, it was to bear testimony to the greatness of Thebes in defeating the Argives. They also pointed out the spot where Amphiaraos (another of the Seven) was swallowed up by the earth (passage 2).

As for Hektor, Pausanias says that his bones were brought to Thebes and buried by the spring of Oidipous in fulfillment of an oracle that urged the Thebans to worship Hektor if they wished their city to prosper. Keramopoullos offered the explanation that there was actually a local hero named Hektor whose story must have been forgotten by the time of Pausanias, and whose identity, somewhere along the line, was confused with that of the Trojan Hektor (1917:397-398). Schachter (1979) has recently proposed that the tomb was created in the Hellenistic period in response to renewed interest in epic poetry. Similar opinions have been expressed in the past (see Ziehen 1934:1514-1515 for a discussion of the subject). The tomb was probably another cenotaph like those of Tydeus and Teiresias, mentioned in this passage.

The tomb of Asphodikos, located near the spring of Oidipous, may have been on the side of the Kastellia hills that is closest to the area of this spring (cf. fig. 5.1, cemetery at site 140, spring at site 244). In fact, all the tombs of this passage may have been located at the major Mycenaean cemetery at Kastellia (Catalogue, site 25). One of the tombs in that cemetery is of monumental size and appears to have been prepared for a royal burial (site 254); it has two entrances and a very large chamber. It could be that the tomb shown to Pausanias was that of the children of Oidipous, to whom the Thebans offered sacrifice (Pausanias 9.18.3-4; Robert 1915, 1:361-362).

If Pausanias was shown other tombs in this area, he did not describe them, either because they were of lesser importance, or because they could not be gracefully incorporated into his literary design. It is truly remarkable that the Mycenaean cemetery of Kastellia was remembered even in the time of Pausanias, and related, in however distorted a fashion, to the War of the Seven against Thebes, a major event in Theban mythohistory (see chap. 2 for a discussion of the cemetery). The Oidipodia spring mentioned in this passage is identified with some certainty as the modern fountain at Agioi Theodoroi (see Catalogue, site 244).

At this point in his tour, Pausanias leaves Thebes to visit northeastern Boiotia, returning after having visited the town Anthedon, north of Thebes. Presumably, he came back on the road from Anthedon that is still in use, which cuts through the Aonian plain leading to Thebes in a south-southwest direction, just east of the modern railway station (fig. 5.1).

PASSAGE 14 (9.23.1)

Θηβαίοις δὲ πρὸ τῶν πυλῶν ἐστι τῶν Προιτίδων καὶ τὸ ᾿Ιολάου καλούμενον γυμνάσιον καὶ στάδιον . . . ἐνταῦθα δείκνυται καὶ ἡρῷον ᾿Ιολάου.

"In front of the Proitides gates" the gymnasion and the stadium named for Iolaos; . . . also, the heroon of Iolaos.

Pausanias has already described the monuments closest to the Proitides gates and has covered the areas to the east, north, and northwest of the Kadmeia. When he locates the gymnasion and stadium of Iolaos "in front of the Proitides gates," we must, rather than take him literally, understand that he is using the gates as a point of reference. Keramopoullos (1917:404) realized that these monuments must have been located by the road to Anthedon, inside the walls of Greater Thebes; he placed the heroon of Iolaos at the site where the church of Agia Paraskevi stands today (site 224, fig. 5.1).

The heroon that Pausanias saw was designed in association with the newer and larger gymnasion and stadium of Thebes built within the walls during the Classical period. In the area north of the theater are scattered remains of isodomic walls that could easily have belonged to public buildings of this type (Catalogue, sites 65, 67, 69, 106). In fact, if we agree that the Iolaeion was indeed north of the theater, then the following topographical clue makes sense.

PASSAGE 15 (9.23.2)

῾Υπερβάντι δὲ τοῦ σταδίου τὰ ἐν δεξιᾷ δρόμος ἵππων καὶ ἐν αὐτῷ Πινδάρου μνῆμά ἐστι.

"After one crosses over to the right side of the stadium" the hippodrome and the tomb of Pindar within it.

Here again is a problem of right and left! In this instance, the right side of the stadium is determined as one approaches Thebes from Anthedon, and not as one comes from the Proitides gates. This is clear because Pausanias subsequently tells us that the road to Akraiphnion goes from the hippodrome through the plain (see passage 16) and this road is certainly northwest of the Kadmeia (fig. 5.1). Pausanias mentions the hippodrome in passing, and we are quite certain that it did exist and was associated with the house of Pindar and with Poseidon Hippodromios. The area northwest of the theater, in modern Pyri, is flat and open, suitable for horse racing, yet within the Classical walls (Keramopoullos 1917:403, 409; Schober 1934:1447).

PASSAGE 16 (9.23.5)

Ἐντεῦθεν ἐς Ἀκραίφνιόν ἐστιν ὁδὸς τὰ πλείω πεδιάς.

From here [the hippodrome] goes the road to Akraiphnion, mostly through the plain.

This passage, as we have already indicated, is topographically important although no monuments are described. Here, Pausanias again interrupts his tour of Thebes to visit the towns of northwestern Boiotia. On his return, he describes the area of the Neistai gates.

PASSAGE 17 (9.25.1-2)

Θηβαίοις δὲ τῶν πυλῶν ἐστιν ἐγγύτατα τῶν Νηιστῶν Μενοικέως μνῆμα τοῦ Κρέοντος. . . . Τοῦ δὲ Μενοικέως ἐπιπέφυκε ῥοιά τῷ μνήματι· . . . Τοῦ δὲ Μενοικέως οὐ πόρρω τάφου τοὺς παῖδας λέγουσιν Οἰδίποδος μονομαχήσαντας ἀποθανεῖν ὑπὸ ἀλλήλων· σημεῖον δὲ τῆς μάχης αὐτῶν κίων, καὶ ἀσπὶς ἔπεστιν ἐπ' αὐτῷ λίθου. Δείκνυται δέ τι χωρίον ἔνθα Ἥραν Θηβαῖοί φασιν Ἡρακλεῖ παιδὶ ἔτι ἐπισχεῖν γάλα κατὰ δή τινα ἀπάτην ἐκ Διός· καλεῖται δὲ ὁ σύμπας οὗτος τόπος Σύρμα Ἀντιγόνης· ὡς γὰρ τὸν τοῦ Πολυνείκους ἄρασθαί οἱ προθυμουμένῃ νεκρὸν οὐδεμία ἐφαίνετο ῥαστώνη, δεύτερα ἐπενόησεν ἕλκειν αὐτόν, ἐς ὃ εἵλκυσέ τε καὶ ἐπέβαλεν ἐπὶ τοῦ Ἐτεοκλέους ἐξημμένην τὴν πυράν.

"Very close to the Neistai gates" the tomb of Menoikeus, son of Kreon, . . . with a pomegranate tree growing on it; . . . "not far from that" the site where the sons of Oidipous killed each other in a duel; the site is marked by a pillar with a stone shield on it; the site where Hera was tricked by Zeus into giving her breast to Herakles; the whole area is called the Syrma of Antigone because from here she dragged the body of Polyneikes to the funeral pyre of Eteokles.

Pausanias must have visited these sites *before* crossing the river Dirke, because he introduces the subsequent passage with the words, "after crossing the river Dirke." The Neistai gates must have been on the west side of the Kadmeia; the river Dirke is there and that is where the road to Kabeirion starts. In fact, the ancient road can still be seen, and the site of the gates has been accurately identified (Keramopoullos 1917:409 471; site 104, fig. 5.2). Between the river and the slopes of the Kadmeia is a stretch of land, 50 to 100 m wide. This must have been the area where Pausanias was shown several sites.

First, the tomb of Menoikeus, who, in a gesture comparable to that of the daughters of Antipoinos, committed suicide to ensure the victory of Thebes over the Seven. According to Euripides (*Phoin.* 913, 1009-1011), as he died he fell into the spring of Ares. Yet this cannot be, for the spring of Ares is on the other side of town from the tomb (Keramopoullos 1917:414); Euripides must have meant the spring of Dirke. Wilamowitz (1922:31) believed that the whole story of Menoikeus' self-sacrifice was a fabrication of Euripides. Be that as it may, there is no reason to doubt that the Theban guides showed Pausanias a site that they themselves connected with the death of Menoikeus. Perhaps the most striking detail of the tomb is the pomegranate tree growing on it:

> A pomegranate tree grows on the tomb of Menoikeus. When the fruit is ripe and one breaks open the outer layer one finds inside a blood-like substance. This pomegranate tree flourishes to this day. The Thebans claim that they were the first to grow the grapevine, but they no longer have a memorial of this to show. (Pausanias 9.25.1, my translation)

The pomegranate is a known symbol of the chthonic gods and was sacred to the dead (Keramopoullos 1917:415). The juice of its fruit was associated with the blood of the dead; the fruit is a frequent funerary representation, not only in Boiotia, but in all of Greece (e.g., Higgins 1967, pls. 18-19). What particularly interests us here is the seemingly unrelated interjection of the Theban claim to have been the first to grow the grapevine. Why bring up the vine unless one wished to imply that although the Thebans no longer had a memorial to prove they introduced viticulture, they did have a memorial to prove they were the first to cultivate the pomegranate and to use it as a funerary symbol? One may conclude that the tomb of Menoikeus served as a testimonial to the introduction by the Thebans of the cultivation of the pomegranate tree, and perhaps indirectly of the grapevine as well. There is also the implication that the pomegranate was first used as a funerary symbol in Thebes.

Not far from the tomb of Menoikeus, Pausanias was shown the site where Eteokles and Polyneikes killed each other in a duel. According to Euripides (*Phoin.* 1570) the duel took place at the Elektrai gates; according to Aischylos (*Hepta* 631, 800) it happened at the Hebdomai gates. It is unclear whether there was a gate named Hebdomai, or whether Aischylos simply meant the seventh gate of Thebes. There is no point speculating whether or not the duel occurred, and there is no reason to believe either one of the tragedians regarding its location. We can surely believe, however, that Pausanias' guides showed him a site that they believed was associated with the story. Pausanias even describes the commemorative pillar "upon which is a stone shield." The pillar was clearly of later date than the mythohistorical time of the duel, and the shield is a well-known emblem of Thebes and Boiotia.

Not far from the site of the duel is the place where Antigone dragged the body of Polyneikes onto the funeral pyre. The entire area was called *Syrma* ("dragging") for this reason, and I would locate it in the southern section of Pyri, near the pyres of the Seven (see passage 11). Pausanias' version of Antigone's ordeal differs from that of Sophokles in that Antigone does not bury the traitor Polyneikes, but burns his corpse on the pyre of Eteokles. Pausanias has already mentioned the tomb of the children of Oidipous (i.e., Eteokles and Polyneikes). As Keramopoullos (1917:417) pointed out, we are dealing here with a discrepancy that is probably the result of two conflicting traditions; Pausanias presents both without attempting to elucidate either one. Assuming that there is an element of credibility in each tradition, we can tentatively suggest a possible explanation of the apparent conflict between them. In the historical context of the War of the Seven, it would appear reasonable for Antigone to burn the corpse of Polyneikes rather than bury him (a highly rebellious act). By the same token, it would seem reasonable to afford the loyal Eteokles proper inhumation burial in the family tomb. I think it far more plausible to assume that Polyneikes was cremated not on the pyre of Eteokles (as Pausanias reports) but on the pyre that the traveler attributed to the Niobids, which seems more likely to have been that of the army of the Seven (see passage 11 in which the question of cremation is also discussed). The notion of a common tomb and a common pyre for both brothers could have come centuries later when the actual details of the war of the Seven were forgotten, but the preservation of its memory was still of great importance to the Thebans.

Within the general area of the Syrma was the place where Zeus tricked Hera into breastfeeding Herakles. This spot was marked by no monument and cannot be pinpointed by any feature of the geography. We must assume that the Thebans, in their wish to show the great importance of their Herakles, pointed to the very spot where they believed he became invincible and immortal.

PASSAGE 18 (9.25.3)

Διαβάντων δὲ ποταμὸν καλούμενον ἀπὸ γυναικὸς τῆς Λύκου Δίρκην . . . οἰκίας τε ἐρείπια τῆς Πινδάρου καὶ μητρὸς Δινδυμήνης ἱερόν, Πινδάρου μὲν ἀνάθημα, τέχνη δὲ τὸ ἄγαλμα Ἀριστομήδους τε καὶ Σωκράτους Θηβαίων . . . Τὸ ἄγαλμα εἶδον λίθου τοῦ Πεντελῆσι καὶ αὐτὸ καὶ τὸν θρόνον.

"After crossing the river Dirke" . . . the ruins of the house of Pindar; the sanctuary of Mother Dindymene with a [cult] statue and a throne of Pentelic marble, dedicated by Pindar and made by the sculptors Aristomedes and Sokrates of Thebes . . .

Keramopoullos (1917:418) proposed that the house of Pindar was in an area called Kynos Kephalai. Indeed, the only other area that would conform with Pausanias' account is that of the valley and the hills west of the Kadmeia, which are near the hippodrome and Pindar's tomb. Archaeological remains are scanty there, but they do exist.

The sanctuary of Mother Dindymeme (a Theban form of Kybele) was an important one; not only was the mother goddess worshipped, but also Pan and the Nymphs (Philostratos, *Ikones* 2.12). Pindar (*Pyth.* 3.78) implies that the sanctuary was near his house.

Keramopoullos (1917:424) placed it near the house of Pindar in the fields opposite the Neistai gates. I would suggest the site of the modern church of Agia Trias (site 26, fig. 5.1), not only because it is the only major religious site west of Thebes, but also because remains of a Classical temple were seen there by Fabricius (1890.28). It is about 500 m south of the Neistai gates, yet still within the area Pausanias is describing. Also, the sites of this passage are the only ones in Pausanias' entire text that can possibly be attributed to the valley west of the Kadmeia, a valley through which Pindar traveled to Delphi (Keramopoullos 1917:419-420).

It is curious that Pausanias says nothing about the spring of Dirke, which is about 300 m south of the Neistai gates (site 53). Perhaps he thought it sufficient to mention the river Dirke and the fact that it was named for the wife of Lykos. Neither does he say anything about the heroon of Alkmaion, son of Amphiaraos, which Pindar mentions (*Pyth.* 8.55-60), and which Keramopoullos preferred to locate within the sanctuary of Amphiaraos (1917:419; see chap. 3).

Pausanias has come full circle in his tour of Thebes and is very close to his starting point. If the sanctuary of Dindymene were southwest of the Kadmeia, it is reasonable that Pausanias returned to the area of the Neistai gates after visiting the sanctuary, and then took the road that passes south of Pyri toward Kabeirion (passage 20). This is the last area he must cover, and after describing it, he leaves Thebes permanently.

PASSAGE 19 (9.25.4)

Κατὰ δὲ τὴν ὁδὸν τὴν ἀπὸ τῶν πυλῶν τῶν Νηιστῶν τὸ μὲν Θέμιδός ἐστιν ἱερὸν καὶ ἄγαλμα λευκοῦ λίθου, τὸ δὲ ἐφεξῆς, Μοιρῶν, τὸ δὲ Ἀγοραίου Διός· οὗτος μὲν δὴ λίθου πεποίηται, ταῖς Μοίραις δὲ οὐκ ἔστιν ἀγάλματα.

"Along the road from the Neistai gates [to Kabeirion]" the sanctuary of Themis with a statue of white stone; the sanctuary of the Moirai without statues; the sanctuary of Zeus Agoraios with a statue made of stone.

The sanctuary of Themis is not very well known. Perhaps its existence is implied by Pindar who connects Themis with the Moirai and with Zeus (frag., *Hymn* 29-35). The presence of statues for Themis and Zeus may indicate that there were structures, whereas the Moirai had no statues and were perhaps worshipped in an open-air sanctuary. The best topographical indication we have is the epithet for Zeus Agoraios, which probably indicates the proximity of his sanctuary to the agora of Greater Thebes, alluded to in passage 11. Pausanias would then be south of this agora in the vicinity of the Vranezi spring (now destroyed) where the road from the Neistai gates turns west (200 m west-northwest of the Archaeological Musuem). As the sanctuary of Zeus is mentioned last, the other two may have been on the west side of the northern tip of the Kadmeia, north of the sites described in passage 17.

PASSAGE 20 (9.25.4, 5)

Καὶ ἀπωτέρω μικρὸν Ἡρακλῆς ἕστηκεν ἐν ὑπαίθρῳ Ῥινοκολούστης ἐπωνυμίαν ἔχων.

Σταδίους δὲ αὐτόθεν πέντε προελθόντι καὶ εἴκοσι Δήμητρος Καβειραίας καὶ Κόρης ἐστὶν ἄλσος· ... Τούτου δὲ τοῦ ἄλσους ἑπτά που σταδίους τῶν Καβείρων τὸ ἱερὸν ἀφέστηκεν.

"A little farther [from the sanctuaries]" [the statue of] Herakles Rhinokoloustes stands in the open.

From here it is twenty-five stadia to the grove of Demeter Kabeiraia and Kore, and another seven to the sanctuary of the Kabeiroi.

The statue of Herakles Rhinokoloustes is mentioned by no writer other than Pausanias. Perhaps it was associated with an open-air cult site. It obviously commemorated the occasion on which Herakles cut off the noses of the heralds of Orchomenos who had come to demand tribute of Thebes. Pausanias (9.26.1) also mentions Herakles Hippodetes, who stole and bound the chariot horses of the Orchomenians and then killed the soldiers, and whose sanctuary was probably about 5 km west-northwest of Thebes (Judeich 1888:85-86 places it at Mt. Kotsika, just west of Kabeirion) and not near Onchestos (Schachter 1973:37). In any event, Pausanias clearly makes his departure from the northwest side of Greater Thebes. In describing the sites outside the Kadmeia, he says nothing about a second protective wall. We know that the Classical wall had been destroyed by Alexander in 335 B.C. when he leveled the city, but we do not know whether there were any visible remains of it in the time of Pausanias.

Pausanias' record of his visit to Thebes shows an utter lack of interest in the daily life and living conditions of his Theban contemporaries. His only focus is on those sites and monuments—be they religious, mythological, or historical—that reflect some aspect of the past. While appreciating the fantastic aspects of the myths told to Pausanias, one can believe that there were real monuments associated with them. And although the monuments have, for the most part, been destroyed, Pausanias' record is so orderly that we can follow in his path and assign locations to most of them. In addition, I suggest that there is still a continuity of tradition in Thebes, and it may be illuminated by Pausanias' account.

Pausanias describes seventeen sanctuaries (see table 5.1), other sources inform us that there were certainly another three, giving us a total of twenty sanctuaries. We have also speculated about the existence of additional cult sites: the altar of Apollo Spodios, the site where the cow Kadmos followed sank to the ground, the Oionoskopeion of Teiresias, the temenos of Iolaos, and the site of the statue of Herakles Rhinokoloustes. The inclusion of these gives a possible total of twenty-five cult sites. There are also the sites at which there may have been a heroon: the tomb of Zethos and Amphion, and the tomb of the sons of Oidipous. But even without these, the twenty-five reasonably certain cult sites compare surprisingly closely in number to the thirty churches of modern Thebes. Of

Table 5.1 Sites and monuments of ancient Thebes mentioned in Pausanias, with additions from other writers

A Sanctuaries	B Mythohistorical Sites	C Public Buildings	D Tombs	E Statues
1 Demeter & Kore	Polyandrion of 335 B.C.	Elektrai gates	Kaanthos	2 at A1
2 Dionysos Aigobolos	Kadmos and Spartoi	Proitides gates	Children of Herakles by Megara	5 at A5
3 Amphiaraos	Spring of Ares	Neistai gates	Semele	4 at A6
4 Zeus Hypsistos	House of Amphitryon	Krenaiai gates	Alkmena	4 at A6 pediments at A6
5 Apollo Ismenios	Sophronister stone	Hypsistai gates	Niobids	1 at A7
6 Herakles	Relief of Pharmakides	Ogygiai gates	Antipoinidai	4 at A8
7 Athena Onka	Apollo Spodios	Homoloides gates	Zethos and Amphion	1 at A9
8 Dionysos Kadmeios	Kadmos and cow	Gymnasion (South)	Malanippos	1 at A10
9 Ammon	House of Kadmos	Stadion (South)	Tydeus	3 at A11
10 Tyche	Oionoskopeion	Agora (Kadmeia)	Children of Oidipous	1 at A12
11 Aphrodite	House of Kadmos and his Descendants	Theater	Teiresias	2 at A13
12 Demeter Thesmophoros	House of Lykos	Agora (North)	Hektor	2 at A14
13 Dionysos Lysios	Pyre of the Niobids	Gymnasion (North)	Asphodikos	2 at C12 (?)
14 Artemis Eukleia	Athena Zosteria	Stadion (North)	Pindar	2 at B14
15 Iolaos	Spring of Oidipous	Hippodrome	Menoikeus	1 at A16
16 Dindymene	Duel of sons of Oidipous			1 at A17
17 Themis	Hera feeds Herakles			1 at A19
18 Moirai	Syrma of Antigone			1 at A20
19 Zeus Agoraios	House of Pindar			
20 Herakles Rhinokoloustes				
other writers	*other writers*	*other writers*	*other writers*	
21 Zeus Homoloios	Heroon of Alkmaion	Agora? (West)	Amphitryon	
22 Poseidon	Spring of Dirke	Stoa (North)	Iolaos	
23		Prison	Dirke	
24		Wall of Greater Thebes	Alkmaion	

Note: It is not always possible to know whether a site was a sanctuary or simply a locality, or whether some of the mythohistorical sites and tombs were associated with cults.

these, seventeen are on the Kadmeia, where in antiquity there were, at the very least, fourteen sanctuaries, appearing to confirm the traditional continuity reflected in the use of religious sites. Although it is impossible to propose direct continuity from pagan to Christian worship at one and the same site, we cannot help but remark that not only do the clusters coincide, but also in most instances an ancient male deity has been superseded by a male Christian saint, and a female deity by a female saint (table 4.2).

The identification in modern times of two Mycenaean palaces, the presence of the modern market in close proximity to them, the tenacity of the toponym *Pyri,* and the geographical details (springs, hills, gullies, roads) also attest to the integrity of Pausanias' description of a city that was in his day already 3,000 years old.

6
CONCLUSIONS

A survey of the changing fortunes of Thebes over a period of 4,500 years, as documented by the existing archaeological evidence and the literary tradition, has shown the city's persistent attachment to the land through periods of prominence and decline, and its contribution to Greek civilization in a general sense. There also emerge from the survey cultural characteristics that are peculiarly Theban.

POPULATION CHANGES

The data on the population of Thebes are based on settlement size (cf. figs. 2.14, 3.10; table 4.1). The complete development may be seen in figure 6.1, where population estimates of the Christian period have been added. I have used the standard of 300 inhabitants per hectare throughout, which I consider the norm, perhaps a conservative one, for populations within fortifications (see table 2.6). The resulting population averages show that for 2,800 years (that is, for the better part of the city's history), the size of the population fluctuated between 2,000 and 5,000 (table 6.1). The accuracy of these estimates is underscored by the census of 1897, which showed a population of 3,496, and that of 1920, which showed a population of 4,085. The conditions that prevailed at the turn of this century were probably very similar to those for most of the city's previous history. It was the influx of refugees from Asia Minor after 1922 and modern industrialization that brought the population of Thebes to its current level of over 20,000, a figure almost identical to the estimate I have given for the brief period of the Theban hegemony during the Classical period.

In the middle of the third millennium B.C., a small community was established at the highest point of the Kadmeia. The archaeological remains show that this community maintained a low-level subsistence economy based on exploitation of the rich environment. Many of the reasons for which the Kadmeia was selected as a settlement site have been discussed in chapter 1. Here, I wish to add another consideration that may have prompted the move to the Kadmeia. Although we lack environmental studies of Thebes

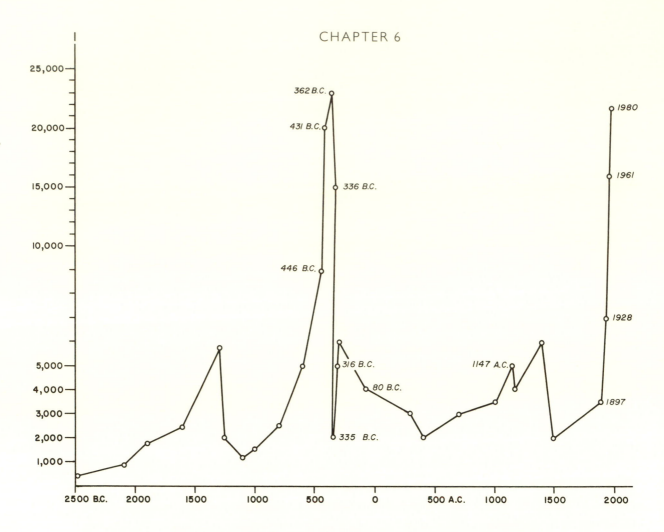

Fig. 6.1. Population estimates for the entire history of Thebes

itself, we do have the results of work that has been done in the Kopaic plain. The richest soils of Boiotia were in the large plains of Thebes and the Kopais. During the Neolithic and Early Bronze Age periods, settlements flourished at the periphery of these plains, as evidenced at Lithares and in Thebes itself (site 87, fig. 1.2). Preliminary studies of the Kopaic plain show that forests existed at or near the edge of the plain. Turner and Greig (1974) believe that the forests were on the hillsides near the plain. Bintliff (1977:79-83) argues, however, that the forests were on the basin floor and were cleared during the third millennium B.C. in order to cultivate the rich soil. Consequently, the settlements moved higher up on the hills. If this view is correct, it would explain the first settlement on the Kadmeia as a movement by the indigenous Boiotian population. The archaeological evidence from Thebes seems, in fact, to be in accord with this view.

The size of the settlement had doubled by the end of EH II, and had quadrupled by the end of EH III. These dramatic increases can be attributed to the influx of additional population, perhaps from Crete, as recorded in local legends about the arrival of Kadmos.

Table 6.1. Average population of Thebes

Average Population	Number of Years
450– 2,000	1,050
2,000– 3,000	1,100
3,000– 5,000	1,700
5,000–10,000	500
10,000–23,000	150

Note: Based on the results shown in figure 6.1.

This new population introduced superior agricultural practices, which gave Thebes, in particular, and Boiotia, in general, new impetus, and made the province an agricultural center. Perhaps future archaeological work will shed light on the nature of these agricultural practices.

The continued growth of Thebes in the Middle Helladic period can be attributed to yet another development: while continuing to advance agriculturally, Thebes seems to have built its first major fortifications, which significantly increased the attractiveness of living in or near the city. Evidence that these fortifications existed is indirect, but it is nevertheless very likely that the famous reference to seven-gated Thebes is to these Middle Helladic fortifications, which must have stood until the fourteenth century B.C. During this period the first Greek-speaking peoples probably arrived in Thebes.

We may attribute the sharp increase in population during the Late Helladic period to the same conditions that brought wealth and prosperity to the rest of Mycenaean Greece: profitable agriculture, maritime trade, and administrative consolidation. There is evidence of all of these in Thebes. Many imported objects have been found in its two consecutive Late Helladic palaces and its rich homes. Local legends tell of conquests that show the city extended its power over a large geographic area. Thebes probably constructed its Cyclopean wall in the fourteenth century B.C. The population then rose sharply: 5,760 inhabitants within the walls is a conservative estimate; houses are known to have stood outside the walls, and a plausible estimate of the total population could be as high as 7,500 to 9,000. As small as this may seem by modern standards, the population of Thebes at the peak of the Mycenaean period was extraordinarily high in comparison with other cities of the time. It is conceivable that Thebes maintained a population of this size for more than a hundred years, during which time the city fought a series of wars against Orchomenos and against a coalition of rival Mycenaean states (remembered in myths about the Seven against Thebes and the War of the Epigonoi). Thebes was conquered and destroyed by the middle of the thirteenth century B.C. and was perhaps the first major Mycenaean city to experience its Dark Age. By 1100 B.C., the population had shrunk to about a thousand, which probably lived in the sparsely inhabited northern tip of the Kadmeia, the low-lying area north of the Mycenaean city, remembered in Greek tradition as Hypothebai.

The ability to exploit the Aonian plain agriculturally allowed Thebes to recover gradually during the Dark Ages and to expand the settlement once more towards the Mycenaean akropolis. Although we lack archaeological evidence of habitation, we can make inferences about the city's development by observing the changing locations of its cemeteries. The population had increased to at least 2,500 by 800 B.C. During the Geometric and Orientalizing periods (ca. 900 to 600 B.C.), Thebes became once more the economic and cultural center of Boiotia. The wars with its archrival, Orchomenos, were renewed; the outcome seems to have favored Thebes, which solidified its domination over eastern Boiotia. The population of Thebes may have been over 5,000 by 600 B.C. While Thebes was consolidating its power in Boiotia, other Greek city-states like Korinth and Athens broadened their agriculturally based economies through extensive trading and colonizing in the Mediterranean. Thebes had little or no participation in these activities. It continued to adhere to its conservative policies and maintained an economy based entirely on agriculture. Consequently, neither the economy nor the population expanded as much as those of other major Greek cities.

The population of Thebes did continue to grow during the sixth century, however, and it is possible that by 500 B.C. it had exceeded the previous high of the Late Helladic period (ca. 7,000 to 9,000). During this time, Thebes had become the most important city of the Boiotian League, an organization that was primarily religious, but that also had political and military functions. Thebes went through one of its worst historical periods from 520 to 446 B.C., a time that coincides with the life of Pindar (ca. 518 to 438 B.C.), perhaps the city's most famous native son. This period saw the humiliation of Thebes during the Persian wars of 480 to 479 B.C., when the city found itself allied with the Persians against the other Greeks. This was also a time of bitter rivalry with Athens, the rich and powerful neighbor to the south. Thebes suffered several military defeats during this period.

In 447/446, however, there was an unexpected change of fortune: after the victory over Athens at Koroneia and the formation of the Boiotian Confederacy, Thebes was in a position of political and military advantage. A wall 7 km long was built around the Kadmeia, and the population swelled to over 20,000. The city's power continued to grow in the early fourth century, a period of friendship with Athens and of increasing rivalry with Sparta. In 371 B.C., Thebes and its Boiotian allies crushed the formidable Spartan army in the battle of Leuktra. For the next ten years, Thebes ruled the Greek mainland from Sparta to Macedonia, under the leadership of Epaminondas and Pelopidas (Buckler 1980).

The period from 446 to 335 B.C. was one of unprecedented affluence: many public buildings were constructed; new sanctuaries were built and old ones renovated or refurbished; a new and longer conduit was added to the aqueduct system; perhaps for the first time in the city's history there were many commissions for sculpture to decorate sanctuaries and public areas. But all of this ended catastrophically in 335 B.C., when

Alexander the Great sacked and destroyed the entire city, leaving only the sanctuaries and the house of Pindar. Most of the population was killed or sold into slavery. The few who escaped eventually returned to rebuild, with the help of contributions from other Greek cities. The population of Thebes shrank to about 2,000. In 316 B.C., Kassandros rebuilt the wall of the Kadmeia and this encouraged new settlers. By ca. 300 B.C., the population of Thebes could easily have reached 5,000 or more.

During the Hellenistic and Roman periods, Thebes was one of the most important cities of Boiotia. The archaeological remains do not show that many public buildings were constructed, although many of the old ones clearly were maintained. Pausanias found most of the sanctuaries still functioning in the second century A.D. Greater Thebes, though unfortified, was inhabited by those who wished to have large properties or orchards, but it was gradually abandoned, probably as a result of warfare in the Hellenistic period. To judge by the few remains of the Roman period found in Greater Thebes, the population continued to decline until the end of antiquity, or to fluctuate between 2,000 and 5,000.

By the Early Christian period, the entire population had withdrawn to the Kadmeia, using the area of Greater Thebes solely for burial. There were even burial sites on the Kadmeia, which shows that the akropolis itself was only sparsely populated, perhaps by about 2,000 people. The population gradually increased after the time of Justinian. The rich land and central location contributed to making Thebes the capital of Greece in the eighth century, and soon after that, Greater Thebes was inhabited once more. Between 800 and 1200, successful agriculture and the silk-weaving industry gave Thebes a long period of prosperity. According to Benjamin of Tudela, the Jews of Thebes, an ethnic minority, numbered 2,000 in 1160, and we can estimate that the total population exceeded 5,000 on the basis of the archaeological evidence, which shows not only that the Kadmeia was occupied in its entirety, but that there were many houses and churches outside it.

There is no indication that Thebes suffered as a result of the Frankish conquest of Greece in 1204. To the contrary, its fortifications were renovated, and for the first time in its Christian history, a palace was constructed on the Kadmeia. It is even likely that the population rose to at least 6,000. Toward the end of this period (late fourteenth and fifteenth centuries), however, there was increasingly frequent warfare, culminating in the Turkish conquest in 1460. It is possible that the population had diminished sharply by 1500, although archaeological evidence of this period is scarce. Under Ottoman rule, Thebes nevertheless must have enjoyed relative prosperity because of its central location, its fortifications, and its rich land. During this period, the population must have been about 3,000.

The population changes of Thebes reinforce the historical and archaeological picture of the city. It has been surprising to note that despite the importance of Thebes, its average population remained rather low, 2,000 to 4,000 people. Out of curiosity, I calculated the total number of people who lived and died in Thebes over a 4,500-year period.

Estimating an average life span of 33 years for the period from 2500 to 600 B.C., and of 50 to 60 years for the period from 600 B.C. to the present, the total comes to about 400,000. There were only five population peaks—three in which the population exceeded 5,000, and two in which the population was just over 20,000. The population peaks of the Mycenaean and Classical periods coincide with the most glorious and best-remembered times of Theban history, periods characterized by economic success and military might, which were expressed through monumental architecture and the construction of extensive fortifications. Ironically, however, these two periods ended in major catastrophes. I would suggest that fortifications on such a scale aroused the intense hostility of neighboring states and were considered provocative. Thus, what was originally built to protect may actually have invited attack.

AGRICULTURE

Throughout its long history, Thebes has maintained an unswerving commitment to agriculture. It is one of the few Greek cities that was able to maintain a high standard of living for its population without ever becoming seriously involved in seafaring. All of Boiotia was agriculturally rich and could satisfy its own material needs, whereas Attica had difficulty providing food for its people. Boiotia not only produced excellent grain, but also provided itself—and Athens as well—with vegetables, game, and eels (Michell 1940:4, 51). Its abundant water supply enabled Boiotia, through irrigation, to produce both winter and spring wheat. Boiotia was also famous for its cattle, horses, and sheep. Even during the Middle Ages, the area around Thebes was one of the best organized agricultural regions of the Byzantine empire (Svoronos 1959). The history, mythology and religion of Boiotia repeatedly show the primacy of agriculture. Hesiod, one of the earliest known poets of Greece, wrote a treatise on agriculture in the seventh century B.C. *(Erga)*. Dionysos, originally a god of fertility, was said to have been born in Thebes. Its fertile land enabled Thebes to experience prolonged periods of prosperity and to rebound after disaster.

One of the most poorly documented periods of Greek history is the Dark Age (ca. 1100 to 800 B.C.). While it is fair to say that most Greek cities revitalized themselves through trade and commerce in the Mediterranean, the Theban recovery may be attributed entirely to agriculture. There were no imported objects in Thebes during this period, and the archaeological evidence attests to a modest life style. Yet, one of the most surprising realizations to emerge from this study has been the fact that during the period from 900 to 600 B.C., Thebes was probably one of the most important cities of Greece and may even have considered itself a cultural center. I have explained the reasons for this in my discussion of Thebes in the Geometric period. I would add here that this now largely forgotten resiliency may be attributed both to the highly successful and profitable agriculture and to the vital and powerful oral tradition.

It is true that the economies of many Greek cities were based on agriculture. The Thebans were unusual, however, in their single-minded preoccupation with the land and their unwillingness to diversify their economy through other kinds of profitable endeavors. No doubt they were so because their land was unusually fertile and amenable to intensive and highly profitable cultivation techniques. With the exception of Epaminondas' naval program in 366 to 364 B.C. (Buckler 1980:160-175), the Boiotians never tried seriously to become a sea power. The Mycenaeans gathered at Aulis before going to Troy not because Boiotia was an important naval base, but because the Mycenaeans of the Peloponnese had just conquered Thebes and were thus the masters of a rich province that could provide them with the necessary supplies for their expedition.

So far as trading goes, it is clear that Thebes received imported goods in many periods of its history, although there is never a clear indication that the Thebans themselves went to sea. It is possible, therefore, that others imported things for them, at least much of the time. The Boiotians were not totally ignorant of the sea, however; there are references to seafaring as early as Hesiod's *Erga,* and there are representations of ships on their Geometric pottery (Williams 1958). It is possible, however, that their fondness for ships was a romantic one, not closely tied to the practical business of sailing.

THE LEGACY OF THEBES

Thebes has made a significant contribution to Greek civilization, and it is important to recall some aspects of Theban culture that are well known and to acknowledge those that are less well remembered. These involve several areas of development, such as religion, social and political organization, economics, and the arts.

Much of Theban influence on religion related in large measure to agriculture, which played a central role in the city's own history. Demeter and Dionysos, originally gods of fertility, may well have been introduced into the Theban pantheon as early as the time of the founding of the Kadmeia, ca. 2100 B.C. The meager evidence of that remote era makes it difficult even to speculate about the circumstances of their introduction, but if it did occur at that time, their Theban cults must have been the earliest on the Greek mainland. The worship of Demeter and Dionysos spread, in all likelihood, from Thebes to other areas of Greece, together with the superior agricultural practices with which these gods were associated. In Thebes, their worship was of primary importance, equaled only by that of Apollo.

Several cults and festivals associated with other gods were uniquely Theban; some of these may have had considerable influence on the development of Greek religion. We cannot fail to call attention to the cult of the secret society of the Kabeiroi and the festival of the *Kabeiria*. The sanctuary was located at the junction of the Aonian and Teneric plains, only 5 km from Thebes (Wolters and Bruns 1940). The only other sanctuary in all of Greece dedicated to the Kabeiroi was on the island of Samothrake. Although little is known about the *Kabeiria* (Hemberg 1950), it appears that the cult resembled that of Dionysos in that it was orgiastic in character and centered around an older man *(Kabeiros)* and a boy *(pais)*.

The *Agrionia,* an agricultural festival famous throughout the Greek world, was celebrated on the Kadmeia in honor of Dionysos and included competitions in tragedy, comedy, and music. Music, of all the arts, was particularly favored by the Thebans. Thebes nurtured the finest musicians of Greece and may well have been the only city to have erected a statue of a musician (Pronomos, the flutist, according to Pausanias 9.12.5) alongside a statue of its most famous statesman, Epaminondas.

Divination appears to have had a very long association with Theban religious practices. It was in Thebes that one of the earliest temples to Apollo as a god of divination was built, probably in the eighth century B.C., at the sanctuary of Apollo Ismenios. The Theban practice of divination (with which Teiresias, the most celebrated of all seers and himself a Theban, is associated), however, was known at least as early as the Mycenaean period. Divination and healing continued to be important religious activities until the end of antiquity. Pausanias recorded the presence of as many as five oracles (Apollo Ismenios, Apollo Spodios, the Bird Observatory of Teiresias, the oracle of Ammon-Zeus, and the oracle of Amphiaraos). I know of no other Greek city with as many oracles and believe that their presence in Thebes attests to a long and traditional association of divination and religious ritual.

A long and relatively uninterrupted tradition allowed Thebes to preserve a wealth of oral literature and one of the richest mythologies in the Greek world. The powerful accounts of the deeds of striking personalities combine historical with religious elements. Several epic poems existed that now survive only in fragments or in later versions, such as the *Thebaid* by Statius, which in turn inspired medieval authors such as Chaucer and Dante (Mozley 1928).

Even the bitter enmity between Thebes and Athens did not prevent Athenian writers from basing some of their greatest plays on Theban legends. It is true that we do not find a comparable preference reflected in the extensive repertory of Athenian vase painting, where the depiction of Theban myths is rare. Theban subjects were common, however, in Etruscan art (Small 1972; Krauskopf 1974), and Theban mythology continued to influence European literature directly or indirectly. In French literature alone, there have been numerous works based on Theban stories (Smith 1974).

No discussion of the Theban legacy could fail to mention Pindar, the first national poet of Greece. Pindar lived just after a period that the Thebans regarded as one of great cultural vitality. This was the later Dark Age and the Geometric period, when, following one of the deepest economic depressions Greece had ever known, Thebes experienced something of a renaissance. The Theban renaissance was not the result of trading or colonization, which revitalized other large Greek cities. It grew, rather, from the rich oral tradition that preserved the memory of a glorious past, from agricultural wealth, and from the renewal of Theban religious institutions. During the Geometric period, Thebes regained a position of prominence in Boiotia and undoubtedly sought broader recognition for her cultural contributions. By the sixth century B.C., however, when Pindar was born, conditions in Greece had changed: economic power and cultural influence had shifted to other centers. The Theban success following the Dark Age had been forgotten. Although Thebes maintained preeminence in Boiotia, her cultural leadership had faded. These circumstances must, I believe, have made the Thebans all the more nostalgic about their great past, and all the more desirous of regaining the admiration of the entire Greek world.

It was in this social environment that Pindar grew up, and he must have been not only inspired by his city's great traditions, but also deeply saddened as he witnessed her glory erode even further during the critical years of the Persian wars. I would suggest that the individual genius of Pindar was most significantly affected by that aspect of Theban culture which, transcending the confines of a single city, touched all those who understood the Greek language: the Theban oral tradition. Nurtured by it, Pindar reiterated in his poetry the Theban ideals of the Geometric period in proclaiming unity among the Greeks. Because he addressed the shared beliefs of the Greeks, his poetry was seen by them as overriding the boundaries of the city-states. He was the first poet to inspire a national audience, and his acknowledged greatness must also be seen to reflect on his native city.

In the sixth century B.C., Thebes became the most important city of the newly organized Boiotian League, which evolved into the Boiotian Confederacy in the fifth century. The Confederacy was one of the earliest and best-organized forms of representative government in ancient Greece (Larsen 1968:16-40). The events that followed the formation of the Confederacy in 446 B.C. demonstrate that Thebes was central to it: the construction of the wall of Greater Thebes, the doubling of its population, its military victories, all led to the hegemony of Thebes over the Greek mainland in the period from 371-362 B.C. This was probably one of the most extraordinary phenomena in Greek history: a city without a broad economic base, with virtually no commerce or major industry, with a small population, and with profitable agriculture as its only advantage, gained the leadership of the Greek mainland. The success of Thebes was undoubtedly the result of superior organization rather than economic power and numerical strength.

Much has been written about the Theban hegemony, not only because of its inherent historical interest, but also because of its influence on Greek political thought. Of most interest have been such things as the effect of the hegemony on the unification of Greece, the military strategies of Pelopidas and Epaminondas, and the history of the hegemony itself. Although the hegemony was a ten-year period of great Theban glory, it has unfortunately given rise to the incorrect notion that Thebes was an important city for those ten years alone. In reality, Thebes experienced many such periods, and these usually coincided with increases in its population (fig. 6.1). We may say, in fact, that Thebes was the most important city of Greece during most of the second millennium B.C., during the Christian era, and during shorter periods in between. Such prolonged prosperity was the result of several factors, but chiefly of the continued attachment to the rich Boiotian land and the successful exploitation of it. Agriculture provided Thebes with remarkable economic stability and helped it recover from periods of deep economic depression. The city flourished also by means of the help it received from other Boiotian communities, which made Thebes their capital.

In a sense, Thebes epitomized Boiotia, a province ridiculed by the Athenians of the Classical period, but one that nevertheless provided the Athenian playwrights with their most inspiring material. Whereas the star of Thebes never did shine as brightly as that of Athens, it did shine more frequently and for longer periods of time.

CATALOGUE OF SITES

All of the archaeological remains are catalogued here according to site. I have included not only those sites where significant remains were discovered, but also those where little or nothing was found. I believe this gives the most comprehensive picture of the depth of deposit, the spread of the remains and their state of preservation. All excavations, including those previously published, have been catalogued, and the locations of the sites charted on topographical maps (Maps A and B). References to the original publications are given; most are to the *Deltion* (through vol. 28, 1973, the latest available to me at the time of writing). Unpublished material is either from my own notes, in which case no reference is given, or from another source credited in the text. The location of each site is indicated in the text by the map coordinates, and by the name of the property owner. Street addresses are given when possible, but many streets are still unnamed. An "archaeological site" is one that is owned by the Greek government. The topographical map of Greater Thebes (Map A) was prepared at a scale of l:5000; that of the Kadmeia (Map B) at a scale of l:2000.

SITE 1. KADMEIA I-11.

Archaeological site, known as "the house of Kadmos," excavated in 1906-1929. Keramopoullos 1909A, 1911, 1912, 1917 (passim), 1921, 1922, 1927A, 1928, 1929, 1930A, 1930B. *Deltion* 21 (1966):191, pls. 197:a-b, 200:c. Schober 1934:1434-1436 (with a plan). On the stirrup-jars with Linear B: Catling and Millett 1965, 1969; Raison 1968, 1977; Godart 1970; Palmer 1972; McArthur and McArthur 1974; Sacconi 1974; Wilson 1976; Catling and Jones 1977; McArthur 1978; Fossey 1978. On the frescoes: Reusch 1948, 1953, 1955, 1957.

This is the most extensively excavated and the most important site in Thebes. The excavation reports were published by Keramopoullos in a fragmentary manner and in Greek, which probably accounts for the general lack of attention given the site itself. A careful study and republication of the excavation would be of value, although it might be very difficult to reexamine the data. Below is my summary of Keramopoullos' published reports; I have prepared a plan based on the descriptions and measurements he gave (cat. fig. 1).

Excavation began in 1906 when Keramopoullos observed ancient remains as construction work progressed north of the Daoutis property. At the time, a street 10 m wide and 55 m long, lined with butcher shops of the central market led from Pindar St. to Epaminondas St., cutting the city block in half (1909A:59-60, figs. 1-2). Keramopoullos excavated part of this street and thought, initially, that he had found a huge Mycenaean kiln, because of the fire-hardened remains and the large quantities of burned pottery (1909A: 61-63, n. 1). He worked for eight seasons at the site (1906, 1911, 1912, 1921, 1922, 1927, 1928, and 1929) interrupted by three wars (1912, 1914-1918, and 1922). His excavations uncovered a major portion of a Mycenaean palace. Keramopoullos sank several trial trenches in the same city block in an attempt to locate the western extension of the palace, but without success. He was constrained by the limited space in which to excavate and by the apathy of both the local population and the national government. His appeals for money to purchase the land and for systematic and extensive excavations went unheeded (1909A:122). The results of his excavations are arranged below by period and, insofar as possible, by rooms and associated finds.

EARLY HELLADIC. One wall was found running through rooms *M, Λ, K,* and *I,* consisting of one layer of large, undressed stones laid directly on the bedrock. Pottery associated with this wall was not published, but samples of the earliest pottery from the site were found and identified as "Pre-Mycenaean" and hand-made as early as the 1906 season (1909A:74, 95-96). More such pottery was found in room 114 (1928:50), four examples of which were subsequently published (1930A:31, fig. 2): these included two pots of Agia Marina style, one tripod-cauldron with impressed decoration, and one hand-made chytra. They date to EH III, which may be the earliest period of the site.

MIDDLE HELLADIC. Even fewer remains dating to this period were published. Two small sections of a wall in rooms *Λ* and *K,* which run parallel to the later building, are Middle Helladic, as revealed by the typical Middle Helladic construction using small, undressed stones (1909A:65, fig. 5). There is no mention of pottery, but it is likely that some was found with that called "Pre-Mycenaean" (1909A:74, 95; 1928: 50). Middle Helladic pottery is referred to in the discussion of the finds from the long trench west of the palace (1922:29).

LATE HELLADIC. I retain here the Greek letters used by Keramopoullos to label the rooms. Keramopoullos published only the measurements of room *Π*; I myself measured those remaining rooms that are well preserved.

Room A. Only the southwest corner is preserved. It was probably 7.49 m wide, similar to room *B.* This room may have belonged to a megaron, as Keramopoullos

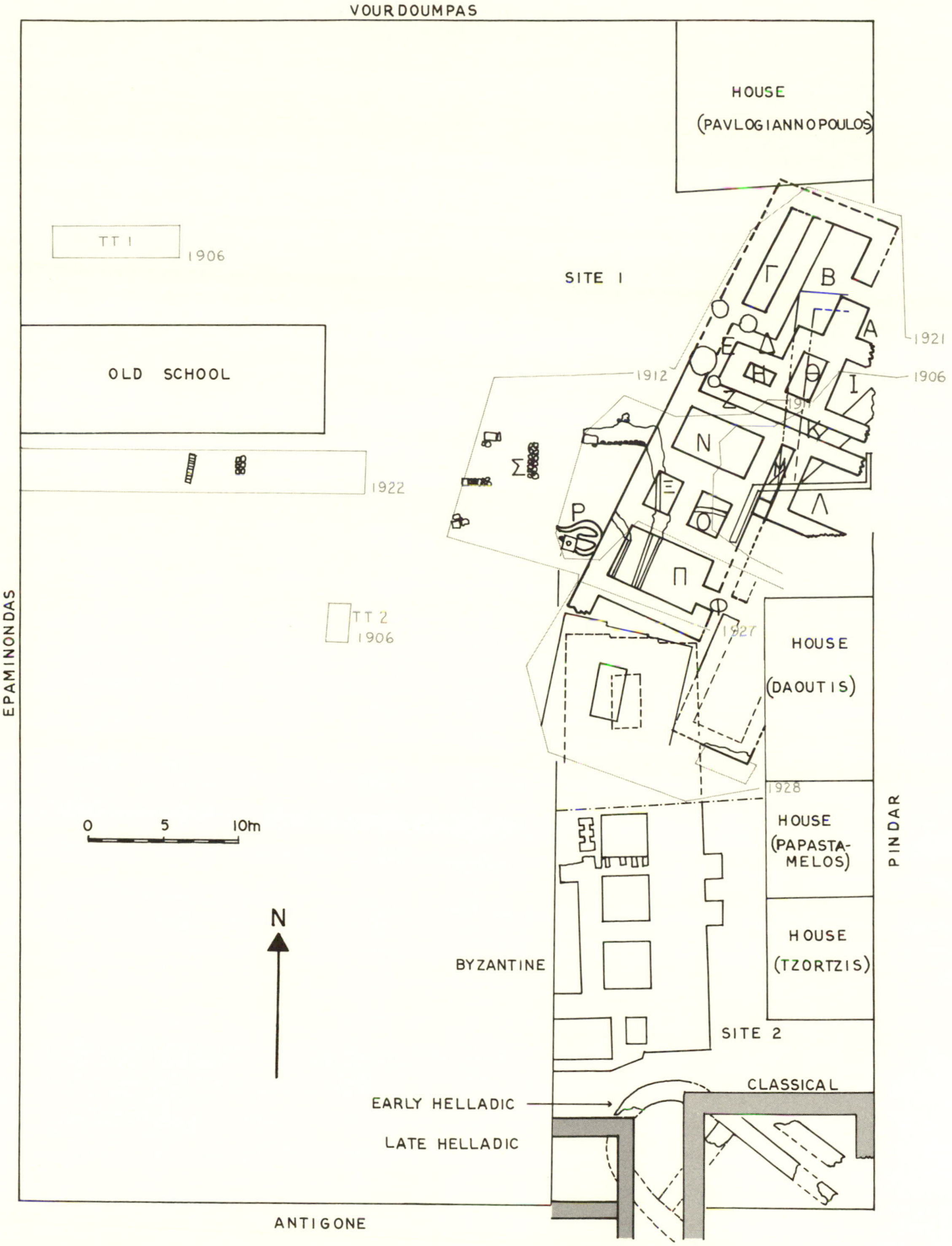

VOURDOUMPAS

HOUSE
(PAVLOGIANNOPOULOS)

TT 1
1906

SITE 1

Γ B
A
1921
OLD SCHOOL
1912
Θ 1906
I
Ψ
Σ
N
1922
Ξ
Λ
P
O
TT 2
1906
Π

1927

HOUSE
(DAOUTIS)

0   5   10m

1928

HOUSE
(PAPASTA-
MELOS)

N

HOUSE
(TZORTZIS)

BYZANTINE

SITE 2

CLASSICAL

EARLY HELLADIC →

LATE HELLADIC

EPAMINONDAS

PINDAR

ANTIGONE

Cat. Fig. 1. The Kadmeia. A comparison of site 1, as excavated by Keramopoullos,
with the main buildings of site 2 (for a reconstructed plan of site 1,
see figs. 2.9 and 2.10)

suggested (1921:33-34), and it is unfortunate that so little of it has remained.

Room B. One enters room *B* from room *A* through a doorway ca. 1.40 m wide. The estimated size of the room is 7.49 m x 2.64 m. At the south end, it opens onto a long corridor; there should have been a doorway towards room *Γ*; Keramopoullos was often unable to find doorways in this building. Only a few sherds were found; the function of the room is unclear.

Room Γ. Keramopoullos lamented that there were practically no walls left (1921:33). If we extend the walls of the adjoining rooms, the reconstructed area may measure 7.49 m x 1.50 m. No finds were reported, but Keramopoullos, in a later report (1922:30), referred to a doorway from the west courtyard. The northern end was damaged before Keramopoullos' excavations when the adjoining modern house was constructed (1909A: 59, fig. 4).

Corridor ΔEZK, MΦ. This long, winding corridor is one unit. What Keramopoullos called two "walls" between *Z* and *K* (1927A:33, fig. 1) proved to be burned debris, which was cleared in 1965 (*Deltion* 1966:191). The narrow corridor measures 1.12 m in width; section *Δ* communicates with the south side of room *B*. Keramopoullos found eighty stirrup-jars here, which bore inscriptions in Linear B (1921:33). Keramopoullos believed they were made at the palace (see kiln *P*, west of the palace) and stored in the corridors (1930A:33-34). In section *E*, which was not as well preserved because of later in-

trusions, fragments of additional stirrup-jars were found (1921:33). Section *Z* yielded not only more stirrup-jars, but also cups and bowls. Furumark studied this pottery (1941A, 1941B) but the first extensive publication of it was prepared by Raison (1968). Among the finds from Section *K*, Keramopoullos mentions two fragments of stirrup-jars and some cups, one of which was published in the first report (1909A:73, figs. 7, 8, FS264). Three stone fragments carved with the running spiral and the scale pattern in shallow, delicate relief were also found here (1909A, figs. 7:1-3, 19). A cup FS230 was found in an area where the fire-hardened layer had been broken (1909A:100, pl. 3:10) and this could be the place where yet another decorated sherd was found (pl. 3:6). Nothing else is reported to have been found here except the typical accumulation of burned debris. Section *M* of the corridor was destroyed before Keramopoullos' excavations. In the "clay layer" he found only some "fired bricks" (1909A:72). In section *Φ*, excavated at a later date, Keramopoullos found again a fire-hardened layer on top and a "burned layer" below it. The latter yielded some burned wood (one beam seemed to belong to the wooden floor of the corridor), a great deal of pottery, and some fresco fragments (1928:47). But most interesting by far was the find of a hoard of onyx jewelry in front of room *Π*, which was published in detail (1930A). A fragmentary wall, described but not shown in the plan, revealed that the corridor continued further south at least 6 m beyond room *Π* (1928:49-50; here, fig.

2.10, room *Π3*). Keramopoullos considered this long corridor similar to those of Minoan palaces (1930A:33).

Room H. This room is approximately 1.80 m x 0.90 m. No objects were found here. Keramopoullos reports only the presence of burned beams lying in a north-south direction inside the "clay-layer" (1921:32). He later interpreted the room as a light-well, an influence of Minoan architecture (1930A:33; 1930B).

Room Θ. This is a small space, 3.08 m x 1.80 m, perhaps opening to room *I*. Here Keramopoullos found one complete stirrup-jar (1921:32) and fragments of thirty others. It is likely that this was a storage room.

Room I. This partially preserved room, approximately 3.50 m wide and of unknown length (see discussion of room *Λ*), was excavated in 1906. There were three basic layers, the uppermost consisting of fire-hardened material, the middle of ashes and burned wood ("burned layer"), and the lower mostly of clay ("clay layer"). There were no finds in the top layer but there were stones within the extremely hard debris. In the second layer, which was at least 0.50 m thick, three well-preserved beams, 0.13 m thick, were found lying north-south and spaced 0.35 m apart. Other more poorly preserved beams were found, some of which Keramopoullos determined went north-south, and others east-west. There were some thin planks (cf. room *Π*). Associated with the burned wood were fire-hardened mud-bricks and thin, poros stone slabs. Beneath this, but still within the "burned layer" and above the "clay layer,"

were five large stirrup-jars (1909A:67, fig. 5; pp. 96-99, figs. 16-17) and other pottery, including a shallow bowl FS295 (1909A:75, Fig. 7:7). The lower layer was not excavated until 1921. Keramopoullos did not describe it in detail, but did mention some pottery, a stone vase, and stone fragments showing the same relief design as that seen on the fragments found in corridor *ZK* (1921:32).

Room Λ. This partially preserved room is approximately 3.60 m wide. The east wall, which Keramopoullos seems to have found here, appears in the figure 5 plan of 1909A, but does not appear in the later, more accurate plans (1927, fig. 1; 1930, fig. 1). Either Keramopoullos doubted that it was Mycenaean, or thought it pointless to include it because it had been damaged by the locals (about whom he vaguely complains, 1927A:32). I suspect that it was demolished by the locals, but that it was indeed Mycenaean and would complete the measurement of room *Λ* to ca. 3.60 m x 3.70 m. If the same wall line extended beyond corridor *K* to room *I*, the latter would be of comparable size, 3.50 m x 3.70 m. The stratigraphy of room *Λ*, as described by Keramopoullos, is comparable to that of room *I*, and shows the same basic layers: the uppermost of fire-hardened debris, at least 0.80 m thick; the second, yielding bones, charcoal, and pottery beneath the ashes, only 0.20 to 0.30 m thick; and the third "clay layer," red in color and ca. 1 m thick. The archaeologist Christos Tsountas was at the site when it was excavated and confirms the observations made by Keramopoullos (1909A:70):

there were many "fired bricks," two of which were found intact and measured 0.32 m x 0.32 m, 0.03 to 0.05 m thick, and 0.27 m x 0.26 m, 0.02 m thick. Many "Pre-Mycenaean" potsherds were also found, presumably lower down in the third layer. A large quantity of Mycenaean pottery was found in the second layer; the stems of over a hundred cups were counted. All of the pottery was plain with the exception of a few decorated sherds, which were not published but were later mentioned in reference to other such sherds found elsewhere on the site (1909A:71, 100-101). Finally, a few fragments of frescoes were found on the south wall of the room (1909A:69).

Unlabeled room. The room south of room Λ was dug during the construction of a house (property of Daoutis). Keramopoullos was told that a section of the aqueduct of Thebes tall enough for a man to walk in was found here (1909A:71-72).

Room N. The room is of irregular rectangular shape: 2.73 m (west), 2.84 m (east), 5.34 m (north), and 5.54 m (south). There was an entrance to corridor *M* (1909A:76). The preserved remains, most of which were the destruction debris of the palace, were over 2 m deep. Here Keramopoullos found the numerous fragments of the fresco showing a procession of women that was reconstructed by Reusch (1948, 1955, 1957). There were also numerous sections of unpainted plaster, bricks, a lot of burned wood and pottery, gold scraps, and hundreds of glass-paste beads. This, the best-preserved room of the site, was excavated in four seasons (1906, 1911, 1921, and 1929). Keramo-

poullos gave most of his energy and attention to clarifying the stratigraphy, identifying the building materials, and determining the original height of the palace. But the different layers were not uniform throughout the room, and the excavation procedure made interpretation even more difficult. Keramopoullos removed three uneven slices: the first between corridor *M* and the eastern end of the room (1909A:76-77) the second in the eastern half of the room (1909A:77-80, 88), and the third in the western half of the room (1911:144-145). These three sections were excavated down to the floor level and, if we are to judge from the only photograph of the room, were composed of strata totaling about 2 m (1909A:78, fig. 8). The northwest corner of the room was excavated at a much later date (1921:33), and the layers below the floor down to the bedrock, still later (1929:60-61).

Keramopoullos initially believed that he had uncovered a multistoried palace (1909A:89-90), but then changed his mind (1927A:42). His first report of a second burned layer (1909A:88) he later considered an error (1911:145). It is by no means an easy task to follow Keramopoullos' descriptions because he neither numbered nor named the layers he excavated. But if we tabulate his information as shown in catalogue table 1, columns A through C, we observe seven distinct and fairly homogeneous strata, and we get a quite coherent picture of the layers of room *N*. On the east wall of the room (col. A), most of the burned layer (no. 2) was found near the inner portion of the room. The fresco layer (no. 4) was not found here because

Catalogue Table 1. The stratigraphy of room *N* as described by Keramopoullos (1909A, 1911)

Layer no.	*1906 season: layers on east wall of room (1909A:76)*	*1906 season: layers of eastern half of room (1909A: 77-80, 88)*	*1911 season: layers of western half of room (1911: 144-145)*	*Observations*
1	fire-hardened sur-face (burned clay, stones)	fire-hardened sur-face (burned clay, stones)	same? not mentioned, implied	surface layer cover-ing the entire site
2	closer to the room: similar burned layer to that in the room	thick, burned layer (wood, wall-plaster, pottery, glass-paste beads)	painted wall-plas-ter, a lot of pot-tery, burned wood, ashes, jewelry, soil, baked bricks	building materials, wall-plaster and objects; first burned layer
3	"red soil" with pottery and a few objects	soil, sand, and some pottery	layer of thick plas-ter, mostly mono-chrome	intermediate layer of debris thoroughly disintegrated by fire
4	——	numerous frescoes and monochrome plaster	numerous frescoes	layer of frescoes and plaster
5	burned layer 30 cm thick (pottery, bones, seashells, wood)	burned wood, a lot of pottery, some jewelry(?), some lead; beams ori-ented north-south	sand and pottery, burned layer missing	not uniform layer of wood and debris; second burned layer
6	clay layer, baked bricks, sun-dried bricks	clay layer, some baked bricks	soil layer	bottom layer of clay, soil, and bricks
7	east wall of room *N*	(did not excavate any further in 1906)	layer with Pre-Mycenaean pottery	Pre-Mycenaean layers
8	——	——	bedrock	bedrock

there were frescoes only inside the room. There is no layer of Pre-Mycenaean ma-terial (no. 7) because the east wall of room *N* occupied its place.

The layers of the eastern half of room *N* (col. B) show the entire stratigraphy, per-haps the best record of the destroyed building: layers 2 and 5 (both "burned layers", layer 2 the thicker) contained a lot of burned wood. Above each of the burned layers were the remains of building materials (layers 1, 3-4).

In the western half of room *N* (col. C) we see the same distribution of layers, except for the absence of burned layer 5. This bewildered Keramopoullos. But layer 2 in the same western section contained less burned material than layer 2 in the eastern section. The explanation for this must be that we are closer to the western end of the building, and the wood collapsed toward the middle of the room. It is clear, in any case, that not only were the layers not uniform throughout the room, but they were not of the same thickness in all areas. The bottom layer (no. 6), beneath which was a rather thick layer of Pre-Mycenaean material resting on the bedrock, was not quite uniform either and caused some confusion. Layer 6 was interrupted on the south side of the room by a mysterious wall shown only in the plan of the 1906 season (1909A:68, fig. 5, wall *Ξ*). This wall was 0.45 m high and 0.45 m wide, of unknown length, but presumably continuing another 1.75 m from the west wall where a step 0.45 m high was cut in the bedrock (1929:61), resulting in two different levels of bedrock within the same room. Keramopoullos believed that this was originally the south wall of room *N*, which was later remodeled and enlarged (1929:61). I think it more meaningful, however, to interpret this wall as evidence of the terracing of uneven ground in preparation for construction. In this area, the ground sloped to the south, where wall *Ξ* was needed to support the south wall of the room, and to the east, where the irregular ground was cut away and then filled with clay. The clay layer (no. 6) is more substantial in the eastern part of the room (cols. A, B) than

in the western part (col. C). Beneath the "mystery wall," Keramopoullos found decorated Mycenaean pottery of Late Helladic II date (1929:61), which suggests an approximate date of construction for the palace.

Room Ξ. Approximately 2.14 m x 2.80/2.62 m, this badly preserved room was damaged by the construction of a recent (Byzantine?) wall. In the burned layer Keramopoullos found a few gold scraps, masses of lead, glass-paste beads, and "fired bricks" (1911:147).

Room O. This room is comparable in size to room *Ξ* but much better preserved. The burned layer (which is the way Keramopoullos refers to it from 1911 on) contained two large burned beams, one lying north-south, the other east-west, some poorly preserved fresco fragments, sun-dried bricks (within one of which was the stem of a cup), many glass-paste beads, a bronze spearhead, bronze arrowheads, masses of lead, a piece of gold jewelry made of flat discs connected by wires, a gold wing, a gold flower (lily?), and three unfinished objects of rock crystal (two multi-sided prisms, one oblong) (1930A:35-36, figs. 3, 4). Here too, Keramopoullos found pottery and evidence of damage (and perhaps theft) resulting from the construction of a Byzantine wall (1911:146-147).

Room Π. This is a large room, 3.75/ 3.80 m x 6.20/6.40 m. It is possible that part of room *Π* was excavated when trial trenches 4 and 5 were sunk (1909A:83-84). The excavation of the room was the focus of the sixth season. The work was done very carefully here, yet using the same procedure as that used in the excavation of room *N*, this time taking slices from west to east. Instead of verbally describing the stratigraphy, Keramopoullos made two drawings: the first after he had completed the excavation of the west side of the room (1927A: fig. 3), the second when he neared the east wall (1927A: fig. 4). The drawings show that the extensive debris had fallen into the room and had been preserved at an angle, rather than in neat horizontal layers (see especially fig. 4). Figure 3 gives an even more interesting picture of the stratigraphy, which we can compare with the strata in room *N* (cat. table 1). Keramopoullos completely omits some of the layers in the drawing of the section. He clearly omits the first "fire-hardened" layer (mentioned in 1927A:35-36). The "clay layer" is mentioned only in the text (1927A:35), and the "fresco layer" is described but not associated with the stratigraphy (1927A:41-42).

But a definite similarity in the destruction pattern emerges from the comparison shown in catalogue table 2: the materials of the upper structure collapsed and sealed the large quantity of wood used in the construction below. However, enough air circulated for the wood to continue burning slowly for a long time (layer 5). As the wood disintegrated, other materials sank into its place to be in turn disintegrated by the continuing heat (layers 3, 4). Above all of this, a second layer of wood collapsed and burned in some areas (layer 2). The building debris was transformed by the great heat into a hard, thick crust that sealed the entire site (layer 1).

The west half of room *Π* was damaged by penetrations during the Roman and medieval periods (1927A:33-34). Three gold objects were found in the soil disturbed by these penetrations: a reclining deer, 4 cm long (1927A, fig. 6); an ornament in the form of a jug, 2.5 cm high (1927A, fig. 7); and a necklace (?) made of rings and discs (1927A, fig. 8). Other finds from the room included a bronze attachment, 9 cm

Catalogue Table 2. Comparison of the stratigraphy of room *N* and
the section of room *Π*

Stratigraphy of Room *N* (Catalogue Table 1)	Section of Room *Π* (Keramopoullos 1927A:fig. 3)
1. Fire-hardened layer	not shown in the section
2. First burned layer	4 (?)
3. Fire-dissolved debris	5, 8
4. Frescoes and wall plaster	missing?
5. Second burned layer	1, 2, 3, 7
6. Clay layer	not shown
7. Pre-Mycenaean	not shown
8. Bedrock	not shown

Note: Although the section of room *Π* is poorly drawn, it is possible to identify layers found elsewhere in the excavation. Keramopoullos' nos. 6 and 9 in the section are not tabulated here because no. 6 refers to the walls, and no. 9, to the foundation of a modern building.

in diameter, decorated with 23 nautili and 24 shells (not shown) and lots of pottery, most of it badly fragmented.

Keramopoullos gave most of his attention to identifying building materials and understanding construction methods. He realized that the floor consisted of a layer of clay, perhaps the same "clay layer" found elsewhere in the excavation. On top of this was a wooden floor made of longitudinal beams 0.20 m thick, laid at intervals of 0.75 to 0.79 m, and of similar transverse beams laid at intervals of 0.85 m. On top of the beams, he was even able to find the remains of planks 0.03 m thick (1927A:39). He was quite certain that he had identified wooden reinforcements for the interior walls and published a drawing of his reconstruction (1927A:36-37, fig. 5). This drawing he later revised to show rows of short, transverse beams set in the wall instead of vertical beams (1929, figs. 1-2; 1930A: 30), an acknowledged method of Mycenaean wall construction (Mylonas 1966:48, fig. 11). The reinforcement beams were approximately 0.14 m thick. Keramopoullos identified yet a third kind of timber, about 0.35 m thick as roof material (1927A:39). He also found a great many roof tiles (1927A:40), perhaps the same as the "fired bricks" found in previous seasons.

A few fresco fragments were found: a human eye, a feline paw, and a spiral are the only examples mentioned. Keramopoullos differentiated two kinds of fresco (1927A:41-42) and realized that the room had undergone remodeling. During the following season, a doorway to the room was found in the east wall (1928:48).

Rooms Π_1-Π_5. The work of the 1928 season revealed the existence of at least four, perhaps five, rooms south and east of room Π. Of these, only three were included in the final plan of 1930; remains of the others may have been considered too scanty (1930A, fig.1). The plan presented here is based on Keramopoullos' measurements and descriptions (cat. fig. 1, figs. 2.9-2.10).

Room Π_1, south of room Π, had been almost completely destroyed by the structure which Keramopoullos refers to as the "Turkish bath" (cat. fig. 1). Only a small triangular area of it remained (1930A, fig. 2); the unidentified building south of room Π is the so-called "Turkish bath" (1928:45-46). Although not much was left of this room, Keramopoullos thought he had found a section of its southern wall 1.10 m from room Π (1928:47). This would make Π_1 a corridor, and an entrance should have been found from the west courtyard, but Keramopoullos neither discusses it nor indicates it in the plan. Excavation in the light-well area of the "Turkish bath" convinced Keramopoullos that there was at least one other room south of this corridor (room Π_5; 1928:46, 50).

Fragmentary walls indicate the existence of rooms Π_2, Π_3, and Π_4. A portion of the east wall of corridor Φ was found during the excavation of the onyx hoard (1928:47), which clearly showed the continuation of corridor $M\Phi$ and the presence of a room, Π_2, opposite Π. The corridor was destroyed when the so-called "Turkish bath" was built, but Keramopoullos excavated a small area east of the "bath" and discovered a section of a wall that apparently belonged to the southern border of yet another room, Π_3; according to Keramopoullos, the wall turned a corner, showing that rooms Π_2 and Π_3 were each approximately 3 m wide. He also thought that the area he had excavated was the inside of yet another room, Π_4, in which he found a lot of Mycenaean pottery, and in the layers below it, well-preserved Early Helladic pottery (1928:49-50; 1930A, fig. 2 for the Early Helladic pottery).

West of the Palace. The area west of rooms N, Ξ, and Π was excavated in 1911, 1912, and 1922. Most interesting was the discovery of a horseshoe-shaped structure west of room Π (1927A, fig. 1, structure P), built of stones and covered on the inside with hard white plaster. A small interior wall was built of mud-brick and covered with the same plaster. At a height of 0.60 m there was a plaster cover with holes, supported by the interior wall. Mycenaean pottery was found within, and a nearby depression was filled with clay. Keramopoullos concluded that the structure was a pottery kiln (1911:148-149). A small area of this structure had been damaged through the construction of what appeared to be a well, the stone cover of which was found on the kiln (1911:149-150). Within the "well" at a depth of 3.60 m, were five branching tunnels, each 1.10 m high and 0.50 m wide. The "well" was in reality a water main of the Theban aqueduct.

North of the kiln, Keramopoullos found a thick, undisturbed Mycenaean layer, but only poor architectural remains unrelated to the palace (1912:85-86; 1927, fig. 1:Σ). Ashes showing extensive burning were

found in this area. Most important was the find of a large, irregular stone slab, approximately 2.10 m square, and 0.75 m thick. On the one flat side, an oval, raised 0.05 m was very precisely carved to measure 1.54 m x 1.36 m (1912:86-87, fig. 1). Keramopoullos thought it might be the keystone of a tholos tomb, but Kavvadias (1912:76) identified it as a column base. The carved surface is comparable in size to the base found in the monumental propylon at Phaestos (Pernier and Banti 1951:320-321) and bases similar in form are known from many Minoan-Mycenaean sites (see chap. 2). Keramopoullos found in the same area five column bases, which he attributed to the Roman agora, and a space with floor and walls of hard plaster that may have been a cistern (1912:86).

Trial Trench 1. During the first season, Keramopoullos opened five trial trenches: two considerably west of the palace (trenches 1 and 2), one in the west area discussed above (trench 3), and two somewhere within room Π (trenches 4 and 5; see cat. fig. 1). Trench 1, located north of the abandoned school on Epaminondas St., was 8 m x 2 m (1909A, fig. 1). On the east side of the trench the bedrock was found at 4 m; on the west side, at 5.40 m. The bedrock clearly sloped toward the west. Below 2 m, a lot of Mycenaean pottery was found in a thick layer of ashes, bones, bricks, and frescoes. Although the palace did not extend as far as trial trench 1, Keramopoullos published for purposes of comparison three decorated sherds from this trench (1909A, pls. 3:7-9) in the same plate as two sherds from corridor *K* of the palace, one a fragment of a cup FS230, found where the burned layer had been disturbed (1909A:100, pl. 3:10), and one a fragment decorated with FM58 (1909A, pl. 3:6). It is very important to note that the actual provenance of the three sherds from trial trench 1 is clearly given in Keramopoullos' discussion of the finds (1909A:101), *not* in the discussion of the trench itself (1909A:80-82). These three sherds have been erroneously included for dating purposes among the finds of the palace (for a discussion of the problem, see Symeonoglou 1973:73). Further confusing the issue is a typographical error in the original publication that refers the reader to plate 2 instead of plate 3 (Keramopoullos 1909A:101, pl. 3, sherds 7, 8, 9). The three sherds from trial trench 1 clearly date to the end of LH III B, but are in no way related to the palace (Furumark 1941B:52). Also found in trench 1 was an animal figurine of the Spine type, probably LH III B (1909A, fig. 18; French 1971:156-157).

Trial Trench 2. Approximately 15 m west of room *Π*; roughly 1.20 m x 2.40 m (see plan in 1909A:82, fig. 13). In this trench Keramopoullos found a Mycenaean wall (1909A, fig. 13, *β-β*) with pottery similar to that of the palace, and earlier walls (1909A, fig. 13, *γ-γ*) associated with Pre-Mycenaean pottery. The depth of the deposit was over 2.50 m.

Trench of the 1922 Season. West of the palace, Keramopoullos opened an enormous trench all the way to Epaminondas Street, measuring 22.50 m x 2.50 m (cat. fig. 1). At a distance of 14.30 m from Epaminondas Street, a substantial wall going north-south was found. It was 0.60 m thick and was preserved from a depth of 2 m to the bedrock found at 4.50 m. On the east side of this wall, the Mycenaean layer, 2.50 m deep, contained pottery "like that of the palace" and a lot of ash "from the pottery kiln" (1922:29). On the west side of this wall, Middle Helladic, Late Helladic, and recent materials were found in disarray. Keramopoullos suggested that this wall could have belonged to the perimeter of the palace. Approximately 3 m west of it, several brick walls were found from a depth of 3 m to over 5 m. Keramopoullos concluded that these were the walls of houses of an undetermined period. Throughout the trench, he found a lot of debris similar to that of the palace. He interpreted its presence as evidence that the site was cleared after the destruction of one palace to make room for a second (1917:353, 1922:29). The trench of 1922 proved that the palace did not extend to the west. It may more likely have extended to the east where the locals reported finding the burned layer during the construction of Pindar St. (1909A:111). The palace may have extended to the north as well (see sites 103, 204, 260, 261).

General Remarks. In my reconstructed plan of the palace (figs. 2.9-2.10) I have completed the partially preserved rooms, and I have drawn the rooms that Keramopoullos discussed but did not include in his plan. I have shown the corridor as it appeared when it was cleared in 1965, and I have added doorways. The building that emerges is an impressive one, some 40 m long and 18 m wide, with 17 rooms on either side of a long corridor.

There were probably additional rooms to the south, and additional units may have extended to the north and east. The palace was clearly destroyed by a sudden and thoroughly devastating fire (for a full discussion of the archaeological problems related to the house of Kadmos, see chap. 2).

BYZANTINE REMAINS OF SITE 1. Keramopoullos excavated part of a large structure that he called the "Turkish bath" (1928:45-46, 50-52) and published a plan two years later (1930A, fig. 1). The orientation of the building is not quite precisely given; if we correct it, we see that the portion Keramopoullos excavated is part of the large structure found in site 2 (see cat. fig. 1). The building in site 1 is not clearly visible today. An interpretation of it is given in the discussion of site 2; it is certainly not a "Turkish bath."

SITE 2. KADMEIA I-11.

Archaeological site. Platon and Touloupa 1964A. Touloupa 1964. *Deltion* 19B (1964):194-195, 212, pls. 224-230; *Deltion* 20B (1965):230-232; *Deltion* 21B (1966):177-180, pls. 189-193; *Deltion* 26B (1971): 202-207. Grumach 1965; Porada 1965, 1966, 1981.

The Archaeological Service ordered a halt to construction work when Mycenaean finds were uncovered here in the winter of 1963-1964. Most of the site was excavated then; a narrow strip at the south side was excavated in 1965 in order to con-

struct a supporting wall. In 1970, excavation down to the Early Helladic levels was carried out at the southwest corner of the site (western extension of the Mycenaean room) and at the northeast area. The discovery of Near Eastern cylinder seals was widely publicized in newspapers and periodicals and drew attention to the importance of Thebes in the Mycenaean period.

EARLY HELLADIC. The remains of a large, apsidal building (cat. fig. 2) were poorly

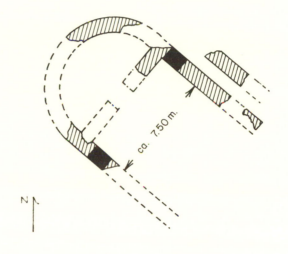

EH BLG.
SCALE 1:200

Cat. Fig. 2. Site 2, remains of two Early Helladic apsidal houses

preserved because of later intrusions. The reconstructed plan (fig. 2.2) shows an interior space approximately 7.50 m wide, with a dividing wall towards the horseshoe-shaped end of the building. The walls are 1.10 m thick and made of large, undressed stones. No traces of interior columns were found. There is possibly a door on the north wall. Parallel to the north side are remains of a wall that may belong to a building of the same size and form (see *Deltion* 1966:178, fig. 1, for a detailed plan of the site). It is most probable that the building dates to the middle of three phases of the Early Helladic period observed at the site (*Deltion* 1966:181, fig. 3, layers 17-19). A hoard of bronze tools was reported to have been found in a crude pot in the uppermost Early Helladic layer and included a double axe, a shaft-hole axe, flat axes, awls, and chisels (Platon and Touloupa 1964B, fig. 5). The tools could date to EH II or III (Renfrew 1967:9; Branigan 1974:23-24, 134). A lot of pottery was found at the site, most of it dating to EH III, although there was some dating to EH II. The floor, found at 5.15 m below the surface, was well preserved in one area, and intact pottery was found on it (*Deltion* 1971: 206, pl. 181: B).

MIDDLE HELLADIC. Architectural remains were scarce and fragmentary, having been damaged by later occupation. A layer only 0.50 m thick was found intact at the southeastern end of the excavation (*Deltion* 1966:181, fig. 3; layer 14). However, Middle Helladic pottery was found in several successive layers, mixed with later material. In fact, throughout the site, a great deal of Middle Helladic pottery representative of all phases of the period was found. In the published plan of the excavation (*Deltion* 1966:178, fig. 1) walls *Y* and *Σ* are the earliest, wall *Z* is slightly later, and structures *Θ*, *Π*, and *P* belong to a third phase. Of greatest importance are the remains of a large building (walls *B, H, Θ, K*), 6.50 m wide, which was destroyed by fire at the beginning of the Late Helladic period (*Deltion* 1964:195, 1965:230). It was probably built in the latter part of the Middle Helladic period and may have been a megaron. It was built of dressed masonry, and its southern wall showed evidence of reconstruction. The earlier phase probably dated to MH III.

LATE HELLADIC. The important architectural remains of the "Treasury Room" (so named by the excavators because of the impressive collection of objects) were found at the southwest corner of the site. The massive foundations, 1.12 m thick, were preserved to a height of 2.50 m and go all the way down to the bedrock. They were of large limestone boulders and constructed in Cyclopean style (see *Deltion* 1966:178, fig. 1, for a plan of the site). The room was 4.30 m wide and of unknown length. To the south, a storage room was partially excavated. Narrow clay partitions subdivided it into four compartments, each containing two storage jars (*Deltion* 1966: pl. 191). The lower halves of some of the jars were found in situ and a few contained olive pits. Also found in the room were numerous animal bones. East of the building there were remains of a pebble floor, perhaps that of a courtyard, and, beneath it, a Mycenaean drain built of stone (*Deltion* 1966:179, fig. 2).

The finds summarized here have been widely publicized. In addition to numerous fragments of frescoes, two hoards of objects were found: The first included a collection of objects made of lapis lazuli and of onyx, and a hematite seal. The second included jewelry made of gold, glass paste, and ivory. A few more objects were found in 1970 (*Deltion* 1971:206). Most interesting was the find of 38 cylinder seals, all but two of lapis lazuli. Ten of them were quickly published by the excavators (*Deltion* 1964, pls. 228B, 229; Platon and Touloupa 1964A, figs. 2-3, 5, 7-10; Touloupa 1964, figs. 6-8) and the same ten were then republished in various journals and newspapers. Several styles and periods are represented in this group, most of them from Mesopotamia: Early Dynastic (1), Akkadian (2), Isin-Larsa (1), Old Babylonian (3), Mitannian (6), and Kassite (12); there are also Hittite seals (1), Cypriot (11), and one of uncertain origin. Thirteen of the cylinder seals bear cuneiform inscriptions. There is little doubt that they came to Thebes as the commodity lapis lazuli (Porada 1981). The lapis group also included 26 uncarved cylinders, eleven large pendants of palm-tree motif (Platon and Touloupa 1964A, fig. 11), seven small axe-shaped beads, a necklace (?) of sixteen figure-of-eight shields, and seven beads of various shapes.

In the onyx group were 100 perforated beads of various shapes (Platon and Touloupa 1964A, fig. 12), one flattened cylinder carved with a representation of bull-leaping (Platon and Touloupa 1964A, fig. 4), and another showing a griffin (Touloupa 1964, fig. 5). The lentoid seal of hematite was carved with a representation of two horses (Platon and Touloupa 1964A, fig. 6). The second hoard included 52 gold beads of various shapes (Platon and Tou-

loupa 1964A, fig. 13; Touloupa 1964, fig. 4) along with two ivory diadems (?), 12 bottle stoppers (?) and at least 50 glass-paste beads of different shapes.

The treasury and storage rooms were clearly in the basement of a palace that is strikingly different in size, orientation, and manner of construction from the palace of site 1. The building was destroyed by fire at the end of the Late Helladic III B:1 period; a preliminary study of the pottery shows that it is identical in style to the pottery of the similarly constructed Mycenaean building of site 4. The hoards, which were in boxes, must have fallen from an upstairs room with the debris of the destruction (see chap. 2 for further discussion).

PROTOGEOMETRIC. A solitary trefoil-lipped oinochoe was found above the Mycenaean room. Most of the remains of the Protogeometric and Geometric periods seem to have vanished from Thebes, making the find of this vase a rare delight. It dates to the last phase of the Protogeometric period (Desborough 1952:48, 52, pl. 7).

CLASSICAL. In the southern half of the site, the foundations of a large building were found, continuing south underneath Antigone St. (*Deltion* 1964:194, pl. 225; 1966: 177, pls. 189:B, 190:a-b). The stratigraphy of the site had been disturbed by Roman and Byzantine reoccupations. The three preserved walls form part of a rectangle 13 m long (north side) and at least 10 m wide (west side); the east side is preserved to only 5 m. The west wall is best preserved, eight courses deep, 3.45 m high. The two uppermost courses are arranged in isodomic construction; in the courses below, the blocks are transverse to the direction of the wall and are clearly the foundation. Between the foundation and the isodomic layers is a short course of leveling blocks. The building material is local conglomerate, soft and crumbly.

The function and date of the building are not clear. It is probably Classical, of the fifth or fourth century. The excavators identified the building as the sanctuary of Demeter, which, according to Pausanias, occupied the site of the House of Kadmos and his Descendants (the second Mycenaean palace of Thebes). Unfortunately, the excavated remains do not conform to the plan of a conventional Greek temple; these may be the foundations of a portico of the Agora of Thebes, which, according to Pausanias, was in this vicinity, or of a square public building like the Telesterion of Eleusis. Finds of the Classical period were few and included very little pottery. Most important were two marble statuettes (Thebes Museum nos. 149, 150), one a headless figure of the Athena Parthenos type (*Deltion* 1964, pl. 226:a), 0.22 m high, found near the north wall of the Classical building. The other was a female head, 0.15 m. high, which could be a Demeter (*Deltion* 1964, pl. 226:B).

ROMAN. A hypocaustum built of ashlar masonry was found at the southwest corner of the site. The structure was only partially preserved; a section 3.20 m x 1.45 m was found in 1964 but was demolished by the excavators in order to reach the Mycenaean building below. A small section of the hypocaustum was found in the 1965 excavation (*Deltion* 1966:181, fig. 3, marked "Roman wall"). From this area came a few coins and numerous potsherds.

CHRISTIAN. No major structures were found in the deep, extensive strata of the southern half of the site, although the large quantities of pottery indicate heavy use of the area during the ninth to fourteenth centuries. A large wall was found in the southwest corner (*Deltion* 1966:181, fig. 3). Occupying the northwest quarter of

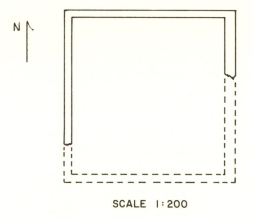

SCALE 1:200

Cat. Fig. 3. Site 2, plan of the Classical building

the site, however, was a most impressive building with massive concrete foundations going all the way to the bedrock. The presence of a hypocaustum in one of its rooms gave rise to the suggestion that the building was a Byzantine bath (*Deltion* 1964:195, 212). But the building was enormous (its eastern exterior foundation is 4 m thick) and there were no other remains of bathing facilities in the numerous rooms beyond the area of this hypocaustum. The building can be seen as a continuation of the so-called "Turkish bath" excavated by Keramopoullos (1930A, fig. 1; for a complete plan showing the corrected orientation of the "Turkish bath" in relation to the Byzantine building of site 2, see cat. fig. 1); the entire structure is at least 29 m long. No other building of this period found in Thebes can approach this one in size, which, in addition to its central location, suggests that it was built by someone of great wealth.

We know that shortly after 1287, a famous palace was built in Thebes by Nicholas II de St. Omer, and was underwritten by the vast fortune of his wife, Princess Marie of Antioch (Miller 1921:76; Ziehen 1934:1492). That palace was said to be large enough to house an emperor and his court, and was decorated with frescoes depicting the conquest of the Holy Land. It was destroyed by the Catalans in the fourteenth century (Miller 1921: 77). The Byzantine remains of sites 1 and 2 may well be the foundations of this palace, the hypocaustum being part of its facilities.

Site 2 is clearly at the center of the Kadmeia, where major structures continued to be built up to Byzantine times.

SITE 3. KADMEIA I-11.

Archaeological site. *Deltion* 19B (1964):197, pl. 231; *Deltion* 20B (1965):233-235, pls. 277:C-280:a; Platon and Touloupa 1964B. Touloupa 1964:27, fig. 9. *Deltion* 26B (1971):209. *Athens Annals of Archaeology* 8 (1976):86-90, K. Demakopoulou (Submycenaean tomb).

Linear B tablets, *Ug* series; Chadwick 1969; Godart and Sacconi 1978.

The site was one of the first to be excavated during the modern construction boom of Thebes. Excavation followed the discovery of a hoard of Mycenaean bronze weapons. Most of the work was done in 1964, but more has been done since then (1965, 1966, 1970, 1975).

EARLY HELLADIC. Little was found because only in a very small area did excavation proceed to the bedrock on which rested a very thin layer of Early Helladic remains. There was one foundation built of large river stones, and some pottery.

MIDDLE HELLADIC. In the northern half of the site, the Mycenaean remains were very poorly preserved and excavation continued beneath them. Seventeen cist graves numbered T 1 to T 17 were found here (see plan of the site in *Deltion* 1965:234, fig. 2), most with single burials, although T 13 contained a man and a woman in embrace, and T 15, a mother and infant. Tomb 1 was the largest (2.53 m x 1.15 m, 1.20 m. deep) and contained several burials; it was in poor condition because of the collapse into it of the Mycenaean building above. Mycenaean bronze objects were found in it (*Deltion* 1964, pl. 231:c).

The cemetery dates to the latter part of the Middle Helladic period. Three more tombs (T 18-T 20) were discovered east of the main excavated area by Demakopoulou (oral communication). Tombs 6 and 18 each contained a vase of the Late

Helladic 1 period in addition to pottery of developed Middle Helladic style (*Deltion* 1964, pl. 231:b). Tomb 3 contained two vases, one gold ring, carnelian beads, and glass-paste jewelry. The cemetery was extensive and continued to the north and west.

LATE HELLADIC. The Late Helladic architectural remains may be subdivided into two phases (cat. fig. 4), the earlier represented by several walls that do not fall into a reconstructable plan, but that are clearly beneath a later building. The eastern half of the later building shows the clearest plan: one can distinguish a megaron-type building with three rooms, one like a narrow porch (room I) and two others of equal size (rooms II and III). The building is 13 m long. A great many pithos fragments were found in the destruction layer. The area west of this building is not as well preserved, but one may distinguish an-

other three rooms alongside those of the first building (rooms IV to VI). Room IV is a corridor 1.80 m wide, which preserved for us not only evidence of the fire that caused the final destruction, but also some unique objects.

The finds included two papyrus-shaped furniture columns, 0.40 m high, made of solid ivory (*Deltion* 1965:233, pl. 278:a; Platon and Touloupa 1964B, fig. 4; Richter 1966:6-7, figs. 4-5), a large quantity of military equipment including spears (*Deltion* 1965, pl. 278:b), different types of arrowheads, parts of horse and chariot equipment, and a lot of pottery. Room V was poorly preserved except for a small area (cat. fig. 4, south of the earlier Mycenaean remains) that yielded Linear B tablets in the destruction layer (*Deltion* 1965:233, pl. 278:c; Platon and Touloupa 1964B:896, fig. 7; Chadwick 1969). In the area of the tablets, a small section was dug that revealed an earlier destruction layer,

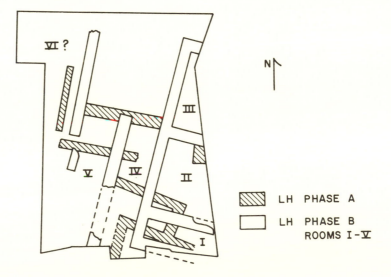

Cat. Fig. 4. Site 3, plan of the Late Helladic remains

also showing traces of fire, 0.20 m below the first floor. The earlier floor yielded two fragments of Linear B tablets, and pottery that was almost certainly of Late Helladic III A date; there was not enough of it for secure dating. But it is important to realize that there were Linear B tablets in an earlier layer than that of the final destruction of the building. Room V also yielded fragments of frescoes decorated with yellow spirals between red and black lines, and some terracotta figurines.

At the northwest corner of the site (where room VI once was), a collection of bronze objects had collapsed into Middle Helladic tomb 1, consisting of vessels (*Deltion* 1964:197, pl. 231:c; Platon and Touloupa 1964B, fig. 8) and parts of Mycenaean body armor like that found at Dendra (Åstrom et al. 1977, pls. 12-22). In 1971, an area 5 m x 9 m was excavated east of the main site. Architectural remains were not well preserved. The destruction layer was found and yielded bronze weapons, a stone vessel, a reclining calf of ivory (*Deltion* 1971, pl. 183:f), and two Linear B tablets (pl. 183:c-e, photographs of the destruction layer). In 1974, further excavation to the east uncovered more of the destruction level and possibly an earlier destruction layer similar to the one of room V. The final destruction level yielded pottery dating to the end of the LH III B:1 (oral communication by Demakopoulou).

This Late Helladic building is not necessarily part of the Mycenaean palace complex. As Chadwick observed (1969: 127), the tablets cannot be part of the main archive of the palace. The finds from this building suggest that it belonged to a wealthy individual who owned a large collection of weapons, a chariot, body armor, bronze vessels, and other possessions in large enough quantity to necessitate record keeping. The building was destroyed during the last major disaster in Thebes at the end of the Late Helladic III B:1 period. It is not necessary to associate its destruction with that of the House of Kadmos (site 1) simply because the two buildings have the same orientation. As I have already suggested (Symeonoglou 1973:73-74), the end of this building has no connection with the disaster that completely destroyed the first palace. But it is remotely possible that the earlier destruction layer seen in room V is related to that disaster.

SUBMYCENAEAN. A cist grave was found at the west side of the property, 1.10 m below the surface and 0.40 m above the Mycenaean level. It was a child's grave. Along with the poorly preserved skeleton were a few potsherds, one of which was Mycenaean, and two intact vases of Submycenaean style.

SITE 4. KADMEIA I-12.

14 Oidipous St., property of A. Kordatzis. Ancient remains preserved in the basement. *Deltion* 20B (1965): 235-236, fig. 3 (plan), pls. 280B-281B); *Deltion* 21B (1966):183, pl. 194B; Platon and Touloupa 1964B, figs. 3-4; Symeonoglou 1973 (monograph on the Mycenaean finds from

this site). Rutter 1974. Snodgrass 1975. Courtois 1976. Raison 1977.

EARLY HELLADIC. Remains of a house were excavated in one foundation pit. The house, found at 5.50 m, was built directly on the bedrock and yielded only some pottery.

MIDDLE HELLADIC. The substantial Middle Helladic remains amounted to an accumulation of deposit 1.50 m thick. At the south side of the site, where preservation was good, three walls were found, two of which must have belonged to a large structure (Symeonoglou 1973, pl. 3, walls IV and V) and were of a later phase (MH III?). Three infant burials were associated with this structure. Of an earlier phase was a long, narrow wall that ran parallel to the other two, but was deeper. The finds included only a few minor objects and a great deal of pottery that has not been studied.

LATE HELLADIC. There were architectural remains of three phases: walls III and X are earliest (Symeonoglou 1973, pl. 3), followed by building A and walls XI and XII; building B-C represents the third phase for which a destruction date at the end of the Late Helladic III B:1 period has been firmly established. This period saw the collapse of palatial Thebes (see chap. 2). The find of a hoard of ivory and pottery almost certainly associated with building B-C dates to the last part of LH III A:2 and constitutes a terminus ante quem for the building's construction. I have tentatively suggested a construction date earlier in the Late Helladic III A:2 period for this building (and consequently for the second palace of Thebes, 1973:74) because it seemed to me that the apparently vast second palace could not have been completed within one or even two generations. But there are admittedly some problems with this dating, as has been pointed out (Rutter 1974; Snodgrass 1975). Nevertheless, as new sites are excavated and studied (see sites 2, 3, 165, 196), it appears more and more untenable to date the destruction of the second palace to the end of LH III B:2 (Spyropoulos 1970).

Building B-C included a workshop in which gold jewelry and objects of semiprecious stones were made. The finds included beads and scraps of gold, gold wire from which pieces could be cut for processing, and flat gold pieces that may have been used as inlays; beads, inlays, and scraps of lapis lazuli; inlays of rock crystal; beads of glass paste (one of clear, blue glass), amber, amethyst, agate, and bronze. A few scraps of bronze tools and an iron drill-bit were also found.

The pottery-ivory hoard included 112 vases of various shapes, 28 of which were decorated. Of the ivories, the largest number consisted of running decorative patterns for furniture; most interesting were the bands of figure-of-eight shields and the three large handles of the same design. There were also carved attachments for daggers and combs, and many types of inlays. The pieces with figured representations included three plaques, each decorated with a pair of crossed goats, and poorly preserved fragments of a frieze showing Minoan "genii" carrying stags on their backs and spaced between palm trees (Symeonoglou 1973, chap. 4).

CLASSICAL THROUGH ROMAN. Very few remains of this period have survived. Most important was a long wall along the eastern border of the site. Its lower courses show that it was originally Classical, but it was rebuilt several times. This wall might be related to the large structure found in 1975 a few meters to the northeast (see site 229).

CHRISTIAN. Four successive stages of the use of the site were distinguished. Earliest was a flimsily constructed building, the foundations of which were the walls of Mycenaean building B-C. Too little of it was preserved to determine its function. It dates to the fourth to sixth centuries. During the seventh to eighth centuries, the site was used as a cemetery. In the third phase (perhaps ninth to fourteenth centuries) the area was used for storage, thereby causing major disturbance of the remains of earlier periods; the deep silos descended to Late or Middle Helladic levels. The last phase is represented by two well-built walls (fourteen to fifteenth centuries) whose function is unknown.

The site has been in continuous use up to modern times. The remains of recent periods are found in the form of mixed debris because of the nineteenth- and twentieth-century custom of constructing a basement, which necessitates penetration 1.50 to 1.00 m below the surface.

SITE 5. KADMEIA I-11.

72 Pindar St., property of C. Antoniou. Ancient remains preserved in the basement. *Deltion* 19B (1964): 196-197, fig. 3 (plan), pl. 230:c; *Deltion* 20B (1965):233. Platon and Touloupa 1964B:896.

EARLY HELLADIC. Pottery was found, but it was not possible to excavate to the lower levels.

LATE HELLADIC. Remains of buildings showing the same orientation as the first palace of Thebes were found in the northeast and southeast areas. South of the northeast group of walls, three successive layers of pavement were distinguished: The uppermost layer, 0.13 m thick and covered with pebbles, was 4.20 m below the surface. Beneath the pavement, a few bronze objects, stone buttons, terracotta tiles and figurines were found. The second layer, 0.20 m thick and made of small stones and potsherds, was 4.95 m below the surface. There was a skeleton found on it, and beneath it were many pieces of brightly colored wall plaster. The third layer was made of large pebbles and was found at 5.35 m, resting directly on the Early Helladic material. The largest preserved width of the pavement was 5.50 m; it may have been a courtyard or a street. Its proximity to sites 1 and 2 (site 5 lies east of these) makes it likely that the pavement belonged to the palace complex, although the chronological relationship of these sites is not clear. The large quantities of pottery have not yet been studied, and the architectural remains were not well enough preserved to permit comparison with other buildings. However, the walls found seem to belong to the period before the construction of the second palace. The pottery above the second pavement was dated to LH III B by the excavators (*Deltion* 1965:233).

SITE 6. KADMEIA H-12.

61 Epaminondas St., property of P. Theodorou. *Deltion* 19B (1964):192, fig. 1 (plan of the site), pl. 221 (architecture), pl. 222:a-d (objects from the site); pp. 210-212, fig. 5 (plan of Byzantine remains). Schachermeyr 1971, fig. 82 (foundations), fig. 83 (Early Helladic askos-jug). *Arch. Reports* 1965-66:12, fig. 20 (same Early Helladic jug).

EARLY HELLADIC. Substantial remains of houses, preserved to a height of 1 m, were found; one wall was 8 m long and 0.50 m thick. There may have been two buildings representing two consecutive phases, but the plan of neither could be reconstructed. The floors were of packed clay. There were five circular pits lined with clay, probably representing an earlier phase. Under the floor was a well-preserved burial of an adult, the remains of which were carried intact to the Museum of Thebes. There was a large quantity of pottery; at least ten vases were put together, including the published askos, which is certainly of Early Helladic II date. Other finds included stone and bone tools, a pair of copper tweezers (*Deltion* 1964, pl. 222:a), and a glass-paste bead with the representation of a lion (pl. 222:c) that was found near the burial.

CLASSICAL. The only Classical find was a marble stele showing a female arm carved in relief with incised wreaths in the background (*Deltion* 1964, pl. 222:d). The stele was found in the debris of the upper layers and seemed to have been used in recent construction.

HELLENISTIC-ROMAN. Foundations of buildings were found under a Byzantine chapel (*Deltion* 1964:210).

CHRISTIAN. Interesting remains of a chapel were found in which two construction phases were identified: the earlier was represented by one nave ending in an apse to the east. The exterior dimensions were 7.75 m x 3.75 m. The walls were beautifully constructed with bricks and poros stones; it is likely that the roof was vaulted. This chapel dates to the tenth or eleventh century (according to P. Lazarides, *Deltion* 1964:210, fig. 5). In the later phase, the width of the chapel was increased to 4.75 m; the south wall of the earlier structure continued to be used. The ultimate length was not established. The floor of this chapel was at least partially covered with marble (28 pieces were transferred to the Museum), and there were frescoes dating to the Late Byzantine period (fifteenth and sixteenth centuries). The chapel itself could, of course, be earlier than the frescoes. Numerous burials were associated with this church, both within and without.

SITE 7. KADMEIA I-13.

Archaeological site, Elektrai gates. Keramopoullos 1917:7-24 (architecture and finds), fig. 3 (plan of the site), figs. 4-18; pp. 25-32 (cemetery at the site). Desborough 1952, 1972. Snodgrass 1971. Keramopoullos' excavation yielded remains of almost every period, though only the Submycenaean cemetery and the Classical gates were in a decent state of preservation.

MIDDLE HELLADIC. Middle Helladic pottery was found inside the west tower of the gates (1917:22).

LATE HELLADIC. Late Helladic remains were limited to the layers beneath the east tower and were, according to Keramopoullos, clearly Mycenaean, packed with Mycenaean pottery and roof tiles (1917:14); similar finds came from the area of the west tower (1917:22). Keramopoullos thought that the poorly preserved remains of a wall, found south of the east tower, might have belonged to the Mycenaean fortification of Thebes (1917:27, 32, fig. 3; wall 10 to the south of tomb 3). Although it is not made of the usual Cyclopean-size boulders, the wall could have been part of the fortification system, not only because it is near the Classical gates, but also because it is in this vicinity that the wall would have turned west to enclose the south side of the Kadmeia. Unfortunately, neither its thickness nor any indicative length of it was preserved.

SUBMYCENAEAN AND PROTOGEOMETRIC. Part of a cemetery was found in and around the east Classical tower. Eleven single inhumation cist burials were found (T 1-T 4; T 4a-T 9; for the eleventh, see 1917:25, no. 1). Two of the preserved skeletons were

of adults, the others of children. In addition to pottery, the finds included an iron ring, bronze rings, sheets of lead, seashells, a few terracotta figurines, and a piece of gold wire. The floor of one of the tombs was covered with clay plaques (T 4). The cemetery has been dated on the basis of the pottery to the Submycenaean and Protogeometric periods (Desborough 1972:69; Snodgrass 1971:158). Tomb 3 yielded some surprises: a large domestic jar (1917, fig. 23) and a jug (1917, fig. 24) of uncertain date: Snodgrass considers it LH III B (1971:383), Furumark, LH III C:1 (1941A, FS121, no. 6), and Desborough, Submycenaean (1952:196). Keramopoullos reports that "above the soil covering these objects (but presumably inside the tomb) there were ashes" where the sheet of lead was found (1917:27).

Keramopoullos believed that this cemetery was within the area originally protected by the Mycenaean fortifications of the Kadmeia (represented by wall 10 in his excavation: 1917, fig. 3). But because there were no intramural burials during the Submycenaean period, he believed that wall 10 must have been in ruins by the time this area became a cemetery. Consequently, there must have been a later wall beyond which this cemetery lay (1917:32).

ARCHAIC AND CLASSICAL. A fragment of an inscription may indicate that the site was in use during the Archaic period (1917:24). Most important were the remains of two round towers, 11 m in diameter and 8 m apart. Most of the gate itself lies under the modern road (Amphion St.), but one stone from the doorsill of the east tower was found in situ. Starting from the towers was a large, circular wall, ca. 20 m in diameter, that opened toward the interior of the city and may have been meant to trap an invading army (1917, fig. 3, wall Ξ). Attached to the west tower was a well-built isodomic wall, 2 m thick (1917, fig. 3, wall Λ), which Keramopoullos interpreted as the wall of the Kadmeia turning west to enclose the south side of the akropolis (1917:17). By the west tower, Keramopoullos found an undisturbed deposit of pottery, apparently from the time of the tower's construction. On the basis of this pottery and his knowledge of the city's history, Keramopoullos attributed the towers to the period of the reconstruction of Thebes by Kassandros in 316 B.C. (1917:23, 269-270). The famous prehistoric walls were clearly not extant in this area at that time; they were replaced by isodomic walls. The absence of the prehistoric wall in this area raised once more the possibility that the isodomic walls might belong to the Classical wall enclosing Greater Thebes. Keramopoullos rejected this possibility (1917:267-276; see chap. 3).

HELLENISTIC AND ROMAN. Some Hellenistic pottery (1917:22) and two Roman inscriptions (1917:24) were found.

CHRISTIAN. Byzantine remains were found in several areas but were not described in detail. Walls *M, P, Y,* were identified as medieval (1917:17, 20, fig. 3). Of four successive layers of houses, two seem to date to the Byzantine period (earlier two layers) and two to the eighteenth and nineteenth centuries (later two; 1917:21, figs. 13-15, with mosaics from one of the recent houses).

SITE 8. GREATER THEBES K-13.

Archaeological site. Keramopoullos 1917:34-37 (inscriptions), 37-79 (temple), 80-98 (Late Helladic tombs). *Deltion* 16 (1960):147, pl. 125:a (inscription; cf. site 105); *Deltion* 22B (1967):227 (Late Helladic tomb), 232-233 (Christian tombs). Keramopoullos 1926 (Christian tombs). Schober 1934:1441-1442. Ziehen 1934:1498-1501. Schachter 1967B. Dinsmoor 1950:218. Jeffery 1961:94. Pl. 18.

According to Pausanias, the sanctuary of Apollo Ismenios was near the Ismenos River, to the right of the Elektrai gates as one approaches Thebes from the south (9. 10.2; here, see chap. 2, passage 5). According to Pindar, the sanctuary was near the Melia spring (*Pyth.* 11.6), which was in the same general area. The sanctuary was excavated by Keramopoullos in 1910 and is indeed located on a small hill, 200 m east of the southeastern tip of the Kadmeia. Even those most unwilling to identify archaeological remains with monuments known through literature must acknowledge the inscriptions confirming the fact that this is the site of the famous oracle of Apollo Ismenios at Thebes. Keramopoullos, who had to convince an unusually large number of skeptics, began his discussion of the site with the inscriptions. It is unfortunate that this important cult center of Thebes is very poorly preserved.

LATE HELLADIC. Keramopoullos excavated six tombs (numbered T 1-T 6) under the west foundation of the temple (see 1917:33, fig. 30, for plan of the site). The tombs remained open until 1966 when they were filled with soil to prevent them from collapsing. Most of them had been used over a long period ranging from LH II B to LH III B. Tombs 2, 4, and 5 date to the LH III A, while tomb 3 had been in use by LH II B and was used again in LH III B. The Geometric pottery found in tomb 3 had fallen into it from the temple of Apollo (1917:86) and is not related to the hero cult in the Geometric period (Blegen 1937). Tomb 1 was in poor condition, having been used as an ossuary during the Byzantine period. Tomb 6 was completely empty (perhaps a result of earlier excavations 1917:82-83), though its vases might have gotten mixed with those of tomb 2. LH III A seems to be the main period of the cemetery (see Furumark 1941B for these dates). The chambers are large, the best-preserved tomb 3 a rectangle 4.30 m x 2.80 m and 2.80 m high; tomb 3 contained seven burials. The finds from the tombs included a good deal of pottery (52 vases from tombs 2 through 5 have been published), a few terracotta figurines, many steatite buttons, an ivory comb (T 3), two pieces of boar's tusk (T 5), and a bronze dagger (T 5; Sandars 1963:150, class Eii). One other tomb (T 7) appeared as a result of erosion on the south side of the hill and

was excavated in 1966 (*Deltion* 1967:227). It yielded very few finds; steatite buttons, glass-paste beads, three gold rosettes, a bone comb, and some pottery.

GEOMETRIC AND CLASSICAL. Keramopoullos' excavation revealed three major construction phases of the temple of Apollo Ismenios, the only preserved structure of the sanctuary. There was some evidence that a temple existed in the Late Geometric period. Adjoining the west side of the foundations of the Classical temple was a layer 0.40 m thick containing some Mycenaean and Geometric pottery; directly above this was another layer 0.40 m thick, of burned debris containing ashes, poros stones, mud-brick, and lots of Geometric and Protocorinthian pottery (figs. 56-57; a terracotta horse in fig. 55) indicating a destruction at the end of the eighth century B.C. Keramopoullos concluded that there was an eighth-century temple built of wood and mud-brick, perhaps without columns, but with poros stone somewhere in the structure. He suggested that the temple may have been established at the site of a Mycenaean ancestor cult (1917:77-79).

The second temple is better known. It was built of light-colored poros in the Doric style, had terracotta roof tiles, and was decorated with colored terracottas. A column fragment painted red and showing twenty flutings was found (1917:59, fig. 52). According to Keramopoullos, this temple was smaller than the Classical one. The following inscriptions were associated with Apollo Ismenios; the first three were found in this building:

1. A bronze oinochoe (sixth century B.C.) found here before Keramopoullos' excavation (Athens Nat. Mus. 12343) bears a dedication to Apollo Ismenios (1917, fig. 32).

2. A bronze phiale (Athens Nat. Mus. 12344, sixth century B.C.) found with the oinochoe, bears a dedication to Athena Pronaia (1917, fig. 33).

3. A poros fragment (sixth century B.C.) found at the site is perhaps from a dedicatory base (1917, fig. 53). This is the oldest of these inscriptions.

4. A votive Doric column was found in the wall of the modern cathedral (site 216) with a dedication to Apollo (1917, fig. 54).

5. A poros fragment of a votive column from the vicinity of the temple preserves the beginning of the word "Ismenios" (cf. site 105; *Deltion* 1960:147, pl. 125:a).

6. A stone with two fragmentary inscriptions was found in 1929 near the chapel of Metamorphosis tou Soteros (site 232). Keramopoullos interpreted the first as a dedication of the Koroneans to Apollo Ismenios in the fifth century B.C., the second as a dedication of Lucius Mummius (second century B.C.; Keramopoullos 1931).

Ancient literature records other offerings associated with this temple, such as the treasury of golden tripods (Pindar, *Pyth.* 11.5), and the famous inscribed tripods seen by Herodotos (1.52, 1.92, 5.59-61) and Pausanias (9.10.4).

The construction date of the second temple is uncertain. Archaeological evidence indicates that it was in use by 600 B.C. Keramopoullos thought it unlikely that the Thebans would have remained very long without a temple after the first one

was destroyed. Although there is no direct archaeological evidence, he suggested that the second temple could have been built ca. 700 B.C. If his suggestion is correct, this would be the earliest poros temple of the Doric style in the Greek world. In 1966, Keramopoullos' notion was confirmed to some degree when the refilling of Mycenaean tombs necessitated excavation at the site. What was thought to have been debris from Keramopoullos' excavations turned out to be undisturbed strata. A trench 2 m wide and 6.50 m long was opened by N. Pharaklas. The stratigraphic section of this trench (*Deltion* 1967:232, fig.2) shows a Byzantine layer on top, a thick second layer with Archaic pottery, and beneath it three successive layers of packing material arranged on a slant as though intended to form a terrace for the temple. The amount of pottery found in the packing was insufficient for dating, but related to the packing layers was an ancient trench that lay along the west krepis of the temple (marked Z in the section); in this trench, Pharaklas found a lot of pottery of Geometric and Orientalizing styles; mixed with it were fragments of poros stone in the Doric style. All of this indicates a significant effort, perhaps in preparation for the construction of a large temple. The importance of the site in the Geometric period clearly requires a detailed study, but Keramopoullos' suggestion that Thebes had the earliest poros temple might have some validity after all.

The second temple lasted into the fourth century when it was replaced by a Doric peripteros, which was perhaps never completed but was still in use in the time of

Pausanias. This hexastyle Classical temple had twelve columns on the flanks and measured 46.25 m x 22.83 m at the stylobate; the cella was 21.60 m x 9.30 m. Only the deep foundations of the west side are preserved, but the foundation trenches were found and carefully measured by Keramopoullos (1917:37-42). Some carved architectural pieces were preserved and helped determine the size of the building (1917:42-55, fig. 37 shows the reconstructed plan of the temple). Keramopoullos dated the third temple to the first half of the fourth century B.C. on the basis of a mason's inscription on a capital (1917:56, fig. 36) and the style of the preserved architectural fragments. Dinsmoor (1950:218) has classified the temple among those of the fourth century B.C., pointing to the short opisthodomos, which he considered the first stage in a series of innovations in fourth-century Doric architecture.

CHRISTIAN. Keramopoullos (1926) excavated several tombs here, which were of two types: pit graves, usually covered with slabs and sometimes lined with slabs, and tile-covered tombs of the poor. The tombs were always dug in east-west orientation, with the head of the deceased at the west side. Offerings to the dead were few; finds included bronze fibulae, finger-rings, and earrings, and a few vases and lamps. On top of the tombs, there were usually plates and cooking ware, jugs, lamps, and candle holders; these objects were probably deposited after ceremonies honoring the deceased. Keramopoullos dated the cemetery to the twelfth to thirteenth centuries on the basis of the few coins he found. Six additional pit graves were found in 1966, approximately 10 m east of the temple. This is a large cemetery, and tombs have been found here many times, though not always recorded.

SITE 9. KADMEIA I-11.

Archaeological site. Keramopoullos 1917:306-307. *Deltion* 20B (1965): 237, n. 3, pl. 282:a (photograph of site). Pl. 17.

The site was excavated by Keramopoullos in 1915 in an attempt to locate the Proitides gates. Two considerations led him to this location: first, this is a natural exit leading from the Kadmeia to Chalkis. Secondly, a bridge (called the bridge of Mouchlinas, still extant) and a Frankish tower (demolished a few years before Keramopoullos' excavation) were here. Keramopoullos found substantial remains of the Cyclopean fortifications of Thebes, the only section of the famous wall visible today. The wall is preserved to a length of 6.30 m and is 3.50 m thick. The undressed stones are approximately 1 m long and exhibit an early form of Cyclopean masonry. The wall, preserved two courses high, was built against the slope in such a way that it has no inner face in these lower courses. This means that it could have gotten thicker as it went up. Keramopoullos found some pottery in an "undisturbed layer around the wall" and he published a photograph of four sherds (1917:307, fig. 185); these are not sufficient to date the wall.

SITE 10. KADMEIA I-11.

34 Pelopidas St., property of P. Ziomas. *Deltion* 20B (1965): 237-239, pl. 283:a (Protogeometric amphora, mistakenly labeled Submycenaean). Snodgrass 1971:207. Desborough 1972:203, 368.

The hill is steep in this area. Bedrock was found at 10 to 11 m below the surface. Archaeological work was limited to observing the opening of foundation pits.

LATE HELLADIC. There were remains of houses showing the same orientation as that of the first palace, and a great deal of pottery. It is possible that this area was terraced even in Mycenaean times in order to build houses.

PROTOGEOMETRIC. A pit grave dug in the bedrock contained an extended skeleton. Between its legs was a Protogeometric amphora within which were the cremated remains of another person. The opening of the amphora was covered by two bowls.

SITE 11. KADMEIA I-11.

Chapel of Agios Vasileios built on the remains of a Byzantine church. Soteriou 1924. Strzygowski 1894. Keramopoullos 1917:65, n. 1. Delvenakiotis 1970:22, 23. Pl. 44.

The site was excavated in 1921-22 by Soteriou (1924, figs. 1-45). The twentieth-century Thebans erroneously dedicated the modern chapel to Agios Vasileios because that name appears twice in the dedicatory inscription of the Byzantine church. This inscription, imbedded in the east wall of the chapel, identifies the builder as a certain Vasileios, a local official (*candidatos*) of the three Byzantine emperors: Vasileios of Macedon, Constantine, and Leon. The original church was actually dedicated to Agios Gregorios Theologos and was built in A.D. 872. The locals also refer to the chapel as the Church of the Three Hierarchs (Vasileiou 1967:58-60), perhaps because Vasileios and Gregorios were two of the three fathers of the Greek Orthodox church.

BYZANTINE. The original single-nave basilica measured 11.50 m x 5.20 m. Attached to the west side was a room, 5.85 m x 5.20 m that could have been used as a crypt. The building is of isodomic construction, the large blocks probably taken from an earlier building (an ancient temple?), perhaps of the Classical period. The roof was probably vaulted. The interior was richly decorated: the floor was covered with marble in geometric designs, and there were wall frescoes (1924, fig. 10). One large tomb was found within the church, and there were at least five others south of the church where a marble sarcophagus was also found (1924, fig. 12). Soteriou considered the church a private chapel attached to the residence of its builder, Vasileios. He judged it a typical example of Eastern Orthodox architecture. Its rich decoration attests to the growing importance of Thebes in the ninth century.

was, in all likelihood, only 50 m to the south (site 217).

SITE 12. KADMEIA I-12.

The corner of Pindar and Dirke Sts., property of the brothers I. and G. Tzortzis. *Deltion* 19B (1964): 192-194, fig. 2 (plan of Roman apse); p. 212, pl. 223:a-c (apse and capitals).

EARLY HELLADIC. A few remains of Early Helladic habitation were found in an area not occupied by the Roman building: two foundation walls, five pits lined with clay and containing pottery and ashes, and a skeleton.

ROMAN. Remains of a building from Imperial times were preserved to a height of 2.56 m. The apse, 7.20 m in diameter was built of alternating poros stone and bricks. In a few spots, some of the original stucco, which has been painted, was preserved. The floor was covered with terracotta tiles 0.50 m square. Also found were two capitals, one of which was carved out of an older inscribed stone. Some of the writing is preserved, and joins were made at the Museum with two other fragments of the same inscription, one of which had already been published (*IG* 7:2422). All three fragments have now been published by Koumanoudis (1970:130-134). The inscription records a list of donors and their offerings to a god whose name is not preserved. It is possible that the inscription refers to Zeus Hypsistos, whose sanctuary

SITE 13. KADMEIA I-12.

Pindar St., south of site 12; property of A. Theodorou. *Deltion* 21B (1966):188-189, pl. 196:a (Mycenaean aquaduct); *Deltion* 22B (1967): 226-227, pl. 159:a (view of the site).

EARLY HELLADIC. Two successive layers of clay-lined pits and post-holes were distinguished directly above the bedrock. Some intrusive pottery was found in the top layer, which was originally published as Middle Helladic (*Deltion* 1967:226). There is now no doubt that these early remains on the Kadmeia were Early Helladic. The clay-lined pits were either shallow or deep, always neatly lined; there were also pits dug into the bedrock without a clay lining. There were bones in some of the pits, and pottery was found in both layers.

MIDDLE HELLADIC. Only some pottery was found associated with the uppermost Early Helladic layer.

LATE HELLADIC. The extensive Late Helladic remains were, unfortunately, purposely and badly damaged by the property owner, but we were able to establish the existence of a Mycenaean house decorated with frescoes. In a small area where the strata were left undisturbed, it was possible to distinguish five successive floors that may have belonged to this building. Each floor yielded pottery, which remains to be studied. The second floor from the top seemed to correspond stratigraphically to the upper level of the magnificent Mycenaean aqueduct, remains of which were found throughout the entire 12.50 m of the property (*Deltion* 1966, pl. 196:a). The conduit was carved into the bedrock and differs from the later Classical aqueduct in that its sides were both stone-lined and tapered as they went up. The opening cut in the bedrock measured 1.30 m wide and 2 m high, whereas the constructed interior was 0.50 m wide and 1.10 m high. Within the aqueduct was a huge quantity of Mycenaean pottery.

CLASSICAL. Only a section of an isodomic wall was found, made with poros blocks 0.70 m wide. No finds were associated with this wall (*Deltion* 1967, pl. 159:a, *upper right*).

SITE 14. KADMEIA I-10.

53 Pelopidas St., property of D. Adrianos. *Deltion* 20B (1965):239.

LATE HELLADIC. A few potsherds were found scattered among the Byzantine remains.

BYZANTINE. One wall of a house dating to the ninth to twelfth centuries was preserved. Associated with it was a large silo of typical pear shape, 9 m in depth, dug mostly into the bedrock. The upper half was empty, the lower filled with debris. It was cleared to about 7 m and yielded some 25 vases. Above this building was a large structure of hard, white concrete, which

in Thebes is usually associated with the period of the Frankish occupation. One foundation wall, 1.20 to 1.30 m thick, was well preserved.

SITE 15. KADMEIA I-10.

50 Pelopidas St., property of V. Matthaios. Not published.

BYZANTINE. One trench, 3.30 m x 1.30 m was opened. At a depth of 1.80 m was a Byzantine wall (ninth to twelfth centuries), 1.80 m high and 0.60 m thick. There were no other finds.

SITE 16. KADMEIA I-12.

16 Pelopidas St., property of N. Stamatis. *Deltion* 20B (1965):239.

MIDDLE HELLADIC. No walls were found, but the large amount of Middle Helladic pottery indicated the existence of habitation that was disturbed by subsequent occupation of the site.

CLASSICAL. In a large foundation pit, a portion of the Theban aqueduct was found carved in the rock. It was 0.60 m wide and 4 m deep, rather than the expected 1.20 m x 1.50 m depth. Perhaps a modification of depth was needed in this area to facilitate the flow of the water. The aqueduct lay in a northeast-southeast direction. Only a few Byzantine sherds were found within it, but in all likelihood, the original construction dates to the Classical period (see chap. 3).

ROMAN. A few fragmentary walls and pottery associated with them attested to the presence of habitation during the Roman period.

CHRISTIAN. There was evidence of habitation in the form of pottery and building debris, but most of the Christian remains at this site were destroyed in the course of contruction work of the last hundred years.

SITE 17. KADMEIA H-10.

143 Epaminondas St., property of P. Giannopoulos. *Deltion* 21B (1966): 183-187, figs. 5-10, pl. 195:a-c (frescoes). *Athens Annals of Archaeology* I, 1 (1968), frontispiece (frescoes). *Bulletin de correspondence hellénique* 94 (1970):1031-1037, figs. 309-311 (frescoes).

This site is situated on a steep slope; bedrock was found 11 to 15 m below the surface. Only the areas intended for the foundation shafts of a modern building were excavated (*Deltion* 1966:184, fig. 5, marked 2-14, and T 1-T 6).

MIDDLE HELLADIC. In one of the shafts was a wall forming an angle, with which some Middle Helladic pottery was associated. Under the wall was a female skeleton (fig. 5, T 2, fig. 10), which rested on the covering slab of a small cist tomb containing the remains of an infant. This manner of burial signifies that both mother and infant died at childbirth. In the same area was another wall curved at one end, belonging to an apsidal house. The burial was obviously earlier than either of the two structures, which date to the end of the Middle Helladic.

LATE HELLADIC. Deposits containing Mycenaean pottery were as deep as 3 m. In foundation shafts 12 and 14, two walls of similar construction were found at a depth of 10 m. Each had an exterior but not an interior face, indicating that they were retaining walls (*Deltion* 1966, figs. 8, 9). A very large wall, 2 m high and 1.15 to 1.17 m thick, which lay northwest-southeast was found in two consecutive shafts (4, and T 3-T 6; *Deltion* 1966, fig. 6). It was built on leveled bedrock and also seems to have been a retaining wall. Just east of it was a great amount of building debris containing a large quantity of fresco fragments, most of them from a large seascape representation, in a good state of preservation. More frescoes were found east of this area in foundation shafts 9 and 10 (at a depth of 11.20 m). At a depth of 10 m in the same shafts were remains of a house: there was a wall and a floor on which there were traces of the destruction (burned mudbrick, ashes, and pottery in disarray). In T 3-T 6 an unusual burial was found: a pit grave cut in the rock contained the skeletons of five infants arranged radially with feet pointing towards the center. There was only one alabastron in the tomb. The skeletons were covered with soil, on top of which were ashes and then a layer of clay. On top of the clay was a thin stone slab and on that a square poros stone, obviously a grave marker.

The most plausible interpretation of the Mycenaean material from this site is that the three retaining walls were constructed to terrace the area. The beautiful frescoes did not originate here but were brought from elsewhere, perhaps the palace of Thebes itself (the house of Kadmos is only 100 m away), to fill in and level the ground. Frescoes were also found in the adjoining properties (sites 120, 181) in the same sort of debris (see also chap. 2).

CLASSICAL. No Classical remains were found at the site. However, Classical architectural materials were reused here (*Deltion*1966:186, fig. 7).

CHRISTIAN. At a depth of 9 m in shafts 9 and 10 were walls of three different Early Christian structures that seemed to rest on foundations of the Roman period. The reuse of Classical material is particularly characteristic of Late Roman/Early Christian buildings in Thebes. In the levels above, however, there was only debris; the site seemed to have become a dumping ground for demolished buildings. Only in the eleventh to twelfth centuries was a substantial building constructed here at a depth of 6 m. Remains of it were found in shaft 7-8: one wall, 0.90 m thick, was preserved to a height of 1.20 m. Unfortunately, it was too fragmentary to determine its nature. Thick Byzantine deposits were found in shaft 2.

SITE 18, KADMEIA H-11.

6 Plutarch St., (also called I. Metaxa St.), property of S. Stamatis. *Deltion* 20B (1965):237, 253-255, pls. 309-313 (mosaics); *Deltion* 21B (1966): 189-191, 210, pl. 196:B; *Deltion* 24B (1969):188, pls. 196:B, 197:a-c. *Arch. Reports* 1966-1967:13, cover photograph. *Bulletin de correspondance hellénique* 92 (1968):858-866, figs. 4-10 (mosaics).

The discovery of beautiful Early Christian mosaics could not have been made without the help of a special team of workers headed by D. Phountouzis. The property owner had secretly begun to destroy them in an attempt to avoid involvement with the Archaeological Service. Fortunately, very little was lost; the mosaics were properly excavated and transferred to the Thebes Museum. Below the mosaics, it was possible to excavate only a 5-meter square without threatening the neighboring houses with collapse.

EARLY HELLADIC. Remains of a building longer than our 5-meter trench were partially excavated beneath the Middle Helladic level. The packed earth floor was found at 6.40 m below the surface; remains were preserved 0.30 m above the floor. The one wall found was 0.60 m thick, covered on the interior surface with smooth plaster. Two clay partitions 0.25 m thick divided the room into sections. The entrance was 1.10 m wide; on either side of it and outside the house were low stone benches, originally covered with smooth clay. The plan of the building could not be determined, but it seemed to have been a rich and well-built house. It was destroyed by an intense fire. The finds included some terracotta bobbins, charred grains of wheat, and a wonderful collection of pottery including examples of the Agia Marina style, which date the building to EH III.

MIDDLE HELLADIC. The substantial Middle Helladic deposit amounted to a total accumulation of 1.40 m. Three layers were distinguished, each with some architecture (*Deltion* 1966:190, fig. 11, plan of the trench). The earliest layer yielded a long wall at the north side of the trench (marked *Γ*) at a depth of 5.20 m below the surface. Pottery was associated with it. The middle layer at 4.95 m contained the stone foundation of a house; attached to it on the outside was a cist grave containing a child burial with a vase and a necklace of terracotta beads. The upper layer yielded the corner of a house at a depth of 4.60 m. It had well-built stone foundations and a packed earth floor. Only some pottery was found in the room. The Middle Helladic remains were found directly beneath the Byzantine mosaics.

CLASSICAL. The corner of a structure (drain?) found at the southwest corner of the trench may date to the Classical period (*Deltion* 1966, fig. 11).

CHRISTIAN. A mosaic floor of an Early Christian basilica was found here. More of the mosaics were reportedly found and destroyed during the construction of an apartment house east of this site (see site 40). The church itself must have extended east of this site because the long, well-preserved rectangle of the mosaics lies in a north-south direction, indicating a transverse room, perhaps a narthex. The mosaic rectangle was 3.40 m wide and about twice as long, but incomplete at one end. Most striking were the representations of four months (February, April, May, and July), and an oblong panel showing a hunting scene, the right end of which was missing. Left of the hunting scene was a dedicatory inscription mentioning Demetrios, the designer of the mosaics; Epiphanes, the technician who made them; and Paulos, the priest who supervised the work. East of this area were poorly preserved mosaics with elaborate borders and representations of birds in circles within squares. Another inscription identified the donor of the mosaics as Konstantinos.

Above the mosaics was a cemetery. Numerous tombs of the tile-covered type were found without offerings; they must date to the seventh to ninth centuries A.D.

SITE 19. KADMEIA H-13.

21 Epaminondas St., property of N. Ktistakis. *Deltion* 21B (1966): 187-188, pl. 194:c (Byzantine tower).

LATE HELLADIC. A few Late Helladic potsherds were found under the Byzantine tower. The sherds themselves are of little interest, but their association with the large tower is significant topographically. The tower was positioned at the natural exit leading south from the Kadmeia, and there may have been a gate here. Other towers situated at natural exits from the Kadmeia include the two Classical towers of site 7, which were associated with the Elektrai gates, and the two other known Byzantine towers of sites 9 and 52, which were almost certainly associated with gates (see chap. 2). The tower of site 19 was only 70 m from the highest point of the Kadmeia, where the sanctuary of Zeus Hypsistos was located (see chap. 2, passage 6), and may well have been associated with the Hypsistai gates.

CHRISTIAN. Remains of a tower were found, built with large blocks taken from Classical buildings. Only two sides, 1.50 to 1.70 m thick and forming a right angle, are partially preserved. The longer side measures 7.50 m. The tower was erected on a steep slope and was best preserved on the downhill side to a height of 3.50 m. It may have been square in shape, and perhaps as large as the Museum tower (see site 52), and it must have been built during the Frankish occupation of Thebes (thirteenth to fourteenth centuries). The remains of the tower were not demolished; a modern building was constructed on top of them. The Byzantine aqueduct, no longer extant, was also associated with this area, perhaps with this very site; it came from the hills of Kolonaki and ended somewhere here. It was built on arches (called Kamares by the locals) like a Roman aqueduct. Twenty arches were still preserved in 1895 (Frazer 1898:32). It was demolished by the Thebans in the late nineteenth century (Keramopoullos 1917:123, n. 2).

SITE 20. KADMEIA G-11.

15 Kithairon St., property of the Association of Agios Ioannis Kaloktenis (also called Christianike Enosis Thevon). *Deltion* 21B (1966):193.

LATE HELLADIC. Four foundation shafts on an east-west axis were opened in 1965. The western shaft yielded a huge amount of debris mixed with a lot of Mycenaean pottery. Unfortunately, no other remains were found to help us interpret the original character of this debris.

CHRISTIAN. In the eastern shaft were remains of a house of undetermined date. It is reported that during the excavation of the main building in 1963, tile-covered tombs were found (Thebes Museum notebook (1963): 1, 15).

SITE 21. KADMEIA G-11.

30 Plutarch St. (now called I. Metaxa); property of N. Stavropoulos. *Deltion* 21B (1966):192-193. On the east side of the property, which is located on a steep slope, the bedrock was found at 3.50 m, whereas at the third and last row of shafts to the west, it was found at 7.50 to 8 m.

MIDDLE HELLADIC. Scanty remains of habitation were found in the first row of shafts at 3.50 m, directly on top of the bedrock.

LATE HELLADIC. There were only scattered remains; the Late Helladic levels were damaged during the Byzantine period.

CHRISTIAN. The discovery of a large pithos in situ caused great excitement among the locals, but it contained unimportant bronze and iron objects perhaps of the Frankish period. Only in the southwest area of the site were there undisturbed layers in which a small corner of substantial Byzantine structure was found.

SITE 22. KADMEIA I-11.

3 Zegginis St., property of I. Liakos. *Deltion* 20B (1965):239, pl. 283:b (Middle Helladic pithos frag.). In this property, bedrock was found at 1.50 m; most of the ancient remains were obliterated.

MIDDLE HELLADIC. Two cist graves and one pit grave were found. A large amount of pottery was found in mixed strata and included fragments of pithoi, some of which were used as bricks in Byzantine times (*Deltion* 1965, pl. 183:b).

EARLY CHRISTIAN. Poorly preserved foundations built of reused Classical masonry, and numerous coins from the Early Christian period were found.

BYZANTINE. A few foundations and five pear-shaped silos were the only remains of habitation. Four of the silos were cut in the rock; and fifth and largest was built like a well, 3.50 m deep, with a lower diameter of 2.60 m and narrowing at the top to 1.20 m.

SITE 23. KADMEIA I-10.

2 Tsevas St., property of I. Malathounis. Some remains preserved in the basement. *Deltion* 20B (1966):237, fig. 4, pl. 282:b: *Deltion* 21B (1967): 180-183, fig. 4 (plan and section of Classical building), pl. 194:a.

LATE HELLADIC. One exploratory trench 3 m square was opened in order to determine the depth of deposit. At a depth of 7 m was the upper surface of a massive wall that was wider than the trench itself, making it impossible to proceed without demolishing it. The property owner decided to set his foundations at 2.50 m. There is no doubt that the wall belonged to the famous fortifications of the Mycenaean period: its thickness was greater than needed for any building foundation, and it was too massive to have been a retaining wall. The method of construction was clearly Cyclopean, with boulders of medium size (0.40 to 0.60 m long). Although it was impossible to expose the sides of this wall, its direction appeared to be northwest rather than north; this was surprising because one would have expected it to follow the line of the hill and the road. Above the wall was a clear Mycenaean stratum with a lot of pottery, leaving no question about the period of the wall.

CLASSICAL THROUGH ROMAN. Above the Mycenaean level in the exploratory trench was an ancient fill containing pottery of many periods, to the clear level of the Classical period at a depth of 2.90 m. At this level there was a well-made pebble floor associated with a well, the interior opening of which was 0.95 to 1.05 m. It was lined mainly with undressed stones, within which some architectural stones were incorporated. Inside the well was pottery of the Roman, Hellenistic, and Classical periods in successive layers, indicating continuous use. The mouth of the well was gradually raised as the floor build-up accumulated.

The Classical level was 0.40 m thick and yielded not only a lot of local pottery, but also a collection of beautiful Red Figure potsherds imported from Attica dating to the first half of the fifth century B.C. This pottery is being studied by Barbara Philippaki. Also found in the Classical level was a small column 0.78 m high with a conical top bearing the inscription *FOROS* (boundary), which lends credence to the idea that this was a public place.

Sometime at the end of the Classical or the beginning of the Hellenistic period, an L-shaped wall was constructed, the longer leg measuring over 12 m, continuing beyond the limits of the property toward the west; it was built of ashlar blocks (0.90 m long, 0.50 m wide, and 0.45 m high). The wall was two courses high and clearly not intended to support a heavy upper structure. South of this wall was a water main constructed of small poros stones, and of the same date as the wall. This was clearly designed to bring an even more abundant supply of water to the site, probably from the underground aqueduct constructed in the Classical period. A well-made floor of packed earth at 2.40 m below the surface marked the beginning of the Hellenistic period, the total accumulation of which was 0.40 m. At 2.00 m below the surface was the earliest Roman floor. The site continued to be used until the end of antiquity, by which time the L-shaped wall was completely covered by the floor build-up. This site was clearly an outdoor sanctuary, and with the help of Pausanias' description of the Kadmeia (see chap. 5, passage 8), we can identify it with some confidence as the *oionoskopeion of Teiresias* (chap. 3, p. 131). Its excavated remains are preserved in the basement of the newly built house.

BYZANTINE. The remains of this period were not preserved, but a slab with a cross carved on it attested to its one-time presence.

SITE 24. GREATER THEBES H-13 to H-16.

The long hill of Kolonaki, south of the Kadmeia. Philios 1897 (three Late Helladic tombs). Keramopoullos 1910: 209-244 (two Late Helladic tombs, Agia Anna T 1 - T 2); 1917:123-209 (28 Late Helladic tombs, Kolonaki T 1 - T 28), 210-252 (20 Classical-Hellenistic tombs T 1 - T 20). *Deltion* 22B (1967):230-231 (11 Classical tombs).

Most of the tombs in this cemetery are classified here with site 24. Some recently found tombs are classified with sites 136, 150, 151, 174, and 210.

LATE HELLADIC. Kolonaki is the largest known Mycenaean cemetery of Thebes. Keramopoullos (1910:209) reported that over one hundred tombs were visible before he started excavations in 1905; all had been looted during the previous forty years. Keramopoullos excavated thirty tombs, and another six were excavated by other archaeologists (Philios 1897, and see site 151). A double-chamber tomb was excavated somewhere here by Pappadakis (1919).

The tombs of Kolonaki are cut in the soft bedrock; most have rectangular chambers, the size of which varies from

1.20 m x 1.30 m (smallest, T 24) to 4.70 m x 7.35 m (largest, T 4). Half the tombs have a chamber larger than 3 m x 3 m, which indicates the wealth of the cemetery. The tombs cover the entire span of the Mycenaean period from LH I to LH III; some of them were used several times. The study of pottery from the well-preserved tombs (Furumark 1941B) has made possible their chronological classification, which in turn enables us to determine that the cemetery's main period of use was LH II to LH III A:1; most of the large tombs date to this period (cat. table 3; T 25 is the sole exception). Keramopoullos (1917:208), who published the tombs in detail, also observed that the largest tombs were the earliest.

The cemetery was in a generally poor state of preservation, but did produce small quantities of the usual finds: gold jewelry, glass-paste beads, semiprecious stones, a few seals, arrowheads, and daggers. Some of the Kolonaki tombs also produced surprises: a collection of 23 terracotta figurines (T 25), a collection of 41 vases (T 14), a cremation burial (T 16), a single Protogeometric skyphos (T 27), and a dog burial in the dromos (T 6).

CLASSICAL-HELLENISTIC. Kolonaki became the burial ground of the poor. Three Mycenaean tombs were reused in Classical times (Kolonaki T 4, T 14, T 17); another pit grave was cut within T 25. Keramopoullos (1917:210) mentions a Classical burial in T 9. He excavated another twenty tombs, all but one pit graves, five of which

Catalogue Table 3. Dates of tombs at the cemetery of Kolonaki

	Tomb Number	
Period	Keramopoullos 1910	Keramopoullos 1917
LH I	2(19)	
LH II	2	4(34.5), 14(16.1), 26(15.4) 9(21.6)
LH IIIA:1		14, 15(18.1) 26
LH IIIA:2		17(8.1), 21(14) 14, 4
LH IIIB	2	1(5.2) 25(19.9), 4
LH IIIC		10(3.2), 12(4.4), 16(6.2), 15, 14

Note: Dates are based on the study of pottery. The tomb numbers are those of Keramopoullos; the chamber floor space in square meters is indicated in parentheses.

were shallow and lined with tiles. There were also five cremations. Those tombs that had remained intact contained pottery, in the main, but there were also several terracotta figurines of humans and animals. A well-preserved painted stele was found in T 20 (Keramopoullos 1917:246, fig. 177).

Eleven pit graves were found in 1966 (*Deltion* 1967:230-231). The fact that all the known tombs were discovered accidentally leads one to believe that there must have been many more of this type. The Classical Kolonaki cemetery was used from the fifth to the third century B.C.

CHRISTIAN. There is evidence that the Mycenaean cemetery was reused during the Christian period. Many skeletons were found in Kolonaki T 5; there were burials in the dromos and chamber of T 6; Byzantine pottery was found in tombs 8, 9, 16, and 23. Kolonaki T 17 has been used continuously up to modern times. Keramopoullos (1917:207-208) found evidence that the Mycenaean tomb 28 had been transformed into a chapel.

SITE 25. GREATER THEBES
J-K, 9-11.

The Kastellia hills, northeast of the Kadmeia. Keramopoullos 1917:99-122 (Christian tombs and catacombs), 108-111, (Mycenaean tombs). *Deltion* 22B (1967):228-229 (Mycenaean tombs); *Deltion* 26B (1971):209, 211.

This site essentially comprises the excavations of Keramopoullos on the Kastellia

hills in the area of the present-day high school of Thebes. I have added a few tombs excavated near the high school in 1966 and 1970. Other sites on the Kastellia hills have been assigned different numbers. The hills are divided into the Megalo Kastelli to the south and the Mikro Kastelli to the north; in antiquity, the road to Chalkis ran between the two (Keramopoullos 1917:361). They were used mainly for burials, but also for habitation in the Classical and Byzantine periods. The finds of the two hills are summarized in catalogue table 4. Keramopoullos excavated in several places in this area, but mostly on the west slopes of the hills where he suspected the existence of the theater.

LATE HELLADIC. On the west side of Megalo Kastelli, Keramopoullos (1917:108-111) excavated two chamber tombs, poorly preserved. On Mikro Kastelli he saw remains of three Mycenaean tombs but did not excavate them. It is possible that these tombs were among the six excavated in 1966. All of them were very poorly preserved; three were connected by a tunnel in Classical or Hellenistic times (*Deltion* 1967, pls. 161:a-b, 162:a). They yielded a lot of Mycenaean and Classical pottery, and a few objects such as a lentoid seal (*Deltion* 1967, pl. 162:b), a circular ivory plaque with the representation of a lion attacking a bull (*Deltion* 1967, pl. 162:c), remains of a helmet made of boar's tusks, and two glass-paste plaques showing such helmets. The connecting tunnel and the presence of many additional cuts in the rock raised the possibility that the tombs were not used for burial in Classical times, but may have been used for cult purposes.

Catalogue Table 4. Summary of excavated sites on the Kastellia hills
(Megalo Kastelli and Mikro Kastelli)

Site number	Kastellia location	Tombs		Habitation	
		Mycenaean	Byzantine	Classical	Byzantine
25	both hills	X	X	-	X
122	megalo	X	X	X	-
138	mikro	-	X	X	X
139	mikro	X	X	-	X
140	mikro	X	X	-	-
141	mikro	-	-	X	-
176	mikro	X	-	X	X
180	mikro	-	-	-	modern chapel
191	megalo	X	-	-	-
235	mikro	X	-	X	-
254	megalo	X	-	-	-

Note: The hills were used mainly for burials, except in the two periods of the city's great expansion.

Because of the poor state of preservation, however, no evidence of cult practice could be found.

CHRISTIAN. Keramopoullos (1917:102-103) found remains of habitation on the southwest side of Megalo Kastelli. There were also Early Christian tombs in the same area. The main target of Keramopoullos' excavation was on Mikro Kastelli, where the high school of Thebes is today. The west side of the hill was occupied by a large Christian catacomb, approximately 25 m long (1917:113-119, figs. 79-88). Its plan consists of a large cross-shaped room, a small irregular room, and a long corridor connecting the two. There were traces of a fresco of Christ in the larger room. The catacomb was dug in Early Christian times, according to Keramopoullos (1917:119-120), but was probably in use for several centuries thereafter.

A group of fourteen Byzantine tombs was found in 1970 in the courtyard of the high school (*Deltion* 1971:209, 211). They were shallow pit graves, some of them covered by stone plaques. The tombs contained pottery and silver and bronze jewelry.

SITE 26. GREATER THEBES G-14.

Church of Agia Trias, southwest of the Kadmeia.

The present church may have been built in the late nineteenth century. The locals report that materials from the nearby spring of Dirke were incorporated in the construction. Fabricius (1890:28) reports that the remains of an ancient temple were found here, and Frazer (1898:48-49) confirms that the church rests on ancient foundations. Both authors suggest that the ancient temple was that of Athena Onka (cf. Robert 1909:100-103). Keramopoullos (1917:334-336) disagreed and placed Athena

Onka close to the southwest edge of the Kadmeia. My interpretation of Pausanias' text leads me to place the sanctuary of Mother Dindymene at this site (see chap. 5, passage 18).

SITE 27. GREATER THEBES J-13.

3 Polyneikes St., property of M. Euthymiou. *Deltion* 19B (1964):197.

Excavation was limited to the area of the foundation shafts.

CLASSICAL-HELLENISTIC. Remains of houses were found at a depth of 3.10 m, just above the bedrock. There was pottery and a pebble floor.

BYZANTINE. There were remains of at least one house, including a silo and a well-made plaster floor, and a lot of pottery. One wall combined brick and mortar with stones from an ancient building.

SITE 28. GREATER THEBES J-13.

3 Seventh St., property of A. Stamelakis.

BYZANTINE. Scanty remains of house(s) were found near the surface.

Site 29. GREATER THEBES J-12.

Nea Sphageia. 20 22d St., property of S. Karaoulanis.

BYZANTINE. One tomb is reported, perhaps Byzantine (Thebes Museum notebook 1 [1963]:7-8).

SITE 30. GREATER THEBES J-12.

Nea Sphageia. Property of D. Vrekas (just south of site 29).

BYZANTINE. Six tombs were reportedly found here, but there are no details about them.

SITE 31. GREATER THEBES J-12.

Nea Sphageia. 20 19th St., property of K. Hatzidouros.

EARLY CHRISTIAN?. I saw part of an underground chamber that seemed to belong to a Christian catacomb.

SITE 32. KADMEIA H-12.

Oidipous St., directly west of the town hall; property of Petros Klokas.

EARLY CHRISTIAN AND BYZANTINE. During construction activity in 1962, nine tombs were observed. Six of these were tile-covered, perhaps Early Christian; the other three were cist graves, built with stones and mortar and covered with slabs, perhaps Early Byzantine. The presence of a Byzantine wall above the graves was reported orally, but could not be confirmed.

SITE 33. KADMEIA I-12.

11 Pindar St., property of Photios Soteriou. Thebes Museum notebook 1 (1963):19.

BYZANTINE. Two fragments of carved marble from a church were found in no apparent association with the site, but perhaps brought here from neighboring Agios Andreas (site 217) or from a different church.

SITE 34. KADMEIA H-10.

Corner of Epaminondas and Vourdoumpas Sts., property of Demetrios Vozis and Demetra Stamatis. Thebes Museum notebook 1 (1963):21, 36-38.

BYZANTINE. In 1963, substantial habitation remains were found near the surface. No clear plan was observed, but there were many walls built of stones, brick, and mortar, sometimes with pieces of good ashlar masonry in reuse.

SITE 35. KADMEIA H-10.

147 Epaminondas St., property of Nikolaos Margonis.

Foundation pits related to construction activity in the late 1950's did not reach the bedrock, but walls of various materials, including large stones, were found near the surface; the walls are perhaps Byzantine.

SITE 36. KADMEIA H-10.

135 Epaminondas St., property of Ioannis Tsingos. Thebes Museum notebook 13 (1966):133ff.; 14 (1966):3ff.

BYZANTINE. Construction activity in 1966 revealed a building with two rooms in the southern part of the property. Byzantine walls and four silos were found in the northern part, together with tombs and ossuaries, perhaps of Byzantine date. A stone sarcophagus without carving (perhaps Hellenistic) was found in second use.

SITE 37. KADMEIA H-10.

44 Vourdoumpas St., property of Nikolaos Selekos. *Deltion* 21B (1966):194.

Sixteen foundation pits were opened in 1965 for house construction.

LATE HELLADIC. Some pottery was found directly beneath the Byzantine layer. Bedrock was found at 4.20 m.

CLASSICAL. In one of the foundation pits, a duct was found at a depth of 3.80 m, running east-west and built of clay plaques (bottom), stone (sides), and covered with stones. Interior dimensions were 0.32 m in width and 0.25 m in depth.

SITE 38. KADMEIA H-11.

13 I. Metaxa St., property of Argyrios Tzouvelakis.

BYZANTINE. Scanty remains of a house with a large silo were found as well as some pottery.

SITE 39. KADMEIA I-13.

Southern end of Pindar St.

The bedrock is above the surface of the street and there are no ancient remains in the immediate vicinity. Some regular cuttings in the bedrock date to World War II.

SITE 40. KADMEIA H-11.

91 Epaminondas St., property of Stylianos Hatziioannou, formerly property of Parapoulis. House construction in 1959. *Deltion* 16B (1960):147 (inscription published by I. Threpsiades).

Bedrock for the foundations was reached at approximately 7 m, but there is no record of what was found.

HELLENISTIC. A statue base, 1.55 m long, 0.745 m wide, and 0.365 m thick was found here and delivered to the Museum of Thebes. It had been used at this site as a doorsill. The fragmentary inscription tells us that the statue it supported was one of Philokrates and was made by Teisikrates of Sikyon. Threpsiades pointed out that the sculptor is known from another inscription found in Thebes, *IG* 7:2470, and that Pliny (34.8:19) mentions an important work by Teisikrates of an elderly Theban. Koumanoudis (1970:138-139) proposes a new reading of the inscription.

EARLY CHRISTIAN. According to persistent reports, mosaics were uncovered in some of the pits and were destroyed. They must have belonged to the same building that was excavated nearby a few years later (see site 18).

SITE 41. KADMEIA H-11.

39 Kadmos St., property of Vasileios Maranis. Thebes Museum notebook 1 (1963):250-252.

LATE HELLADIC. There were scanty remains of habitation: fragmentary walls and Mycenaean pottery.

ROMAN. A large wall, oriented east-west, constructed of ashlar masonry alternating with layers of bricks was preserved to a height of 1.30 m.

SITE 42. KADMEIA H-11.

Elektra St., property of Alexandros Samartzis.

BYZANTINE. Remains of a house with a silo were found near the surface.

SITE 43. KADMEIA.H-10.

57 Kadmos St., property of Gerasimos Katapodis.

BYZANTINE. Two foundation pits were opened to a depth of 2.50 m. No bedrock was found. Remains consisted of a few fragmentary walls and Byzantine pottery.

SITE 44. KADMEIA H-12.

11 Kadmos St., property of Soterios Spourlis.

BYZANTINE. Many roof tiles, a silo, and some pieces of marble were found near the surface.

SITE 45. KADMEIA H-10.

Keves St., near Kadmos St., property of Spyridon Karagatsoulis. *Deltion* 21B (1966):194; *Deltion* 22B (1967):227.

A total of 12 foundation pits and a sewer were opened. Bedrock was found at 1.20 to 1.50 m except at the northeast corner of the property where it was found at 2.40 m.

LATE HELLADIC. In the deeper pit, a strong Mycenaean wall was found, 1.18 m wide, established on the bedrock. Having no clear inner face, the wall looked more like terracing than part of a building. It continued to the east. There was a floor of packed earth associated with it. A lot of Mycenaean pottery was found at this property, mostly on the north side. A smaller wall of good construction belonged to the foundation of a Mycenaean house.

CLASSICAL. A small section of a well-constructed building was found in the south part of the property. It consisted of two rows of ashlar blocks.

ROMAN. Near the Classical building was a small fragment of another structure, built of ashlar masonry, bricks, and mortar. It could have been Late Roman/Early Christian.

SITE 46. GREATER THEBES I-10.

Mouchlinas Bridge, near the Proitides Gates (site 9). Keramopoullos 1917:361, 372.

According to reliable local informants, here were a Frankish tower, a gate, and a bridge. The tower was demolished shortly before 1904. To the west there was an arched gate with a vertically sliding door. The bridge stood in the same place as the current one, and could have been Turkish, or even Frankish (Gell 1819:128; Ross 1851:23). The dates of the other monuments are not clear, but the tower could have been from the period of the Latin occupation, as is the only remaining tower, which is at the Museum (site 52). Keramopoullos excavated in the area, searching for the ancient theater; he found some theater seats that had been used in the construction of one of these monuments. North of this area, Keramopoullos found an isodomic wall (1917:273, 307-308), possibly belonging to the Classical restoration of the wall of the Kadmeia.

SITE 47. GREATER THEBES I-10.

2 Delaidou St., property of Nikolaos Baronas.

According to reliable local informants, there were Mycenaean architectural remains, perhaps related to the fortifications, a strong Classical wall, and a Byzantine wall similar in construction to the Frankish tower.

SITE 48. KADMEIA H-10.

38 Vourdoumpas St., property of Soterios Karastathis.

BYZANTINE. One foundation pit was opened; there were only remains of a few silos cut in the bedrock.

SITE 49. KADMEIA I-11.

54 Amphion St., property of Vasileios Asimakis.

A few foundation pits were opened.

LATE HELLADIC. There was some Mycenaean pottery near the bedrock.

BYZANTINE. Remains of a house and a well-built silo were found.

SITE 50. KADMEIA H-12.

Dirke St., just east of Epaminondas St., property of Angelos Katzelis. Thebes Museum notebook 1 (1963):1ff.

BYZANTINE. There were poorly preserved remains of a house with an ancient column drum incorporated in its construction. There were three large silos cut in the bedrock, very little pottery and no other finds.

SITE 51. KADMEIA H-11.

6 I. Metaxas St., property of G. Dougekos and D. Akrivakis. House construction in the late 1950's.

EARLY HELLADIC. Local informants gave reliable reports of habitation remains. There are well-preserved Early Helladic remains in the area (cf. site 18).

SITE 52. KADMEIA H-9.

Archaeological Museum of Thebes and Frankish tower.

Keramopoullos (1917:2-5, fig. 2, pottery) excavated in the courtyard of the old Museum where he had observed early Mycenaean pottery. South of the Museum he opened two trenches 2 m x 1.50 m, and found bedrock at 1 m. North of the Museum he opened one trench, 3.60 m x 1.70 m, that went 5 m deep without reaching bedrock.

NEOLITHIC. Mylonas (1928:74-75) reports that he examined the material from the excavation and found monochrome and painted, hand-made Neolithic pottery. This is the only evidence of a Neolithic presence on the Kadmeia, and it is interesting that it comes from the area of the Museum, close to the other suspected Neolithic settlement of site 87.

MIDDLE HELLADIC. Keramopoullos mentions the presence of Minyan pottery several times in both areas. It is possible that he found some Early Helladic pottery as well, though he makes no such distinction. He mentions no habitation remains, and it is possible that he found prehistoric debris. This area was a dumping ground in several periods. Keramopoullos himself dumped the debris from his "house of Kadmos" excavation (1917:4, n. 1).

LATE HELLLADIC. Keramopoullos did not find Mycenaean remains here. Leake (1835:226) reports seeing a wall, 30 m long, of Cyclopean construction preserved four courses high, similar to those of Mycenae and Tiryns. Keramopoullos (1917:304) expressed doubt as to whether the wall seen by Leake was part of the fortifications, or simply a supporting wall. However, he accepted the locating of the Borraiai gates in the vicinity of the Frankish tower (1917:386).

CLASSICAL. Keramopoullos (1917:309, fig. 186) reports the presence of an isodomic wall from the fortifications of the Kadmeia.

FRANKISH. The Frankish tower is the only monument of the period still standing in Thebes. It was part of the fortifications built by Nicholas II de St. Omer (1287-1294), who also constructed a grand palace in Thebes (Miller 1921:76; Keramopoullos 1917:310, figs. 186, 210; cf. site 2). The tower is 15.40 m square, with walls 3 m thick, constructed mainly of ancient ashlar masonry, including theater seats and some inscriptions.

THE MUSEUM OF THEBES. The old museum of Thebes was inaugurated in 1885 (Fraser and Rönne 1957:3). The collection consisted of material assembled by Epaminondas Koromantzos, a local antiquary, and was augmented by objects from Thespiai. The early collection was published by Körte (1878). The only other publication of the collection was by Karouzos (1934). The old museum was demolished to make room for the present one, completed in 1962 under the administration of Ephoros Ioannis Threpsiades.

SITE 53. KADMEIA G-12.

West end of Dirke St., under the cliff.

The site of the spring is called *Paraporti* ("by the gate"). The present structure dates from the Turkish period. The water of the spring was diverted for a different purpose in the late 1950s and no longer flows. The existing structure is a wonderful monument, even without water. It was cleaned and studied in 1965 (*Deltion* 21B [1966]:202-203, figs. 21-22, pl. 207B). There must have been a spring here in antiquity as well. The *Krenaiai* ("by the spring") gates may have been located near here (fig. 2.7) as Keramopoullos (1917:426-434) has shown. The name *Dirke* was used to signify both the spring, and the river that flowed west of the Kadmeia. Pindar frequently referred to Dirke without specifying which he meant; in certain passages, however, he seems to mean the spring (*Pyth.* 9.86; *Isth.* 6.74; *Isth.* 8.19).

SITE 54. GREATER THEBES K-14.

The cemetery and church of Agios Loukas, east of the Kadmeia.

Local tradition has it that the Evangelist Luke was buried here (Keramopoullos 1917:318, n. 1). Delvenakiotis (1970:24) says that the modern church is built on the site of an eleventh-century church. A church of Agia Loukia is mentioned during the Frankish period (Keramopoullos 1917:34, n. 2). Evidence for the antiquity of the cemetery are three coins found there—one of Manuel Komnenos (1143-1180), and two Frankish coins of the thirteenth century (Keramopoullos 1926). There are also numerous burials in the area dating to Christian times (see site 8).

SITE 55. GREATER THEBES K-13.

Nea Sphageia.

Just north of site 54 there are surface indications of large ashlar blocks, roof tiles, Hellenistic-Roman pottery, and Byzantine pottery as well. No excavating was done, but I suspect there was once some sort of public building in the area.

SITE 56. GREATER THEBES B-6.

West Pyri. Roadbridge over the railroad. *Deltion* 20B (1965):240, pls. 284:b, 285:a. *Bulletin de correspondance hellénique* 92 (1968):865, fig. 15 (the site).

Six large foundation pits were opened in the ancient cemetery of Thebes. One of the pits was dug up by the contractor. A great number of tombs were destroyed, and hundreds of vases were collected. The tombs found in three of the foundation pits were poorly preserved. Two pits were properly excavated. Two types of burial were observed: the majority were cremations in shallow pits; the rest were pithos burials. The offerings included a great number of vases and small numbers of terracotta figurines, bronze daggers, glass beads, and the like. The offerings for the cremation burials were sometimes placed inside large vases that were then placed beside the cremation pit; the pottery was found broken. As a rule, complete vases were placed inside the pithos burials.

Large quantities of pottery came from the site, and it has not been possible either to catalogue it or to study it in detail. My impression is that the excavated area ranges in date from the late seventh to the late sixth or even early fifth century B.C.

SITE 57. GREATER THEBES FIG. 1.2, E-8.

Kazi, west of Pyri. *Deltion* 20B (1965):239-240, pl. 284:a (Hellenistic tomb); *Deltion* (1969):185 (one stele). *Bulletin de correspondance hellénique* 92 (1968):865, fig. 14 (stelai).

The area is part of the vast cemetery of Thebes. In 1964, six farms in the area were plowed to a depth of 0.80 m, turning up a huge quantity of pottery, funerary stelai, and tombs ranging in date from the Archaic to the Hellenistic periods. Only a few of the tombs were excavated and their contents salvaged. Several inscribed stelai were transferred to the Museum, including the seven that had been used to cover a Hellenistic tomb (*Deltion* 1965, pl. 284:a).

SITE 58. GREATER THEBES L-4.

The location is called Gephyra Basiakou ("Basiakou's bridge"). *Deltion* 19B (1964):202-203, pls. 246:b, 247:a-b, 248:a-c (12 funerary stelai found by I. Threpsiades in 1961-1962 were published by Evi Touloupa); *Deltion* 20 (1965):240, pl. 285:b (Korinthian pottery).

Forty-one tombs were excavated in 1961 by Evangelos Pentazos and Sokrates Symeonides under the supervision of I. Threpsiades. A great quantity of pottery was found and twelve funerary stelai were transferred to the Museum; the stelai range in date from the sixth to the first century B.C.

Nine more tombs were excavated in 1964. Five were cremations, three were pithos burials, and one was a large cist grave, built of dressed poros stones and containing a large male skeleton. Some of the burials dated to the late seventh century B.C. This area is just outside the Classical fortifications of Greater Thebes; we did find a small section of an isodomic wall that could have belonged to those fortifications. Next to the wall we found a group of Boiotian kantharoi and terracottas.

SITE 59. GREATER THEBES
FIG. l.2, F-6.

Kanapitsa, 2 km north of the railroad station. *Deltion* 19B (1964):200, pls. 235:a (lion), 235:b (papyrus capital), 235:c (calyx crater), 235:d (inscribed base), 236:a-c (three funerary reliefs); *Deltion* 22B (1967):234, pl. 164:b, d-f (finds from Classical tomb); *Deltion* 23B (1968):223, fig. 16. *Ephemeris* 1967, Chronika 15-19 (Hellenistic tomb).

CLASSICAL-HELLENISTIC. A rich cemetery was established here in the Classical period. Parts of it were accidentally discovered during road construction and opening of irrigation canals. In 1962, a monumental lion was found, which was transferred to the Museum courtyard three years later. The head, carved from a separate piece, was missing. The name *FASTIAS* is written on the breast. The lion belonged to an important monument of the fourth century B.C. Evi Touloupa searched the area in 1963 and collected pottery, terracottas, and funerary stones. There were numerous black-glazed kantharoi, architectural reliefs, a papyrus capital decorated with leaves painted red. A beautiful calyx crater had a representation of young Herakles flanked by Dionysos, Hermes, Apollo, and Athena (*front panel*) and four athletes (*back panel*). In 1967, three tombs of the Classical period were found and a "Macedonian" Hellenistic tomb was excavated by Nikolaos Pharaklas; the curious structure consisted of a dromos 10 m long, and an irregularly shaped chamber approximately 5.50 m x 4.00 m. The roof was missing and the interior almost empty.

SITE 60. GREATER THEBES H-16.
South Kolonaki

BYZANTINE. In 1964, we observed on the surface cuttings in the bedrock that are no longer visible. There was some Byzantine pottery associated with them. In all likelihood, these were remains of burials (see site 136).

SITE 61. GREATER THEBES H-14.
Kolonaki, surface observation.

CLASSICAL OR HELLENISTIC. A small section of a wall built of ashlar masonry was visible in 1964, it was perhaps part of a house.

SITE 62. GREATER THEBES L-12.

Myloi, west of Konakia.

LATE HELLADIC. The presence of a cemetery is documented by Philios (1897:95), who reports that all visible tombs had been robbed. Keramopoullos (1910B:210, 1917:100) also reports seeing over 60 tombs, all of which had been robbed.

SITE 63. GREATER THEBES K-8.

Palaios Synoikismos, surface observation in 1965.

BYZANTINE. A few silos were visible on the surface indicating the presence of habitation, perhaps during the Byzantine period.

SITE 64. GREATER THEBES H-15.

Kolonaki, property of A. Stouraitis.

BYZANTINE. A few foundation pits were opened in 1965. We observed remains of houses and two silos of the Byzantine period.

SITE 65. GREATER THEBES J-7.

Neos Synoikismos.

CLASSICAL? Isodomic walls were visible in 1965 in the area marked on the map. They seemed to belong to a large public structure.

SITE 66. GREATER THEBES J-7.

Neos Synoikismos, west of site 65.

CLASSICAL. According to reliable local informants, theater seats were found in two properties, that of Thomas Hatzithomas and that of Emmanouel Panagiotides. A stone carving (perhaps a relief) was found in the latter property.

SITE 67. GREATER THEBES K-7.

Polygyra, northeast of site 65: property of Adrianos.

CLASSICAL? In a large open area we observed at three points the presence of ashlar masonry, perhaps related to the walls seen in site 70.

SITE 68. GREATER THEBES I-7.

On the main street (Leophoros Venizelou) of Neos Synoikismos. *Deltion* 22B (1967):235, pl. 165:a; *Deltion* 26B (1971):211, pl. 184:a; *Deltion* 28B (1973):248, pl. 204:c.

CLASSICAL. Remains of stone walls were known in the area; a huge man-made fill seemed to be supported by them. Some of these walls were destroyed during the opening of Venizelos Avenue, and more of them appeared when the street was widened in 1966. At that time, five foundations of ashlar masonry were revealed, preserved one or two courses high. There were four walls oriented north-south, and one east-west. The longest was 14.50 m.

No plan was made because the remains were quickly covered by the contractor. In 1970, another wall, preserved four courses high, was found at the east side of the street. A similar section was found in 1972, and another in 1976. These substantial remains attest to the presence of large public structures in the area. They are probably related to the theater complex of Thebes. Unfortunately, no clear remains of the theater have been found, and it is likely that it has been almost entirely destroyed.

SITE 69. GREATER THEBES K-7.

Polygyra, north of site 67.

CLASSICAL. Remains of walls made of good ashlar masonry were visible in 1965. These may be related to the ones in sites 65 and 67.

SITE 70. GREATER THEBES K-6.

Polygyra, northeast of site 67.

CLASSICAL? Foundations built of small stones were visible here in 1965. They probably belonged to small structures (houses?) of the Classical period or later.

SITE 71. GREATER THEBES K-5.

Neos Synoikismos, excavation at the site of the Agricultural Cooperative storehouse. *Deltion* 21B (1966):194-197, figs. 15-17, pls. 198:a-c, 199, 200:a-b, 201:a-b. Hackens 1969 (on the coin hoard from the site).

In an area of 3,600 square meters, a total of 85 foundation pits were opened and properly excavated by Evi Touloupa, who was assisted by Evangelos Pentazos and Nikolaos Pharaklas. Bedrock was found 0.70 to 2.50 m below the surface.

ORIENTALIZING. The area had been a cemetery, as was neighboring site 58. Here, however, the cemetery had been cleared for construction in Classical times. Only one tomb was found intact: one burial inside two pithoi contained a skeleton and five vases, three of which were Middle Protocorinthian lekythoi, which date the tomb to the early seventh century B.C. (*Deltion* 1966, pl. 200:a).

CLASSICAL-HELLENISTIC. The area was occupied by houses, some of which lasted into late Hellenistic times. The foundations were built of small stones, generally ca. 0.50 m thick, and the upper structure was of mud-brick. A few houses had foundations of ashlar masonry. White or red plaster was found in some of the houses. The floors were constituted of either the leveled bedrock, or were made of coarse pebbles and flat stones. One house had a hard plaster floor (*Deltion* 1966, pl. 198:a), another a fine pebble floor (*Deltion* 1966, 198:b). Drainage facilities and sewers were well provided; one house had a stone well, 4.80 m deep and 0.80 m in diameter. Another had a small water cistern.

At the northeast side of the excavated area was a substantial structure (*Deltion* [1966]:196, fig. 16): a cistern was cut in the bedrock, topped with ashlar masonry forming a pentagon and lined inside with hard plaster. The interior was shaped like a funnel, 3 m deep and 2.50 m in diameter at the top. There were well-built rooms around the cistern, except to the east where there was a road 4.70 m wide, paved with concrete 0.15 m thick. Beyond the road was a section of the city wall of Greater Thebes, 3.20 m wide, built of two rows of large poros blocks 1.20 m long, and 0.70 m wide; the 1.80-meter gap between them was filled with poros chips and small stones. The wall had been standing in the fourth century when repairs were made, but the date of its construction is not clear. The presence of the wall suggests that the well-built "cistern house" could have been that of a guard, perhaps with an observation tower. The wall seems to turn west at this point (see site 253).

A small hoard of coins was found in pit 48, 16 of silver and 42 of bronze. The bronze coins were all Boiotian, but the silver coins were of various origins: Roman Republic (1), Histiaia (2), Thebes (1), Achaian League (2), Sicyon (1), Megalopolis (1), Rhodes (5), and imitations of Rhodian coins (3). Hackens (1969) dates the hoard to 168 B.C. and observes that Thebes maintained international relations at that time.

SITE 72. GREATER THEBES J-5.

Neos Synoikismos, west of site 71.

CLASSICAL? In 1965, there were remains of ashlar masonry visible on the surface. No excavating took place, but it is likely that the remains are related to the fortifications of Greater Thebes.

SITE 73. GREATER THEBES J-5.

Railroad station, west of site 72.

CLASSICAL? Another wall of ashlar masonry was observed here in 1965, perhaps also part of the fortifications (cf. sites 71, 72, 253).

SITE 74. GREATER THEBES F-7.

Central Pyri, I. Douros St., property of Anastasios Liakopoulos. *Deltion* 21B (1966):197-198, fig. 18, pls. 202:a-b (Geometric pithos), 202:c (Hellenistic tomb); *Deltion* 22B (1967):237 (Classical? house). *Bulletin de correspondance hellénique* 94 (1970), fig. 313 (Geometric pithos).

GEOMETRIC. A child burial was found by construction workers. It had been disturbed, and parts of the pithos including the lid were lost. The Late Geometric pithos has a cylindrical shape with two high handles, decorated with simple geometric designs, and two panels at the top. One panel shows a standing male figure with a lyre, facing a group of six women, and two small figures (male and female) in between (*Deltion* 1966, pl. 202:b); the other panel shows a group of nine female dancers. Two more vases, a kalathiskos and a lekanis, were found in association with the burial.

CLASSICAL? While making street repairs in front of the property of A. Liakopoulos, remains of a house were found; the foundations were of ashlar masonry; there were a column drum, and roof tiles. The original house was probably built in the Classical period.

HELLENISTIC. On the property of A. Liakopoulos was another tomb, built of large poros slabs; interior dimensions were 3.20 m x 2.30 m. It was covered by three large slabs, but there were no finds. Its date may be Hellenistic, or even Late Classical.

SITE 75. GREATER THEBES J-12.

Astegoi. 3 21st St., property of Alexandros Karagiannis. *Deltion* 21B (1966):194.

BYZANTINE. The poorly preserved remains of a small structure were found here; there were many fresco fragments, probably from a chapel. Next to it was a grave cut in the rock measuring 1.76 m x 135 m, and 0.85 m deep, containing a mass of skeletal remains.

SITE 76. GREATER THEBES J-12.

Astegoi, across the street from site 75; property of Pelopidas Manaras. *Deltion* 21B (1966):194.

BYZANTINE. A narrow duct carved in the bedrock led to a shallow square pit; there was Byzantine pottery in both.

SITES 77-79. GREATER THEBES M, 10-11.

Along the road to Konakia.

CLASSICAL. A surface investigation was conducted in 1965: there were visible remains of a wall built of ashlar blocks in each of the three locations. The wall, which was not well enough preserved to make a plan, had appeared and had been damaged when the road was widened. What remained, however, seemed to belong to the Classical wall of Greater Thebes, known from several other locations.

SITE 80. GREATER THEBES M-11.

Konakia. 26 Pege St., property of Konstantinos Balatsos. *Deltion* 21B (1966):193, fig. 14.

CLASSICAL. Foundation trenches were opened on the west side of the road along the line of the fortifications, which were missing here; a related structure was perhaps found in the northeast corner of the foundations. The structure of ashlar masonry formed a small rectangle, 0.50 m x 0.60 m, and was 1.50 m or three courses deep. The lowest course was of hard conglomerate, the upper two of soft poros.

SITE 81. GREATER THEBES N-11.

At the river bed of Moschopodi.

In 1965, we found a poorly preserved and empty grave, which was perhaps a Late Helladic chamber tomb.

SITE 82. GREATER THEBES M-12.

Konakia, ca. 250 m south of site 80.

CLASSICAL. In 1965, there were visible remains here of the Classical wall. It is possible that we saw one of the sections excavated by Kalopais (1892:44), who mentions a semicircular tower, ca. 6 m in diameter, in this area. It is also possible that here, or in the vicinity, Nikolaos Pharaklas investigated the remains of "a gate or a tower" (*Deltion* 22 [1967]: 233).

SITE 83. GREATER THEBES M-15.

The church of Agia Photeini. Orlandos 1939A, 1939B. Pls. 49-50.

BYZANTINE. The present church is the result of a recent restoration by Anastasios Orlandos; it was in ruins at the beginning of this century (Keramopoullos 1917:259-260). Orlandos (1939B) excavated here in 1939 and was able to establish that the earliest church was built at this site in the second half of the tenth century. The original church was of cross-shaped plan and supported a small dome. A square narthex was added at a later time (Orlandos 1939B, fig. 1). Some ancient masonry was used in the construction. Frescoes were found on the lower part of the wall, imitating marble orthostats. Of the original marble decoration, only a small window capital was preserved.

SITE 84. GREATER THEBES L-8.

Just south of the church of Agioi Theodoroi (site 22); property of Bairaktari.

BYZANTINE? According to reliable local informants, there were tombs on this property, perhaps of the Byzantine period.

SITE 85. GREATER THEBES K-12.

Astegoi. 19 Vongini St., property of Christos Xenakis. Thebes Museum notebook 1 (1963):20, 28-29.

CLASSICAL. A section of the underground aqueduct system of Thebes was found here. The duct was carved in the bedrock and was 1.35 m high and 0.47 m wide. There was no evidence regarding its date.

SITE 86. GREATER THEBES D-6.

West Pyri, location Phoros; property of Antonios Tzoumanekas. *Deltion* 22B (1967):236-237, pl. 166:a-b (Siana cup); *Deltion* 23B (1968):221; *Deltion* 26B (1971):226, pl. 199:b (Hellenistic cist grave).

House construction in three stages revealed sections of the ancient cemetery.

ARCHAIC. Several tombs were found in 1966, but only a few contained finds. There were three types of tombs: pit graves, cist graves, and tile-covered tombs. The finds consisted mainly of Boiotian pottery, but there were also Korinthian and Attic vases. Some terracottas and a glass vase were also found. One of the most interesting finds was a Siana cup. The tombs ranged in date from the early sixth to the early fifth century B.C.

HELLENISTIC-ROMAN. Three cist graves were found on this property in 1970. Two were empty; the third contained the remains of a skeleton and ten unguentaria.

SITE 87. GREATER THEBES
FIG. 1.2, E-8.

North of Kazi (cf. site 57), property of Soterios Papademetriou. *Deltion* 22B (1967):236, fig. 3 (plan of cemetery), pl. 165:c (pithos burial); *Deltion* 24B (1969):175-177, fig. 2 (plan of Classical cemetery); *Deltion* 26B (1971):211-213, 220, pls. 184:c-d, 185:a-c (burials and finds).

NEOLITHIC. In 1964, Nikolaos Pharaklas unexpectedly found remains of houses and Late Neolithic pottery, but he decided to postpone systematic excavation. The remains are identified as the Neolithic settlement of Thebes.

GEOMETRIC-ARCHAIC. An important part of the cemetery of Thebes was found with intact tombs yielding large quantities of pottery dating from the eighth to the early fifth century B.C. A total of 18 tombs was excavated: eleven pithos burials and seven pit graves, one of which was a cremation. Three large vases were found outside the tombs; they had been used as grave markers. A great number of vases—including amphoras, kraters, Boiotian kantharoi and kylikes, Corinthian vases—and many terracotta figurines were found. An undetermined number of tombs was excavated by Spyropoulos in 1970. Most of them prob-ably date to the same periods as those found in 1966. I believe that at least one amphora is Middle Geometric (*Deltion* 1971, pl. 185:b).

CLASSICAL. Pharaklas found 16 tombs in 1968, but investigated only nine of them: seven cremations, one inhumation, and one vacant tomb. Four were rich in offerings (pottery and figurines). Above the burned debris of one cremation was a layer of eggshells, a phenomenon known in Greece (Kurtz and Boardman 1971:66, 77, 215).

SITE 88. KADMEIA I-12.

19 Dirke St., property of Andreas Gavriatopoulos. *Deltion* 21B (1966): 191-192, fig. 12 (plan of property); *Deltion* 22B (1967):230.

EARLY HELLADIC-LATE HELLADIC. Only one of the foundation pits was opened down to bedrock, found at 7 m. Because that one was so deep, the other pits were opened only to a depth of 2.50 m. In the deep pit it was clear that there were habitation remains representing the entire Bronze Age, but finds were few because the excavated area was very small.

CHRISTIAN. Remains of a large structure were found in the center of the property: a strong wall, 4 m long, and associated with it, a small portion of a mosaic with geometric decoration, which was transferred to the Museum. The structure could have been a public building or a church (cf. site 11, the church of Agios Vasileios, across the street). Two tombs were found, one built of stone slabs and containing an ossuary, the other a simple cist grave.

SITE 89. GREATER THEBES J-10.

Kastellia. 13 Aulis St., property of Nikolaos Panagainas.

HELLENISTIC? According to reliable information, remains of houses were found during the opening of a sewer, 14 m deep. The date of the houses was not clear, but Hellenistic pottery was reportedly found at the site.

SITE 90. GREATER THEBES M-9.

Suburb of Agioi Theodoroi; property of Panagiotis Karras.

CLASSICAL. Another part of the Classical fortification was found here when a foundation pit was being dug.

SITE 91. GREATER THEBES L-8.

Suburb of Agioi Theodoroi; property of Theodoros Antonakis.

CLASSICAL? According to reliable reports, remains of houses were found here during the digging of foundation pits. The remains were described as Classical or Hellenistic.

SITE 92. KADMEIA I-10.

1 Tsevas St., property of Konstantinos Tsoungas.

BYZANTINE. The area was heavily used in Byzantine times. There were several layers of habitation down to bedrock at 2.20 m. Two large Byzantine silos were found, one dug to a depth of 5.50 m.

SITE 93. KADMEIA H-10.

The church of Agios Georgios in the northern part of the Kadmeia.

MODERN. The present building was begun in 1860 and completed much later. According to local tradition, Osios Meletios (1035-1105) built a monastery here in honor of Agios Georgios (Delvenakiotis 1970:25-26). Remains found nearby support the tradition of the existence of an ancient monastery (cf. sites 135, 236). The use of the site in earlier periods could also be confirmed by the presence of many ancient stones, which seem to have been reused several times. Keramopoullos (1917:365) reports that a Korinthian capital came from here. A Venetian capital, part of a marble throne (*Deltion* 21B [1966]:205) and several other carvings came from this church.

SITE 94. KADMEIA H-9.

Chapel of Agia Eleousa.

MODERN. The chapel was built after 1853, perhaps on the site of an older church. Keramopoullos (1917:120) reports that nearby, under the "new road," a mosaic was found depicting the ocean with fish. There were also tombs in the area. Several Byzantine stone carvings were brought from here to the Museum (*Deltion* 21B

[1966]:204). From the demolition of a wall just north of the church came several architectural elements (capitals, columns, etc.) giving support to the idea that there was an older church, or even a more ancient structure (*Deltion* 22B [1967]:239). For other related remains see site 130.

SITE 95. KADMEIA I-12.

MODERN. The elementary school of Thebes on Pindar St., a small neoclassical building, housed some antiquities before the old museum was built in 1885. A grave stele of a youth was found here in second use and brought to the museum (Mus. no. 39).

SITE 96. GREATER THEBES F-7.

The church of Agios Athanasios in Pyri.

MODERN. This is the major church of Pyri. Three ancient reliefs are known to have come from here: a votive relief of Herakles Ploutodotes (Mus. no. 48), an inscribed grave stele (Mus. no. 87), and another funerary stele (Mus. no. 128). An inscription was also found here (*IG* 7:2537; Keramopoullos 1917:401, n. 1).

SITE 97. KADMEIA H-11.

The church of Agios Kaloktenis, in the center of town.

MODERN. The present church was built in 1900 (Delvenakiotis 1970:77) and named after a celebrated bishop of Thebes who lived in the twelfth century and is credited with bringing about a revival of the city. A great amount of information about the saint was carefully collected and published by Vasileios Delvenakiotis (1970; cf. Kominis 1968). It is possible that the modern building was founded on a twelfth- or thirteenth-century church constructed by the bishop (see site 270). Two ancient monuments are known to have come from the church: the fragment of a relief with a horseman (Mus. no. 115) and a funerary stele showing a female figure on a horse (Mus. no. 210).

SITE 98. GREATER THEBES L-10.

Suburb of Agioi Theodoroi, just west of the water reservoir.

HELLENISTIC. A relief with two figures (Mus. no. 169) was found here, perhaps from a cemetery site nearby.

SITE 99. GREATER THEBES L-10.

By the water reservoir east of Agios Loukas (site 54).

HELLENISTIC. The relief of a horseman (Mus. no. 171) was found here and is included because it probably belonged to a cemetery in this area (see site 124).

SITE 100. GREATER THEBES L-9.

Suburb of Agioi Theodoroi; property of Evangelos Adrianos.

HELLENISTIC. The upper part of a funerary stele (Mus. no. 254) was found in the vicinity of this property and may indicate the presence of a cemetery.

SITE 101. KADMEIA H-12.

43 Oidipous St., property of Ioannis Pelidis. *Deltion* 21B (1966):192, fig. 13 (Early Helladic remains).

A foundation pit was opened to investigate the depth of deposit; bedrock was found at 5.50 m. The rest of the foundation pits were opened to 2.50 m.

EARLY HELLADIC. Directly above the bedrock (5.50 to 5.20 m) there were remains of a house: the walls were relatively thin (0.40 m); the well-made floor was of packed clay. The finds included very fine pottery and terracotta tiles.

MIDDLE HELLADIC. There was a thick deposit (5.20 to 4.00 m) but no architectural remains were found in our narrow trench (1.50 square meters). There was a fair amount of pottery.

LATE HELLADIC. Above the Middle Helladic levels was a thick layer of ashes and sand (4.00 to 3.20 m) with no pottery in it. Above this layer was a thick layer (3.20 to 2.50 m) from the destruction of a building; it contained pottery and a lot of architectural debris.

BYZANTINE. A very deep deposit (2.50 to 0.50 m) of architectural debris owing to the destruction of a single building, perhaps a house.

SITE 102. KADMEIA I-10.

4 G. Tsevas St., property of Petros Delvenakiotis.

LATE HELLADIC. One foundation pit was opened, and bedrock was found at 2 m. Only some Mycenaean pottery was found.

SITE 103. KADMEIA I-11.

On Pindar St., in front of site 1. *Deltion* 22B (1967):226.

LATE HELLADIC. Three shallow pits (1 m) were opened on the dividing island of Pindar St. for the installation of electrical posts. We were curious to see what was preserved there, because at site 1 (only 10 m away), bedrock was 0.50 m above street level. At the bottom of these pits, bedrock had not been reached. We did find walls and Mycenaean pottery. The excavated area was too small to determine the nature of the buildings, but it is very likely that the remains belong to a Mycenaean palace.

SITE 104. KADMEIA G-10.

On the slope of the northwest part of the Kadmeia.

LATE HELLADIC. A bulldozer reopened the road that leads to Pyri from the northwest area of the Kadmeia (in 1966). We saw some loose stones of Cyclopean masonry associated with Mycenaean pottery. This is the suspected location of the Mycenaean fortifications and perhaps of a gate (Keramopoullos [1917:305, 412] placed the Neistai gates here).

SITE 105. GREATER THEBES K-13.

Near the hill of Apollo Ismenios (site 8), exact location not known. *Deltion* 16 (1960):147, pl. 125:a.

ARCHAIC. An inscribed fragment from a poros column was found in the late 1950s. Threpsiades restored the inscription as follows:

Απολλον]ι Ηισμ [ενιοι
Θεσπιε] ιες κα [ι . . .

The word Ismenios is clearly preserved, relating the piece to the sanctuary (see site 8).

SITE 106. GREATER THEBES I-6.

Railroad station. Kalopais 1892:45, 1893:18.

During the construction of the railroad station, a wall was discovered, which was investigated by Kalopais: it consisted of one row of ashlar blocks 0.80 m thick (perhaps of similar height) and continued from east to west for 32 m where it turned south in a wide angle for another 10 m. There it was stopped by a deep well. Kalopais believed it to be a portico, but Keramopoullos (1917:379-380) identified it as the stadion named for Iolaos, and re-

ported seeing pottery of the Classical period by the wall (1930C:69).

SITE 107. GREATER THEBES J-15.

Palaia Sphageia, location Pege; property of Demetrios Koropoulis. *Deltion* 21B (1966):194.

Twelve foundation pits were opened, but only one of them on the west side of the property yielded remains. A Roman hypocaustum was found at a depth of 3.25 m belonging to either a public building or a large private house. Bedrock was found between 5 and 7 m.

SITE 108. GREATER THEBES J-13.

On the road to Agios Loukas (site 54); property of Eustratios Vrontagias.

BYZANTINE. According to reliable reports, the opening of foundation pits revealed habitation remains consisting of reused ashlar masonry and Byzantine pottery.

SITE 109. KADMEIA H-11.

Epaminondas St. Installation of sewer pipes in the central part of the Kadmeia: *Deltion* 22B (1967):230; *Deltion* 23B (1968):207.

LATE HELLADIC. Part of the Mycenaean aqueduct was found in front of the market, going east-west. There was also a well-built wall oriented northeast-southwest that had been damaged by the construction of the Mycenaean aqueduct.

CLASSICAL. Two parallel walls 3 m apart were found in east-west orientation (near Kreon St.).

BYZANTINE. A few walls were found near the Market (houses?); a well-built wall with a column drum in it was at the intersection of Metaxas and Epaminondas Sts., and six silos associated with the walls were found near Kreon St.

SITE 110. KADMEIA H-11.

32 Kadmos St., property of Nikolaos Ioannou. *Deltion* 23B (1968):207-208, figs. 1-2 (plans), pl. 159:a (Mycenaean frescoes). Excavator, N. Pharaklas.

EARLY HELLADIC. Only pottery was found, but habitation remains may have existed beneath the Mycenaean houses.

MIDDLE HELLADIC. There were scattered remains of habitation and a lot of pottery. Three curved walls belonged perhaps to apsidal houses.

LATE HELLADIC. Substantial remains of Mycenaean houses were found on this property, and three phases of construction were distinguished; their relative chronology awaits study. One wall was 1.70 m thick and was probably built to terrace the site. A few good-size fragments of frescoes were found here.

BYZANTINE. Remains of habitation consisted of two silos and pottery.

SITE 111. KADMEIA H-10.

Epaminondas and Loukas Belos Sts. Property of Konstantinos Anadiotis. *Deltion* 23B (1968):210-211, fig. 4 (plan), pls. 159:b-d (pottery), 160: a-b (bronzes). Excavator, N. Pharaklas.

BYZANTINE. There were numerous remains of habitation, three silos, and a well. From the last come a nice collection of twelfth- and thirteenth-century pottery. Bronzes and more pottery were found elsewhere on this property.

SITE 112. KADMEIA I-12.

13 Oidipous St., property of Panagiotis Leontaris. *Deltion* 22B (1967): 230; *Deltion* 23B (1968):208-210, fig. 3 (plan of Byzantine remains); excavator, N. Pharaklas. *Deltion* 24B (1969):183. *Athens Annals of Archaeology* 1 (1968):11, figs. 14, 15 (jewelry); excavator, T. Spyropoulos.

EARLY HELLADIC. On the bedrock were clay-lined storage pits, but no other remains of this period were found.

MIDDLE HELLADIC. Part of a rounded wall belonging to a house destroyed by fire was found.

LATE HELLADIC. The ruined Middle Helladic house was covered by a layer of packed earth, according to Pharaklas. A two-step krepis was found next to the Middle Helladic ruin; no architectural association was apparent. Pharaklas thought it had been built to mark the site of the ruined house. Approximately 1.30 m below this krepis, a pit burial was found and, associated with it, some very nice jewelry and a stemmed cup.

CLASSICAL? There was a two-step krepis described above.

ROMAN. An L-shaped portion of a building dated to the Roman period.

BYZANTINE. There were extensive and well-preserved remains of buildings (*Deltion* 1968:210, fig. 3) that seemed to be part of a very rich house, if we are to judge by the nine silos, the numerous water pipes, and the fine construction. The house must have stood a long time, because there was evidence of numerous repairs.

SITE 113. KADMEIA I-11.

1 Antigone St., property of I. Panagiotopoulos. *Deltion* 23B (1968):211, figs. 5 (plan), 6 (Middle Helladic tomb), pl. 161:a (Late Helladic pottery). Excavator, N. Pharaklas.

The accumulation of deposit was deeper at the northeast corner where the bedrock becomes steep.

MIDDLE HELLADIC. A cist burial was found dating to the end of the period.

LATE HELLADIC. There was a deep accumulation of deposit, which included a lot of Mycenaean pottery. It looked like a fill, perhaps related to the fortifications that should be somewhere in the area. A Mycenaean wall was found in east-west orientation.

HELLENISTIC-ROMAN. Only some pottery was found.

BYZANTINE. Numerous remains of habitation were found: several walls, three silos, and a lot of pottery.

SITE 114. KADMEIA I-10.

49 Pelopidas St., property of Phoiphas. *Deltion* 23B (1968):211-212, pl. 161:b-c (pottery of different periods). Excavator, N. Pharaklas.

The ground sloped sharply from west to east. There was pottery from every period, especially the Middle Helladic, the Late Helladic, and the Hellenistic. The nature of the deposits (habitation? fill?) was not clear.

BYZANTINE. There were remains of a house with a silo.

SITE 115. KADMEIA I-12.

36 Pindar St., property of Sinis. *Deltion* 23B (1968):212, pl. 162:a (Byzantine pottery); excavator, N. Pharaklas. *Deltion* 24B (1969):183, pl. 193:a (fragment of pithos or sarcophagus?); excavator, T. Spyropou-

los. *Bulletin de correspondance hellénique* 95 (1971), fig. 275.

This site promised much because of its location. The first indications were that there were rich deposits from several periods as far down as the Middle Helladic levels. But excavation of the site never materialized, and an apartment house was built over it. There was pottery representing every period, and a "recent" (Byzantine?) building that incorporated ancient marbles. A surface find was subsequently reported: a fragment from a Late Helladic large pithos or sarcophagus (?) showing a fish and a fisherman's net.

SITE 116. KADMEIA H-11.

12 Kreon St., property of Olga Lekkou. *Deltion* 23B (1968):212. Excavator, N. Pharaklas.

BYZANTINE. A duct that had been cut in the rock and built afterwards was found on the property when digging for a sewer began. The duct opening was 0.70 m wide and 0.80 m high. It contained Byzantine pottery.

SITE 117. KADMEIA J-12.

2 Dirke St., property of Georgios Pagonas. *Deltion* 23B (1968):213. Excavator, N. Pharaklas.

BYZANTINE. One foundation pit was opened on this property; only a wall was found, constructed of large, rough stones, and some Byzantine pottery at a depth of 2 m.

SITE 118. KADMEIA I-10.

51 Pelopidas St., property of Perikles Drakos. *Deltion* 23B (1968):213. Excavator, N. Pharaklas.

BYZANTINE. There was a wall of six ashlar blocks on top of large, rough stones (earlier wall?). Only Byzantine pottery was found. The wall was oriented north-south and was 3.40 m long and 0.60 m wide.

SITE 119. KADMEIA I-13.

South end of the Kadmeia; property of Demetrios Kalampakas. *Deltion* 23B (1968):213. Excavator, N. Pharaklas.

BYZANTINE. Only some Byzantine pottery was found here.

SITE 120. KADMEIA H-10.

145 Epaminondas St., property of the Dagdeleni brothers. *Deltion* 23B (1968):213; excavator, N. Pharaklas. *Deltion* 24B (1968):180-182, fig. 2, pls. 191:b (Middle Helladic tomb and finds), 189:b (Byzantine remains), 190-191 (Late Helladic frescoes and finds); *Deltion* 25B (1970):211-212, fig. 1 (plan of Late Helladic walls), pls. 199, 201:b (Late Helladic walls), 200, 201:a (frescoes); *Deltion* 26A (1971):104-119,

pls. 21-23 (frescoes): excavator T. Spyropoulos. *Bulletin de correspondance hellénique* 95 (1971), figs. 272-274, 276-277; 96 (1972), figs. 260-262 (frescoes and pottery).

This property is directly north of site 17, where Mycenaean frescoes were found at great depth.

MIDDLE HELLADIC. A few cist tombs were found more than 12 m deep. In the deep layer of earth above there were no remains.

LATE HELLADIC. Above the layer of earth was a thick layer (ca. 1.30 m) of debris that contained a great quantity of fresco fragments in disorder. A group of finds (*Deltion* 1968, pl. 191) may have been associated with a burial. Above these were remains of Late Helladic walls.

EARLY CHRISTIAN. There were 13 tile-covered tombs at the site.

BYZANTINE. There was pottery and perhaps remains of buildings. A marble thorakion and an ancient stele (in second use?) were transferred to the museum.

SITE 121. GREATER THEBES H-8.

The Amphion hill, north of the Thebes Museum. Keramopoullos 1917:381-392. *Deltion* 22B (1967):229 (Late Helladic tombs), 229-230 (excavation on the hill); excavator, N. Pharaklas. *Deltion* 27B (1972):307-308 (Middle Helladic tomb), pl. 250:f,h (pottery), 251:a (the tomb); *Deltion* 28B (1973):248-252, pl. 206 (the tomb); excavator, T. Spyropoulos. *Bulletin de correspondance hellénique* 96 (1972), fig. 259 (jewelry); *Arch. Reports* 1971-1972:12, fig. 22 (jewelry).

EARLY HELLADIC. Pharaklas found pottery of the period in his excavation at the east-central part of the hill. The presence of domestic pottery may be an indication of habitation. According to Spyropoulos (*Deltion* [1973]:249), the empty pit graves found here had Early Helladic pottery in them.

MIDDLE HELLADIC. Pharaklas found Middle Helladic pottery. The most important find of this period is the monumental cist tomb, which Spyropoulos dates Early Helladic, although the pottery found inside the tomb and the style of the jewelry from it are Middle Helladic. Outside the tomb there was Early Helladic pottery (*Deltion* 1972, pl. 250:f), the earliest found by Spyropoulos, Middle Helladic pottery (*Deltion* 1927, pl. 250:h), and Late Helladic, the latest found. The tomb had been robbed in antiquity. According to the excavator, the cist tomb was found underneath a pile of sun-dried mud-brick, which, at the time of excavation, was ca. 2 m high. No data are given about the size of the tomb, but it was over 2 m long, lined on three sides with huge single slabs; the north, short side had two slabs that were not found in situ, as they had been removed by tomb robbers. Also not found in situ was a huge slab of black limestone, apparently the coverstone. The skeletal remains were too meager, according to Spyropoullos, to assess the number of burials, but he thinks there were two because there were two depressions in the bedrock that may have been used for offerings. Despite its poor state of preservation, this tomb is monumental in character and makes one wonder whether it might have been the celebrated tomb of Amphion and Zethos, seen by Pausanias (see chap. 5, passage 12).

LATE HELLADIC. Keramopoullos (1917: 370-371) reports excavating a Mycenaean tomb "on the right side of the Strophia stream." Although he discusses the tomb in connection with the Amphion hill, it is clear that the tomb is closer to the Kastellia hills and may be the one marked on his map, just east of the Borraiai gates. Two chamber tombs were found by Pharaklas on the west side of the hill. The first had an oval-shaped chamber, ca. 3 m x 1.50 m. Only a few potsherds were found. The second had a large chamber, but was not excavated because of the danger that the soft bedrock might collapse. Its dromos was only partially preserved.

CLASSICAL? There was a shaft dug in the bedrock, 15 to 20 m deep; additional tunnels were opened to the east and west from the bottom of the shaft. I suspect that these tunnels were part of the Classical aqueduct of Thebes.

CHRISTIAN. Pharaklas excavated two burials on the east side of the hill.

SITE 122. GREATER THEBES K-10.

Kastellia; property of Demetrios Kyriakos. *Deltion* 22B (1967):230; *Deltion* 23B (1968):213-214, fig. 7 (plan), pl. 162:b-c (Red Figure oinochoe). Excavator, N. Pharaklas.

LATE HELLADIC. A chamber tomb was found on the west side of the property; its roof had collapsed, and the east part of the chamber had been damaged by later construction. The dromos was 3.60 m long; the chamber measured 2 m x 2.40 m. Two pit graves were within the chamber. The finds included 13 vases and three Phi-figurines, which may date the tomb to LH III A2.

CLASSICAL. There was a level of occupation 1 m thick, with two separate rooms, the foundations of which were built of ashlar masonry. A portion of the south room, 2.60 m x 1.84 m, was uncovered; the room was filled with roof tiles, Classical pottery, and a group of eight bronze vessels. From the other areas came some terracottas, pottery, including a Red Figure oinochoe with a representation of Dionysos, maenads, and a satyr.

BYZANTINE. The level was 1.20 to 1.70 m thick, and included traces of habitation and a lot of pottery.

SITE 123. KADMEIA G-12.

Just southwest of Paraporti spring; property of Alexandros Kordatzis. *Deltion* 22B (1967):230.

CLASSICAL? A long foundation pit was opened in the courtyard. A wall of ashlar masonry was found, but no pottery.

SITE 124. GREATER THEBES J-15.

Palaia Sphageia; property of Alexandros Tsakonas. *Deltion* 22B (1967):231-232.

CLASSICAL? A carving in the bedrock proved to be an air hole for the ancient aqueduct. Water still flowed beneath it, and therefore it was impossible to enter and investigate.

CLASSICAL-HELLENISTIC. A pit grave cut in the bedrock yielded no finds, but it may have been Late Classical or Hellenistic as two funerary stelai of the Boiotian architectural style were found. A name was inscribed on each: *MEΛΩN* and *KAΛΛINIKA* (another stele from this area is described in connection with site 99).

SITE 125. GREATER THEBES 0-6.

The factory of the Choundri brothers, on the road to Chalkis. *Deltion* 22B (1967):233-234.

CLASSICAL. Several broken funerary stones were found in disarray, perhaps discarded in a riverbed in antiquity. Some of the stelai preserved their original color, especially those of the Boiotian architectural type. There were a few made of black stone with incised representations. Most bore the name of the deceased. A complete name was preserved on only four: *MIKYΛA*, *ΔIOTIMA*, *KAΠIΛO*, and *HEP-*

MAIOΣ. None of the monuments dated later than the second half of the fourth century B.C., and it is likely that they were destroyed during the Macedonian wars.

SITE 126. GREATER THEBES J-6.

South of the railroad station; flour mill of Petros Delvenakiotis. *Deltion* 22B (1967):235.

HELLENISTIC. Remains of a poorly constructed house were found associated with Hellenistic pottery. There was also some Byzantine pottery at the site.

SITE 127. GREATER THEBES I-7.

Palaios Synoikismos, location Gypsolakkos; property of Christos Theodorou. *Deltion* 22B (1967):235, pl. 165:b (photograph of site).

HELLENISTIC-ROMAN. A large building was found, made of large ashlar masonry, preserving some of the original red plaster in the interior; the floor consisted of small bricks set in concrete. The pottery included Hellenistic, Roman, and some Byzantine. It was unclear whether this was a public building or a rich house.

SITE 128. GREATER THEBES E-8.

South Pyri; property of Charalampos Roussos. *Deltion* 22B (1967):237.

HELLENISTIC-CHRISTIAN. Part of a house associated with Hellenistic pottery showed evidence of repair; it seemed to have lasted into the Byzantine period, as indicated by pottery. A hoard of 620 Byzantine bronze coins was not clearly related to this house.

SITE 129. GREATER THEBES F-7.

Central Pyri; property of Ioannis Stamelos. *Deltion* 22B (1967):237.

CLASSICAL? Part of an aqueduct was found (cut in the rock?) running northeast-southwest. There was Classical, Roman, and Byzantine pottery (no other details available).

SITE 130. KADMEIA H-9 to H-10.

Epaminondas St. Installation of telephone lines. *Deltion* 22B (1967):237.

BYZANTINE. A narrow channel was opened to a depth of 1 m. At the intersection of Kevis and Epaminondas Sts. there was a stone-paved street going north-south, dating, according to Pharaklas, to the eleventh century A.D. Where Epaminondas St. passes the church of Agia Eleousa (site 94), there were remains of a building, perhaps a church: many frescoes, a wall, Byzantine pottery, and an ossuary. These finds may possibly relate to a church that preceded Agia Eleousa.

SITE 131. KADMEIA I-11.

Vourdoumpas St., near Pelopidas St.; property of Epaminondas Anadiotis and Aikaterini Stamati. *Deltion* 22B (1967):237-239, fig. 4 (plan), pl. 165:d (photograph).

EARLY HELLADIC-LATE HELLADIC. There was pottery from these periods, but architectural remains were obliterated by intensive use of the site in Byzantine times. Only a small Mycenaean wall was found (*Deltion* 1967, fig. 4:XIV).

BYZANTINE. Pharaklas divides the numerous remains into three consecutive phases dated between the eleventh and fourteenth centuries. The remains belong to houses, but no complete plan was distinguishable in the excavation. There were small finds and a lot of pottery.

SITE 132. KADMEIA I-11.

48 Pindar St., property of Vasileios Delvenakiotis. *Deltion* 22B (1967): 239.

A two-storey structure was erected with foundations only 2 m deep.

BYZANTINE. Remains of houses (?) were found, some constructed of reused poros masonry, others of typical Byzantine brick and stone construction.

SITE 133. KADMEIA I-11.

Corner of Amphion and Zengini Sts., property of Evangelos Lingos. *Deltion* 22B (1967):239, pl. 167:a (photograph).

BYZANTINE. A large structure was found, perhaps a public building. Unfortunately, preservation was poor because the remains were so close to the surface.

SITE 134. GREATER THEBES L-8.

Suburb of Agioi Theodoroi; property of Nikolaos Kalokyris (near the elementary school). *Deltion* 22B (1967): 234-235.

HELLENISTIC-ROMAN. There were remains of a large house: one wall was over 12 m long, built of ashlar masonry in north-south orientation. A space 2 m square was covered with small tiles (west side). There was a small cistern on the east side of the house.

SITE 135. KADMEIA H-10.

Corner of Epaminondas and Kevis Sts., property of the Phasoulopoulos heirs. *Deltion* 22B (1967):239, pls. 167:b (photograph of site), 168:a (oven), 168:b (mosaic), 169:b (cistern).

LATE HELLADIC. A wall was found in the southeast corner of the property, together with pottery.

BYZANTINE. Substantial remains of habitation, perhaps public buildings, were found in the western half of the property: a large water cistern, kitchen facilities, a large oven, and part of a mosaic floor. There were traces of other rooms in the poorly preserved eastern half of the property. Be-

cause of its proximity to the church of Agios Georgios (site 93), one should consider the possibility that local tradition is correct in identifying this as the site of a monastery (see also site 236).

SITE 136. GREATER THEBES H-17.

Kolonaki, just south of the settled area, on the west side of the main road; property of Athanasios Houhoumis. *Deltion* 22B (1967):239.

EARLY CHRISTIAN. Illicit digging activity uncovered large underground passages. Pharaklas found lamps in them, but was unable to excavate because of collapsed bedrock; he believed the passages belonged to a large catacomb.

SITE 137. GREATER THEBES J-12.

Nea Sphageia, central street. Road construction. *Deltion* 22B (1967): 239-240, figs. 5-6 (plans).

CLASSICAL-HELLENISTIC? A rectangular stone platform, 4.90 m x 2.00 m, of unknown function was built directly on the bedrock in north-south orientation. Its date is not clear (*Deltion* 1967, fig. 6).

BYZANTINE. Part of an apsidal building made of stone and mortar was found; it was probably a church (*Deltion* 1967, fig. 5, *left*). At another location, there were remains of structures from two different periods, also built of stone and mortar (fig. 5, *right*).

SITE 138. GREATER THEBES J-10.

Kastellia; property of Demetrios Mattas. *Deltion* 23B (1968):214. Excavator, N. Pharaklas.

LATE HELLADIC. some pottery was found.

CLASSICAL. A lot of pottery was found, in no apparent association with any structure.

EARLY CHRISTIAN AND BYZANTINE? Three tile-covered tombs were found, perhaps Early Christian. A poorly preserved structure was built of reused ashlar masonry; its date and function were unclear.

SITE 139. GREATER THEBES J-10.

Kastellia; the High School of Thebes. *Deltion* 23B (1968):214-216, fig. 8 (plan), pl. 163 (Byzantine pottery). Excavator, N. Pharaklas.

LATE HELLADIC. Part of an empty chamber tomb was found.

CLASSICAL. There were only scattered remains of pottery.

HELLENISTIC. A few small objects including fragments from skyphoi were found beneath the Byzantine building.

EARLY CHRISTIAN. There was an extensive cemetery of tile-covered tombs beneath the Byzantine building.

BYZANTINE. Part of a large building was found, with rooms centered around a courtyard 8 m x 9.5 m. This is one of the best-preserved Byzantine buildings found in Thebes, but its plan is not clear because the rooms are partly unexcavated; there are at least ten rooms around the courtyard. The pottery dates from the eleventh to the fourteenth centuries and is of excellent quality. The building was probably a villa.

SITE 140. GREATER THEBES K-9.

Kastellia; property of I. and A. Adrianos. *Deltion* 23B (1968):216-217, fig. 9 (plan). Excavator, N. Pharaklas.

LATE HELLADIC. Five empty chamber tombs were found, which may have been reused for storage in Byzantine times.

SITE 141. GREATER THEBES K-10.

East side of Kastellia, on Oplarchigos Voglis St. *Deltion* 23B (1968):217, pl. 164:a (Hellenistic pottery), 164:b (poros carving and roof tile). Excavator, N. Pharaklas.

HELLENISTIC. Two rooms were cut in the rock and thickly plastered with white mortar; they were partly preserved and contained only Hellenistic pottery.

SITE 142. GREATER THEBES M-14.

South of Konakia. Kalopais 1892:42.

CLASSICAL. Remains of the ancient fortifications of Greater Thebes are visible on the east side of the modern road. They were excavated by Kalopais who described part of a wall of isodomic construction with two buttresses that were preserved to a height of almost 2 m at the time of the excavation, but are very poorly preserved today. The wall was similar in construction to that found in site 71; the buttresses were 3 m apart.

SITE 143. GREATER THEBES J-13.

Nea Sphageia, northwest of the Ismenion (site 8); property of Emmanouel Ioannou. *Deltion* 23B (1968):217-218, figs. 9-10 (plans); *Deltion* 24B (1969):177. Excavator, N. Pharaklas.

CHRISTIAN. There were architectural remains, perhaps of houses of three successive phases. The lowest level yielded a mosaic floor showing a floral composition in five colors; it was transferred to the Museum. In the same level but of slightly later construction was a structure built in part over the mosaic. Above these remains were several empty tile-covered tombs. The third and highest level yielded remains of two houses, one of which was well built: a stone duct for a sewer may have belonged to it (fig. 10). Above these remains were several empty tile-covered tombs.

SITE 144. GREATER THEBES J-11.

Astegoi; property of Demetrios Kotzias. *Deltion* 23B (1968):218, pl. 164:c (Byzantine pottery). Excavator, N. Pharaklas.

BYZANTINE. Remains of one or more houses were found with Byzantine pottery, some with figured representations.

SITE 145. GREATER THEBES K-15.

Palaia Sphageia; property of A. Koligiannis. *Deltion* 23B (1968):218. Excavator, N. Pharaklas.

BYZANTINE. Remains of a house and a silo were found with Byzantine pottery.

SITE 146. GREATER THEBES J-12.

Nea Sphageia; property of P. Hatzidiakos. *Deltion* 23B (1968):218. Excavator, N. Pharaklas.

BYZANTINE. A small excavation yielded remains of a house and some pottery. The walls were built of undressed stones and were preserved to a height of 1.35 m.

SITE 147. GREATER THEBES J-11.

Astegoi; property of Christos Tzintzilidas. *Deltion* 23B (1968):218. Excavator, N. Pharaklas.

HELLENISTIC AND ROMAN. There was some pottery, which may indicate habitation. The well found on the property may date to this period as well.

BYZANTINE. A well was investigated to a depth of 3.20 m. The date of its construction was not clear. A silo and Byzantine pottery were found elsewhere on the property.

SITE 148. GREATER THEBES K-8.

Palaios Synoikismos; property of Ioannis Kaskavelis. *Deltion* 23B (1968):218-219. Excavator, N. Pharaklas.

ROMAN. A cistern cut in the rock measured 5.20 m x 2.20 m and was 0.60 m deep. Its function was not clear, but it contained a lot of Roman pottery.

SITE 149. GREATER THEBES J-9.

Palaios Synoikismos; property of Emmanouel Manolakakos. *Deltion* 23B (1968):219. Excavator, N. Pharaklas.

BYZANTINE OR LATER? Eight pit burials of unclear date were found cut in the rock.

SITE 150. GREATER THEBES H-16.

Kolonaki; property of Georgios Stephas. *Deltion* 23B (1968):219, pl. 165:a-c (finds from a tomb). Excavator, N. Pharaklas.

CLASSICAL. Three pit graves were found here. Only one was intact, but with its covering slab collapsed; finds from it included a small double-axe, an iron strigil, two bronze bands decorated with figured representations, a small Red Figure calyx crater (*Deltion* 1968, pl. 165:b-c), and other small objects. The tomb dates to the fourth century B.C.

SITE 151. GREATER THEBES H-14.

Kolonaki; property of Alexandros Marlasis. *Deltion* 23B (1968):219-220, fig. 12 (plan of tomb), pls. 166:a-b (Mycenaean pottery), 166:c (Byzantine pottery). Excavator, N. Pharaklas.

LATE HELLADIC. Three chamber tombs were found, only one in good condition; its dromos was 2.80 m long and 1 to 1.20 m wide; the entrance was still closed, and the irregularly shaped chamber measured 2.10 m x 2.94 m. A skeleton was found in the center. On the west side of the chamber was a burial in a shallow pit. There were a few finds in the dromos, several vases and figurines in the chamber.

HELLENISTIC. Some pottery was found.

BYZANTINE. Some interesting pottery came up: bowls and dishes with figured representations, including a dragon and a hare. In all likelihood, these were finds related to habitation.

SITE 152. GREATER THEBES H-15.

Kolonaki; property of Spyros Kyriazis. *Deltion* 23B (1968):220, fig. 15 (plan of cistern). Excavator, N. Pharaklas.

CLASSICAL-HELLENISTIC. Remains of a house were found, including two poorly constructed walls and a small cistern. The pottery found at the site was Late Classical and Hellenistic.

SITE 153. GREATER THEBES M-15.

Near Agia Photeini (site 83). *Deltion* 23B (1968):22. Excavator, N. Pharaklas.

A duct cut in the rock was followed for some distance leading to a rectangular cut in the rock, perhaps a simple fountain. It is not clear whether this was part of the aqueduct system of Thebes.

SITE 154. GREATER THEBES K-9.

Suburb of Agioi Theodoroi; property of Soterios Karampitzakos. *Deltion* 23B (1968):220, pl. 166:d (Byzantine pottery). Excavator, N. Pharaklas.

BYZANTINE. A pit or silo cut in the rock contained debris of this period, especially pottery. A few Classical potsherds were also found (strays?).

SITE 155. GREATER THEBES N-7.

Suburb of Agioi Theodoroi; property of Kanaris. *Deltion* 23B (1968):220. Excavator, N. Pharaklas.

CHRISTIAN. Five empty tile-covered tombs were found.

SITE 156. GREATER THEBES F-8.

Pyri, location Alonia. Public works over the Vrysoula creek. *Deltion* 23B (1968):221, pls. 167-168 (pottery). Excavator, N. Pharaklas.

CLASSICAL-ROMAN. A building of ashlar masonry was found; it had several small rooms and yielded a lot of Hellenistic and Roman pottery and lamps. Some vases were distorted in shape, as though they had been misfired. Pharaklas thinks this may have been a pottery factory.

SITE 157. GREATER THEBES F-7.

Central Pyri; property of Georgios Liakopoulos. *Deltion* 23B (1968):221, fig. 14 (plan). Excavator, N. Pharaklas.

HELLENISTIC-ROMAN. An L-shaped wall was found, perhaps the foundation of a house, partly built of ashlar masonry. The pottery was Hellenistic and Roman.

SITE 158. GREATER THEBES G-6.

North Pyri; property of Konstantinos Koutoumanos. *Deltion* 23B (1968):221-222, fig. 15 (plan), pl. 169 (pottery). Excavator, N. Pharaklas.

CLASSICAL? Two rooms of a well-built house were partially excavated. One room, 4.10 m long and over 2.50 m wide, had a floor of packed earth and a small hearth. The second room had a similar hearth, a pebble floor, and a slightly raised bench on one side. An earlier phase is represented by a rectangular pit lined with stone slabs. There were no other architectural remains, but the pottery ranged from Archaic (period of the rectangular pit?) and Classical (main house?) through Hellenistic (continued habitation?) and as late as Byzantine.

SITE 159. GREATER THEBES F-7.

Central Pyri; property of Spyros Kordopatis. *Deltion* 23B (1968):222. Excavator, N. Pharaklas.

EARLY CHRISTIAN? A tile-covered tomb without offerings may date to this period.

SITE 160. GREATER THEBES G-7.

North Pyri; property of Loukas Toutouzas. *Deltion* 23B (1968):222, pl. 170:a-b (pottery). Excavator, N. Pharaklas.

CLASSICAL. There were no architectural remains on this property, but a concentration of objects from the fourth century B.C. may be an indication of habitation. In addition to pottery and three lamps, there was a terracotta male figurine and fragments from a terracotta perirranterium (*Deltion* 1968, pl. 170:b).

SITE 161. GREATER THEBES F-7.

North Pyri; property of Petros Toutouzas. *Deltion* 23B (1968):222, pls. 170:c, 171:a (pottery). Excavator, N. Pharaklas.

CLASSICAL. A wall of ashlar masonry was probably from a house built in the Classical period, but the pottery indicated that it was in use through the Hellenistic period. The pottery included many Classical Boiotian kantharoi and kylikes, and two horse figurines, as well as some Hellenistic vases.

BYZANTINE. Two stone walls were associated with Byzantine pottery.

SITE 162. GREATER THEBES I-8.

Palaios Synoikismos, location Gypsolakkos; property of P. Panagiotides-Parapoulis. *Deltion* 27B (1972): 322, pls. 276:c (bronze lamp), 277:a (terracotta sima). Excavator, A. Ioannidou.

ROMAN? An L-shaped wall of reused ashlar masonry seemed to belong to a house, perhaps Roman. The finds included a bronze lamp and a terracotta sima with light-on-dark decoration.

SITE 163. GREATER THEBES G-10.

South Pyri, location Hebraika; property of N. Angelopoulos. *Deltion* 23B (1968):223. Excavator, N. Pharaklas.

HELLENISTIC? In the bedrock was an irregularly shaped cut with Hellenistic pottery in it.

SITE 164. KADMEIA H-11.

87 Epaminondas St., property of Athanasios Pavlogiannopoulos. *Deltion* 24B (1969):177 (brief mention of the site by N. Pharaklas).

LATE HELLADIC. Although details have not been published, it is certain that Mycenaean remains were found here in 1969.

There were architectural remains and finds, perhaps of the earlier part of the period.

SITE 165. KADMEIA I-12.

Pindar St., just south of the City Hall; property of Nikolaos Koropoulis. *Athens Annals of Archaeology* (1974):162-173, figs. 1-3 (molds), 4-6 (tools), 7 (rock crystal), 8 (idol), 9-14 (pottery); excavator, K. Demakopoulou. *Bulletin de correspondance hellénique* 99 (1975):642, figs. 114-117. *Arch. reports* (1974-1975):17, figs. 27 (jeweler's mold), 28 (deep bowl from destruction level).

LATE HELLADIC. The Mycenaean levels were undisturbed on the west side of the property. There were two layers: the upper consisted of debris 1.50 m thick with no architectural remains, but containing characteristic Late Helladic III B:2 pottery; the layer below yielded a 6 m x 3 m portion of a room that preserved a shallow (0.30 to 0.50 m) accumulation resulting from a devastating fire. In this lower layer were carbonized wooden beams, bricks, tiles, colored stucco, and lead sheets; mixed with the debris were stone molds, various tools, rock crystal beads, steatite buttons, and a few objects of faience, onyx, and ivory. There was also the hand from a large terracotta idol. The pottery from the destruction level includes several examples of "type A" deep bowls, kylikes of Zygouries style, and much other pottery, which dates the destruction firmly to the end of LH III B:1. The finds show that the building was part of the palace complex of Thebes (second palace); its destruction date coincides with that of the other royal workshop found in the vicinity (see site 4).

ROMAN. There was a poorly preserved building with mosaic floors.

BYZANTINE. Remains of habitation were found in the uppermost level of this site.

SITE 166. KADMEIA I-12.

28 Pindar St., property of Xenophon Panagiotopoulos and Charalampos Papageorgiou. Demakopoulou and Konsola 1975 (with numerous drawings and photographs of Bronze Age pottery).

EARLY HELLADIC. The earlier of two phases preserved remains of habitation directly on the bedrock (2.70 to 2.90 m below the surface here): no buildings were found, but there were cuts in the rock, and pits containing food remains, ashes, pottery, and obsidian. A destruction by fire marks the end of this phase. The second phase preserved remains of houses built on stone foundations. There was a cist burial with two skeletons, but no offerings. The pottery from the site shows that occupation began in the second part of EH II and continued to the end of EH III.

MIDDLE HELLADIC. Two phases were distinguished. The earlier preserved remains of two rooms built on stone foundations. The first room had a mud floor, beneath which was a pithos burial of a child, and some small objects. The second room may have ended in an apsidal wall; it had a white plaster floor, two cist burials, and a few small objects including an ivory plaque. The first tomb contained the skeleton of a mother and infant, two vases, two bracelets, one ring, all made of bronze, and one bobbin; the second tomb had been disturbed. The second phase preserved no buildings, probably because of Late Helladic construction activity. Only a pithos burial was found intact with its child skeleton and the offerings—three amethyst beads and two faience beads.

LATE HELLADIC. The Late Helladic buildings had been disturbed by later construction. There was only part of a room with walls 0.65 m thick, and a poorly preserved wall with a small portion of its floor.

BYZANTINE. Remains of a house(?) were found, which used walls of earlier structures as foundations.

SITE 167. GREATER THEBES FIG. 1.2, D-8.

West of Pyri; property of Christos Stephaniotis. Thebes Museum notebook 1 (1963):6. Excavator, K. Kostoglou.

CLASSICAL AND HELLENISTIC? Several fragments of funerary stelai were unearthed as a result of deep cultivation.

SITE 168. GREATER THEBES Q-5.

Panousi Bridge, on the road to Chalkis. Thebes Museum notebook 1 (1963):9-10. Excavator, K. Kostoglou.

CLASSICAL. A funerary stele with the name ΑΜΦΙΣΣΘΕΝΙΑ (Mus. no. 82) was found in a creek; it may have been discarded here in antiquity, as it is unlikely that there was a cemetery so far from the city (cf. site 125, for other discarded monuments).

SITE 169. GREATER THEBES J-7.

Polygyra; property of Ioannis Petroglou. Thebes Museum notebook 1 (1963):16-17. Excavator, K. Kostoglou.

CLASSICAL. An ancient structure of ashlar masonry was partly excavated (see site 65).

SITE 170. GREATER THEBES FIG. 1.2, E-8.

West of Pyri, by the Wine Cooperative. Thebes Museum notebook 1 (1963):18-19. Excavator, K. Kostoglou.

HELLENISTIC. A funerary stele was found here (Mus. no. 1963/91).

SITE 171. KADMEIA H-10.

58 Kadmos St., property of M. Chronopoulos. Oral communication, K. Demakopoulou.

EARLY HELLADIC. Some pottery was found at great depth, 9 to 10 m below the surface. There was also a burial with a typical Early Helladic II cup.

MIDDLE HELLADIC. A deep accumulation of deposits included a lot of pottery, some architectural remains; a cemetery was found directly below the Mycenaean levels.

LATE HELLADIC. There was a lot of debris down to between 8 and 8.50 m below the surface, which included great quantities of pottery, a set of bronze horse-bits, and a knife. In a large trench (6 m x 6 m), which was systematically excavated, there were remains of three rooms, representing three consecutive phases. The buildings of the last two phases were oriented north-south.

SITE 172. GREATER THEBES K-8.

Polygyra; property of Nikolaos Grontas. Thebes Museum notebook 8 (1965):107. Excavator, K. Kostoglou.

CLASSICAL? A large duct cut in the bedrock might be part of the aqueduct system of Thebes. It was 0.50 m wide and 1 m deep, oriented north-south.

BYZANTINE. Two plastered silos cut in the bedrock were found, indicating habitation.

SITE 173. GREATER THEBES J-14.

Palaia Sphageia, location Pege.

This is the site of a natural spring south of the Kadmeia. The names *Lagoumi* or *Pege* (literally, "spring") are still used by the locals. It is the only spring in Thebes that has remained in its natural position. Because of its proximity to the sanctuary of Apollo Ismenios, we may identify this spring as the famous *spring of Ares*. This identification was first proposed by Pagidas (1882:13-17), but was not accepted by Keramopoullos (1917:318-324) who thought that there was another spring closer to the sanctuary. That spring, however, was an artificial one, emerging from the aqueduct of Classical Thebes (see chap. 5, passage 5, for additional information on this spring).

SITE 174. GREATER THEBES H-13.

18 Agia Trias St., property of Nikolaos Kokontinis. *Deltion* 24B (1969): 177. Excavator, N. Pharaklas.

CLASSICAL. Two pit burials were found here, cut in the bedrock. The first was covered with tiles but empty; the second was better preserved but without cover. It contained one skeleton and numerous Classical vases and figurines.

SITE 175. GREATER THEBES J-8.

Polygyra; property of Demetrios Vathis. *Deltion* 24B (1969):177. Excavator, N. Pharaklas.

CLASSICAL. There was a poorly preserved portion of the aqueduct of Thebes going north-south. An air hole was found leading to the main aqueduct.

SITE 176. GREATER THEBES K-9.

Kastellia; property of Evangelos Konsolakis. *Deltion* 24B (1969):177-178, fig. 3 (plan). Excavator, N. Pharaklas.

LATE HELLADIC. There were three empty, poorly preserved chamber tombs.

CLASSICAL. Only some pottery was found.

HELLENISTIC. A cistern and a duct bringing water to it probably date to this period. There were also post-holes indicating light construction.

BYZANTINE. There were remains of habitation: partially preserved floors, small circular pits, and other cuts in the rock.

SITE 177. GREATER THEBES M-8.

Suburb of Agioi Theodoroi, location Alonia; property of Nikolaos Trikallitis. *Deltion* 24B (1969):178. Excavator, N. Pharaklas.

CLASSICAL? Pharaklas mentions a duct with a barrel roof, cut in the rock and going north-south. The size of the opening is not given, but this could be part of the aqueduct system of Thebes.

HELLENISTIC-ROMAN. There was pottery of these periods in a rectangular cut in the rock. The cut was plastered and measured 1 m x 0.55 m; the depth was 0.95 m. It may have been used for refining clay.

SITE 178. GREATER THEBES K-7.

Polygyra; property of S. Lymperiou. *Deltion* 24B (1969):178-179. Excavator, N. Pharaklas.

CLASSICAL-ROMAN? A circular pit 1.10 m in diameter, and two rectangular shafts (1.20 m x 0.47 m and 1.10 m x 0.50 m) were found here. They were investigated to a depth of 2.50 m at which point the bottom had not been reached. These openings are probably related to the aqueduct system of Thebes. There was also a looted pit burial. Only some Roman pottery was found at the site.

SITE 179. KADMEIA I-13.

Archaeological site. Just south of the Metropolis (site 216); property of Konstantinos Douros. *Deltion* 24B (1969):180, fig. 1 (plan), pls. 187 (Late Helladic pottery), 188 (frescoes), 189:a (Middle Helladic tomb); excavator, T. Spyropoulos. *Athens Annals of Archaeology* 1 (1968):11, frontispiece (frescoes). *Bulletin de correspondance hellénique* 95 (1971), fig. 271 (frescoes).

EARLY HELLADIC. The excavator, T. Spyropoulos, mentions the presence of pottery.

MIDDLE HELLADIC. There were architectural remains (of houses?) and a lot of pottery. Three cist burials were also found.

LATE HELLADIC. Substantial architectural remains were found below the surface, representing two phases. One building was oriented north-south. There was a lot of Mycenaean pottery, and also fresco fragments from the representation of a seascape.

BYZANTINE. A large silo with a lot of pottery is the only evidence of habitation at this site.

SITE 180. GREATER THEBES J-10.

Kastellia.

MODERN. The small chapel of the recently built high school of Thebes is included in the Catalogue not only for the sake of completeness in the listing of religious sites, but also to call attention to the fact that no church stood here in the past.

SITE 181. KADMEIA H-10.

141 Epaminondas St., property of Aikaterini Lalioti. *Deltion* 24B (1969):182-183, pl. 182 (photograph of the site). Excavator, T. Spyropoulos.

LATE HELLADIC. A deposit 4 m deep included large quantities of pottery, a few fresco fragments, but very little in architectural remains.

BYZANTINE. There were rich remains of habitation (pl. 182); some walls were constructed of reused ashlar masonry.

SITE 182. GREATER THEBES M-7.

Suburb of Agioi Theodoroi, location Alonia; property of Demetrios Adrianos. *Deltion* 24B (1969):183, pl. 192:c (Classical walls). Excavator, T. Spyropoulos.

CLASSICAL. A part of the fortifications of Greater Thebes was found: the foundation was 0.76 m wide, 0.46 m (one course) high, and was preserved here to a length of 7.70 m. This was apparently one of two sides making up the casing of the wall.

SITE 183. KADMEIA I-11.

36 Pelopidas St., property of the Spourli brothers. *Deltion* 25 (1970):212-213, fig. 2 (plan). Excavator, T. Spyropoulos.

LATE HELLADIC. Architectural remains were very deep (7 to 8 m below the surface; cf. neighboring site 10).

ROMAN? There was some pottery, but it was not clear whether the architectural remains in figure 2 belong to this period.

BYZANTINE. Remains of houses were found here.

SITE 184. KADMEIA I-12.

17 Pindar St., property of Demetrios Staikos. *Deltion* 25B (1970):213-214, pl. 202:a (ivory handle), 202:b-d (Early Helladic remains). *Athens Annals of Archaeology* 3(1970):268-273,

figs. 1-3 (ivory handle). Excavator, T. Spyropoulos.

According to Spyropoulos, there were "Subneolithic" remains on this property. It is not clear what is meant by this term: at the adjoining property (site 13), the earliest remains looked very similar to the "Subneolithic" and "Early Helladic" of this site, but were, in fact, Early Helladic. The earliest remains, consisting mostly of pottery, were found on the bedrock. In a second layer, there were pits, post-holes, hearths, and on a well-preserved floor, a great quantity of pottery, perhaps a hundred vases.

LATE HELLADIC. The aqueduct found in site 13 was preserved at this site as well. There were also remains of houses: frescoes, an ivory handle with the representation of a griffin, and several objects of bronze, steatite, bone, and glass paste. In addition, there were some figurines, and a lot of pottery.

SITE 185. KADMEIA I-11.

19 Antigone St., property of the Stavri brothers. *Deltion* 25B (1970):214-216, pl. 203 (Late Helladic remains). Excavator, T. Spyropoulos.

LATE HELLADIC. Spyropoulos distinguished Mycenaean buildings of two phases. The earlier phase preserved substantial structures with frescoes and pottery; the end of this phase was marked by a destruction by fire "shortly before

the end of LH III B" (p. 215). The later phase was represented by "poorly constructed walls" 0.50 m above the earlier remains. No date is given for the later phase.

SITE 186. KADMEIA I-12.

17 Pelopidas St., property of Ioannis Vryzakis. *Deltion* 25B (1970):216-217, pl. 204 (prehistoric remains). Excavator, T. Spyropoulos.

EARLY HELLADIC. There were post-holes and clay-lined pits. Finds included a great amount of pottery, obsidian, a gold earring, bone tools, and other small objects.

MIDDLE HELLADIC. No architectural remains were identified, but the Middle Helladic level was thick (approx. 1 m) and contained a lot of pottery.

LATE HELLADIC. A wall was preserved beneath the Classical remains.

CLASSICAL? A wall composed of one row of ashlar masonry was resting on a layer that included Black Figure pottery.

SITE 187. KADMEIA J-13.

Anapausis St., property of Eleutheria Katsiou. *Deltion* 25B (1970):217. Excavator, T. Spyropoulos.

ORIENTALIZING. A group of Protocorinthian vases was found here, although their context is not known. Other objects associated with the pottery included some tools, and fragments of iron and bronze.

SITE 188. GREATER THEBES I-9.

Gypsolakkos. Property of Nikolaos Thalassinos. *Deltion* 25 (1970):217-218. Excavator, T. Spyropoulos.

LATE HELLADIC? Nine large boulders were found here, perhaps from a collapsed Cyclopean wall (cf. site 52).

SITE 189. KADMEIA H-11.

Archaeological site. Corner of Epaminondas and Antigone Sts., former property of A. Phasoulopoulos. *Deltion* 25B (1970):218. Excavator, T. Spyropoulos.

MIDDLE HELLADIC. A wall was found 1.10 m below the surface in an exploratory trench. The property was expropriated by the Archaeological Service.

SITE 190. KADMEIA I-11.

Amphion St., property of Argyrios Samiotis. *Deltion* 25B (1970):218. Excavator, T. Spyropoulos.

LATE HELLADIC. The accumulation of deposit was very shallow, but there were some remains of the Mycenaean period.

SITE 191. GREATER THEBES K-11.

Kastellia, southeast of the Megalo Kastelli. *Deltion* 22B (1967):227-228,

pls. 160:a (glass-paste vase), 160:b-c (lentoid seals), 160:d (steatite lamp), 160:e (gold ring), 160:f (stone vase); excavator N. Pharaklas. *Deltion* 25B (1970):218-220, fig. 4 (plan); excavator, T. Spyropoulos.

LATE HELLADIC. Five chamber tombs were excavated in 1966. The one that was intact is described in detail: the dromos was 18 m long and 5.50 m wide; the entrance was 2.40 m deep; the chamber measured 7.40 m x 5.40 m; a high bench ran along three sides of the chamber, but not along the side opposite the entrance. There were two deep niches on the right side of the chamber. At least twenty skeletons were recognized, all poorly preserved. A square stone plaque might have belonged to a table. Among the numerous finds from the tomb were eleven complete vases, including a Canaanite amphora, two terracotta sarcophagi, five alabaster vases, one of which was decorated with a figure-of-eight shield (*Deltion* 1967, pl. 160:f), a stone vase, a glass-paste vase, a steatite lamp, a lentoid seal of agate showing a cow with calf (*Deltion* 1967, pl. 160:c), a lot of jewelry made of gold, amber, glass-paste, and faience, and objects made of bone, iron, and bronze.

The fourth tomb excavated by Pharaklas yielded some interesting finds: two terracotta boats, a gold ring decorated with a bee (*Deltion* 1967, pl. 160:e), and a lentoid seal of rock crystal showing an agrimi (*Deltion* 1967, pl. 160:b).

One more tomb was excavated on this side of the hill by T. Spyropoulos in 1969. It was very well preserved, though partly robbed. Among the finds were 27 vases, and jewelry made of gold, semiprecious stones, and glass paste.

SITE 192. KADMEIA I-12.

15 Pindar St., property of Evangelos Philos. *Deltion* 25B (1970):220, pl. 204:c (fresco), 204:d (Late Helladic wall); *Deltion* 26A (1971):109-119, pls. 24-25 (Late Helladic frescoes); excavator, T. Spyropoulos. *Bulletin de correspondance hellénique* 96 (1972), fig. 263 (Late Helladic fresco).

LATE HELLADIC. This site is located south of sites 184 and 13, where there were Mycenaean buildings with fresco decoration. Similar remains were found here: a poorly preserved building, but some interesting fresco fragments, including those showing the head of a warrior with a boar's tusk helmet.

BYZANTINE. There were substantial remains of habitation that had penetrated deep into prehistoric levels.

SITE 193. KADMEIA I-11.

Corner of Pelopidas and Vourdoumpas Sts., property of Evangelos Voglis. *Deltion* 26B (1971):207, fig. 9 (plan), pls. 183:a-b (head of marble statuette). Excavator, T. Spyropoulos.

MIDDLE HELLADIC. Spyropoulos reports the presence of walls and two burials (remains in fig. 9?).

CLASSICAL? A marble Ionic capital and the head of a marble statuette were found, apparently not associated with the other remains.

SITE 194. KADMEIA I-10.

Corner of Vourdoumpas and Tsevas Sts., property of Nikolaos Selekos. Oral communication, K. Demakopoulou. *Teiresias* 4 (1974):9.

MIDDLE HELLADIC. There were remains of houses directly on the bedrock.

LATE HELLADIC. Remains were 5 to 6 m below the surface. A round structure was found in the southeast corner. In the center was a great heap of stones and a lot of pottery. On the north side of the property, the depth of deposit exceeded 12 m.

CLASSICAL AND HELLENISTIC. There were remains of habitation, a duct built of poros stones, and pottery.

BYZANTINE. Remains of habitation included silos, a few walls, and a lot of pottery. There were also remains of post-Byzantine habitation.

SITE 195. KADMEIA I-11.

4 Antigone St., property of Ioannis Gogos. Oral communication, I. Gogos.

According to the property owner, bedrock was very close to the surface.

BYZANTINE. Some cuts in the bedrock and part of a silo were the only remains of habitation.

SITE 196. KADMEIA H-11.

Corner of Epaminondas and Metaxas Sts., property of Soteriou and Dougekos. *Deltion* 26B (1971):195-202, pls. 178, 179:a,d (photographs of site), 179:b (Middle Helladic tomb), 179:c (deep bowl); *Deltion* 28B (1973):247, pl. 204:a-b (photographs of site). *Kadmos* 9(1970):170-172, pl. I:a-b (deep bowl and stirrup-jar). Excavator, T. Spyropoulos. *Bulletin de correspondance hellénique* 95 (1971), fig. 278 (Linear B tablet). Linear B tablets, *Of* series: Chadwick and Spyropoulos 1975; Godart and Sacconi 1978; Hooker 1977.

MIDDLE HELLADIC. The earliest excavated remains date to this period. There were traces of houses, and some burials.

LATE HELLADIC. Remains of an imposing building that was either part of the large second palace of Thebes, or related to it, was found here. Three rooms were partially uncovered, two of which were 4 m wide. The rooms were filled with burned debris: mud-brick, stone, wood, frescoes, etc. The destruction layer was as thick as 0.90 m. The southernmost of the three rooms, which contained 17 Linear B tablets, was divided from the second room to the north by a thin brick wall. In the second room was a terracotta bathtub. The third room was only partially excavated. This building, like the second palace of Thebes, was oriented north-south. Finds from the site included a large quantity of pottery, figurines, tools of bone and bronze, and some frescoes.

Spyropoulos, the excavator, dated the destruction of this building to LH III B:2, thereby disagreeing with the destruction date LH III B:1 given for sites 2, 4, and 165, which belong to the same phase. However, the pottery published by Spyropoulos dates to the end of LH III B:1; among the material selected for publication are deep bowls of "open style" and stirrup-jars FS171-172 (*Kadmos* 1970, pl. 1: Chadwick and Spyropoulos 1975, figs. 60, 60:a, 61, 69), and Psi-figurines (Chadwick and Spyropoulos 1975, figs. 94, 95:a, 97).

SITE 197. KADMEIA I-11.

Corner of Amphion and Zeggini Sts., property of Konstantinos Papaseraphim. *Deltion* 25B (1970):218 (T. Spyropoulos), 246 (P. Lazarides).

BYZANTINE. A large wall built of reused ashlar masonry, bricks, and mortar probably belonged to a large church that preceded the modern chapel of Agios Stephanos (site 219).

SITE 198. KADMEIA H-10.

131 Epaminondas St., property of Nikolaos Pelekanos. Oral Communication, K. Demakopoulou.

MIDDLE HELLADIC. Pottery was found in deep layers.

LATE HELLADIC. A wall built of large stones was found in one foundation pit at 4.20 m. There was a lot of Mycenaean pottery at the site.

SITE 199. KADMEIA H-12.

Corner of Epaminondas and Drakos Sts., property of Stamelos Papastamelos. *Deltion* 25B (1970):220. Excavator, T. Spyropoulos.

BYZANTINE. Only some pottery was found. Bedrock was reached at 1.50 m, and most of the ancient deposits had been destroyed by modern construction activity.

SITE 200. GREATER THEBES F-8.

Central Pyri: property of Ioannis Stamelos. Oral communication, K. Demakopoulou.

HELLENISTIC-ROMAN? A long wall was found, built of ashlar masonry, perhaps reused. There was pottery from these periods, and also some Byzantine pottery.

SITE 201. GREATER THEBES H-17.

Just south of Kolonaki; property of Thomas Douros-Agatsas. Keramopoullos 1917:261-266, figs. 179 (bronze phiale), 180 (pottery), 181 (roof tile), 182-183 (figurines of seated females, standing nude boys, and animals).

Here, Keramopoullos excavated a partially preserved room, at least 2.60 m long, with a tile floor. A wall consisting of one row of ashlar masonry was found in another part of the property. In a different area, there was a rectangular cut in the bedrock that contained pottery of the fifth century B.C. Finds from the excavation included a bronze phiale, a small piece of a column, terracotta figurines of seated females, a bearded head with torso, standing boys, and animals (pigs, cows, and birds). The pottery included three Mycenaean and two Geometric potsherds, a lot of Archaic, Black Figure, and Red Figure pottery, and two inscribed sherds. Objects similar to these were found recently on the property of S. Laliotis (*Ephemeris* 1976, Parartema 12-17; the exact location of the site is unspecified). I am told that the finds included Geometric pottery.

The excavated material clearly points to the existence of a sanctuary in this area of Thebes. Keramopoullos identified it as the sanctuary of Amphiaraos referred to by Pausanias (9.8.3), but the nature of the finds support its identification as the double sanctuary of Demeter and Dionysos also mentioned by Pausanias (9.8.1-2; see chap. 5, passages 1-2). This southern part of Thebes is the area in which several roads meet and may perhaps be identified with the fateful crossroads in the story of Oidipous (see chap. 5, passages 1, 18).

SITE 202. GREATER THEBES K-14.

South of H. Loukas (site 54).

CLASSICAL. Keramopoullos (1917:284-296) discusses in detail a fortification wall, oriented north-south (see his map of Thebes), perhaps with a tower, south of the cemetery of Agios Loukas. According to Keramopoullos, the fortifications of Greater Thebes went in an east-west direction on the north side of the cemetery; he believed that this wall was an addition, built in 457 B.C., but it is possible that this wall was part of the original fortifications of Greater Thebes (see chap. 3).

SITE 203. GREATER THEBES J-13.

Just southeast of the Kadmeia.

Keramopoullos (1917:314-315) excavated here in an attempt to locate the Polyandrion.

LATE HELLADIC. Under the Classical remains was a lot of Mycenaean pottery.

CLASSICAL. A wall of ashlar masonry was found forming an angle. The conglomerate blocks were more than 1 m long: the wall was 1.45 m thick and was excavated to a length of 15 m; it was preserved to a height of 2 m. Another wall built for terracing was uncovered to a length of 11.50 m. Keramopoullos took both walls for part of the fortifications of Greater Thebes, which he thought continued east along the road to Agios Loukas.

SITE 204. KADMEIA I-10.

Intersection of Pindar and Vourdoumpa Sts. Underground installa-

tion of electric wires. Oral communication, K. Demakopoulou.

LATE HELLADIC. A lot of Mycenaean pottery (mostly kylikes) was found in the street. Digging reached a depth of 1.20 m, but in some spots, bedrock was only 0.50 m below the surface.

SITE 205. KADMEIA H-12.

Epaminondas St., property of Panagiotis Meletiou. Oral communication, K. Demakopoulou.

EARLY HELLADIC. There were remains of houses and a lot of pottery (cf. site 6).

MIDDLE HELLADIC. There were numerous remains of houses, pottery, and a pithos burial.

SITE 206. KADMEIA I-11.

Narrow street between Pelopidas and Pindar Sts., property of Christos Ploumis. Oral communication, K. Demakopoulou.

MIDDLE HELLADIC. There were scanty remains of habitation on the bedrock.

LATE HELLADIC. Two architectural phases were distinguished here; in each, the orientation of the buildings (northwest-southeast) was similar to that of the palace of site 1 (cf. neighboring site 3). The Mycenaean level was thick and yielded a lot of pottery, frescoes, and a bronze cup.

BYZANTINE. Remains of habitation were found above the Late Helladic levels.

SITE 207. KADMEIA I-11.

39 Pelopidas St., property of Helene Salta. Oral communication, K. Demakopoulou.

LATE HELLADIC. A lot of pottery was found on the south side of the property, including some examples of the pictorial style.

HELLENISTIC? A structure of ashlar masonry was partially preserved; it had been built on the bedrock (north side of the property).

SITE 208. KADMEIA I-12.

Just southeast of the Metropolis (site 216); property of Stelios Phloris. Oral communication, K. Demakopoulou.

EARLY AND MIDDLE HELLADIC. While digging for a sewer, pottery of these periods was found to a depth of 3 m. Included was an Early Cycladic vase.

SITE 209. KADMEIA I-13.

South end of Pindar St., property of the Nikolidaki brothers. *Deltion* 22B (1967):239, pl. 169:a (photograph of site).

LATE HELLADIC. The property sloped sharply towards the east, where sand was found, perhaps indicating the presence of an ancient riverbed. Some Mycenaean pottery was found in the sand. There were also some very thick, crude walls, possibly built as supports for a bridge (Pharaklas), or for terracing. Part of the aqueduct was cut in the bedrock; size and date are unknown, but it might be part of the Mycenaean system.

SITE 210. GREATER THEBES H-15.

Kolonaki, church of Taxiarchon. *Deltion* 22B (1967):227, pls. 159:a (lentoid seal), 159:b (faience head of a ram).

LATE HELLADIC. During construction activity in the courtyard of the church, a large chamber tomb was found. The chamber was preserved to a height of only 0.20 to 0.30 m above the floor; its maximum width was 5.30 m. Within were two pit burials, both disturbed. Finds included a lentoid seal with the representation of a lion; a faience bead in the shape of a ram's head; a fragment from a sarcophagus; a fragment of painted plaster; obsidian arrowheads, glass-paste beads, bone implements, and some pottery.

CLASSICAL AND BYZANTINE. Pottery of these periods was found, indicating later use of the chamber.

MODERN. The church of Taxiarchon, small and secluded, belongs to the Old Calendarite sect (adherents to the old Gregorian calendar), which also has a second church in Thebes (site 251).

SITE 211. GREATER THEBES J-12.

Astegoi, on 19th St; property of Georgios Triperinas. *Deltion* 27B (1972):319-321, fig. 1 (plan), pl. 275:b (Late Helladic pottery). Excavator, A. Ioannidou.

LATE HELLADIC. At 1.40 m below the surface, a wall, 0.10 m thick and 7.50 m long, oriented northwest-southeast, was found with another perpendicular to it. The excavator (A. Ioannidou) dates pottery from the building to LH III B.

CLASSICAL. There were remains of ashlar masonry walls and a cut in the bedrock dressed with ashlar masonry. Pottery dates the building (a house?) to the second half of the fourth century B.C. In a limited area of the property, in a burned layer unrelated to the other remains was a group of figurines (seated female figures, birds, and animals) and pottery dating to the end of the fifth century B.C.

SITE 212. KADMEIA H-12.

The church of Agios Demetrios, also called Megali Panagia. Strzygowski 1894. Vasileiou 1972 (monograph on the church). Pl. 42.

MODERN. The present church was built in 1867 on the site of an older one (Megali Panagia). The new church was renamed Agios Demetrios, perhaps because the chapel of Agios Demetrios (our site 226) was the only church left standing after the earthquake of 1853. The architect, Ioannis Philippotis of Tinos, and his son Demetrios collected and incorporated into the structure a great number of ancient stones: inscriptions, capitals, funerary stones, architectural parts, and Byzantine sculptures.

SITE 213. KADMEIA H-12.

Corner of Kadmos and Drakos Sts., the small chapel of Agios Charalampos. Pl. 47.

MODERN. This small structure (2.40 m x 4.50 m) might occupy the site of an older church; although there are no visible remains, there is a large courtyard to the north and west.

SITE 214. GREATER THEBES H-14.

Kolonaki, a high point, ca. 500 m from the south end of the Kadmeia; church of Agia Anna.

MODERN. According to Philios (1897:94, n. 1), there was once a small chapel here. It may have been destroyed along with all the other buildings in the earthquake of 1853; it was never rebuilt. As no remains are visible, it is not even remembered by the present-day locals. Keramopoullos (1917:334, n. 1) thought it possible that the church may have occupied the site of the sanctuary of Athena Onka. He preserved the memory of the chapel by naming part of the cemetery of Kolonaki for it (1910B).

SITE 215. GREATER THEBES I-14.

Just east of Kolonaki and site 214; the church of Agios Nikolaos. Delvenakiotis 1970:24. Vasileiou 1967:74. Pl. 48.

MODERN. The present church was probably built on the site of an older structure, destroyed in the earthquake of 1853. That church was seen in ruins by Pagidas (1882:14). Some Byzantine sculptures are used in the interior, and there are architectural stones in the courtyard. The location of the church (on the main road and in a depression) may support the notion that somewhere here was the sanctuary dedicated to Amphiaraos (see chap. 5, passage 2). Somewhere in the vicinity, Pappadakis (1911:140-141) excavated a few empty tombs, possibly of the Hellenistic period.

SITE 216. KADMEIA I-12.

The Metropolis (Cathedral) of Thebes, called Koimesis Theotokou and Panagia Lontza. Keramopoullos 1917:65, n. 1, 120. Delvenakiotis 1970:72. Pl. 43.

MODERN. The present church was built in 1833 and was extensively damaged in the earthquakes of 1853 and 1914; it was rebuilt around 1920. Ancient columns, capitals, and other stones were incorporated in its construction. An ancient votive column, perhaps originally from the temple of Apollo Ismenios, was taken from the

wall of the church (Keramopoullos 1917:64, fig. 54). During construction of the church, a Christian cemetery was found beneath the Holy of Holies (Keramopoullos 1917:65); this means that if there had been an earlier church dedicated to the Panagia, it must have been smaller or in a different location. Keramopoullos reports that according to local tradition, there was once a smaller church. The name *Lontza,* from *Loggia,* could indicate that a church of this name existed during the Frankish occupation of Thebes. Vasileiou (1967:61-63) records yet a different name for the current church: *Portaitsa,* "by the Gates." The Cathedral is located just 50 m from the Elektrai gates (site 7). For information about the old cathedral of Thebes see site 270.

SITE 217. KADMEIA H-12.

The church of Agios (or Apostolos) Andreas. Vasileiou 1972:108-109.

MODERN. The church was completed in 1959. There are a few large ashlar blocks in the courtyard, and it is possible that a Byzantine church once stood here. This is the highest point of the Kadmeia, where Keramopoullos (1917:337) placed the temple of Zeus Hypsistos (cf. chap. 5, passages 3, 6).

SITE 218. KADMEIA H-12.

The chapel of Agia Aikaterini, on Epaminondas St. Pl. 34.

MODERN. According to Keramopoullos (1917:207), the church had been recently renovated (i.e., before 1917). Before its renovation, he had seen cuts in the bedrock that were either catacombs, or Early Christian places of worship. Delvenakiotis (1970:23) also refers to a catacomb.

SITE 219. KADMEIA I-11.

The chapel of Agios Stephanos, on Amphion St.

MODERN. This small chapel probably occupies the site of an older church (see site 197). Delvenakiotis (1970:24) says that Agios Stephanos was the Cathedral of Thebes in 1563 but does not explain his reasons for believing so. Keramopoullos (1917:308, 464) mentions the existence of a Frankish tower and a Cyclopean wall in the vicinity (perhaps site 46).

SITE 220. GREATER THEBES L-8.

The church of Agioi Theodoroi, after which the suburb is named. *Deltion* 25B (1970):228. Vasileiou 1967:76-77. Pl. 51.

MODERN. The church built in 1842 was destroyed in the earthquake of 1893. It has now been completely rebuilt on plans by the local architect, Themis Papatheodorou. It is possible that an even earlier church had been built on the site of a catacomb. Several ancient stones are in the courtyard, and some have been incorporated in the construction. Some stones were transferred to the Museum in 1969.

SITE 221. KADMEIA I-11.

Corner of Vourdoumpas and Amphion Sts., chapel of Agios Georgios. Keramopoullos 1917:364-366. Delvenakiotis 1970:23-24.

LATE HELLADIC. Some Mycenaean pottery appeared in the lower levels of Keramopoullos' excavations.

CLASSICAL? Keramopoullos found three terracotta figurines, poorly preserved, but probably Classical (1917, fig. 195).

BYZANTINE. Keramopoullos excavated west of the chapel in his search for the ancient theater of Thebes; he found instead the remains of an older church, perhaps Byzantine. He also found a Corinthian capital, an Ionic base, and a marble carving showing a fish. Four capitals in the Museum of Thebes are similar to the one from this site (Mus. no. 521; cf. no. 135, "from the house of Kalopais" on the corner of Vourdoumpas and Pindar Sts.). Elsewhere, Keramopoullos (1917:120) mentions that he found Early Christian tombs at this site.

MODERN. The existing chapel had just been completed at the time of Keramopoullos' excavations in 1915. Although the chapel is small, it occupies a large property. There are some ancient architectural stones in the courtyard.

SITE 222. KADMEIA H-10.

Location Gourna; chapel of Agioi Apostoloi. Delvenakiotis 1970:25.

MODERN. Some ancient material has been incorporated in the chapel's construction; there is a small relief of the Apostles on the west side of the main entrance. There may have been an earlier church at this site.

SITE 223. GREATER THEBES J-8.

Palaios Synoikismos; church of Agios Konstantinos.

MODERN. The church was built in recent times (since the 1920s) to be the main religious center for the refugees from Asia Minor. We do not know whether anything was found here during the period of construction. A Byzantine church was found at site 234, approximately 150 m to the south.

SITE 224. GREATER THEBES I-6.

Just south of the railroad station, the chapel of Agia Paraskevi. Pl. 52.

MODERN. The chapel is located in the middle of a nineteenth-century cemetery, now inactive. There are some ancient stones in the courtyard. Keramopoullos (1917:403) placed the heroon of Iolaos here.

SITE 225. KADMEIA H-12.

Corner of Kadmos and Dirke Sts., chapel of Agios Nikolaos.

MODERN. A very small and simple chapel with no ancient architectural stones stands here. It is doubtful that there was once an older church.

SITE 226. KADMEIA G-11.

Elektra St., chapel of Agios Demetrios. *Deltion* 21B (1966):210. Excavator, P. Lazarides. Pl. 46.

MODERN. There is a one-room chapel with a sloping roof; ancient material is incorporated in its construction, including a carving in marble above the south window. More ancient material is visible in the courtyard. According to tradition, this was the only church left standing after the earthquake of 1853 (cf. site 212). Ten icons were taken from here to the Byzantine Museum in Athens in 1965 as a precaution against vandalism; two were in eighteenth-century Russian style, the rest in nineteenth-century style. The chapel is the only religious site in the area of west-central Thebes.

SITE 227. KADMEIA H-11.

Corner of Epaminondas and Antigone Sts., property of Charalampos Stamatis. *Deltion* 26B (1971):202, pl. 180:a (photograph of site). Excavator, T. Spyropoulos.

MIDDLE HELLADIC. Scanty remains of poorly preserved houses were found at the north side of the property: some foundations, pottery, a dozen terracotta bobbins, a couple of bone tools. There were also some storage pits cut in the bedrock.

LATE HELLADIC. The basement of the modern house had penetrated 2.25 m deep, the depth of the accumulated ancient deposits, and bedrock was found directly beneath it. But because of the property's central location, there must have been important ancient structures on it. Only some Mycenaean pottery was found here.

SITE 228. GREATER THEBES J-11.

Astegoi, Daglaridis St., property of Pavlogiannopoulos. *Athens Annals of Archaeology* 8(1976):25-28, figs. 1-3; excavator, K. Demakopoulou. *Bulletin de correspondance hellénique* 100(1976):640, figs. 118-119.

MIDDLE HELLADIC. A pithos burial was found in a pit cut in the bedrock. The handmade, undecorated pithos measured 1.10 m high and contained the remains of a child. The offerings were a Minyan kylix and three terracotta balls. The burial was 1.60 m below the surface.

LATE HELLADIC. Some Mycenaean pottery was found near the bedrock.

BYZANTINE. Most of the deposits at this site consisted of Byzantine debris, ca. 1 m thick on the average.

SITE 229. KADMEIA I-11.

25 Pelopidas St., property of Demetrios Stephas. Oral communication, K. Demakopoulou.

MIDDLE HELLADIC. There were remains of houses within which was some pottery, and a child burial.

LATE HELLADIC. Two rooms were found, their walls 0.65 to 0.70 m thick and plastered with clay. They could belong to the palace complex because they are so near to site 4. They were oriented north-south, and the destruction date was clearly LH III B:1, according to K. Demakopoulou.

CLASSICAL. Unfortunately, not much more than the foundations were preserved of what was clearly a large and important structure. There was a long wall oriented east-west, built of poros ashlar masonry, parallel to which was a solid wall built of limestone. The excavator considers this building a temple.

BYZANTINE. Very close to the surface was a large, well-built structure of unknown function.

SITE 230. KADMEIA H-12.

South of the city hall, property of Konstantinos Phloris. *Deltion* 27 (1972):321. Excavator, A. Ioannidou.

BYZANTINE. There were habitation remains, a built silo, and two poorly preserved burials. Most important were the remains of a large building: a wall 1 m thick was preserved to a length of 4.30 m and with which a thinner wall formed a right angle (cf. site 266, adjoining to the north, and site 270).

nearby in 1929 (Keramopoullos 1931, see site 8).

SITE 231. GREATER THEBES E-12.

Western Thebes; chapel of Agios Minas. Pl. 53.

MODERN. This little-known chapel is cut in the rock and looks very much like a Mycenaean chamber tomb. The area where the dromos would have been is terraced with a modern cement platform. The interior of the chamber is roughly rectangular, approximately 2 m x 3 m, and there is a bench carved out of the living rock.

SITE 232. KADMEIA H-13.

Southwest end of the Kadmeia; church of Metamorphosis Soteros ("Christ the Savior"), also called Agia Sotera. Vasileiou 1972:107-108.

MODERN. The present church was built in 1961 at the site of an earlier chapel. According to local tradition, there was a monastery here, the lands of which were distributed to the people of Thebes after the Greek revolution of 1821 (in the 1830s). According to local tradition, an old icon called *Megali Panagia* was painted by the Evangelist Luke and was kept here before it was transferred to the church of Agios Demetrios (Vasileiou 1972, fig. on p. 9; see site 212). A stone bearing two dedicatory inscriptions to Apollo Ismenios was found

SITE 233. KADMEIA H-12.

Corner of Kadmos and Oidipous Sts., chapel of Agios Athanasios.

MODERN. This chapel has no access to the street and is hard to find. One enters through the property of I. Pelides (site 101). There are two large unfluted columns in the courtyard, perhaps an indication that an older church once existed here.

SITE 234. GREATER THEBES J-9.

Palaios Synoikismos; property of Georgios Giannoutsos. *Deltion* 26B (1971):247, figs. 1-2 (plans), pls. 225:a (wall), 225:b (fresco). Excavator, P. Lazarides.

BYZANTINE. The remains of a church were partially excavated. The building probably had a single room and was preserved to a height of 1.60 m. It was built of ashlar masonry, bricks, and thick mortar. A great amount of its fresco decoration was preserved and was transferred to the Thebes Museum. The building dates to about A.D. 1200. Nine tombs were found in the floor of the church, which had apparently been dug after the church had been abandoned. The tombs contained three to five burials each, and there were offerings of potsherds, bronze rings, arm bands, and some beads. The tombs were covered with vaulted roofs; they probably date to the late fifteenth century.

SITE 235. GREATER THEBES K-10.

Kastellia; property of Sophia Arvaniti. *Deltion* 26B (1971):226, fig. 20 (plan), pl. 199:a (fresco). Excavator, A. Ioannidou.

LATE HELLADIC. The dromos of an unfinished Mycenaean tomb was found.

BYZANTINE. Poorly preserved remains of a house that was once decorated with frescoes imitating colored marbles were found. There was also a pebble floor (courtyard?).

SITE 236. KADMEIA I-10.

Corner of Keves and Pindar Sts. *Deltion* 26B (1971):227. Excavator, A. Ioannidou.

BYZANTINE. Bedrock is very close to the surface of the street. Only two silos were found here, cut in the rock and joined to one another through an opening of 0.28 m. The first silo had a maximum diameter of 2.40 m and a depth of 1.75 m; the second was slightly smaller. Both were stuccoed inside. It is possible that the silos belonged to a larger establishment, such as the monastery remembered in local tradition (cf. sites 93, 135).

SITE 237. GREATER THEBES J-12.

Astegoi; property of Charalampos Konstas. *Deltion* 26B (1971):227. Excavator, A. Ioannidou.

BYZANTINE. Four pit burials were found cut in the rock and covered with tiles: one contained two skeletons. The offerings were poor: rings, painted potsherds, and cheap jewelry. The tombs probably date to the eighth to tenth centuries.

SITE 238. KADMEIA I-11.

Street repairs on Zeggini St. *Deltion* 26B (1971):227, fig. 21, pl. 199:c (Doric architrave). Excavator, A. Ioannidou.

LATE HELLADIC. Some Mycenaean pottery (mostly stirrup-jars) was found at the bottom (0.60 m below the surface) of the excavated area.

CLASSICAL. There were substantial remains of walls built of poros and limestone. A few architectural stones were also found: parts from an architrave and a cornice.

SITE 239. GREATER THEBES F-8.

South Pyri; property of Demetrios Mpakas. *Deltion* 26B (1971):227. Excavator, A. Ioannidou.

CLASSICAL. A wall made of two rows of poros ashlar masonry was found and was excavated to a length of 6.60 m. The small quantity of black-glazed pottery found is not sufficient to date the building, but a Classical date is likely (cf. site 156, nearby).

SITE 240. GREATER THEBES K-17.

South of Agios Loukas, on the Ismenos River.

MODERN. There is a narrow (ca. 0.50 m) arched bridge over the river, built of stone and mortar, that is no longer used and is in disrepair. It seems to be an aqueduct bridge. A large, deserted farmhouse stands next to it; it was probably constructed in the nineteenth century.

SITE 241. GREATER THEBES L-17.

Just south of the bridge of site 240.

MODERN. Here is another bridge, wide enough to carry pedestrians, though its primary function is to carry water. It spans a side stream of the main river, and is similar in construction and date to the bridge in site 240.

SITE 242. GREATER THEBES L-18.

South of sites 240 and 241.

CLASSICAL. There are numerous visible remains of the ancient aqueduct system of Thebes, which still carries water from the source of the Ismenos River to the suburb of Tampakika and the mill of Koropouli. Today, the bedrock has collapsed to reveal the aqueduct, which would have been completely concealed in antiquity. The tunnel averages 1.55 m in height and 0.55 m in width; it is beautifully carved out of the living rock. The top is arched, and at regular intervals near the top, there are small shelves that were used for the placement of oil lamps needed during the construction and cleaning operations. The aqueduct system seems to branch out in different directions.

SITE 243. GREATER THEBES L-18.

South of sites 240 to 242; the spring of "Agianni" (Agios Ioannis, ancient Ismenos).

This spring is the largest single source of water in Thebes; it surfaces here to create the Ismenos River named for it. The true source is perhaps further south near the military camp where remains of tunneling are still visible. Where the water surfaces today, there is a modern cistern and pump to control the flow of water towards the city and the Plain of Thebes. The only water allowed to flow in the Ismenos riverbed is a small quantity still used by the flour mill of Koropouli (just east of the cemetery of Agios Loukas). The ancient name of the spring is not clearly given. Pausanias does not mention it; he discusses instead the spring of Ares (see chap. 5, passage 5). It is likely that the spring shared the name *Ismenos* with the river; an Ismene spring is mentioned by the scholiast to Euripides *Phoinissae* 53 and 101 (Unger 1839:243). The river was also called "Ladon" (Pausanias 9,10.6). The name "Kadmos' foot" occurs in Pseudo-Plutarch *De Fluviis* 1, and probably refers to this spring.

SITE 244. GREATER THEBES K-9.

Suburb of Agioi Theodoroi, just east of the Agianni River; public fountain.

This was the site of a spring, probably natural, although it may be artificial, resulting from the construction of the ancient aqueduct (cf. fig. 3.9). Pausanias (9.18.5) calls the spring "Oidipodia," and there are other references to it by this name (cf. chap. 5, passage 13; Unger 1839:243-245). The present fountain was built in 1902, but it is now capped. In the nineteenth century, there was here a 12-spout fountain (Ulrichs 1840:269) that was the loveliest in Thebes, according to Pagidas (1882:22).

SITE 245. KADMEIA I-12.

Corner of Oidipous and Pelopidas Sts., property of Stelios and Nikolaos Manisalis. *Athens Annals of Archaeology* 8 (1975):192-199. Excavator, K. Demakopoulou.

EARLY HELLADIC. An apsidal house of monumental size was found here in 1975. The walls were 0.80 m thick: the floors were either covered with tiles (original floor) or packed earth (later repairs). A rectangular stone base near the apsis might have supported a column. A clay hearth was found in the rectangular room filled with ashes and bones. The building had been destroyed by a raging fire. Ten complete vases and numerous sherds date the destruction to the end of EH II. Other finds from the house were a fragment from a pithos, three bone tools, two stone tools, and numerous flints. Of particular interest is an imported Cycladic vase.

The Early Helladic III period was represented by a deposit 0.50 m thick, which yielded no architectural remains. The Early Helladic remains were found 4.50 to 5.50 m below the surface.

MIDDLE HELLADIC. Remains were scanty, only enough to indicate habitation, and poorly preserved.

BYZANTINE. There were several silos, indicating that the site was used for habitation.

SITE 246. KADMEIA I-12.

Corner of Dirke and Amphion Sts., property of Konstantinos Manisalis. Oral communication, K. Demakopoulou.

The depth of deposit was 7 to 8 m, mostly debris of various periods. There was pottery of the Early and Middle Helladic and Roman periods, but only the Late Helladic and Byzantine periods preserved architectural remains.

LATE HELLADIC. There was only one wall of Cyclopean construction, seemingly meant to support a terrace. Many loose stones were found, and a lot of pottery, including a Late Helladic III A:2 krater.

BYZANTINE. Many walls of houses were found in the upper levels.

SITE 247. KADMEIA I-11.

Corner of Pelopidas and Antigone Sts., property of G. Tsigris and S. Makris. Oral communication, K. Demakopoulou.

The accumulation of deposit was shallow at the southern part of the property, but as deep as 8 m in the northern part. There was much debris from the Late Helladic period, including roof tiles and pottery dating to LH III B:1 (according to K. Demakopoulou). No walls were found.

BYZANTINE. The only habitation remains at this site dated to the Byzantine period.

SITE 248. KADMEIA I-10.

Tsevas and Pelopidas Sts., property of Dalekos. Oral communication, P. Dakoronia.

A large foundation pit (5.40 m x 3.20 m) was opened to a depth of over 9 m.

LATE HELLADIC. Near the bottom of the pit was a room built on stone foundations and oriented north-south. East of the room were a curving wall (supporting wall?) and a few flat stone slabs (a stairway?). Mycenaean pottery was found in the room.

SITE 249. KADMEIA I-10.

92 Pindar St., property of Tourikis-Baronas. Oral communication, P. Dakoronia.

Bedrock was very near the surface here (0.30 to 1.50 m below street level).

BYZANTINE. There were numerous remains of habitation, mainly poorly preserved houses with some walls built with reused ancient masonry. There were several silos, one of unusual cylindrical shape.

SITE 250. GREATER THEBES E-8.

South Pyri, Kabiron St.; property of Stroggylis. Oral communication, K. Demakopoulou.

CLASSICAL-HELLENISTIC. Two walls from a large building were built of ashlar masonry and had been restored in antiquity. Most of the pottery was Hellenistic. These were probably public buildings.

SITE 251. KADMEIA I-13.

Just south of the Cathedral, the chapel of Agios Georgios.

MODERN. This concealed structure is the second church of the Old Calendarites (cf. site 210). The building looks like a one-room house and is entered through a small courtyard. It is not clear whether an older structure might have stood in precisely this location.

SITE 252. GREATER THEBES G-8.

Eastern Pyri, near the Amphion hill; the Evangelistria chapel.

MODERN. This small chapel is located just west of the Amphion hill and the Chlevino spring. There is no other religious monument in the area.

SITE 253. GREATER THEBES I-5.

Just north of the railroad station. Ancient fortifications. Kalopais 1893:18-19.

CLASSICAL. Kalopais excavated here and found part of the ancient wall of Greater Thebes 115 m north of the railroad station. The wall was 3.50 m thick and was built of isodomic masonry and a "hard stone" (conglomerate?); a section 15 m long was uncovered, but it is no longer visible.

SITE 254. GREATER THEBES J-10.

Kastellia; chamber tombs on the Megalo Kastelli. *Deltion* 27B (1972):309-312, pls. 251 (photograph of large tomb), 252:a (ivory pyxis), 252:b (Late Helladic pithoid jar), 252:c (Archaic vase), 253:a (interior of large tomb), 253:b-c (frescoes), 254 (frescoes, spirals, and papyrus), 255 (frescoes of mourning women, 256 (view of large tomb); *Deltion* 28B (1973):252-258, pls. 207:a-c, 208 (views of the site); excavator, T. Spyropoulos. *Archaeological Reports* 1970-1971:14, fig. 26 (ivory pyxis); 1976-1977: 36, fig. 62 (Late Helladic pithoid jar). Chadwick and Spyropoulos 1975, figs. 120-121. *Bulletin de correspondance hellénique* 101 (1977):586, figs. 159-161 (site, fresco, pyxis).

LATE HELLADIC. Five or six chamber tombs were excavated, one of monumental size with two dromoi (ca. 25 m long and 4 m wide) and a huge chamber (11.50 m x 7 m, 3.50 m high). One side of the chamber had a gabled ceiling; the other side had a sloping ceiling. Only two burials, one of which was Mycenaean, were found in the

tomb: a cist burial sunk in the floor contained a skull and an ivory pyxis decorated with four sphinxes in relief. A large Mycenaean pithoid jar was found filled with ashes and bones. Unique to this tomb was the presence of frescoes: the lower parts of the double chamber and the entrances were painted with floral and geometric motifs; on the walls were a fresco depicting a funeral procession (first chamber) and one including a landscape (second chamber). There was evidence that the chambers were used from the Archaic to the Hellenistic period, and also in the Byzantine period.

The other tombs were not in good condition, all having been reused in Byzantine times. One of them (*Deltion* 1973:252-253) preserved fragments of painted decoration; another (*Deltion* 1972:311-312) contained some Mycenaean objects.

SITE 255. GREATER THEBES K-12.

Location Tekes, in Nea Sphageia; Late Helladic cemetery. Keramopoullos 1917:80, 99.

LATE HELLADIC. On the hill north of the sanctuary of Apollo Ismenios (site 8), there was, according to Keramopoullos, a Mycenaean cemetery.

CLASSICAL? Keramopoullos also reports the presence of a large cut in the rock, part of the aqueduct system of Thebes.

POST-BYZANTINE. In the time of Keramopoullos, the name *Tekes* was justified by the presence of the ruins of a mosque; its existence cannot be verified today. The word *Tekes* is Turkish and identifies a public/religious place.

SITE 256. GREATER THEBES J-11.

Just east of Agios Stephanos (site 219); an old bridge, no longer standing. Keramopoullos 1917:465, fig. 207 (photograph of the area).

MODERN? There used to be a bridge bearing traffic from the eastern part of the Kadmeia over the Strophia stream and the Koile Hodos to the Ismenion. Keramopoullos considered it very useful and important. There is no bridge here today, but a modern bridge was built one block south.

SITE 257. GREATER THEBES. FIG. 1.2, E-9.

About 800 m west of Paraporti; ancient fortifications. Kalopais 1892:42. Frazer 1898:33-34. Keramopoullos 1917:478.

CLASSICAL. On the road to Ampelosalesi, there were once some foundation stones that, according to Keramopoullos, belonged to the fortifications of Greater Thebes.

SITE 258. GREATER THEBES N-15.

Just east of Agia Photini, fortifications. Kalopais 1892:44-45; 1893:19. Keramopoullos 1917:299, 481.

CLASSICAL. Important remains were excavated here by Kalopais. The polygonal foundations of towers and gates were preserved beneath the debris of disintegrated conglomerate blocks. The wall in this area was destroyed in 1898 (Soteriades 1914:27). In another trench (5 m x 15 m), Kalopais found some ashlar masonry not in situ, large roof tiles, and some "curved masonry" that seemed to him to belong "to the arches of the gates."

SITE 259. GREATER THEBES. FIG. 1.2, E-8.

Western Thebes; fortifications. Kalopais 1892:41-42. Keramopoullos 1917:479.

CLASSICAL. Kalopais excavated here, midway between site 257 and northern Pyri, and found remains of fortifications. According to him, the line of the wall in western Thebes ran about 1,000 m (actually only 800 m) from the river Dirke. In site 259, the wall was 3 m thick.

SITE 260. KADMEIA I-10.

Corner of Pindar and Vourdoumpas Sts., property of Liakopoulos-Kyrtsis. *Athens Annals of Archaeology* 1(1968):241-244, fig. 1. Excavator, N. Pharaklas.

LATE HELLADIC. Bedrock was very near the surface, and only near the northwest corner of the property were any remains preserved. Two shallow ditches were found, 0.65 to 0.80 m wide, and over 5 m long (see plan of fig. 1); there were 15 circular cuts in the ditches containing the remains of storage jars, some of which were recognizable as stirrup-jars like the ones from the "house of Kadmos" (site 1). There were clear indications of a destruction by fire, but the date was not established.

SITE 261. KADMEIA I-11.

Corner of Pindar and Vourdoumpas Sts., property of Mpasiakos.

LATE HELLADIC. According to the locals, S. Marinatos excavated here in 1937 and found remains of the "house of Kadmos." The only reference to this excavation is that made by N. Platon (Platon and Touloupa 1964:859) who succeeded Marinatos as curator of the Thebes Museum in the 1930s.

SITE 262. GREATER THEBES F-11.

Western Thebes, location Kalogeros; property of Gounaras. *Deltion* 22B (1967):240. Excavator, N. Pharaklas.

LATE HELLADIC. Remains of three chamber tombs were visible here in 1966, all poorly preserved and empty. Keramopoullos (1910B:210) also reports seeing one tomb "on the left side of the river Dirke."

SITE 263. KADMEIA I-10.

94 Pindar St., property of the National Bank of Greece. Pl. 38.

LATE HELLADIC. According to the locals, Mycenaean remains were found here during construction activity in the late 1920s, but no details have been recorded.

SITE 264. GREATER THEBES M-13.

Konakia, near Agia Photini. *Deltion* 22B (1967):233. Excavator, N. Pharaklas.

A small tomb(?) of unknown date was found here, 1.80 m x 1 m, and 1.70 m deep; it originally had a vaulted roof and was built of poros ashlar masonry. There were no finds.

SITE 265. KADMEIA I-12.

Just south of the cathedral, property of Konstantinos Gikas. *Deltion* 27B (1972):307, pl. 249:a, 250:g (frescoes). Excavator, T. Spyropoulos.

LATE HELLADIC. Poorly preserved remains of a house were found here, perhaps related to those of the adjoining site 179. Some frescoes and pottery are mentioned among the finds.

SITE 266. KADMEIA H-12.

Just west of the city hall, property of Charalampos Loukos. *Deltion* 27B (1972):321; excavator, A. Ioannidou. *Deltion* 28B (1973):285-286; excavator, P. Lazarides.

BYZANTINE. A mosaic floor was found at a depth of 5.60 m; the design consisted of squares filled with geometric motifs, a bird, and Solomon's knot. The mosaic was transferred to the Museum. It is said that a similar mosaic was found during construction of the city hall in 1939 (Delvenakiotis 197-0:71-72; cf. site 270).

SITE 267. KADMEIA I-11.

East end of Zegginis St., property of the Theodorou brothers. *Deltion* 27B (1972):321, fig. 2 (plan), pls. 275:a (Byzantine remains), 276:a (fragment of stele), 276:b (Late Helladic potsherd). Excavator, A. Ioannidou.

LATE HELLADIC. Mycenaean pottery and a pair of bronze tweezers were found at a depth of 5 m.

CLASSICAL. A small fragment from the upper part of a funerary stele was found in the topsoil; the representation shows two griffins attacking a deer.

EARLY CHRISTIAN. A marble carving was found in the topsoil.

BYZANTINE. The remains of a large building were partially excavated; there were two walls, drain pipes, and domestic pottery.

SITE 268. KADMEIA I-12.

14 Pelopidas St., property of Athanasios Stamatis. *Deltion* 28B (1973):274, 276, pls. 230:a-c (views of site), 231:a, c, e (finds). Excavator, A. Ioannidou.

Bedrock was found at 4.80 to 7.50 m below the surface.

EARLY HELLADIC. Some pottery was found, including a one-handled "Trojan cup" (pl. 231:e).

MIDDLE HELLADIC. There were deposits especially rich in pottery, but no architectural remains. A cist tomb was found at 7.30 m with the skeleton poorly preserved and a vase at the feet of the skeleton (pl. 231:a).

CLASSICAL. The same deep aqueduct of neighboring site 16 was found here as well: it measured from 0.46 to 0.55 m in width, and 4 m in depth. There were two separate cuts in the bedrock, not connected to one another and going in two different directions. They contained Middle Helladic and Byzantine pottery.

BYZANTINE. A poorly preserved structure was found 0.50 m below the surface, containing small quantities of Late Byzantine pottery.

SITE 269. KADMEIA H-11.

114 Epaminondas St., property of Pantelis Karamangiolis. *Deltion* 28B (1973):247-248, 276. Excavators, T. Spyropoulos and A. Ioannidou.

Three trial trenches were opened here; no construction took place.

LATE HELLADIC. Some frescoes and pottery were found at a depth of 7 to 8.50 m, beyond which the excavation did not proceed.

CLASSICAL-HELLENISTIC. Parts of buildings of unknown function were found at depths of 5 to 7 m.

BYZANTINE. There were remains of habitation, evidently between 2 and 5 m: poorly constructed walls, pottery, and silos.

POST-BYZANTINE. Habitation remains were found just below the surface: silos and many small objects.

SITE 270. KADMEIA I-12.

Corner of Pindar and Oidipous Sts., the city hall of Thebes. Keramopoullos 1917:66. Orlandos 1939A:121; 1939B:144, n. 1. Delvenakiotis 1970:71-72.

BYZANTINE. Remains of a church were found here during the construction of the city hall. There were walls and frescoes 6 m below the surface. One of the frescoes depicted *Christ's Entry into Jerusalem;* according to Orlandos, it was transferred to the Museum. Keramopoullos (1917:65, n. 1) believed that the Byzantine cathedral of Thebes, called *Katholikon,* had been located in this vacinity. That famous church, built by Bishop Ioannis Kaloktenis in the twelfth century, was dedicated to the Panagia Theotokos. It is possible that it was the church seen by Spon in 1676 (1678-1680, vol. 2, p. 18) and by Wheler (1723, vol. 2, p. 83), which they referred to as Panagia Chrysophoritsa or Christophoritsa. Remains related to this church have been found at nearby sites west of the city hall (sites 32, 230, 266), and perhaps east of the city hall (site 115). The modern church, dedicated to Agios Ioannis Kaloktenis (site 97), may occupy part of the cathedral complex, which would have included an administration building.

REFERENCES

Adcock, Frank, and D. J. Mosley. 1974. *Diplomacy in Ancient Greece.* New York: St. Martin's Press.

Albright, William F. 1961. The role of the Canaanites in the history of civilization. In *The Bible and the Ancient Near East,* edited by G. E. Wright, 438-487. New York: Garden Books.

Amit, M. 1970. La date de l' alliance entre Athènes et Platées. *L' antiquité classique* 39:414-426.

Åström, Paul, Nikolaos Verdelis, N-G. Gejvall, and H. Hjelmqvist. 1977. *The Cuirass Tomb and Other Finds at Dendra. In Studies in Mediterranean Archaeology,* vol. 4. Göteborg: Åström Förlag.

Barnett, Richard D. 1975. The Sea Peoples. In *Cambridge Ancient History,* 3d ed. vol. II, part 2, 359-378.

Bartoletti, Vittorio. 1959. *Hellenica Oxyrhynchia.* Leipzig: Teubner.

Beattie, Arthur J. 1975. Some notes on the Spensitheos decree. *Kadmos* 14: 8-47.

Beloch, Julius. 1886. *Die Bevölkerung der griechisch-römischen Welt.* Leipzig: Duncker & Humbolt.

Bérard, Jean. 1941. *La colonization grecque de l' Italie méridionale et de la Sicile dans l' antiquité.* Paris: Boccard.

———1960. *L' expansion et la colonization grecques jusqu' aux guerres médiques.* Paris: Aubier.

Bethe, Erich A. J. 1891. *Thebanische Heldenlieder; Untersuchungen über die Epen des thebanisch-argivischen Sagenkreises.* Leipzig: Hirzel.

Bielefeld, Erwin. 1968. Statue des Apollon, Rom Museo Antiquario Forense. *Antike Plastik* 8:13-17.

Biesantz, Hagen. 1958. Mykenische Schriftzeichen einer böotischen Schale des 5. Jahrhunderts v. Chr. In *Minoica; Festschrift zum 80. Geburtstag von J. Sundwall,* edited by E. Grumach, 50-60. Berlin: Akademie Verlag.

Billingmeier, Jon-Christian. 1976. *Kadmos and the Possibility of a Semitic Presence in Helladic Greece.* Diss., University of California at Santa Barbara. Ann Arbor: University Microfilms 77-05235.

Billot, M-F. 1977. Le Sphinx du Louvre CA 637. *Bulletin de correspondance hellénique* 101:383-421.

Bintliff, John L. 1977. *Natural Environ-*

ment and Human Settlement in Prehistoric Greece. Oxford: British Archaeology Reports.

Blegen, Carl W. 1921. *Korakou: a Prehistoric Settlement near Corinth.* Boston: American School of Classical Studies at Athens.

———1937. *Prosymna: the Helladic Settlement Preceding the Argive Heraeum.* Cambridge: Cambridge University Press.

———1945. The roof of the Mycenaean Megaron. *American Journal of Archaeology* 49:35-44.

Blinkenberg, Christian. 1926. *Fibules grecques et orientales.* Copenhagen: Host.

Boardman, John. 1957. Early Euboean pottery and history. *Annual of the British School at Athens* 52:1-29.

Böhlau, Johannes. 1888. Böotische Vasen. *Jahrbuch des deutschen archäologischen Instituts* 3:325-364.

Bossert, Helmuth T. 1948. Die phönizishhethitischen Bilinguen. *Oriens* 1:163-192.

Bouché-Leclercq, A. 1879. *Histoire de la divination dans l' antiquité,* vol. 1. Brussels.

Bourguet, Émile. 1929. *Épigraphie. Fouilles de Delphes,* vol. III, fasc. 1, Paris.

Bousquet, Jean. 1961. Les technites de l' Isthme et de Nemée. *Bulletin de correspondance hellénique* 85:78-85.

Brandis, Johannes. 1867. Die Bedeutung der sieben Tore Thebens. *Hermes* 2:259-284.

Branigan, Keith. 1974. *Aegean Metalwork of the Early and Middle Bronze Age.* Oxford: Clarendon Press.

Bréhier, Louis. 1950. *Le monde byzantin,* vol. 3. Paris: Albin Michel.

Brillante, Carlo. 1980. Le leggende tebane e l'archeologia. *Studi Micenei ed Egeo-Anatolici* 21:309-340.

Bruce, I. A. F. 1967. *An Historical Commentary on the Hellenica Oxyrhynchia.* Cambridge: Cambridge University Press.

Buck, Robert J. 1979. *A History of Boiotia.* Alberta: The University of Alberta Press.

Buckler, John. 1980. *The Theban Hegemony, 371-362 B.C.* Cambridge, Mass.: Harvard University Press.

Burrows, R. M., and Percy N. Ure. 1908. Excavations at Rhitsona. *Annual of the British School at Athens* 14:226-318.

———1909. Excavations at Rhitsona in Boeotia. *Journal of Hellenic Studies* 29:308-353.

Bursian, Konrad. 1862. *Geographie von Griechenland,* vol. 1. Leipzig.

Burstein, Stanley M. 1972. *A Political History of Heraclea Pontica to 282 B.C.* Diss., University of California at Los Angeles.

Bury, John B. 1951. *A History of Greece.* 3d ed. Revised by R. Meiggs. London: MacMillan.

Canciani, Fulvio. 1965. Böotische Vasen aus dem 8. und 7. Jahrhundert. *Jahrbuch des deutschen archäologischen Instituts* 80:18-75.

Carothers, Joan, and William A. McDonald. 1979. Size and distribution of the population in Bronze Age Messenia: some statistical approaches.

Journal of Field Archaeology 6:433-454.

Caskey, John L. 1956. Excavations at Lerna. *Hesperia* 25:147-173.

———1957. Excavations at Lerna, *Hesperia* 26:142-162.

———1958. Excavations at Lerna, *Hesperia* 27:125-144.

———1960. The Early Helladic period in the Argolid. *Hesperia* 29:285-303.

———1971A. Greece, Crete and the Islands in the Early Bronze Age. In *Cambridge Ancient History,* 3d ed., vol. 1, part 2, 771-807.

———1971B. Investigations in Keos: Excavation and exploration 1966-1970. *Hesperia* 40:358-386.

Caskey, John, and E. G. Caskey. 1960. The earliest settlement at Eutresis: supplementary excavations. *Hesperia* 29:126-167.

Caskey, Miriam E. 1976. Notes on the relief pithoi of the Tenian-Boiotian group. *American Journal of Archaeology* 80:19-41.

———1980. Dionysos in the temple at Ayia Irini, Keos. *American Journal of Archaeology* 84:200.

Catling, Hector W., and R. E. Jones. 1977. A reinvestigation of the provenance of the inscribed stirrup-jars found at Thebes. *Archaeometry* 19:137-146.

Catling, Hector W., and Ann Millett. 1965. A study of the inscribed stirrup-jars from Thebes. *Archaeometry* 8:3-85.

———1969. Theban stirrup-jars: questions and answers. *Archaeometry* 11:3-20.

Chadwick, John. 1969. Linear B tablets from Thebes. *Minos* 10:115-137.

Chadwick, John, and Theodoros Spyropoulos. 1975. *The Thebes Tablets II.* Salamanca: University of Salamanca Press.

Chatzidakis, Manolis. 1956. *Byzantine Monuments in Attica and Boeotia.* Athens: Athens Editions.

Cloché, Paul. 1952. *Thèbes de Béotie, des origines à la conquête romaine.* Namur: Secrétariat des publications, Facultés universitaires.

Coldstream, J. N. 1968. *Greek Geometric Pottery; a Survey of Local Styles and their Chronology.* London: Methuen.

———1976. Hero cults in the Age of Homer. *Journal of Hellenic Studies* 96:8-17.

———1977. *Geometric Greece.* London: E. Benn.

Coldstream, J. N., and G. L. Huxley, eds. 1972. *Kythera, Excavations and Studies Conducted by the University of Pennsylvania Museum and the British School at Athens.* Park Ridge, New Jersey: Noyes Press.

Comstock, M. B., and C. C. Vermeule. 1976. *Sculpture in Stone.* Boston: Museum of Fine Arts.

Courbin, Paul. 1966. *La céramique géometrique de l' Argolide.* Paris: Boccard.

Courtois, Jacques Claude. 1976. Review of Symeonoglou 1973. *Syria* 53:169-173.

Dawson, Christopher A. 1970. *The Seven Against Thebes.* Englewood Cliffs, New Jersey: Prentice Hall.

Decharme, M. 1869. *De Thebanis Artificibus.* Thesis presented at the University of Paris.

Defradas, Jean. 1954. *Les thèmes de la propagande delphique*. Paris: Klincksieck.

Deltion (Greek periodical). Ἀρχαιολογικόν Δελτίον. Athens, Greece: Ὑπηρεσία Ἀρχαιοτήτων καὶ Ἀναστηλώσεως.

Delvenakiotis, Vasileios. 1970. Ὁ μητροπολίτης Ἰωάννης Καλοκτένης καὶ αἱ Θῆβαι. Athens: printed privately.

Demakopoulou, Kaiti, and Dora Konsola. 1975. Λείψανα Πρωτοελλαδικοῦ, Μεσοελλαδικοῦ καὶ Ὑστεροελλαδικοῦ οἰκισμοῦ στὴ Θήβα. *Deltion* 30A:44-89.

Demand, Nancy. 1979. *Thebes in the Fifth Century*. Diss., Bryn Mawr College. Ann Arbor: University Microfilms 79-5596.

Deonna, Waldemar. 1909. *Les Apollons archaiques*. Geneva: Georg & Co.

Desborough, Vincent R. d'A. 1952. *Protogeometric Pottery*. Oxford: Clarendon Press.

———1972. *The Greek Dark Ages*. London: E. Benn.

DeVries, Keith. 1972. Incised fibulae from Boiotia. *Forschungen und Berichte* (Staatliche Museen zu Berlin) 14:111-129.

———1974. A grave with a figured fibula at Lerna. *Hesperia* 43:80-104.

Dinse, H. 1856. *De Antigenida Thebano Musico*. Berlin.

Dinsmoor, William B. 1942. Notes on Megaron roofs. *American Journal of Archaeology* 46:370-372.

———1950. *The Architecture of Ancient Greece*. 3rd ed. London: Batsford.

Ducat, Jean. 1971. *Les kouroi du Ptoion:*
le sanctuaire d' Apollon Ptoieus à l' époque archaique. Paris: Boccard.

———1973. La Confédération béotienne et l' expansion thébaine à l' époque archaique, *Bulletin de correspondance hellénique* 97:59-73.

Dull, Clifford J. 1975. *A Study of the Leadership of the Boeotian League from the Invasion of the Boiotoi to the King's Peace*. Diss., University of Wisconsin at Madison. Ann Arbor: University Microfilms 75-18587.

Edwards, G. Patrick, and Ruth B. Edwards. 1974. Red letters and Phoenician writing. *Kadmos* 13:48-57.

Edwards, Ruth B. 1979. *Kadmos the Phoenician: a Study in Greek Legends and the Mycenaean Age*. Amsterdam: Hakkert.

Einarson, Benedict. 1967. Notes on the development of the Greek alphabet. *Classical Philology* 62:1-24.

Ephemeris (Greek periodical). Ἀρχαιολογικὴ Ἐφημερίς. Athens, Greece: Ἡ ἐν Ἀθήναις Ἀρχαιολογικὴ Ἑταιρεία.

Fabricius, Ernst. 1890. *Theben; eine Untersuchung über die Topographie und Geschichte der Hauptstadt Boeotiens*. Freiburg i. B.: Akademie Antrittsprogramm.

Fairbanks, A. 1928. *Catalogue of Greek and Etruscan Vases*, vol. 1. Cambridge, Mass.: Boston Museum of Fine Arts.

Felsch, Rainer. 1979. Boiotische Ziegelwerkstatten archaischer Zeit. *Athenische Mitteilungen des deutschen archäologischen Instituts* 94:1-40.

Feyel, Michel. 1942A. *Polybe et l' histoire*

de Béotie au IIIe siècle avant notre ère. Paris: Boccard.

———1942B. *Contribution à l'épigraphie béotienne.* Le Puy: Imprimerie de "La Haute Loire."

FGrHist. *Die Fragmente der griechischer Historiker.* Edited by Felix Jacoby.

FHG. *Fragmenta Historicorum Graecorum.* Edited by Carl Müller.

Fimmen, Diedrich. 1912. Die Besiedlung Boeotiens bis in frühgriechische Zeit. *Neue Jahrbücher für das klassische Altertum* 15:521-541.

Forchhammer, Peter W. 1854. *Topographia Thebarum Heptapylarum.* Kiel: Akademische Buchhandlung.

Forsdyke, John. 1957. *Greece before Homer; Ancient Chronology and Mythology.* New York: Norton.

Fossey, John M. 1971. Therapnai and Skolos in Boiotia. *Bulletin of the Institute of Classical Studies* (London) 18:106-109.

———1974. The end of the Bronze Age in the south west Copaic. *Euphrosyne* 6:7-21.

———1978. Chemical analysis of Boiotian ceramics. *Teiresias* (Archaeologica), 4-7.

———(Forthcoming.) *The Topography and Population of Ancient Boiotia.* 2 vols. Chicago: Ares.

Franke, Paul R., and Max Hirmer. 1964. *Die griechische Münze.* Munich and New York: Hirmer Verlag.

Frankfort, Henri. 1950. Town planning in ancient Mesopotamia. *Town Planning Review* 21:98-115.

Fraser, P. M., and T. Rönne. 1957. *Boeotian and West Greek Tombstones.* Lund: Gleerup.

Frazer, J. G. 1898. *Pausanias's Description of Greece,* vol. 5. London: MacMillan.

French, David H. 1972. *Notes on Prehistoric Pottery Groups from Central Greece.* Athens: circulated privately.

French, Elisabeth. 1971. The development of Mycenaean terracotta figurines. *Annual of the British School at Athens* 66:101-187.

Frickenhaus, August. 1912. *Lenäenvasen.* Berlin: G. Reimer.

Furumark, Arne. 1941A. *The Mycenaean Pottery; Analysis and Classification.* Stockholm.

———1941B *Chronology of Mycenaean Pottery.* Stockholm.

Gelb, I. J. 1963. *A Study of Writing.* 2d ed. Chicago: The University of Chicago Press.

Gell, William. 1819. *The Itinerary of Greece,* vol. 2. London.

Godart, Louis. 1970. Les tablettes de la série Co de Knossos. *Minos* 12:418-424.

Godart, Louis, and Anna Sacconi. 1978. *Les tablettes en linéaire B de Thèbes.* Rome: Edizioni dell' Ateneo.

Goldman, Hetty. 1931. *Excavations at Eutresis in Boeotia.* Cambridge, Mass.: Harvard University Press.

———1940. The acropolis of Halae. *Hesperia* 4:379-514.

Gomme, Arnold W. 1910. The literary evidence for the topography of Thebes. *Annual of the British School at Athens* 17:29-53.

———1911. The topography of Boeotia

and the theories of M. Berard. *Annual of the British School at Athens* 18:189-210.

———1913. The legend of Cadmus and the Logographi. *Journal of Hellenic Studies* 33:53-72, 223-245.

———1945. *A Historical Commentary on Thucydides,* vol. 1. Oxford: at the Clarendon Press.

Gossage, A. G. 1975. The comparative chronology of inscriptions relating to Boiotian festivals in the first half of the first century B.C. *Annual of the British School at Athens* 70:115-134.

Grace, Frederick R. 1939. *Archaic Sculpture in Boeotia.* Cambridge, Mass.: Harvard University Press.

Graham, James W. 1962. *The Palaces of Crete.* Princeton: Princeton University Press.

Gregorovius, Ferdinand. 1889. *Geschichte der Stadt Athen im Mittelalter.* 2 vols. Stuttgart.

Grenfell, B. P., and A. S. Hunt. 1908. *The Oxyrhynchus Papyri,* vol. V. London: Egypt Exploration Fund.

Grumach, Ernst. 1965. Theben und das Alter von Linear B. *Kadmos* 4:45-57.

Guarducci, Margherita. 1967. *Epigrafia greca,* vol. 1. Rome: Libreria dello Stato.

Guillon, Pierre. 1943. *Les trépieds du Ptoion.* Paris: Boccard.

———1963. *Le Bouclier d' Heraklès et l' histoire de la Grèce centrale dans la période de la première guerre sacrée.* Aix en Provence: Ophrys.

Guthrie, W. K. C. 1955. *The Greeks and their Gods.* Boston: Beacon.

———1975. The religion and mythology of the Greeks. In *Cambridge Ancient History,* 3d ed., vol. II, part 2, 851-905.

Hack, Harold M. 1975. *The Rise of Thebes: a Study of Theban Politics and Diplomacy, 386-371 B.C.* Diss., Yale University. Ann Arbor: University Microfilms 75-24543.

———1978. Thebes and the Spartan Hegemony, 386-382 B.C. *American Journal of Philology* 99:210-227.

Hackens, Tony. 1969. La circulation monétaire dans la Béotie hellénistique: trésors de Thèbes 1935 et 1965. *Bulletin de correspondance hellénique* 93:701-729.

Hammond, N. G. L. 1973. *Studies in Greek History.* Oxford: at the Clarendon Press.

———1975. The literary tradition for the migrations. In *Cambridge Ancient History,* 3d ed., vol. II, part 2, 678-712.

Hampe, Ronald. 1936. *Frühe griechische Sagenbilder in Böotien.* Athens: Deutsches Archäologisches Institut.

Haury, J. 1908. *Über die Herkunft der Kabiren und über Einwanderungen aus Südpalästina nach Böotien.* Munich.

Head, Barcley V. 1881. On the chronological sequence of the coins of Boeotia. *Numismatic Chronicle* 3:177-276.

Heimberg, Ursula. 1973. Boiotische Reliefs im Museum von Theben. *Antike Plastik,* 12:15-35.

Hemberg, Bengst. 1950. *Die Kabiren.* Upsala: Almqvist & Wiksell.

Heurtley, William A. 1923. Notes on the harbours of S. Boeotia and sea-trade between Boeotia and Corinth in Prehistoric times. *Annual of the British School at Athens* 26:38-45.

Heyder, W., and A. Mallwitz. 1978. *Die Bauten im Kabirenheiligtum bei Theben*. Berlin: de Gruyter.

Higgins, Reynold. 1967. *Greek Terracottas*. London: Methuen.

Holleaux, Maurice. 1895. Sur une inscription de Thèbes. *Revue des études grecques* 8:7-45.

————1898. Ἀπόλλων Σπόδιος. In *Mélanges Henri Weil*, 193-206. Paris.

————1938. *Études d'épigraphie et d'histoire grecques,* vol. 1, 1-40 (sur une inscription de Thèbes).

Hood, Sinclair. 1978. *The Arts in Prehistoric Greece*. New York: Penguin.

Hooker, John T. 1977. The language of the Thebes Of tablets. *Minos* 16:174-178.

Hope-Simpson, R., and J. F. Lazenby. 1970. *The Catalogue of the Ships in Homer's Iliad*. Oxford: Clarendon Press.

Hoppin, J. C. 1924. *A Handbook of Greek Black-Figured Vases*. Paris: E. Champion.

Howell, Roger L. 1974. The origins of the Middle Helladic culture. In *Bronze Age Migrations in the Aegean,* edited by R. A. Crossland and A. Birchall, 73-99. Park Ridge, New Jersey: Noyes Press.

Huxley, G. L. 1969. *Greek Epic Poetry from Eumelos to Panyassis*. Cambridge, Mass.: Harvard University Press.

Iakovides, Spyridon. 1969, 1970. Περατὴ· τό νεκροταφεῖον, vols. 1-2. Athens: Archaeological Society of Athens.

IG. *Inscriptiones Grecae*.

Imhoof-Blumer, F. W., and Percy Gardner. 1887. *A Numismatic Commentary on Pausanias*. (Reprint of three articles published in the *Journal of Hellenic Studies* vols. 6-8, 1885-1887. London.

Jardé, Auguste F. V. 1925. *Les céréales dans l'antiquité grecque*. Part 1: *la production*. Paris: Boccard.

Jeffery, Lilian H. 1961. *The Local Scripts of Archaic Greece*. Oxford: Clarendon Press.

————1976. *Archaic Greece: the City States c. 700-500 B.C.* New York: St. Martin's Press.

Jeffery, Lilian H., and Anna Morpurgo-Davies. 1970. Ποινικαστὰς and ποινικάζειν BM 1969.4-2.1, a new Archaic inscription from Crete. *Kadmos* 9:118-154.

Judeich, Walther. 1888. Das Kabirenheiligtum bei Theben; die Lage des Heiligtums. *Athenische Mitteilungen des deutschen archäologischen Instituts* 13:82-87.

————1931. *Topographie von Athen*. 2d ed. Munich: C. H. Beck.

Kalopais, Eustratios. 1892. Untitled report. *Praktika*, 41-46.

————1893. Untitled report. *Praktika*, 18-22.

Karouzos, Christos. 1926. Β΄ Ἀρχαιολογικὴ Περιφέρεια: Θῆβαι. *Deltion* 10, Parartema 7-11.

————1934. Ὁδηγός Μουσείου Θηβῶν. Athens.

Kavvadias, Pavlos. 1912. Λογοδοσία τοῦ συμβουλίου. *Praktika,* passim.

Kayser, Bernard, and Kenneth Thompson.

1964. *Economic and Social Atlas of Greece.* Athens: National Statistic Service of Greece.

Keramopoullos, Antonios. 1907. Λείψανα τοῦ τείχους τῆς Καδμείας. *Ephemeris,* 205-208.

———1909A. Ἡ οἰκία τοῦ Κάδμου. *Ephemeris,* 57-122.

———1909B. Δεύτεραι φροντίδες. *Bulletin de correspondance hellénique* 33:440-442.

———1910A. Ἀνασκαφαὶ τάφων ἐν Θήβαις. *Praktika,* 152-158.

———1910B. Μυκηναϊκοὶ τάφοι ἐν Αἰγίνῃ καὶ ἐν Θήβαις. *Ephemeris,* 209-252.

———1911. Ἀνασκαφή τοῦ ἀνακτόρου τοῦ Κάδμου. *Praktika,* 143-152.

———1912. Ἀνασκαφή τοῦ ἀνακτόρου τοῦ Κάδμου. *Praktika,* 85-87.

———1917. Θηβαϊκά. *Deltion* 3:1-503.

———1918. Θηβαϊκά Εὐριπείδια. *Ephemeris;* 60-65.

———1920. Εἰκόνες πολεμιστῶν τῆς ἐν Δηλίῳ μάχης. *Ephemeris,* 1-36.

———1921. Ἀνασκαφή τοῦ ἀνακτόρου τοῦ Κάδμου. *Praktika,* 32-34.

———1922. Ἀνασκαφή τοῦ ἀνακτόρου τοῦ Κάδμου. *Praktika,* 28-31.

———1926. Παλαιαὶ χριστιανικαὶ καὶ βυζαντιακαὶ ταφαὶ ἐν Θήβαις. *Deltion* 10:124-136.

———1927A. Ἀνασκαφή τοῦ ἀνακτόρου τοῦ Κάδμου. *Praktika,* 32-44.

———1927B. Ἡ Μινωϊκή-Μυκηναϊκή θρησκεία καὶ ἡ ἐπιβίωσις αὐτῆς ἐν τῇ ἑλληνικῇ θρησκείᾳ. *Πρακτικά τῆς Ἀκαδημίας Ἀθηνῶν,* 423-435.

———1928. Ἀνασκαφαὶ τοῦ Καδμείου ἀνακτόρου. *Praktika,* 42-52.

———1929. Ἀνασκαφαὶ Θηβῶν. *Praktika,* 60-63.

———1930A. Αἱ βιομηχανίαι καὶ τὸ ἐμπόριον τοῦ Κάδμου. *Ephemeris,* 29-58.

———1930B. Lichtschächte in festlandischen mykenischen Palästen. In *Bericht über die Hundertjahrfeier,* 252-253. Berlin: Gruyter.

———1930C. Ἀνασκαφαὶ ἐν Θήβαις. *Praktika,* 69-74.

———1931. Ἀνάθημα [Κορω]νέων ἐν Θήβαις· ὁ Λεύκιος Μόμμιος ἐν Βοιωτίᾳ. *Deltion* 13:105-118.

———1935. Ἐπιγραφαὶ ἐκ Βοιωτίας. *Ephemeris,* Chronika 1-16.

———1936. Ἐπιγραφαὶ ἐκ Βοιωτίας. *Ephemeris,* Chronika 23-47.

———1941. Θηβαϊκόν χαλκοῦν ἔλασμα. In *Ἐπιτύμβιον Χρήστου Τσούντα, Ἀρχεῖον Θρακικοῦ Γλωσσικοῦ καὶ Λαογραφικοῦ Θησαυροῦ* 6:519-523.

Kilian, Klaus. 1978. Ausgrabungen in Tiryns 1976. *Archäologischer Anzeiger* 93:449-470.

———1979. Ausgrabungen in Tiryns 1977. *Archäologischer Anzeiger* 94:379-411.

Kilinski, Karl. 1974. *Boeotian Black-figure Vase-painting of the Archaic Period.* Diss., University of Missouri at Columbia. Ann Arbor: University Microfilms 75-20131.

———1977. Boeotian Black-figure lekanai by the Protome and Triton Painters. *American Journal of Archaeology* 81:55-65.

———1978A. The Boeotian dancers group. *American Journal of Archaeology* 82:173-191.

———1978B. The Istanbul Painter. *Antike Kunst* 21:12-16.

Kirk, G. S. 1970. *The Bacchae of Euripides.* Cambridge: Cambridge University Press.

Kominis, Athanasios. 1968. Ἐπισκοπικοὶ κατάλογοι Θηβῶν. Ἐπετηρίς Ἑταιρείας Στερεοελλαδικῶν Μελετῶν, vol. 1.

Körte, G. 1878. Die antike Skulpturen aus Boeotien. *Athenische Mitteilungen des deutschen archäologischen Instituts* 3:301-422.

———1879. Bemerkungen zu den antiken Skulpturen aus Boeotien. *Athenische Mitteilungen des deutschen archäologischen Instituts* 4:268-276.

Koumanoudis, Stephanos. 1970. Ἐκ τοῦ Μουσείου Θηβῶν. *Deltion* 25A:126-142.

———1979. Θηβαϊκή Προσωπογραφία. Athens: Archaeological Society of Athens.

Krauskopf, Ingrid. 1974. *Der thebanische Sagenkreis und andere griechische Sagen in der etruskischen Kunst.* Mainz: Zabern.

Kurtz, Donna C., and John Boardman. 1971. *Greek Burial Customs.* Ithaca, New York: Cornell University Press.

LaCroix, Leon. 1958. Le bouclier emblème des Béotiens. *Revue belge de philologie et d' histoire,* 5-30.

Langlotz, Ernst. 1927. *Frühgriechische Bildhauerschulen.* Nürnberg: E. Fromann.

Larsen, J. A. O. 1955. The Boeotian Confederacy and fifth-century oligarchic theory. *Transactions of the American Philosophical Society* 86:40-50.

———1968. *Greek Federal States: their Institutions and History.* Oxford: at the Clarendon Press.

Leake, William M. 1835. *Travels in Northern Greece,* vol. 2. London.

Legras, Léon. 1905. *Les légendes thébaines dans l' epopée et la tragédie grecques.* Paris.

Lorimer, H. L. 1950. *Homer and the Monuments.* London: MacMillan.

McArthur, John T. 1978. Inconsistencies in the composition and provenance studies of the inscribed jars found at Thebes. *Archaeometry* 20:177-182.

McArthur, John, and Jennifer McArthur. 1974. The Theban stirrup-jars and East Crete: further considerations. *Minos* 15:68-80.

McCarter, P. Kyle. 1975. *The Antiquity of the Greek Alphabet and the Early Phoenician Scripts.* Missoula, Montana: Scholar Press.

McDonald, William A. 1967. *Progress into the Past; the Rediscovery of Mycenaean Civilization.* Bloomington, Indiana: The Indiana University Press.

McDonald, William A., and George R. Rapp, Jr., eds. *The Minnesota Messenia Expedition: Reconstructing a Bronze Age Environment.* Minneapolis: University of Minnesota Press.

Maffre, Jean-Jacques. 1975. Colléction Paul Canellopoulos: vases béotiens. *Bulletin de correspondance hellénique* 99:409-520.

Martin, Roland. 1965. *Manuel d' architecture grecque.* Part 1: "matériaux et techniques." Paris: A. & J. Picard.

Michell, Humphrey. 1940. *The Econom-*

ics of Ancient Greece. Cambridge: Cambridge University Press.

Miller, William. 1921. *Essays on the Latin Orient*. Cambridge: Cambridge University Press.

Mitsopoulos, Konstantinos. 1894. Die Erdbeben von Theben und Lokris in den Jahren 1893 und 1894. *Petermanns geographische Mitteilungen*, 217-227.

Mollard-Besques, Simone. 1954. *Catalogue raisonné des figurines et reliefs en terre-cuite grecs, étrusques et romains du Louvre*, vol. 1. Paris: Éditions des Musées Nationaux.

Mommsen, August. 1878. *Delphika*. Leipzig.

Mozley, J. H. 1928. *Statius*. New York: The Loeb Classical Library.

Mylonas, George. 1928. Ἡ νεολιθική ἐποχή ἐν Ἑλλάδι. Athens: Archaeological Society of Athens.

———1962A. Ἡ ἀκρόπολις τῶν Μυκηνῶν· οἱ περίβολοι, αἱ πύλαι, καὶ αἱ ἄνοδοι. *Ephemeris*, 1-199.

———1962B. Τὰ Μυκηναϊκὰ ἔθιμα ταφῆς. Ἐπιστημονικὴ Ἐπετηρὶς τῆς Φιλοσοφικῆς Σχολῆς τοῦ Πανεπιστημίου Ἀθηνῶν, 291-356.

———1966. *Mycenae and the Mycenaean Age*. Princeton: Princeton University Press.

Myres, John. 1930. *Who Were the Greeks? Sather Classical Lectures*, vol. 6. Berkeley: University of California Press.

Naveh, Joseph. 1973. Some Semitic epigraphic considerations on the antiquity of the Greek alphabet. *American Journal of Archaeology* 77:1-8.

Nilsson, Martin. 1950. *The Minoan-Mycenaean Religion and its Survival in Greek Religion*. 2d ed. Lund: Gleerup.

Nisetich, Frank J. 1980. *Pindar's Victory Songs*. Baltimore: Johns Hopkins University Press.

Noack, F. 1894. Arne. *Athenische Mitteilungen des deutschen archäologischen Instituts* 19:405-485.

Notopoulos, James. 1960. Homer, Hesiod, and the Achaean heritage of oral poetry. *Hesperia* 29:177-197.

Orlandos, Anastasios. 1939A. Γλυπτὰ τοῦ Μουσείου Θηβῶν. Ἀρχεῖον τῶν Βυζαντινῶν Μνημείων τῆς Ἑλλάδος 5:119-143.

———1939B. Ἡ Ἁγία Φωτεινὴ τῶν Θηβῶν. Ἀρχεῖον τῶν Βυζαντινῶν Μνημείων τῆς Ἑλλάδος 5:144-147.

Overbeck, Johannes. 1868. *Die antiken Schriftquellen zur Geschichte der bildenden Künste bei den Griechen*. Leipzig.

Pagidas, Georgios. 1882. *Τὰ τῆς τοπογραφίας τῶν ἑπταπύλων Θηβῶν*. Athens.

Palmer, Leonard R. 1972. Mycenaean inscribed vases II: the Mainland finds. *Kadmos* 11:27-46.

Pappadakis, Nikolaos. 1911. Ἀνασκαφαὶ τάφων ἐν Βοιωτίᾳ. *Praktika*, 132-142.

———1919. Μικραὶ σκαφαὶ. *Deltion* 5, Parartema 33-34.

———1923. Ἐκ Βοιωτίας. *Deltion* 8:182-256.

Paton, James M. 1951. *Chapters on Medieval and Renaissance Visitors to Greek Lands*. Princeton: American School of Classical Studies at Athens.

Payne, Humphrey G. G. 1931. *Necroco-rinthia; a Study of Corinthian Art in the Archaic Period.* Oxford: Claren-don Press.

Pelon, Olivier. 1976. *Tholoi, tumuli et cir-cles funéraires.* Paris: Boccard.

Pernier, Luigi, and Luisa Banti. 1951. *Il palazzo minoico di Festos, II, Il se-condo palazzo.* Rome: Libreria dello Stato.

Philios, D. 1897. Προϊστορικοὶ τάφοι παρὰ τὰς Θήβας. *Praktika,* 94-104.

Philippart, H. 1922. Pausanias à Thèbes. *Revue de l' université de Bruxelles,* 140-157.

Philippson, Alfred. 1951. *Die griechischen Landschaften,* vol. I, part 2. Frank-furt a. M.: V. Klostermann.

Platon, Nikolaos, and Evi Touloupa. 1964. Oriental seals from the palace of Cad-mus: unique discoveries in Boeotian Thebes. *Illustrated London News* (Nov. 28):859-861.

———1964B. Ivories and Linear B from Thebes. *Illustrated London News* (Dec. 5):896-897.

Pollard, John. 1977. *Birds in Greek Life and Myth.* London: Thames & Hud-son.

Pollitt, Jerome J. 1965. *The Art of Greece 1400-31 B.C., Sources and Docu-ments.* Englewood Cliffs, New Jersey: Prentice Hall.

———1976. The ethos of Polygnotos and Aristeides. In *In Memoriam Otto J. Brendel,* edited by L. Bonfante and H. von Heintze, 49-54. Mainz: Za-bern.

Popham, Mervyn R., ed. 1980. *Lefkandi I, The Iron Age; the Settlement and Cemeteries.* London: Thames & Hudson.

Popham, Mervyn R., and L. H. Sackett, eds. 1968. *Excavations at Lefkandi, Euboea 1964-1966.* London: Thames & Hudson.

Porada, Edith. 1965. Cylinder seals from Thebes. *American Journal of Archae-ology* 69:173.

———1966. Further notes on the cylin-ders from Thebes. *American Journal of Archaeology* 70:194.

———1981. The cylinder seals found at Thebes in Boiotia, with contributions on the inscriptions from Hans G. Gü-terbock and John A. Brinkman. *Ar-chiv für Orientforschung* 28:1-78.

Pritchett, William K. 1965, 1969. *Studies in Greek Topography,* pars 1 and 2. Berkeley: University of California Press.

Raison, Jacques. 1968. *Les vases à inscrip-tions peintes de l' âge mycénien et leur contexte archéologique.* Rome: Cen-tro di Studi Micenei.

———1977. La Cadmée, Knossos et le li-néaire B; à propos de plusiers ouv-rages ou articles recents et d' un livre de S. Syméonoglou. *Revue archéolo-gique,* 79-86.

Raubitschek, Anthony E. 1949. *Dedica-tions from the Athenian Akropolis.* Cambridge, Mass.: Archaeological Institute of America.

Renfrew, Colin. 1967. Cycladic metal-lurgy and the Aegean Early Bronze Age. *American Journal of Archaeol-ogy* 71:1-26.

———1972. *The Emergence of Civiliza-tion; the Cyclades and the Aegean in* the Third Millennium B.C. New York: Barnes & Noble.

———1978. The Mycenaean sanctuary at Phylakopi. *Antiquity* 52:7-15.

Renfrew, Jane M. 1973. *Palaeoethnobotany; the Prehistoric Food Plants of the Near East and Europe.* New York: Columbia University Press.

Reusch, Helga. 1948. Der Frauenfries von Theben. *Archäologischer Anzeiger* 63-64:240-253.

———1953. Ein Schildfresco aus Theben, *Archäologischer Anzeiger* 69:16-25.

———1955. Die zeichnerische Rekonstruktion des Frauenfrieses im böotischen Theben. *Abhandlungen der deutschen Akademie der Wisseschaften zu Berlin, Klasse für Sprachen, Literatur und Kunst,* Jahrgang 1955: no. 1.

———1957. Ein Frauenfries der kretisch-mykenischen Epoche aus dem böotischen Theben. *Forschungen und Fortschritte* 31:82-87.

Richter, Gisela M. A. 1960. *Kouroi; Archaic Greek Youths.* London: Phaidon.

———1966. *The Furniture of the Greeks, Etruscans, and Romans.* London: Phoidon.

Ridder, A. de. 1984. Fouilles de Gha [Gla]. *Bulletin de correspondance hellénique* 18:271-310.

Ridgway, Brunilde S. 1977. *The Archaic Style in Greek Sculpture.* Princeton: Princeton University Press.

Robert, Carl. 1894. *Die griechische Heldensage.* Berlin: Weidmann.

———1909. *Pausanias als Schriftsteller; Studien und Beobachtungen,* Berlin: Weidmann.

———1915. *Oidipus; Geschichte eines poetischen Stoffs im griechischen Altertum,* volumes 1 and 2. Berlin: Weidmann.

Robert, Louis. 1977. Les fêtes de Dionysos à Thèbes et l' amphiktionie. *Ephemeris,* 195-210.

Roberts, W. R. 1895. *Ancient Boeotians: their Character and Culture, and their Reputation.* Cambridge: Cambridge University Press.

Rocchi, Maria. 1978. Po-ti-ni-ja e Demeter Thesmophoros a Tebe. *Studi Micenei ed Egeo-Anatolici* 19:63-67.

Roesch, Paul. 1965A. *Thespies et la Confédération béotienne.* Paris: Boccard.

———1965B. Notes d' épigraphie béotienne. *Revue de Philologie* 39:252-265.

———1970. Inscriptions béotiennes. *Bulletin de correspondance hellénique* 94:139-160.

———1972. Pouvoir fédéral et vie économique des cités dans la Béotie hellénistique. *Vestigia, Beiträge zur alten Geschichte* 17:259-270.

———1975. Les Herakleia de Thèbes. *Zeitschrift für Papyrologie und Epigraphik* 17:1-7.

Ross, Ludwig. 1851. *Wanderungen in Griechenland im Gefolge des Königs Otto.* Halle.

Rutter, Jeremy. 1974. Review of Symeonoglou 1973. *American Journal of Archaeology* 78:88-89.

Sacconi, Anna. 1974. *Corpus delle iscrizioni vascolari in Lineare B.* Rome: Ateneo.

Salmon, Paul. 1953. L' armée fédérale des Béotiens. *L' antiquité classique* 22: 347-360.

Salviat, François, and Claude Vatin. 1971. *Inscriptions de Grèce centrale*. Paris: Boccard.

Sandars, N. K. 1963. Later Aegean bronze swords. *American Journal of Archaeology* 67:117-153.

Schachermeyr, Fritz. 1971. Forschungen zur ägäischen Frühzeit. *Archäologischer Anzeiger* 86:387-419.

Schachter, Albert. 1967A. The Theban wars. *Phoenix* 21:1-10.

———1967B. A Boeotian cult-type. *Bulletin of the Institute of Classical Studies* 14:1-16.

———1973. The Boiotian Herakles. In the *Proceedings of the Second International Conference on Boiotian Antiquities* (held in Montreal), 37-43.

———1979. The tomb of Hector at Thebes, paper presented at the *Third International Conference on Boiotian Antiquities* (held in Montreal, not yet published).

Schefold, Karl. 1966. *Myth and Legend in Early Greek Art.* New York: Abrams.

Schild-Xenidou, W. 1972. *Boiotische Grab- und Weihreliefs archaischer und klassischer Zeit.* Diss., Munich.

Schläger, Helmut, David Blackman, and Jörg Schäfer. 1968. Der Hafen von Anthedon mit Beiträgen zur Topographie und Geschichte der Stadt. *Archäologischer Anzeiger* 83:21-102.

Schlumberger, George. 1889. Sceaux byzantins inédits. *Revue des études grecques* 2:245-259.

Schmaltz, Bernard. 1974. *Terrakotten aus dem Kabirenheiligtum bei Theben.* Berlin: Gruyter.

Schober, F. 1934. Thebai, Topographie und Geschichte. In *Real Encyclopädie* vol. V, part A2, 1423-1492.

Scoufopoulos, Niki. 1971. *Mycenaean Citadels.* In *Studies in Mediteranean Archaeology* 22. Göteborg: Åström Förlag.

SEG. Supplementum Epigraphicum Graecum.

Shaw, Joseph W. 1973. *Minoan Architecture: Materials and Techniques.* In *Annuario della Scuola Archeologica di Atene e delle Missioni Italiane in Oriente* 49 (1971):1-256.

Simon, Erica. 1957. Beobachtungen zum Apollon Philesios des Kanachos. In *Charites für Ernst Langlotz,* edited by K. Schauenburg, 38-46. Bonn: Athenaeum.

Sinos, Stefan. 1971. *Die vorklassischen Hausformen in der Ägäis.* Mainz: Zabern.

Six, J. 1913. Myron de Thèbes. *Bulletin de correspondance hellénique* 37:359-377.

Skouphos, T. G. 1894. Die zwei grossen Erdbeben in Lokris. *Zeitschrift der Gesellschaft für Erdkunde zu Berlin,* 409-474.

Small, Jocelyn. 1972. *Studies Related to the Theban Cycle on Late Etruscan Funerary Urns.* Diss., Princeton University.

Smith, E. Baldwin. 1942. The Megaron and its roof. *American Journal of Archaeology* 46:99-118.

Smith, Nicole M. F. 1974. *Le cycle de Thèbes dans la literature française des origines à la revolution.* Diss., University of Nebraska at Lincoln. Ann Arbor: University Microfilms 74-23944.

Snodgrass, Anthony M. 1971. *The Dark Age of Greece: an Archaeological Survey of the Eleventh to the Eighth Centuries B.C.* Edinburgh: Edinburgh University Press.

———1975. Review of Symeonoglou 1973. *Gnomon* 47:313-316.

Sodini, Jean-Pierre. 1970. Mosaiques paléochrétiennes de Grèce. *Bulletin de correspondance hellénique* 94:699-753.

Soteriades, Georgios. 1900. Περί τῆς τοπογραφίας τῶν ἀρχαίων Θηβῶν. *Φιλολογικός Σύλλογος Παρνασσός, Ἐπετηρίς* 4:140-170.

———1914. Περί τῆς τοπογραφίας τῶν ἀρχαίων Θηβῶν. 2d ed. Athens.

Soteriou, Georgios. 1924. Ὁ ἐν Θήβαις Βυζαντινός ναός Γρηγορίου τοῦ Θεολόγου. *Ephemeris*, 1-26.

Sparkes, Brian A. 1967. The taste of a Boeotian pig. *Journal of Hellenic Studies* 87:116-130.

Spon, Jacob. 1678-1680. *Voyage d' Italie, de Dalmatie, de Grèce et du Levant fait en années 1675 et 1676*, vols. 1-3. Lyons.

Spyropoulos, Theodoros. 1970. The discovery of the palace archives of Boeotian Thebes. *Kadmos* 9:170-172.

———1975. See Chadwick 1975.

Strzygowski, J. 1894. Inedita der Architektur und Plastik aus der Zeit Basileios I (867-886). *Byzantinische Zeitschrift* 3:1-16.

Stubbings, Frank H. 1973. The rise of Mycenaean civilization. In *Cambridge Ancient History*, 3d. ed., vol. 2, part 1, 627-658.

———1975. The expansion of the Mycenaean civilization. In *Cambridge Ancient History*, 3d. ed., vol. 2, part 2, 165-187.

Symeonoglou, Sarantis. 1972. Thebes, Greece: an archaeological and sociological problem. *Architectura* 2:81-91.

———1973. *Kadmeia I: Mycenaean Finds from Thebes, Greece.* In *Studies in Mediterranean Archaeology*, vol. 35. Göteborg: Åström Förlag.

Svoronos, Nikolaos. 1959. *Recherches sur le cadastre byzantin et la fiscalité aux XI et XII siècles; le cadastre de Thèbes.* Athens: École Française.

Tataris, Athanasios, Georgios Kounis, and Nikolaos Marangoudakis. 1970. *Geological Map of Greece, Thebes Sheet.* Athens: Greek Institute of Geology.

Taylour, Lord William. 1970. New Light on Mycenaean Religion. *Antiquity* 44:270-280.

Theochari, Maria. 1962. Δοκιμαστική σκαφή εἰς Χασάμπαλι Λαρίσης. *Θεσσαλικὰ* 4:35-50.

Thompson, Homer. 1937. Buildings on the west side of the Agora. *Hesperia* 6:1-226.

———1968. Activity in the Athenian Agora. *Hesperia* 37:36-72.

Threpsiadis, Ioannis. 1955. Ἀνασκαφαὶ ἐν Ἄρνῃ Κωπαίδος. *Praktika*, 121-124.

——1958. Ἀνασκαφαὶ Ἄρνης (Γκλᾶ) τῆς Κωπαΐδος. *Praktika*, 38-42.

——1960. Ἀνασκαφαὶ Ἄρνης (Γκλᾶ) τῆς Κωπαΐδος. *Praktika*, 23-38.

——1963. Ἡ ἐπανέκθεσις τοῦ μουσείου Θηβῶν. *Ephemeris*, Chronika 5-16.

Touloupa, Evi. 1964. Bericht über die Ausgrabungen in Theben. *Kadmos* 3:25-27.

Travlos, Ioannis. 1960. *Πολεοδομικὴ ἐξέλιξις τῶν Ἀθηνῶν*. Athens.

——1971. *Pictorial Dictionary of Ancient Athens*. New York: Praeger.

Tsevas, Georgios. 1928. Ἡ ἱστορία τῶν Θηβῶν καὶ τῆς Βοιωτίας. Athens.

Turner, J., and J. R. A. Greig. 1974. Some pollen diagrams from Greece and their archaeological significance. *Journal of Archaeological Science* 1:177-194.

Ulrichs, Heinrich N. 1840 and 1863. *Reisen und Forschungen in Griechenland*. Part 1, Bremen; part 2: Berlin: Weidmann.

Unger, Robert. 1839. *Thebana Paradoxa*. Halle.

Ure, Anne D. 1932. Boeotian Orientalizing lekanae. *Metropolitan Museum Studies* 4:18-38.

Ure, Anne D., and Percy N. Ure. 1933. Boeotian vases in the Akademisches Kunstmuseum in Bonn. *Archäologischer Anzeiger* 48:1-42.

Ure, Percy N. 1910. Excavations at Rhitsona in Boeotia. *Journal of Hellenic Studies* 30:336-356.

——1913. *Black Glaze Pottery from Rhitsona in Boeotia*. Oxford: Oxford University Press.

——1927A. *Boeotian Pottery of the Geometric and Archaic Styles*. Paris: Classification des céramiques antiques, no. 12 (Paris).

——ed. 1927B. *Sixth and Fifth Century Pottery from Excavations made at Rhitsona*. Oxford: Oxford University Press.

——1934. *Aryballoi and Figurines from Rhitsona in Boeotia*. Cambridge: Cambridge University Press.

Valmin, Nathan. 1938. *The Swedish Expedition to Messenia*. Lund: Gleerup.

Van Buren, E. Douglas. 1926. *Greek Fictile Revetments in the Archaic Period*. London: J. Murray.

Vasileiou, Antonios. 1967. Αἱ Θῆβαι τοῦ Μεσαίωνος· Ἅγιος Ἰωάννης ὁ Καλοκτένης καὶ ἡ ἐποχὴ του. Thebes.

——1972. Ἡ "Μεγάλη Παναγία" ἐν Θήβαις. Thebes.

Vermeule, Emily. 1964. *Greece in the Bronze Age*. Chicago: The University of Chicago Press.

——1971. Kadmos and the Dragon. In *Studies Presented to G. M. A. Hanfmann*, edited by D. G. Mitten, J. G. Pedley, and J. A. Scott, 177-188. Cambridge, Mass.: Fogg Art Museum.

Wace, Alan J. B. 1932. *Chamber Tombs at Mycenae*. In *Archaeologia* 82 (London).

Waiblinger, Angelica. 1974. *Corpus Vasorum Antiquorum*, France 26, Louvre 17. Paris: Boccard.

Wallace, Paul. 1969. *Commentary on Strabo's Description of Boiotia*. Diss., Indiana University. Ann Arbor,

Michigan: University Microfilms 70-7514.

———1973. The dikes in the Kopais. In the *Proceedings of the Second International Conference on Boiotian Antiquities* (held in Montreal), edited by John M. Fossey and Albert Schachter, 7-9. Montreal, 1979.

Weil, Henri, ed. 1903. *Aischylos' Ἑπτὰ ἐπὶ Θήβας*. Leipzig.

Weinberg, Saul S. 1965. The relative chronology of the Aegean in the Stone and Early Bronze Ages. In R. W. Ehrich, *Chronologies in Old World Archaeology*, 285-320. Chicago: The University of Chicago Press.

Wellenstein, Klaus. 1973. *Corpus Vasorum Antiquorum*, Germany 36, Tübingen 1. Munich: C. H. Beck.

Wheler, George. 1723. *Voyage de Dalmatie, de Grèce et du Levant*. Amsterdam.

Wickersham, John, and Gerald Verbrugghe. 1973. *Greek Historical Documents, the Fourth Century B.C.* Toronto: Hakkert.

Wide, Sam. 1899. Geometrische Vasen aus Griechenland. *Jahrbuch des deutschen archäologischen Instituts* 14:26-43, 78-86.

Wilamowitz-Möllendorff, Ulrich von. 1891. Die sieben Tore Thebens. *Hermes* 26:191-242.

———1895. *Euripides Herakles*, 2d ed. Berlin: Weidmann.

———1922. *Pindaros*. Berlin: Weidmann.

Williams, R. T. 1958. Early Greek ships of two levels. *Journal of Hellenic Studies* 78:121-130.

Wilson, A. L. 1976. The provenance of the inscribed stirrup-jars found at Thebes. *Archaeometry* 18:51-58.

Wolters, Paul. 1892. Βοιωτικαὶ ἀρχαιότητες. *Ephemeris*, 213-240.

Wolters, Paul, and Gerda Bruns. 1940. *Das Kabirenheiligtum bei Theben*. Berlin: Gruyter.

Wycherley, R. E. 1969. *How the Greeks Built Cities*. Garden City, New York: Anchor.

Young, Rodney S. 1969. Old Phrygian inscriptions from Gordion, toward a history of the Phrygian alphabet. *Hesperia* 38:252-296.

Ziehen, L. 1934. Thebai, Kulte. In *Real Encyclopädie*, vol. V, A2, 1492-1553.

INDICES

GENERAL

ANCIENT SOURCES

Map B. The Kadmeia

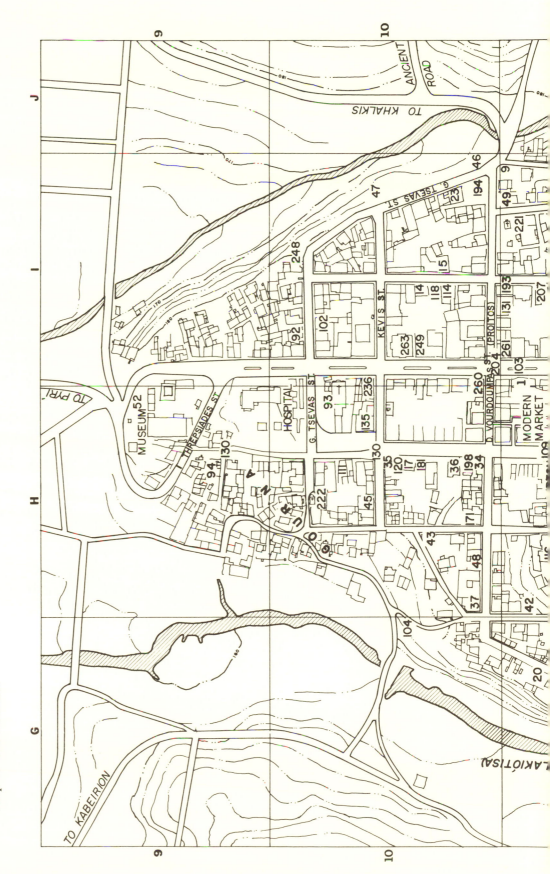

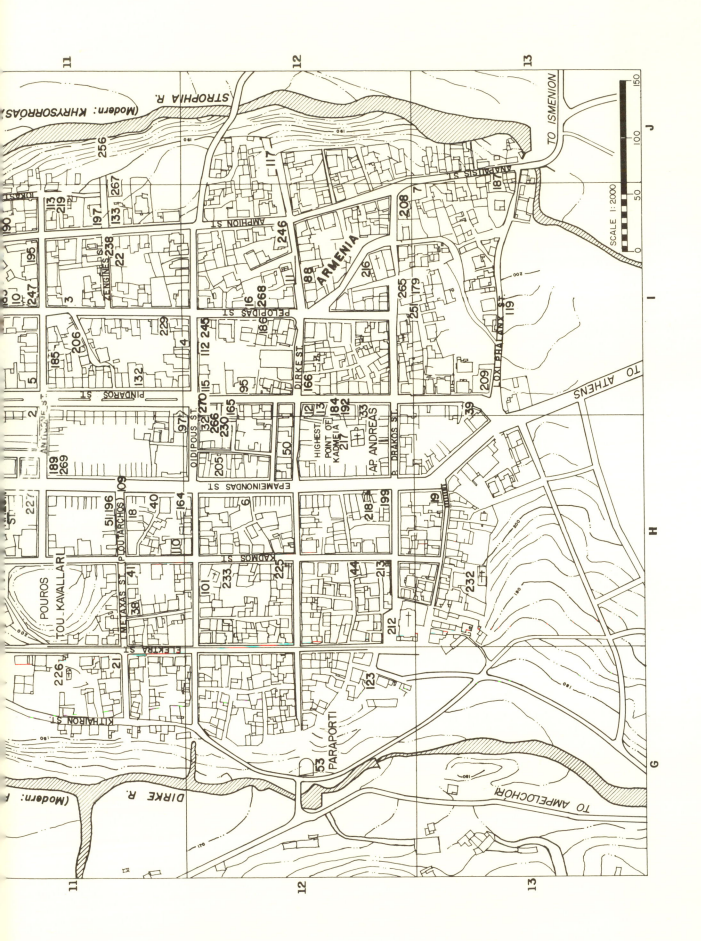

PLATES

1. Aerial view of Thebes: *1*, Kadmeia; *2*, Pyri; *3*, railroad station; *4*, Plain of Thebes; *5*, Palaios and Neos Synoikismos; *6*, Agioi Theodoroi; *7*, eastern limit of Classical Thebes; *8*, Moschopodi River; *9*, barren hills east of Thebes.

2. Aerial view of the Kadmeia (north is upper right): *1*, Dirke River; *2*, Kynos Kephalai, area of the house of Pindar; *3*, Pouros hill; *4*, hill of Apostolos Andreas, highest point of the Kadmeia; *5*, city hall, site of Byzantine Cathedral; *6*, second Mycenaean palace; *7*, first Mycenaean palace; *8*, Agios Georgios (site 93); *9*, Museum and Frankish tower; *10*, Panagia, modern Cathedral; *11*, Elektrai gates; *12*, road to Chalkis and site of Proitides gates; *13*, Oionoskopeion of Teiresias.

3. Aerial view of Thebes: *1*, Kadmeia; *2*, Amphion hill; *3*, Strophia River; *4*, Palaios Synoikismos; *5*, Thebes high school at Mikro Kastelli; *6*, ancient road to Chalkis; *7*, Megalo Kastelli; *8*, Ismenos River; *9*, Oidipodia spring (site 244); *10*, Agioi Theodoroi; *11*, eastern limit of Classical Thebes.

4. Aerial view of Thebes from the northeast: *1*, Kadmeia; *2*, Neos Synoikismos; *3*, Palaios Synoikismos; *4*, Amphion hill (site 121); *5*, Tachy (ancient Potniai); 6, Agioi Theodoroi; 7, Kastellia hills.

5. Aerial view of Thebes from the northeast: *1*, Frankish tower and Museum (site 52); *2*, church of Agios Georgios (site 93); *3*, area of first Mycenaean palace (site 1); *4*, elementary school of Palaios Synoikismos (area of ancient theater); *5*, Thebes high school (site 25); *6*, Ismenion hill (site 8); *7*, Kolonaki hill (site 24).

6. The Kadmeia and eastern Thebes from the northeast: *1*, area of first Mycenaean palace (site 1); *2*, courthouse; *3*, city hall, main area of second Mycenaean palace; *4*, area of Proitides gates (site 9); *5*, area of Oionoskopeion of Teiresias (site 23); *6*, Chrysorroas River (ancient Strophia); *7*, Thebes high school; *8*, monumental Mycenaean tomb (site 254).

7. The Kadmeia and Kolonaki from the northeast: *1*, city hall (site 270); *2*, church of Panagia (site 216); *3*, chapel of Agios Stephanos (site 219); *4*, chapel of Agios Georgios (site 221); *5*, area of Elektrai gates (site 7); *6*, Kolonaki hill (site 24).

8. The southern part of the Kadmeia and Kolonaki: *1*, church of Panagia, Cathedral of modern Thebes (site 216); *2*, church of Apostolos Andreas (site 217); highest point of the Kadmeia; *3*, church of Agios Nikolaos (behind trees), possible area of oracle of Amphiaraos (site 215); *4*, road to Athens; *5*, road to Tachy; *6*, bridge and crossroads of ancient Thebes.

9. View of the Kadmeia from the southwest (1970): *1*, church of Agios Demetrios (site 212); *2*, church of Metamorphosis Soteros (site 232); *3*, highest point of the Kadmeia (site 217); *4*, Pouros tou Kavallari, highest point of the west-central part of the Kadmeia; *5*, Paraporti spring (ancient Dirke, site 53), barely visible behind the trees. The Plakiotissa River (ancient Dirke) is just in front of the spring.

10. View of the Kadmeia from the southeast (1970): *1*, church of Panagia, modern Cathedral (site 216); *2*, highest point of the Kadmeia (site 217); *3*, area of Elektrai gates; *4*, modern bridge over the Chrysorroas River (ancient Strophia), and road to the sanctuary of Apollo Ismenios.

11. The crossroads of Thebes from the northwest. The road to the left leads to Plataiai and Athens, the one to the right to Potniai (modern Tachy).

12. The excavated remains of the first Mycenaean palace, from the south (site 1). The two-storey house was built shortly after 1900, the apartment building behind it in the late 1960s (site 260).

13. Site 2 during excavation. The second Mycenaean palace is in the extreme lower left corner; a Classical building is in the foreground and within it the remains of the Early Helladic III apsidal building; the Frankish palace is at the upper left.

14. The foundations of the second Mycenaean palace. The massive foundations are over 2 m high. The floor belongs to the basement, where a treasury of objects was found in 1963.

15. Site 2, looking south. *Foreground*, massive foundations of Frankish palace; *center*, second Mycenaean palace; *upper center*, early twentieth-century house; *upper left*, three-storey courthouse.

16. Site 2, looking north. *Bottom*, second Mycenaean palace; *center*, Frankish palace with hypocaustum. The site of the first Mycenaean palace is beyond the hypocaustum (cf. pl. 12).

17. Site 9. The poorly preserved remains of the Mycenaean Cyclopean wall are in the middle foreground.

18. Site 8, showing the poorly preserved remains of the west side of the temple of Apollo Ismenios.

19. Site 7, the Elektrai gates, the east circular tower. As many as seven courses are preserved.

20. Site 7, the Elektrai gates; the west circular tower from the south. In the background are two early twentieth-century houses without plaster, showing the stone construction. Much of the stone was taken from ancient ruins.

21. Site 68, a well-preserved portion of a Classical building. Many such walls exist in this area. The ancient theater was nearby.

22. Site 242, a portion of conduit *B* of the Classical aqueduct of Thebes (cf. fig. 3.8). Some water is allowed to flow to the nearby farms and the flour mill at Agios Loukas.

23. Site 242, another portion of conduit *B*.

24. Site 53, the Paraporti spring (ancient Dirke). The Dirke River flows in front of it. The church of Agios Demetrios (site 212) is at the upper right (cf. pl. 9).

25–26. Site 53, the Paraporti spring.

27. Site 240, a footbridge southeast of Thebes.

28. Site 241, a footbridge near site 240.

29. Epaminondas St., east side. This row of houses and shops remains as it was early in this century; it occupies the site of the second Mycenaean palace (view from site 18).

30. Epaminondas St., west side. This row of shops is beyond Antigone St., across from the central market (view from site 189).

31. Antigone St., with the small hill, Pouros tou Kavallari. The Kadmeia slopes sharply towards Gourna to the right (north) of this place (cf. pl. 32).

32. Kadmos St., looking north from Pouros tou Kavallari. The location, Gourna, is at the end of the street.

33. Antigone St., looking east from site 185. The Kadmeia slopes sharply towards the Strophia stream here.

34. Epaminondas St., looking south from Dirke St. (near site 50). A neoclassical style house is on the right; the modern church of Agia Aikaterini (site 218) is on the left.

35. 71 Kadmos St., a typical nineteenth-century style house: whitewashed, one-storey, with storage basement, tile roof, fruit trees, and flowers.

36. 84 Pindar St. This house was built in the late 1930s on Mycenaean ruins, perhaps of the first Mycenaean palace (site 261).

37. 86 Pindar St., neoclassical house.

38. The National Bank of Greece. This imposing structure on Pindar St. (site 263) was constructed in the late 1920s.

39. The Oidipodia spring (site 244) at Agioi Theodoroi. It was built in 1902.
The water wheel in the background belongs to a flour mill.

40. An outdoor cafe at Agioi Theodoroi.

41. Epaminondas St., looking
north during the festival of the
Vlachikos Gamos. The picture
was taken in 1966.

42. The church of Agios Demetrios (site 212), looking west from site 213.

43. The church of Panagia, currently the Cathedral of Thebes (site 216). There are six Corinthian capitals inside it.

44. Chapel of Agios Vasileios (site 11). Byzantine sculptures from the original church of Agios Gregorios are incorporated in the east wall.

45. The chapel of Agios Georgios (site 221).

46. The chapel of Agios Demetrios (site 226).

47. The chapel of Agios Charalampos (site 213).

48. The church of Agios Nikolaos (site 215), located in a depression. The Strophia stream is beyond the church, and the road to Athens, beyond the trees.

49. The church of Agia Photini (site 83) from the east, as restored by Anastasios Orlandos. The entrance (west side) is on the other side of the building (cf. pl. 53).

50. Agia Photini (site 83). In front of the entrance (west side) are the excavated remains of the narthex, with ancient masonry and architectural marbles on the ground.

51. The church of Agioi Theodoroi (site 220) from the south. It is surrounded by the old houses of low-income inhabitants.

52. The chapel of Agia Paraskevi (site 224) located in a cemetery that is no longer used.

53. The chapel of Agios Menas (site 231), which may have been a Mycenaean chamber tomb.

LIBRARY OF CONGRESS CATALOGING IN PUBLICATION DATA

Symeonoglou, Sarantis.
The topography of Thebes from the Bronze Age
to modern times.

Bibliography: p.
Includes index.
1. Thebes (Greece : Ancient city)—Description.
2. Thēvai (Greece)—Description.   3. Thēvai (Greece)—
Antiquities.   4. Excavations (Archaeology)—Greece—
Thēvai.   5. Greece—Antiquities.   I. Title.
DF261.T3S94   1985   938'.4   84-24890
ISBN 0-691-03576-8 (alk. paper)